Voices of the Magi

Enchanted Journeys in Southeast Brazil

CHICAGO STUDIES IN ETHNOMUSICOLOGY

A series edited by Philip V. Bohlman and Bruno Nettl

EDITORIAL BOARD

*Margaret J. Kartomi, Hiromi Lorraine Sakata, Anthony Seeger,
Kay Kaufman Shelemay, Martin H. Stokes, Bonnie C. Wade*

VOICES OF THE MAGI

Enchanted Journeys in Southeast Brazil

SUZEL ANA REILY

THE UNIVERSITY OF CHICAGO PRESS
CHICAGO & LONDON

SUZEL ANA REILY is senior lecturer at Queen's University Belfast.

The University of Chicago Press, Chicago 60637
The University of Chicago Press, Ltd., London
© 2002 by The University of Chicago
All rights reserved. Published 2002
Printed in the United States of America

11 10 09 08 07 06 05 04 03 02   1 2 3 4 5
ISBN: 0-226-70939-6 (cloth)
ISBN: 0-226-70941-8 (paper)

Library of Congress Cataloging-in-Publication Data
Reily, Suzel Ana, 1955–
Voices of the magi : enchanted journeys in southeast Brazil /
Suzel Ana Reily.
p. cm. — (Chicago studies in ethnomusicology)
Includes bibliographical references (p.) and index.
ISBN 0-226-70939-6 (cloth : alk. paper) — ISBN 0-226-70941-8
(paperback : alk. paper)
1. Folk music — Brazil, Southeast — History and criticism. 2. Folk
songs, Portuguese — Brazil, Southeast — History and criticism.
3. Christmas — Brazil, Southeast. 4. Epiphany — Brazil, Southeast.
5. Magi — Folklore. 6. Brazil, Southeast — Social life and customs.
I. Title. II. Series.
ML3575.B7 R36 2002
781.72'4162698 — dc21
2001003290

♾ The paper used in this publication meets the minimum requirements of
the American National Standard for Information Sciences — Permanence of Paper
for Printed Library Materials, ANSI Z39.48-1992.

TO MY PARENTS

Whenever . . . rational knowledge has consistently carried out the disenchantment of the world and its transformation into a causal mechanism, there appears the ultimate challenge to the claims of the ethical postulate, that the world is a divinely ordered cosmos with some kind of ethically *meaningful* direction.

                                        Max Weber

CONTENTS

Preface   xi

Key to Musical Transcriptions   xix

I.   *Preparations*   1

II.   *Folias*   27

III.   *Banners*   63

IV.   *Rehearsals*   88

V.   *Departures*   122

VI.   *Adorations*   143

VII.   *Visitations*   166

VIII.   *Arrivals*   190

IX.   *Visions*   210

Appendix: Musical Examples   223

Notes   231

Glossary   243

Bibliography   249

Index   259

Gallery of photographs follows page 121

Preface

On a Sunday afternoon in May 1986, equipped with a small tape recorder and a notebook, I set off from my flat in São Paulo for São Bernardo do Campo, the heartland of Brazil's car industry. On the way I picked up Waldir, a bright young journalism student who was helping me conduct a survey of rural traditions among migrants in greater São Paulo. Waldir had heard that the *folia de reis* in his neighborhood was planning a rehearsal that afternoon, and he had arranged for us to document it.

Folias de reis—or *companhias de reis* (companies of kings)—are musical ensembles made up predominantly of low-income workers that perform during the Christmas season in various regions of Brazil, particularly in rural communities. These groups reenact the journey of the Wise Men to Bethlehem and back to the Orient, roaming from house to house as they sing to bless the families they visit in exchange for food and money. These offerings are then used to promote a festival on 6 January, Kings' Day, to which all who contributed are invited. Today, folias have become a common feature of many peripheral neighborhoods of the country's large urban centers, brought by the thousands of migrants who have flocked to the cities in search of a better life.

Waldir lived in Baeta Neves, one of the oldest working-class neighborhoods in São Bernardo. He knew where we were going and led the way. From the municipal plaza, we turned up a steep hill leading to Baeta. When the terrain flattened out a bit, he told me to turn left, then right, then left again, and then right, up another hill. By this time I was beginning to wonder whether I would be able to find the place again if I ever had to come alone. After winding our way through several other streets, Waldir finally pointed to a house and told me to park the car. We had arrived.

Seu Owaldir,[1] the leader of the companhia, came to the gate and invited us in. We entered a small living room, which was already quite crowded.

There were about ten people inside—all men—and the rest of the space was occupied by musical instruments, many of them colorfully decorated with ribbons and plastic roses. Waldir knew some of the musicians, and they greeted each other warmly. I was introduced as the reporter from São Paulo, who had come to record the rehearsal. I made my way around the room shaking hands with everyone before I was taken to the kitchen to meet the women, who were preparing coffee and sandwiches for the break.

When I was led back to the living room, a few more people had arrived, and after they were introduced to me, everyone settled back into conversation. I was engaged by Seu Zezo, who began to tell me about how this companhia had first started with a group of migrants from his hometown in Minas Gerais back in the 1940s. He said that although all the original members had died, new migrants had arrived and kept the group in existence. Now, he told me, its survival was under threat, and that was why they were meeting that afternoon: they intended to make a demonstration tape to submit to the municipal Department of Culture in the hope of securing government funds to produce an LP of their music. Through the production of an LP they hoped to rekindle interest in the tradition, particularly among the youth, to guarantee the continuity of the tradition for yet another generation.

When it looked as though all the *foliões* (folia members) had arrived, Owaldir left the room and returned with a banner on which a local artist had painted a scene depicting the Adoration of the Wise Men, which looked much like any representation of the Adoration from anywhere in the Christian world. The banner of the Three Kings (*bandeira dos santos reis*), the sacred object of the folia, was passed around the room, and they all kissed it before crossing themselves. It was then left standing on a side table, as a kind of altar, and it was put away only after everyone had left.

The presence of the banner served to cue the musicians that they should get ready to sing, and they began to tune their instruments and take their performance positions. Although they appeared to be standing in a disorganized cluster, I later learned that each musician had a prescribed place defined by the hierarchical organization of the ensemble. Once everyone was standing, the transition from warm-up sounds to the beginning of the instrumental introduction (*estribilho*) was almost imperceptible. Even though they were making a demonstration tape, Owaldir saw no need for a "clean" beginning; their recording adhered quite closely to their normal performance practices at visitations.

They sang for about twenty-five minutes before stopping, repeating the same melodic structure (*toada*) over and over. Although I found it difficult

PREFACE

to follow the words of the song, I was intrigued by the polyphonic form they used. The vocal organization of the toada was characterized by an accumulation of eight different parts, which led up to a loud and prolonged major chord. It began with a solo by Owaldir, who improvised a text called the *embaixada* (embassy) that would then be repeated by the other voices as they entered the ensemble, each one a register higher than the preceding voices. With each entry the sound became progressively more dense. Later I was told that this cumulative form was called the *mineiro* style (from the state of Minas Gerais), and that most of the foliões in the group had come from Arceburgo, Guaranésia, and Guaxupé, three neighbouring towns in southern Minas Gerais.

When they finished the toada, a young man began reciting a long poem which narrated a unique interpretation of the Christmas story. I was told that he was one of the group's *bastião,* or clowns,[2] who during ritual journeys recited the "prophecy" (*profecia*) in homes with manger scenes, and that this occurred after the "adoration verses" which the group had just been performing. After the prophecy the foliões began singing a different toada in which the solo role was performed by Zezo, but the cumulative structure remained the same. This time, however, the texts transmitted the blessings of the Three Kings to the members of the household the companhia was visiting. Because of my difficulty in understanding the words they were singing, I almost missed the verse they performed for me:

Santo Reis que abençoa	Holy Kings bless
A reporter aqui presente;	The reporter here present;
Tá gravando a companhia,	She is recording the company,
Nosso Pai Onipotente.	Our Omnipotent Father.

The final toada they performed before taking a break followed the same cumulative pattern as the other performances, but it was far more compressed, since there were only two vocal configurations succeeding the soloist. I was informed that this was the style used for the "thanksgiving verses," which occur before the group leaves a house to make their way to the next one, thanking the family for their offering. When they finally stopped singing, the women emerged from the kitchen, only to leave again as soon as they had served the men. While they were eating, Owaldir played back the tape, and everyone was satisfied that it would impress the secretary of culture. After the break the musicians played another round of toadas before they began to disperse, but this time they did not record them.

xiii

PREFACE

There were only five or six musicians left when Owaldir's wife brought out more coffee. As we sipped it, Zezo and Owaldir began discussing a strategy for convincing the Department of Culture to embrace their project. There was something intriguing about the discursive mode they employed in their dialogue, which reminded me of Christian base communities (CEBs) and other politically motivated neighborhood associations I had encountered over the years. It was then that I took note of Zezo's T-shirt: it was stamped with the emblem of the metalworkers' union, calling for a forty-hour week.

When they appeared to have reached consensus on how they would deal with the government officials, I took advantage of the gap in the conversation to ask Zezo about his T-shirt. It turned out that he was on the factory commission at Mercedes-Benz and a leader in the metalworkers' union. Yet when he was a child, his mother had made a promise (*promessa*) to the Three Kings on his behalf, and he had a lifelong obligation to sing for them every year. Owaldir had also participated in the metalworkers' movement until he lost his job at Volkswagen in 1980 because of his militant activities.

I left the folia rehearsal with many questions reverberating in my head. How could it be that these hardened union activists were prepared to take up guitars, tambourines, and drums decorated with colored ribbons and plastic flowers during the Christmas season and sing endless ditties before the manger scenes in their neighborhood? Moved by their obvious devotion to the Three Kings, I was reminded of Mário de Andrade's (1976) poetic accounts of his encounters with popular religious groups on his treks across Brazil during the early part of the century. Several decades later I found myself similarly charmed by the ingenuous aesthetics of Brazil's popular traditions. What was particularly intriguing was that the foliões did not seem to see any incongruity between folia participation and militant activism. Had they merely compartmentalized these two spheres of their lives, or were they linked in some way? One thing was certain: I had found the sort of research context I had been looking for, one in which musical performance was being used to mediate between the migrants' rural backgrounds and their current urban experiences.

Before the end of the week I was back in Baeta Neves, and soon afterward I had contacted the other four companhias de reis in São Bernardo. For the next few years my life was absorbed by the documentation of the music and the aspirations of the members of these five groups. In the beginning I attempted to explain that I was not a reporter, but an anthropologist. This distinction seemed to be of little interest to them, and I have remained "their"

xiv

PREFACE

reporter to this day. Now reconciled to this identity, I hope that I am able to report with accuracy that which they so willingly and generously shared with me: their music and their lives.

Acknowledgments

This book has been over fifteen years in the making, and during this period so many people have passed through my life, leaving an imprint upon these pages, that it would be impossible to name everyone. All that I can do is highlight those to whom I am especially indebted. Since no project of this magnitude can be undertaken without adequate financial backing, I begin by thanking the numerous institutions that provided financial support for the research at various stages of its development; these include FUNARTE, Instituto Metodista de Ensino Superior, Capes, CNPq, the British Academy, NIDevR, and Queen's University Belfast.

The most fulfilling aspect of this project was the opportunity it afforded me to engage with the enchanted world of the folia de reis, into which I was so warmly and openly welcomed. I am very grateful to all the foliões and their families who collaborated with this project. The main protagonists are the members of the five folias in São Bernardo, and I wish to thank them all for their contributions. I am especially grateful to Owaldir, Nair, Paulinho, Careca, André, Seu Januário, Seu Sebastião, Juarez, Tonico, Jacaré, Geraldinho, Cida, Dona Mariinha, Lazinho, Zé dos Magos, Luizinho, Longa, Seu Zé Machado, Dona Francisca, Wanderley, Seu Alcides, Dona Clotilde, João, Mario, Lázaro, and Quim Braz. Along with countless pleasurable experiences, fieldwork also had its moments of sorrow, but none so sad as the death of Seu Zé Quatorze in 1992. I shall always remember his stories, and I especially cherish the memory of our trip to Monsenhor Paulo, where he tried to teach me the footwork of the *cateretê*.

My greatest debt is to Zezo and Conceição, who opened their home to me throughout my research. Zezo's remarkable ability to represent his world in terms which I could understand greatly speeded my entry into the folia universe. Moreover, he embarked upon the project with such enthusiasm that I am rather inclined to see him as a coresearcher, and his voice echoes throughout these pages, both explicitly and implicitly.

I also wish to acknowledge the contributions made by foliões I met in Arceburgo, Batatais, Campanha, Carapicuiba, Cordislândia, Mococa, Monsenhor Paulo, Rio de Janeiro, Santo André, São Gonçalo do Sapucai, São

xv

Luiz do Paraitinga, and many other places. In particular, I thank Seu João Isaias, Seu João Paca, Seu Matias, Antônio Mariano, Seu Vicente, Zé Canhanga, Pedro Cigano, Seu Paulo, and Dito Geraldo. My understanding of the Brazilian popular Catholic ethos was further enhanced by Seu Antônio, Dito, Zé, Cleu, Dona Mariquinha, Dona Dosinha, Jorge Grilo, Pequita, Lucas, Didi, Dona Cinira, and many others.

In the academic world I am indebted to the many people who commented on drafts at various stages of development. In its first incarnation, this book was a doctoral thesis, so I shall begin by thanking my supervisors. My official supervisor was Liana Salvia Trindade, and I am very grateful for her continuous support and openness toward my project. I feel especially privileged for having had the opportunity to work with John Blacking in the last year of his life; although we were able to meet regularly only during the periods he was allowed home from the hospital, he made a very strong and long-lasting impact upon my thinking. Above all, though, I am indebted to Maria Lucia Montes, who devoted countless hours of her time to discuss my work with me, even though she received no official recognition for her efforts. I did not benefit only from her extraordinary mind; I was also greatly inspired by her endless generosity. Others whose comments contributed in some way to the final form of this text include Carlos Rodrigues Brandão, Carmem Cinira Macedo, Rembrant Wolpert, John Baily, Tracey Heatherington, Michael Clendinning, Graham McFarlane, Eurides de Souza Santos, the anonymous referees of the University of Chicago Press, and Erik Carlson; I acknowledge and thank them for their assistance. My writing has also benefited from questions and comments made during aural presentations of sections of this research at a number of conferences and seminars; in particular, I wish to thank the following associations and institutions for providing a forum for these discussions: the British Forum for Ethnomusicology, the Anthropological Association of Ireland, the European Seminar for Ethnomusicology, the School of Anthropological Studies at Queen's University Belfast, the Department of Social Anthropology at the University of São Paulo, the "Eth-noise" seminar series at the University of Chicago, and the Instituto Villa-Lobos at the University of Rio de Janeiro. I would also like to remember a few friends, colleagues, and mentors who, however diffusely, have made an impact on this work: Martin Stokes, Hastings Donnan, Luiz Tatit, Gilberto Velho, Tiago de Oliveira Pinto, Mundicarmo Ferretti, Sergio Ferretti, Philip Bohlman, Martha Tupinambá de Ulhôa, Deborah Schisler, Eliana Magrini Fochi, Jaqueline Camargo, Rowena Robinson, Waldir, and Emer.

PREFACE

Unquestionably, my sharpest critic over the years has been Peter Parkes, whose judicious reading, attention to detail, and challenging interrogations have contributed immensely to the form and tone of the final text; "enchantment," the very pillar upon which this book is based, emerged out of these discussions. But my gratitude to Peter extends well beyond the sphere of intellectual debate. I am especially thankful to him for providing my cats and me with a periodic refuge far from teaching and administrative duties, where I could turn my attention completely to my writing.

Finally, I would never have been able to complete this book without the constant and unwavering support of my family, who always believed that I could actually do it. Alongside this crucial moral and emotional support, several members of my family participated in the project itself and contributed toward its intellectual development. On numerous occasions my mother and my sisters, Celia and Lucia, accompanied me to the field, and invariably their sensitive observations enhanced my understanding of the context we had entered. Even some of my nieces participated in field excursions; Alice was just a one-year-old on her first field trip. I'm especially grateful to my father, the church historian Duncan Alexander Reily, for scouring through my manuscripts for any theological inaccuracies; his comments on a number of other aspects of the manuscript were also extremely useful.

Key to Musical Transcriptions

Pandeiro (Tambourine)

produced by rubbing the skin around the rim of the instrument with the thumb

Triangle

produced by tightening the grip on the instrument

Viola

thumb, downward movement

index finger, upward movement

fingernails, downward movement

CHAPTER I

Preparations

As the Christmas season approaches, *folias de reis,* or *companhias de reis* (companies of kings) begin to make the necessary preparations for their ritual journeys (*jornadas*). Before setting off they plan their itinerary, they check to make sure that there are people to occupy all the ritual and administrative roles required by the tradition, and they meet for rehearsals to guarantee the quality of their performances. While *foliões* (folia members) know what happens on these ritual journeys, no one knows what will happen during the one for which they are preparing themselves. Expectations heighten as foliões reminisce about previous journeys, remembering bygone days when the drama could be conducted "properly"; they remind one another of the various "Herods"—or dangers—they might encounter along the way; they speculate about how they will be received by a particular household, and about the number of manger scenes to be adored along the way. As they prepare for their journey, foliões create an atmosphere of excitement around the days to come, keeping expectations high through to the final festival.

This book is about these journeys, and it follows their sequence from the planning stages to their festive culmination.[1] Folia journeys are both part of and set apart from everyday life. They are embedded in the patterns of everyday social life, but they are also special spaces which enhance social experience through music making and intense sociability. Journeys articulate with the foliões' values and commonsense notions about the world around them while speaking also of their visions and aspirations. These ritual spaces constitute "total social facts," drawing on the dominant themes that mark the daily lives of the foliões: they comment on family and community relations as well as on class and race relations, they refer to the economic conditions of the participants and provide a forum for the elaboration of political views, they create a stage for asserting and proclaiming the values of the devotees, and through their ritual activities they define themselves as a moral community. The investigation of these ritual contexts, then, provides a means of gaining access to the social lives, worldviews, and aspirations of vast sectors of the Brazilian subaltern classes engaged in popular Catholic activities.

My focus is upon the folia tradition in the urban context, where the ritual journeys are set against the backdrop of the journeys made by rural migrants in search of a better life in the city. In the urban setting, many migrants have confronted conditions of extreme poverty and marginality in a highly stratified society, and their adaptation to city life has been hindered by low levels of education and inappropriate skills as well as by value systems radically opposed to the rationality of capitalist enterprise. Within this hostile environment, folia activities have provided a means of creating and sustaining networks of mutual support. Though there is nothing new in this proposition,[2] I shall argue that the efficacy of these networks within the folia universe is predicated on the ethical base that sustains them: the moral principles of popular Catholicism emphasize solidarity and mutual obligations, and a claim to these principles has become a primary means of forging cultural integrity within migrant communities. It is in moral terms that they mark their identity in opposition to the privileged sectors of Brazilian society.

This argument could be made equally with respect to popular Catholicism in rural contexts. Indeed, it is not my intention to suggest that there is anything unique about the urban setting which alters the fundamental dynamics of the folia tradition. On the contrary, the very embeddedness of folia ritual activity in everyday life has hindered its sedimentation, allowing the tradition to be continuously resignified over the centuries in consonance with changing historical circumstances. In moving to the city there certainly has been a shift in the themes highlighted during folia performances, but since colonial times folias de reis have operated in and articulated with a diversity of social formations, the contemporary urban context being only the most recent structural setting into which the tradition has been adapted. One of my objectives is to portray the fluidity with which folia communities have continuously negotiated their ritual life in face-to-face interactions, drawing on their daily experiences on the margins of mainstream Brazilian society.

The resilience of popular Catholicism in Brazil is undoubtedly linked to its continuous ability to engage with the themes of immediate concern to the devotees. But these themes are brought to the fore within an aesthetic environment of intense experiential value, in which music plays a central role. Folia journeys are conducted through participatory musical performances, as are countless other vernacular religious traditions around the world. Music, of course, is used in a number of distinct ways within different ritual contexts, just as musical styles and the conditions of their performance display considerable diversity from one ritual tradition to another. Yet ethnomusicologists have documented numerous cases in which music is the primary medium for organizing ritual activity. The folia de reis is just such a musically directed religious tradition: musical sounds dominate the ritual time-frame; musical performance is conducted by an ensemble with a more or less inclusive participatory orientation; and music is the primary means of integrating the attendants into the ritual drama. Through an in-depth ethnography of this context I hope to show that anthropological perspectives on ritual and ritualization can be significantly enhanced by close attendance to ritual music and music making.

The book is premised on the argument that participatory musical performance within a religious context provides a means of orchestrating ritual enactment in such a way as to allow participants to proclaim their religious truths at the same time as their coordinated interactions during music making re-create the social ideals embodied in their religious tenets. I refer to the musical mode of ritual orchestration as "enchantment."[3] Enchantment creates a highly charged experiential realm in which devotees gain a momentary glimpse of the harmonious order that could reign in society, provided everyone agreed to adhere to the moral precepts outlined in religious discourse. By promoting such intense experiences, musical performance is, I contend, a powerful medium for forging religious conviction and commitment.

In vernacular usage, "enchantment" refers to a seductive world of poetry and fantasy. One of its connotations pertains to the use of magical powers to effect transformations. The concept of enchantment was introduced into social theory through the work of Max Weber, for whom it was the condition of premodernity. Weber contended that enchantment would ultimately be displaced by the rationality of modernity, leaving in its wake a disenchanted world of "icy darkness and hardness" (Weber 1958, 128), a world devoid of meaning. But what I wish to highlight here is the link Weber ([1922] 1963) saw between enchantment and morality. According to Weber, the enchanted sphere of religion articulates a moral order, and when ethically constituted, the world remains warm, fluid, and meaningful. My conceptualization of enchantment draws on these associations, providing a concise way of encapsulating what I consider to be the main thrust of the musical mode of ritual orchestration: the creation of a morally grounded visionary social world through communal music making, the experience of which can have profound transformative implications for the participants.

As an experiential realm, enchantment takes place in the here and now; its efficacy is predicated upon its emergent quality. Such experiences can be promoted through music precisely because music making organizes collective action, while song texts can be endlessly rewritten and brought to bear upon the specificities of the immediate performance situation. By directly linking content to the performance context, I will demonstrate how foliões are able to generate profound personal experiences within an interpretive frame which relates shared discursive representations to the sensory experiences promoted during ritual enactment. Furthermore, within the fluid and decentralized context of the folia universe—and of other vernacular religious settings—musical performance serves to mediate the negotiations involved in staging ritual activity.

My journey into the folia universe began with the enchanted experience I had when I first heard the Folia do Baeta Neves back in 1986. But like the Kings, I did not return by the same route. Once the singing had come to an end, I began the struggle of making sense of their journeys and musical performances, reflecting upon where I had been and what I had heard, seen, done, and read over the years, merging the intensely moving experiences I had among folia communities with the requirements of academic practice. Without doubt it was the memories which my data evoked in me of my time spent with them that sustained my interest as I confronted endless stacks of field notes, transcriptions, photographs, and audio- and videotapes.

Journeys always produce stories—as do reporters. It is, therefore, through stories that I present this account. Some of the stories I will be telling were narrated by foliões; others are my own anecdotal representations of observations and experiences I had during my time in the field. Stories have the potential of bringing an event to life; they demand the readers' identification with the characters, allowing them to sympathetically reexperience an episode with the narrator. Moreover, stories provide eloquent illustrations of the uniqueness and contextuality of an event; they show how shared representations are negotiated in terms of the specificities of the here and now. Stories are perhaps the human way of reconciling the fluidity of experience with the representational mode through which people communicate with one another. But before I can begin my story, I will set out my agenda through a dialogue with relevant literature.

Folias de Reis and Popular Catholicism in Brazil

Numerous popular narratives tell how the Three Kings became musicians, forming the first folia on earth. In one of the most common versions of the narrative it is said that, in exchange for their gifts, Our Lady presented them with musical instruments when they arrived at the crèche. She gave them a *viola* (a stringed instrument slightly smaller than a guitar, with five double courses), a *pandeiro* (tambourine), and a *caixa* (a large double-headed cylindrical drum) and told them to return to the Orient singing along the way to announce the birth of Christ. In accordance with the myth, folias de reis conduct a symbolic dramatization of the journey of the Three Kings, in which a group of musicians and a few clowns—frequently known as *bastião*—roam from house to house with the banner of the Holy Kings. During their journeys—or *giros* (rounds)—the groups bless the families they visit in exchange for donations that will then be used to promote the "festival of the arrival" (*festa da chegada*) that occurs on Kings' Day, 6 January. Companhias normally begin their journeys at midnight between 24 and 25 December in a ritual known as the "departure of the banner" (*saída da bandeira*). This event occurs at the home of the *festeiro* (patron of the festival), who administers the funds the folia collects during the journey and organizes the festival on behalf of the community. The journey ends when the group closes the circuit and "arrives" back at the festeiro's house, where the festival of the arrival is held. All those who contributed with donations during the journey are invited to participate in the event. A good festival is one in which there is an abundance of food and much music and dancing throughout the night.

There can be little doubt that the folia tradition in Brazil came to the country with the Portuguese colonists, but it then began to take on a localized profile. As the tradition diffused throughout the land, it was continuously reinvented and reinterpreted to suit the specific needs and aesthetic preferences of those involved in its performance. As one would expect of any "folk" tradition, there is a considerable degree of variation in the performance practices of different groups from one region to the next, and even from one town to the next within a single geographic area, just as each group is itself in a constant process of transformation. Today folias are also common in the country's large urban centers, brought by the millions of rural laborers who have come to the cities over the past decades in search of work and a better standard of living. This process has brought further transformations to the tradition to adapt it to the migrants' experiences in the new context.

The folia de reis is but one of countless localized lay devotional traditions to have developed in Brazil during the colonial era. *Congados* and *moçambiques,* for example, are drum- and percussion-based dance troupes, made up predominantly of blacks, that perform during festivals in honor of Saint Benedict the Moor and Our Lady of the Rosary, among other saints; Saint Gonçalo dances (*danças de São Gonçalo*) are devotional double-line dances which help guarantee the strength of one's legs; baptisms of Saint John the Baptist involve requests for rain by rural communities to guarantee an appropriate supply of water for crops; festivities in honor of Saint Anthony, the patron saint of "old maids" (*tias*), commonly include social dances and mock weddings. Like the Three Kings, many of the saints who have become the objects of popular devotion in Brazil are depicted with all-too-human characteristics, and quite frequently they are fun-loving musicians and dancers. Devotion to these saints typically involves merrymaking, an abundance of food, and much music and dancing.

The relative homogeneity in the devotional practices associated with a specific saint has led some researchers to suggest that these spheres be viewed in terms of distinct "cycles" (see Brandão 1981), each comprising a cluster of interrelated symbolic units of wider or more restricted diffusion. While it could be argued that a broadly defined popular Catholic ethos underlies them all, the sphere of popular Catholicism is highly fragmented and localized; whatever links there may be across devotional cycles—or even within each cycle—popular Catholic practices constitute local instantiations of an available repertoire, in which, over the centuries, participants have selected, highlighted, and downplayed distinct elements at their disposal, in accordance with their daily lives and aspirations.

What favored the proliferation of these forms of lay religious expression was the limited presence of the institutionalized church in the colony, which left settlers to develop their own forms of devotion to meet their religious needs, particularly in isolated rural communities. These circumstances emerged out of a special relationship between Rome and the Portuguese crown established during the crusade against the Moors, in which a series of papal bulls granted the king patronage concessions over the religious institution, rendering the church subservient to the Portuguese state. In the first years of ecclesiastical patronage, the goals of the state were congruent with those of the church. In time, however, the crown's greater interest in gold than in souls had grave consequences for the expansion of the church. Approximately 250 years after the "discovery," the state had scarcely fulfilled its part of the mission: there were but eight dioceses in the colony and the vast majority of secular clergymen were employed independently by large landowners or urban confraternities, serving a limited part of the population. Throughout much of the colony, religious life was left predominantly in the hands of laymen, who expressed their religious sentiments by drawing upon Portuguese forms of folk devotion, many rooted in late medieval musical practices.[4]

With the separation of church and state in the late nineteenth century, the relationship between local religious communities and the Catholic church entered a new phase, as a progressive sector of the clergy spearheaded a project of ecclesiastic Romanization. Their efforts, however, were unable to eradicate popular Catholic beliefs and practices, particularly among members of the lower classes. Though they invested heavily against vernacular forms of devotion in urban centers, the most they were able to achieve was to push such practices out of the church itself, while in isolated rural areas they remained virtually unaffected by this civilizing onslaught. In any case, the primary targets of Romanization were the members of polite society, so that the rural peasantry remained forgotten and continued to conduct their religious lives much as before. In urban centers the marginalized lower classes either transferred their religious practices out into the churchyard and the street or removed them altogether from the direct gaze of the priests (Brandão 1985, 138–39). It is worth noting, however, that among significant sectors of the clergy, the former state patronage system remained entrenched, such that conservative stances with tolerant and laissez-faire attitudes toward popular Catholicism have continued to be prevalent right up to the present day.

Even since Vatican II, when the church declared a preferential option for the poor, the official church in Brazil has made little headway in displacing popular Catholic worldviews and ritual activities. It has been primarily the groups associated with liberation theology who have made the greatest efforts to absorb the practices of their low-income parishioners into the sphere of the church, but they have often found it difficult to reconcile their projects with the "unorthodoxies" of popular Catholic religiosity. One of the major forces compelling church authorities today to rethink their attitudes toward popular forms of religious expression has been the astounding growth of Pentecostalism among the lower classes, which has resulted in an increased—if guarded—acceptance of the charismatic movement within the church (Iulianelli 1999; Oliveira et al. 1978). Yet while the church has struggled to develop strategies to deal with vernacular modes of religiosity, many devout Catholics actively involved in popular forms of devotion call upon the services of the church only for major sacraments, such as baptisms, first communions, marriages, and funerals.

As this overview indicates, there is no straightforward way of defining the relationship between official Catholicism and popular Catholicism. While popular Catholic practices are highly localized affairs with immediate links to the lives of devotees, the "official" church is hardly a unified institution, sheltering—as it does—a diversity of conflicting and contradictory orientations to theological doctrine, liturgical practice, and vernacular religiosity. Any assessment of the interaction between these two domains must take account of their complexities and of the specificities of the contexts in which they intersect.

Although Brazil is the largest Catholic country in the world, with around 75 percent of the population declaring themselves formally Catholic, the interest in the study of Catholicism among anthropologists has been fairly muted. This contrasts dramatically with research into African-Brazilian possession cults, in which a much smaller proportion of the population is involved but in which the "exotic other" is in clear evidence. It was only after the emergence of liberation theology that Catholicism attracted the attention of social scientists in a significant way (see, for example, Bruneau 1974; Hewitt 1991; Kadt 1970; Macedo 1986; C. Mariz 1994; and Petrini 1984). These studies tend to focus on the effects of the changing attitudes of church officials in the post–Vatican II era, and on the movements these changes have engendered, particularly the emergence of CEBs (Christian base communities), in an attempt to assess their potential as effective instruments of political change.[5]

The same enthusiasm, however, has not been shown toward the investigation of popular Catholicism, which has remained of secondary interest. Along with the material contained in the community studies of the 1950s (see E. Galvão 1955; Mello e Souza 1982; Pierson 1966; Wagley 1964; and Willems 1961, among others),[6] the most extensive documentation of the aesthetic forms of popular Catholic traditions has been conducted by Brazilian folklorists, who have tended to locate their object of research among the rural peasantry. Although folklorists have published extensively, their research methods are those of interested amateurs, and their material is essentially descriptive (Béhague 1982, 1991). Following in a tradition established in the early part of the century, these researchers have conceived of folklore as a repository of national and regional heritage (Rowe and Schelling 1991, 4–6), and the collecting of it was meant to rescue the country's cultural legacy from extinction. Over the past decades, however, anthropological studies have become more prevalent, as researchers have begun looking at the expressive dimension of popular Catholicism as a way of understanding the ethos and aspirations of the subaltern classes of the country.

This interest emerged when Brazilian anthropologists began turning to the ideas of Antonio Gramsci, whose concept of folklore as the expression of popular commonsense notions brought a refreshing alternative to the structural Marxist perspectives prevailing in Brazilian popular Catholic studies. It is worth noting, though, that the term "folklore" was strategically avoided in favor of "popular culture" by "serious" Brazilian scholars. They wished to distance themselves from the country's folklorists not only because they saw them as dilettantes, but also because of their political positions: many folklorists had become directly associated with the projects of the military dictatorship.

Up until the early 1980s, anthropological studies of popular Catholicism had emphasized the fatalistic ethos of popular Catholic forms of devotion, which was seen as an ideological support upholding the exploitative patterns of interclass relations in rural Brazil (see Bruneau 1974, 68). Gramsci, however, had a far more dynamic vision of the popular domain, seeing human beings as historical agents actively involved in the construction of their own destinies. He defined folklore as the conceptions of the world and life of the subaltern classes, and he saw popular Catholicism as a sphere for the articulation of the morality of the people (1985, 190), rooted in their notions of "natural law." While the church authorities were also said to have a concept of natural law, Gramsci saw it as distinct from that held in the popular domain. He argued that the popular masses continuously renew the commonsense categories expressed in their popular traditions in accordance with the "pressures of real living conditions and the spontaneous comparisons between the ways in which the various social strata live" (1985, 193). This renewal is possible, he argued, insofar as folklore is "a confused agglomerate of fragments of all the conceptions of the world and life that have succeeded one another in history," which people continue to appropriate into "the mosaic of tradition" (1985, 189). Ultimately, he posited, this process would al-

CHAPTER ONE

low for the formation of "organic ideologies" that would permit the masses to organize and fight for the transformation of the means of production which limit their access to the goods of society.

Whatever the revolutionary potential of popular religious movements may be, Gramsci's ideas altered the way some Brazilian anthropologists looked at the country's lower classes and their lifestyles, and excellent documents began to emerge showing how popular Catholicism articulates with the moral codes and patterns of sociability prevailing in popular Catholic communities. This perspective is most evident in the work of Carlos Rodrigues Brandão (1981, 1983a, 1985, and 1989, among others), who has dedicated a lifetime of research to the central and southeastern rural peasantry, but it is also found in the work of Francisco Rolim (1980), Alba Zaluar (1983), Rubem César Fernandes (1982), Raymundo Heraldo Maués (1995), and others. These studies, however, focus primarily on the analysis of the symbolic repertoire and normative ritual processes of popular Catholic traditions, paying less attention to the fluidity of social interactions in expressions of religiosity. Thus, they reflect a rather static and essentialist representation of the popular Catholic ethos and subaltern morality, obscuring the intense processes of negotiation and resignification of commonsense categories so integral to Gramsci's ideas. Indeed, in accordance with the perspective so prevalent in community studies and Weberian approaches to popular religion, outside forces, such as the church, agricultural capitalism, and urban migration, are typically portrayed as agents in the erosion of the idyllic pastoral lifestyle of the peasantry, ultimately leading to the impoverishment and disappearance of popular Catholicism.

Without doubt, global forces have had an impact on the lives of rural communities, and popular Catholic forms of expression have clearly been affected by them. But vernacular traditions have also become significant sites for the expression of subaltern responses to these forces (see Bohlman 1997). It is precisely because of the localized nature of popular Catholic practice that religious life can keep pace with all aspects of daily experience; each time devotees stage a ritual, they engage in intense processes of negotiation, bringing the shared symbolic repertoire of the tradition to bear upon their contemporary lives.

Within the folia tradition, ritual journeys are constructed from people's memories of their participation in previous journeys, but this shared template is adapted annually to the specific circumstances, motivations, and interests of the participants at the time, so that folia performances are continuously in an ungraspable state of flux. Each folia journey is a reinvention of past journeys, some involving contemporary musicians, others of generations long gone, their individual biographies woven into the "confused agglomerate of fragments" out of which history is constituted. Thus, each journey is distinct, as pragmatic considerations and new ideals fuse with the archaeological mosaic of past journeys to generate new expressive forms and experiences among participants. The familiarity of the symbolism provides devotees with a sense of the continuity and stability of their rituals, which allows them to perceive them as "their tradition," "their cultural heritage," and to constitute themselves through them as a moral community (Stokes 1994, 3). Each folia journey is the result of intense negotiation among participants, in which together they strive to reenact collectively their interpretations of the journey of the Wise Men. All this investment proves worthwhile when the outcome is the construction of an aesthetic world which greatly enhances the quality of social experience.

Ritual, Music, and Experience

In his discussion of rituals within religious revitalization movements, James Fernandez (1986, 162) has argued that such movements—and possibly even all religions—are in the business of reconstituting the fragments of everyday life by creating an illusion of the relatedness of things associated with disparate domains of experience; their mission is to provide people with a sense of the wholeness of the cosmos in which they live. While it is not entirely clear what Fernandez means by wholeness, it is certainly the case that religious systems typically postulate a vision of cosmic order which links the social world of humanity to the sacred universe of the gods. This sacred domain is commonly portrayed in religious discourse as an idealized utopia of social harmony, and it is detached from the ever-changing terrestrial sphere to protect it from the effects of temporality and human limitations. Morality is defined in terms of this mythic realm, and ritual activity is the primary means available to humans in their struggle to preserve their links with the morally constituted cosmic order.

Religious discourse, however, is typically allusive and figurative in nature, constituting what Richard Bauman and Charles Briggs (1990, 72–76) might call entextualized reality, an independent reality contained within a text. While fictional entextualization calls for only a temporary suspension of disbelief, religious entextualizations are meant to be taken as truth. If they are to be convincing, they must be capable of encompassing their followers within the moral order they construct, and they must also provide the means for people to visualize their relationship to that order. Whatever Fernandez may have meant by wholeness, his work has highlighted the critical significance and persuasive power of what one might call "religious experience," fleeting moments in which the world seems perfect and everything is as it should be. Religious experience circumscribes phenomenological encounters which are interpreted by those who experience them as momentary revelations of the sacred sphere. Such intensely charged affective experiences are highly memorable and deeply cherished, providing inchoate insight into the metaphorical language of religious discourse. As Harvey Whitehouse (1995, 175) has argued, it is out of experiences such as these that a sense of commitment to religious organizations and their doctrines can be forged.

Anthropologists have frequently pointed to ritual as the locus of religious life, and thus it constitutes a privileged context for the orchestration of religious experience. According to Catherine Bell (1992, 74), ritualization is predicated upon establishing a "qualitative distinction between the 'sacred' and the 'profane.'" To achieve this separation, the ritual space is set apart from the pragmatic world of everyday life, so that it can be perceived and experienced as extraordinary, and special framing devices are employed to demarcate its sacredness (Bauman 1975, 1992). For Joel Kuipers (1990, 4) rituals construct the sacred frame through entextualized enactments, and he defined ritual entextualization as "a process in which a speech event (or series of speech events) is marked by increasing thoroughness of poetic and rhetorical patterning and growing levels of (apparent) detachment from the immediate pragmatic context." Ritual entextualization, then, is created through the use of performative devices in which articulations become progressively more formulaic and musical, while the content of the messages draws increasingly upon mythic imagery. In this way ritual constructs a representation of the cosmic sphere.

Kuipers (1990) claims that, among the Weyewa of Indonesia, the ultimate mode of ritual extextualization results in a coherent monologic performance of the ancestors' words, and its persuasive power derives from the ritual specialist's ability to convince the audience that he is but a mediator through which the ancestors speak. In emphasizing the poetic display of the ritual speaker, Kuipers loses sight of the participatory role of the attendants in the enactment, yet as the "ancestor" speaks—though actually he sings— his words are endorsed through choral responses. By focusing exclusively upon the ritual texts, Kuipers disregards the potential of participation as a means of bridging the gap between the entextualized monologue and the attendants' experience of the (enchanted) reality it depicts.

Among the Weyewa, ritual efficacy is predicated upon the proper performance of a strictly prescribed ritual script, but such formal rigidity is far from universal. In fact, it is quite uncharacteristic of revitalization movements and autonomous community-based associations, such as Brazilian popular Catholic ensembles, which are not committed to "well-worn routines and the inertia of institutions" (Fernandez 1986, 183). Indeed, many vernacular ritual traditions are remarkably flexible, and the means of linking performances to the immediate circumstances is often built into the ritual structure itself. Nonetheless, it would appear that some level of prescriptive "ruling" (G. Lewis 1980, 11) or "directionality" (Parkin 1992) is common to all rituals, particularly those with some degree of historical depth. This skeletal framework, however, can be—and often is—padded out and made ever thicker by a complex interplay of various communicative media, which heighten the contrast between the ritual space and everyday life. Along with music, ritual may be accompanied by mythic narrations, prayers, and various other types of text, ritual objects, spatial organization and positionality, phasing, significant colors, foods, smells, and much, much more. At first glance, this symbolic density appears to immerse participants in an ocean of fragmentary sensory stimuli, or motifs, which are combined in a number of ways as the ritual progresses, creating continuous tension between the prescribed ritual script and its elaboration. While the whole may be too complex to be apprehended in its totality, it is designed to affect the senses, enhancing the experiential value of the event.

Fernandez's argument emphasized this interplay of ritual motifs,[7] giving center stage to the way in which it affects the orchestration of ritual experience. He claimed that when people are enveloped by a multiplicity of sensations, their primary perceptions are evoked, and the disparate fragments begin to resonate inchoately with one another, forming ever larger webs of association. Thus, however contradictory and incoherent rituals may be shown to be (Gerholm 1988), an experience of coherence nonetheless can be forged through the emergent associations made by the participants during the ritual event. To illustrate the process of associative resonance, Fernandez resorted to metaphors derived from the musical universe; more specifically, he invoked the relationships between the different parts in orchestral music.[8] Yet he made no mention of how musical performance within the ritual context itself might play a special role in promoting associative experience. If religious systems are indeed in the business of forging a sense of wholeness and group music making is frequently a fundamental part of ritual proceedings, it follows that structural properties specific to music and music making play a central role in orchestrating the ritual experience of relatedness.

Musical sound is, in the first instance, a contentless vessel, since it lacks an immediate semantic base (Blacking 1977, 2; 1980a, 35; 1985a, 65–66). It is articulated through such abstract elements as melody, rhythm, form, timbre, tempo, dynamics, and instrumentation. Because it is nonreferential, any objectified meanings a piece of music may come to acquire at the discursive level can be represented only through metaphoric associations. Within the ritual context, numerous encoded forms of representation are in evidence, such as myths, oratory, song texts, iconography, gestures, and spatial and temporal organization, as well as the formal properties of the style of music employed. These media provide a pool of resources for the construction of associative webs that link the ritual motifs to one another. The very ambiguity and multivocality of symbols (Turner 1967) allow for multiple resonances and for the continuous emergence of new associations, cross-referencing the ritual sphere, the wider social context, and personal life stories, spinning them into complex, interconnected and meaningful webs.

While the ritual motifs embody the potential for endless resonances, musical performance binds the participants to the associative webs they construct, encompassing them within a meaningful—yet ineffable—world. This, I contend, is the critical factor accounting for the prevalence of music—and more specifically of participatory music making—in many communal religious rituals. As "text," it could be said that there is little to distinguish the way music operates within ritual from the associative processes invoked by other ritual motifs, but in performance, music organizes the actions and interactions of the participants, giving a temporal dimension to their ephemeral experience of connectedness. But it does more than this. To perform in an ensemble, participants must act in consort, agreeing to adhere to the performance requirements of the genre which unites them, and this provides a communal focus for forging a sense of shared experience. Through group music making the entextualized reality of the cosmic order is enchanted collectively into existence, and through the participants' engagement in the construction of that order, they create a context for envisaging themselves within it. In the act of making music participants become a part of the very webs they are constructing, and they are able to experience the harmonious social world envisaged within their religious discourse.

As John Blacking (especially 1973a, 1973b, 1980a, and 1985b) insisted throughout his work, the emphasis in participatory music making is on the sociability of the activity, heightening people's awareness of their relationships to other people. To perform as a group musicians must coordinate their behavior with one another, becoming engaged in intense processes of negotiation through nonverbal interaction. During performance, people can become so closely "tuned in" to one another (Schutz [1951] 1977) that they perceive minute inflections in the behavior of those around them, which in other circumstances could go unnoticed. In highlighting the face-to-face relationships that are established among musicians in an ensemble context, Alfred Schutz ([1951] 1977, 117) observed: "The Other's facial expressions, [her] gestures in handling [her] instrument, in short all the activities of performing, gear into the outer world and can be grasped by the partner in immediacy. Even if performed without communicative intent, these activities are interpreted by [her] as indications of what the Other is going to do and therefore as suggestions or even commands for [her] own behavior."

The performance requirements of the style may promote particular modes of social interaction in the very process of music making (Blacking 1980a, 35). The style may involve turn taking during particular sections, which places people in musical dialogues with one another; it may engage them in attempts to mirror each others' behavior simultaneously, as occurs in unison singing; it may call for the coordination of disparate parts; or it may combine these various modes of interaction simultaneously. Many African styles, for example, are structured in a repetitive, cyclical manner, involving turn taking in the form of improvised solo calls and unison choral responses, while polyrhythmic percussion parts coordinate among themselves and with the vocal parts, often adding dialogic variations which draw out their musical relationships to one another. The interactive experience can be further enhanced by the presence of dancers, who also enter into nonverbal dialogues both among themselves and with the musicians (Chernoff 1979). In relation to the Venda, Blacking demonstrated that the modes of interaction promoted during the performance of traditional styles articulated with the patterns of social interaction that were valued by the Venda in extramusical spheres. In the *tshikona,* the most highly cherished of their musical traditions, the Venda enchanted a space for experiencing their social ideal: "individuality in the largest possible community of individuals" (Blacking 1973a, 51).

While certain musical forms are likely to be more conducive than others to generating particular patterns of social interaction during performance, the same musical form can be used in different ways, articulating quite dis-

CHAPTER ONE

tinct orientations to the social relations of musical production (see Turino 1993). Thus, the ways in which musical activities are orchestrated and experienced are implicated in the conceptions held by the participants about music and music making (Merriam 1964; Nettl 1989). In participatory genres the formal properties of the musical style used in a given context articulate dialectically with the conceptual orientations and motivations of the performers, and together they negotiate their performance practices in the very act of music making. Where sociability is the prime objective underlying the musical event, one would expect participants to strive to construct their musical performances in a manner which makes extensive use of the interactive potential of their repertoire, heightening their awareness of their contribution to the collective undertaking.

One could say that participatory music making provides a context for the experience of what Victor Turner (1974) has called *communitas*. Turner made a major contribution to the social sciences by placing the analytical gaze squarely upon those experiences which make life worth living, but he insisted upon a highly problematic methodological dichotomy between social structure and antistructure (Morris 1987, 254–62), which is untenable when applied to any context of group music making, where coordinated interaction is possible only because participants agree to adhere to the structural norms of the genre which unites them. The experience of communitas is dependent upon structure, since it is through structure that the collective gaze can be most efficiently funneled to generate a sense of shared experience. To experience communitas is to experience a sense of intersubjectivity, which neutralizes structure and creates the illusion of antistructure. As Niall MacKinnon (1994) has shown, the informality and "cosiness" experienced by participants of "singarounds" in the British folk scene is the result of considerable management on the part of the organizers of the events.[9]

Clearly not all music making is integrated into religious ritual, but— following Leach ([1954] 1970, 10–14)—one could argue that all musical activity entails ritualized behavior. Drawing on Wittgenstein, Leach ([1954] 1970, 12) argued that aesthetic behavior articulates ethical principles, obscuring the divide between the sacred and the profane. Enchantment, therefore, is not restricted to religious contexts; any setting which promotes experiences of communitas through music making enchants an alternative social reality into existence. The paradigmatic sphere of enchantment, however, is religious ritual. Within the religious context, the musical experience is juxtaposed to religious discourse, thus enhancing the potential that the

16

sensory experiences promoted through ritual enactment be interpreted in moral terms. Through musical performance, religious discourse and aesthetic experience become inextricably intertwined, inclining participants to experience the ritual space as an encounter with the moral order of the sacred. In such an enchanted world, participants construct and simultaneously experience the harmonious order that could reign in their society, if only their natural laws were not being systematically violated.

The Urban Experience

Analysts commonly cite the 1930s as the decade in which the urbanization of Brazil got under way in earnest (Bresser Pereira 1985; French 1992). This was the period in which the economic base of the country started to shift from agricultural to industrial production, and this development was mostly concentrated in the urban complexes of the southeast. But it was not until the 1960s, when a dramatic restructuring of the rural economy led to a mass exodus of the rural labor force, that Brazil was to emerge as an urban nation, as several million destitute and unskilled migrants flooded into the country's major centers in the hope of securing their livelihood. In 1940, 73.65 percent of the population lived in rural areas; by 1991, 77.13 percent resided in urban centers (Santos 1993, 29), the greater part of them in or near absolute poverty.[10] Already in 1960 São Paulo and Rio de Janeiro had absorbed 10 percent of the population of the country; by 1991 greater São Paulo and greater Rio housed nearly 25 million people, approximately 17 percent of the total national population. According to data obtained by the Plano Urbanístico Básico (PUB) for 1968, 88.6 percent of the inhabitants of greater São Paulo at the time had not been born in the municipality. The national census figures for 1980 indicate that the migrant population for São Bernardo do Campo stood at 73 percent (Cardoso 1981, 39). Between 1960 and 1970 São Bernardo accounted for 36 percent of the total population increase in the "Great ABC,"[11] which indicates that it attracted only a minor majority of the incoming migrants to the region; during the following decade, however, when the car industry had focused its activities in the municipality, São Bernardo was responsible for 60 percent of the regional population increase (Krumholz 1982). Although internal migration declined considerably during the 1980s, São Bernardo remained a major pole of attraction; while the national population increase during the decade was 1.8 percent, São

CHAPTER ONE

Bernardo underwent a 3.5 percent increment (Toledo 1992, 60–61), reaching 563,000 people in 1991, although in 1950 there were but 29,000 people in the municipality.

Although industry was growing at an astounding rate, it was unable to keep up with the vast labor supply, most of which was composed of unskilled and illiterate—or semiliterate—rural agriculturalists, arriving daily in search of jobs. The constant influx of migrants was also putting tremendous pressure on the urban infrastructure, which was unable to provide the necessary housing, public services, transport facilities, and so on to meet the new demands. Over the past decades the standard of living of the Brazilian lower classes has been rapidly deteriorating as salaries have been corroded by unimaginable rates of inflation.[12] As Lucio Kowarik (1987, 221) has observed, Brazilian development has not been linked with prosperity for large sectors of the working classes. In 1975, 85 percent of the population of greater São Paulo—the best-paid workforce in the country—received no more than three times the minimum wage. Even though this figure had declined to 79 percent in the early 1990s, the buying power of the minimum wage had fallen by 80 percent since 1960, while since 1985 alone it had lost 40 percent of its buying power ("Pingente da economia" 1993, 22–23).

Today São Bernardo do Campo is the locus of the Brazilian automobile industry. Within sociological literature, it is best known for the militancy of its metalworkers' labor unions, particularly their historic strikes in the early 1980s, which have received considerable academic attention (see Brato 1983; French 1992; Humphrey 1982; Keck 1992; and Rainho and Braga 1983, among countless others). These movements ultimately led to the organization of the Workers' Party (*Partido dos Trabalhadores*), or the PT, which has come to be the largest left-wing political party of the country, with a somewhat stable electoral base of around 33 percent of the national votes. Thus, São Bernardo do Campo stands as more than a paradigm of Brazilian industrialization: with its migrant population, it helped to articulate transformations that marked the political history of the country in the late twentieth century, and local foliões were squarely immersed in this political atmosphere.

Despite my first impressions, however, political militancy among foliões was quite rare. Indeed, the only "real" political activist participating in a companhia in São Bernardo during the period of my research was Zezo.[13] He was directly involved in the metalworkers' union, he had been a member of the factory commission at Mercedes-Benz since 1984, and he stood as a candidate for the PT for a seat as town representative in the municipal elections of Santo André in 1988, though he received only half the number of votes required for the seat. Zezo's militant career was instigated by a family tragedy in 1978. He was on the night shift at Volkswagen while his daughter was in the hospital undergoing a routine operation in São Paulo. The child died on the operating table and the hospital claimed it informed the factory, but Zezo never received the message. The next morning he set off for the hospital to collect the child, but discovered she was dead. He became convinced that the factory managers had deliberately withheld the information because they were short of staff that evening. His attitude toward the company changed dramatically, and—drawing on the discourses of the union activists with whom he worked—he came to see the multinational as being solely preoccupied with extracting labor from the workforce while showing no interest in their families' well-being.

Owaldir had participated in the 1980 strike and lost his job at Volkswagen as a consequence, even though he had not held a leadership role within the movement. He blamed his misfortune and the hardship his unemployment had brought upon his family squarely on the union leaders, and when these same people founded the PT a few years later, he transferred his disdain to the party. His grievance resided in his feeling that the union leaders had placed their personal political aims before the well-being of the workforce they claimed to be defending, while leaving them out in the cold once they had fulfilled their role. Since then he has steered clear of all forms of voluntary political activity, an attitude he continued to hold when I last met him in 1994. With the leadership of the Folia do Baeta Neves thus divided in their political allegiances, party political discussions within the group were systematically avoided.

Their father's disdain for the PT notwithstanding, Owaldir's two sons of voting age declared their support for the workers' party to me in 1992, as did several other members of the group, most notably those employed in the automotive industry. Other foliões, however, sympathized with Owaldir and other acquaintances whose personal lives had been disrupted by militant activism. These foliões tended to cast their votes all across the vast spectrum of political parties registered at the time, so even though only a third of the group's membership supported the PT, it was still the party with the largest representation within the group throughout my years among them. While PT support tended to be somewhat higher in most of the other companhias in São Bernardo, on the whole, foliões' voting patterns closely mirrored the general electoral trends of the municipality at large. Given these figures, it seems inappropriate to pursue a line of inquiry that would attempt to relate folia participation to preferences for particular political parties. Moreover, foliões themselves saw no direct relationships between these domains, and they actively pursued strategies to keep them separate. While this may tell us more about the foliões' conceptions of the public political sphere in Brazil than it does about their ideological stances, it seems clear enough that—at least up to the mid-1990s—none of the country's political parties voiced their aspirations with any clarity.

It seems, then, that folia communities are far more representative of the wider working-class population of greater São Paulo than they are of the more visible militant associations that have so fascinated the academic community. This study, therefore, is of the more commonplace strategies adopted by migrant communities in Brazil's big cities in dealing with a life of urban poverty and marginality. Indeed, James Scott (1985, 1990) has argued that such overt and explosive forms of political opposition as occurred in the 1980 strikes are quite rare, but political activity is not confined to such open manifestations of discontent. Between an apparent quiescence of the status quo and outright revolt lies an immense political terrain marked by countless forms of covert resistance, which Scott refers to as "infrapolitics": like infrared rays, infrapolitics lies "beyond the visible end of the spectrum" (1990, 183), and like the support system implied by the concept of infrastructure, it provides a cultural and structural foundation out of which public forms of political action can emerge when conditions are right. In the interim, infrapolitical activity nibbles away at the edges of the power structures, often to great effect.

It is in the realm of the infrapolitical that Scott (1990) claims that subaltern groups construct their "hidden transcripts," that is, critiques of power containing expressions of their experiences of social injustice. These transcripts are hidden precisely because they are formulated among one's family and peers in spaces that are far removed from the public gaze of the power holders, and like Gramsci, Scott finds them in aesthetic representations that are often called folklore. Scott, however, emphasizes the experience of assaults upon one's dignity and self-esteem that typically accompany material exploitation, pointing out that these themes are prominent in hidden transcripts. Thus, considerable energy is expended within the infrapolitical sphere in creating autonomous social spaces for the reassertion of dignity and the restoration of self-esteem.

Though—at least at present—the folia tradition cannot be connected to public political action, it can be seen as part of the infrapolitical grid, providing a safe cover for the construction of hidden transcripts and the nurturing of cultural integrity. Its discourses may challenge official church doctrine, but they are presented as a form of Catholicism, which reduces surveillance over folia activities; folia journeys take place completely outside the control of the church, circulating within the limits of low-income neighborhoods, where the state apparatus also keeps a low profile; furthermore, they are the basis for the construction of networks of mutual support common to many migrant groups all over the world, encompassing many households within the grid. By structuring the network around religious activity, mutual support can be articulated in ethical terms. By enchanting their social vision into the world during their annual journeys, folia communities periodically reconfirm the truths of their religious tenets, reconstituting themselves as moral communities, where they can reclaim a sense of dignity.

Itineraries

When I began my fieldwork for this project, I had already been investigating Brazilian popular Catholic traditions since 1982, though I had focused on patron saint festivals in the rural southeast. Having been brought up in São Bernardo in an American Methodist missionary family, I was fascinated by what I perceived as the garish baroque aesthetics of Brazilian popular Catholicism. This mystical world of magical realism contrasted so starkly with the austerity and frugality of mainstream urban middle-class Protestant aesthetics that, at least initially, I had little difficulty finding the "exotic other" among its practitioners. Indeed, I was convinced I had just entered the pages of Gabriel Garcia Marques's *One Hundred Years of Solitude* on my first-ever field excursion to document a popular Catholic festival, the Pentecost festival in São Luiz do Paraitinga. There I was, a total stranger to the place, and yet immediately upon my arrival, I was informed of the dreadful tragedy that had just stuck the town: only minutes before my bus rolled into the station, someone had stolen the crown of the Divine Holy Spirit from the festival altar. It had happened, I was told, because the priest had refused to choose a patron for the festival; it was an electoral year and he had not wanted local politicians to use the event to forward their political aims. Without a patron, however, there could be no *afogado,* the local meat stew served as a collective repast to everyone at the festival. Thus, the Holy Spirit had punished the community because there would be no food for the masses on his feast day.

The poetics of popular Catholicism was also not lost on Dona Maria

"Santeira" (Saint-Maker), who painted the banners for the various Catholic festivals in São Luiz. She lived in a tiny, narrow cottage whose walls were lined from top to bottom with clippings and posters of saints, angels, churches, and other religious symbols, and her cabinets overflowed with Catholic paraphernalia. She told me that several years earlier she had converted to Pentecostalism, and the pastor had said she needed to take down all her decorations. And she did. One day, a few months later, she walked into her house and saw the blank white walls and realized that her house was ugly. Then and there she decided to become a Catholic again, and put everything back up.

For all its poetic charm, popular Catholicism is constructed out of representations of wide diffusion throughout the Christian world, and this posed a methodological problem intrinsic to any ethnography of the familiar—or "endo-ethnography" (daMatta 1994): the challenge of "defamiliarization." Having had a strong Christian upbringing, I often found it difficult to distinguish between the readings of Christian symbolism that I held and those of the devotees with whom I worked. Though I strove to estrange myself, I was never entirely sure of the extent to which I was imposing my own commonsense notions upon the material. Moreover, the cultural baggage I shared with Brazilian popular Catholic communities was not limited to a common repertoire of Christian symbolism: we all saw ourselves as Brazilians, and therefore we had been socialized into many of the same dominant narratives and ideologies—or "public transcripts" (Scott 1990)—operating in the wider society; we spoke the same language, despite the differences in our accents; we lived within the same national borders, which made us subject—at least in principle—to the same laws and public policies; we were exposed to many of the same television soap operas and commodities propagated by the mass media; and this is but a small sampling of the vast overlapping spheres in our experiences. This commonality of experience provided us with a mutually recognized repertoire of cultural representations, and one could be easily deceived that we also shared the same understandings of this common ground.

Yet the lifestyles and social experiences of the devotees contrasted dramatically with my own. In Brazil, where the social classes are highly segregated, there is a wide cultural gap separating the rich from the poor, which only appears to be bridged by the national and supranational representations and discourses that make up the public transcripts. The class divisions in Brazilian society are, of course, far more complex and contradictory than this simple dichotomy between rich and poor would indicate, cut across, as it is, by distinctions that emerge from regional specificities, the rural-urban divide, race and ethnic relations, gender and generational differences, and the finer markers of distinction operating within each of these categories. Among the lower classes, however, a gross opposition between rich and poor is basic to their understanding of the social order (Sarti 1995, 117; Scheper-Hughes 1992, 98). In a society thus divided, much of the cultural material available for elaboration by the subaltern classes derives from the public transcripts, since they must negotiate their livelihood and cultural integrity within a wider frame defined by hegemonic discourses. This does not mean, however, that their understandings of the dominant cultural themes necessarily cohere with the dominant views; along with continuity, there is also considerable interpretive discrepancy. While contrasting interpretations can be identified fairly easily, at the interface, where public and hidden transcripts meet, there is a wide, ever-shifting gray area of continuous negotiation and argument that refuses to be disentangled. Indeed, it is the very ambiguity and multivocality of the shared repertoire that enable the continuous dialogue—or argument—across the divide, preserving a façade of national unity.[14]

Given the global nature of Christian symbolism, there are also methodological issues pertaining to the ethnographic representation of the material, since Western readers' understandings of the familiar motifs will also be informed by their cultural backgrounds and their commonsense interpretations of the symbols. Just as the ethnographer must strive toward distanciation to grasp local interpretations when dealing with global phenomena, she must also find the means of constructing the ethnographic narrative in such a way as to elicit defamiliarization from the readership. The danger here is that one can easily overemphasize and fix the interpretive distinctions, losing sight of the ambiguity, multivocality, and contextuality of cultural representations. In response to this problem I have juxtaposed accounts of actual performance events to the normative cultural models that informed them, as a means of illustrating the fluidity with which shared representations are negotiated within immediate situations.

While these matters pertain to the study of popular Catholicism generally, when I transferred the research from the rural to the urban context, I confronted other challenges as well, not the least of which involved overcoming my fear of entering the "dangerous space" of low-income urban neighborhoods, a fear which—as a child of the middle classes—had been repeatedly drummed into me. I had heard countless stories about the violence that was thought to prevail in such places, and it was said that only luck—

and God's protective hand—allowed one to reemerge unscathed. To be sure, the daily lives of the urban poor were marked by violence, but not of the sort portrayed in middle-class myths. Furthermore, their ethos seemed remarkably continuous with that of the rural communities with which I was familiar,[15] for urban life seemed to have made little headway in breaking the enchantment of the popular Catholic aesthetic world which linked the migrants to their rural backgrounds, even though—to me—many aspects of their lives seemed to be far from enchanted.

When I began my project on folias de reis, I held a short-term research fellowship at the Centro de Estudos da Memória Popular do ABC of the Instituto Metodista de Ensino Superior in São Bernardo do Campo, where I was conducting a survey of migrant traditions in the industrial centers surrounding the institute. I was still completing the survey when I entered the doctoral program in social anthropology at the University of São Paulo, which was located at the opposite end of the city. Moreover, I had teaching obligations at three other institutions scattered across São Paulo. This was not an uncommon scenario for Brazilian doctoral candidates, since the buying power of salaries and student grants fluctuated continuously, along with the escalating rates of inflation. Developing strategies for balancing the household budget while trying to prepare a doctoral thesis was a challenge I shared with most of my colleagues in the postgraduate program. These circumstances were far from ideal for conducting field research according to "conventional" anthropological methods, and I never lived continuously for a prolonged period in any of the neighborhoods in which a folia was based. Instead, I remained in my flat in São Paulo, and the bulk of my data were collected during evening visits and weekends, when foliões were off work and free to speak with me. During my vacations I spent time in their hometowns to experience the contexts they spoke about so frequently and with such nostalgia. By working as a part-time field researcher, I collected data in a steady stream of homoeopathic doses extending over a period of three years. Since I moved to Northern Ireland in 1990 I have returned to Brazil on an regular basis, updating my material with each trip.

Anthropologists and ethnomusicologists have become acutely aware that the most any ethnography can achieve is a partial representation of what is there (Clifford 1986). Despite this inescapable truth, exacerbated perhaps by "homoeopathic" research methods, I was guided throughout my work by what I would now call the "holistic ideal of radical empiricism" (Spencer 1997). Clearly, there will always be a gap between what is possible in a pragmatic world and what one would hope for in an ideal setting, but it is only by safeguarding the ideal that we will be able to construct revelatory visions of humanity's humanity. By preserving a holistic orientation, I hope that my partial representation is able to give some insight into the ways folia communities construct experiences of fragmentary wholeness through the contradictory coherence of their enchanted realities.

In the next chapter, "Folias," I discuss the historical background of the tradition. This is followed by descriptions of the various musical styles used by folias in the southeast, which are then related to the mobility, settlement patterns, and economic activities of the population in the region from the colonial era to the present day. I conclude the chapter by introducing the reader to the companhias of São Bernardo.

Chapter 3, "Banners," outlines the hierarchical structure of folias and provides descriptions of each of the roles available to the participants within these associations.

In chapter 4 "Rehearsals," I look at the foliões' conceptions of music, music making, and the social relations of musical production, demonstrating how these conceptions articulate with folia musical performance practices. Through a detailed ethnography of the sociability of music making, I show how an atmosphere of camaraderie is created among the musicians during performance, which neutralizes their internal hierarchies. The chapter concludes with a discussion of how the recent introduction of product-oriented conceptualizations of music is being negotiated within urban companhias.

In "Departures" I discuss the ritual that launches each journey, looking at how its orchestration redefines the social sphere, to construct a sacred sphere distinct from the everyday world. The chapter addresses the ways in which the various motifs in the ritual context articulate with the ritual script to form webs of associations which embody the major themes in the folia worldview. Moreover, I show how the shared representations of the folia repertoire are made meaningful on a personal level by integrating individual biographies into the collective memory of the community.

The sixth chapter, "Adorations," focuses upon the mythic repertoire of the tradition. Folia narratives are viewed in relation to "orthodox" accounts of the Nativity to highlight the ways in which the foliões' (unorthodox) representations of the Three Kings embody the moral values of the Brazilian subaltern classes. In proclaiming their subservience to the saints, folia communities construct their identity in moral terms, marking their distinction from the "rich."

In chapter 7, "Visitations," I describe the ritual exchanges that occur during visitations, in which the blessings of the Kings are reciprocated with do-

CHAPTER ONE

nations to the festival. Reciprocal relations within the context of visitations are further viewed in terms of the logic of the promise, in which the miracles of the Kings are implicated in communal obligations, articulating inter-household solidarity as a divine mandate.

The eighth chapter, "Arrivals," looks at the final festival that ends the annual journey, bringing together a community of fellow townsmen and their friends and neighbors. Together they celebrate their religious tenets, constituting themselves as a moral community. I claim that the apparent naïveté and innocuousness of the folia de reis tradition provides a cover through which foliões have been able to safeguard their cultural capital, while the folklorization of the tradition has allowed for the creation of spaces for its performance in a wider public arena.

In the final chapter, "Visions," I argue that, in contrast to official Catholicism, in the popular Catholic realm the continuous communal resignification of religious representations maintains a degree of coherence between religious life and daily experiences and aspirations. In such a decentralized context, enchantment provides a means of organizing communal action in a manner which re-creates the religious ideals, allowing devotees to visualize themselves within a divine moral order. Within folia communities it is the contrast between experiences within the ritual domain and experiences outside it that reinforces their conviction of the truths articulated in their enchanted worlds. From the margins of society, the infrapolitical realm of popular Catholicism allows the Brazilian underprivileged classes to periodically reinvent the universe in terms of their understanding of God's natural laws and thereby to create and sustain a vision of an equitable social world.

CHAPTER II

Folias

You want to know where the folia de reis comes from? Well, madam, it's from the beginning of the world.

Before Jesus was born . . . there already was Gaspar, because there were three: a Portuguese, a German, and an African. . . . So they had been raised out there. Well, one day before Jesus came, King Herod ruled the earth. So all the people were slaves. . . . Those three boys took care of the sheep out there. . . .

Before Jesus was born, he already performed miracles. The Three Kings were working there, innocently. They were there without a father, without a mother. Not even their father and mother knew each other, because slaves were all bought. They would buy a lot and take it over there; another lot and bring it here. Well, there they were working, working.

So one day Jesus's mother passed by. She and Saint Joseph passed by where they were. . . . Gaspar, who was the oldest, said to his companions: "Look"—he had never met his mother—"look, there's our mother, our mother is coming!"

They looked and looked and looked. And she was coming and coming and coming.

He said to her, "There's no path here"—the fence was high so the sheep couldn't escape—"there's no path here."

She said, "But I can pass."

He said, "There's no path."

CHAPTER TWO

Then she put her hand on the fence, the fence opened and he became sad. He said, "Oh no, our master will beat us. We get beaten a lot. Our master beats us."

She said, "No, I'll fix it," and she fixed it.

And he already had the viola. . . . He said, "Look, mother, I'm going to sing a song for you."

She said, "Not now: in eight days you will sing for me wherever I am." Then she took leave of them and left.

Eight days went by. On the night Jesus was born, at eleven o'clock, she sent an angel to them, a star to get them, an angel and a star. The angel brought the message, the star lit up, and they followed it. . . .

At a certain point they went to speak with King Herod, because at some houses along the way the star stopped shining. The angel moved away and they went to ask which direction the star took to Bethlehem. Nobody knew. They kept going, kept going, until they reached Herod's castle. He wanted to be king. He was king of the world before Jesus came, wasn't he? Well, they kept asking, asking. They arrived at the castle and asked.

The king said, "What are you looking for? What do you need?"

They said, "Well, we are travelling to Bethlehem to find our savior, the king. Our Savior, the King of the World is born."

At this time he wanted to be the king of the world, before Jesus came. He got angry.

So they stayed there a bit, and the Three Kings were leaving. Well, then [the star] started to light up a tiny bit. It rose a little bit. It rose over the castle, and lit up a bit. [Gaspar] saw it, and climbed a few steps and moved backwards. It lit up a bit more and two of them saw it. It lit up even more and all three of them saw it. It moved on.

At this moment the king of the world said to them, "So you go on, and on your way back come by to tell me, because I want to know where the King of the World is, because I want to take him a present, send a present to him."

Now the present [Herod] wanted to send was to kill the boy.

Well, that was when the star lit up. They heard the angel's voice and the star lit up. . . .

So, after that there were no more mistakes. They followed it and arrived.

Now, at that time, after they had been inside the palace, the Eternal Father sent down the gold, the myrrh, the incense. Each one got his present, but they had nothing. It was the divine power that filled their hands with presents so they could arrive there and make the Adoration. One took gold; another took incense; the other took myrrh. It was for the Adoration. From midnight on the twenty-fourth until New Year's, noon, making the Adoration, praying, making the Adoration.

At noon, Jesus's mother gave a little can to one of them and another little can to the other one. So that's how they got the caixa and the tambourine. Gaspar already had the viola, because he took his old viola with him.

Well, on the night before New Year's, the angel talked with them, said to them, "Don't go back the way you came, take another path." . . .

Well, then Jesus's mother had said to them, "Now you go asking for alms and bid thanks for them as you sing."

Well, so they returned singing. They would arrive here, say, six o'clock, saying:

Cheguei na sua casa,	I arrived at your house,
Isso é seis horas.	It is six o'clock.
Vim pra dar notícia	I've come to announce
Que nasceu o Rei da Gróría.	That the King of Glory is born.

They asked for alms and thanked them, . . . making the announcement. Wherever they went, they made the announcement, until they arrived back in the Orient again.

Now, after a certain point, the people were very happy to hear the announcement of the King of Glory, King of the World, Savior, all that crowd. On the sixth of the arrival there were many people. At dawn they were still dancing the *cateretê*.[1] (João Isaias, Monsenhor Paulo, Minas Gerais)[2]

Other Explanations

Historians have suggested that folias de reis and other itinerant ensembles associated with the Christmas season—most notably the *pastoril*, a musical shepherds play[3]—may have emerged in the Brazilian colony as early as the mid-sixteenth century (Azzi 1978, 113). Musicologists such as Renato Almeida (1942), Luiz Heitor Correia de Azevedo (1956), Vasco Mariz (1983), and Gerard Béhague (1979) have continuously commented on the difficulty of dealing with the music of Brazil during the colonial period because of the lack of written records of these activities; documentation is even more scarce in relation to colonial vernacular traditions. It is known that during the first three centuries of the colonial period much musical activity served religious—that is, Roman Catholic—purposes, but very little is known about the repertoire itself.

Mendicant traditions like the folia de reis and the pastoril developed in Spain and Portugal during the Middle Ages, and in time Epiphany—or Kings' Day—became the main feast day of the winter solstice on the Iberian peninsula (Livermore 1972, 142). Oneyda Alvarenga ([1950] 1982, 232) claimed that the folia de reis tradition in Brazil "represents a confluence of two Portuguese traditions: that of the trade guilds that formed processions during public festivals carrying the banner of their patron; and that of the itinerant groups of *janeiras* (Januaries) . . . that commemorated the entrance of the new year . . . not only in Portugal, but throughout Europe."[4]

Already in 1553 a confraternity of the Kings which promoted festivals in honor of the Magi had been founded in the Captaincy of Espírito Santo (Leite 1938–50, 1:217–18). While there are very few early references to itinerant ensembles dedicated to the Three Kings in Brazil, paintings from the early nineteenth century by Jean Baptiste Débret, Johann M. Rugendas and others depict mendicant groups bearing banners and collecting donations for religious festivals in various parts of the country. The early Brazilian folklorist Alexandre José de Mello Morais Filho ([1901] 1979, 58) provided one of the most extensive historical descriptions of itinerant ensembles dedicated to the Magi, drawing on observations from the late nineteenth century in Bahia.[5] While these documents provide some evidence of the historical depth of the tradition in Brazil, I am unaware of any documents which include details of the musical practices of the early Brazilian folias de reis. It was not until the mid–twentieth century that more extensive descriptions and musical transcriptions of folia performances were published (A. Araújo 1949; Bruffatto 1948).

Since then the folia de reis has received a fair bit of attention from folklorists and social scientists, who have studied the tradition in various parts of the country.[6] In this literature the dominant term used to designate these ensembles is *folia de reis,* but numerous foliões throughout the southeast prefer the term *companhia de reis.* In contemporary vernacular Portuguese, the term *folia* connotes loud merriment, chaos, and disorder, carnivalesque associations from which foliões wish to distance their serious religious tradition. To some extent, they use the two terms interchangeably. Yet there is a certain tendency for foliões to speak of folias de reis when they are referring to the tradition in a generic sense, while they often refer to companhias de reis when they are discussing particular ensembles. Nonetheless, when the name of a recognized group is stated, it is most commonly called a folia (e.g., Folia do Baeta Neves rather than Companhia do Baeta Neves). I have attempted to preserve this variable usage throughout my text.

Furthermore, work on the folia tradition indicates that companhias de reis—despite their differences—have a number of common elements. First, the tradition is generally practiced by rural peasants and low-income laborers, but unlike other popular Catholic traditions, such as patron saint festivals, it has rarely received substantial patronage from the dominant classes. Similarly, folias de reis operate completely outside the structure of the institutionalized church, and there are no ritual occasions prescribed by the tradition which require the participation of a priest. They are, therefore, autonomous voluntary associations structured entirely around laypeople, who organize themselves into companhias to express their devotion to the Three Kings.

There is also a remarkable degree of concordance in the overall ritual procedures of these groups: they all conduct ritual house-to-house visitations during the Christmas season in which the Kings' blessings are exchanged for material donations; the myths supporting the tradition are based on similar moral principles, emphasizing reciprocity; the organization of the ensembles always involves some sort of hierarchical structure; and generally folias are accompanied by a few clowns who commonly represent Herod's spies. Moreover, many of the same special rituals are performed throughout southeastern Brazil, such as *pousos* (rest stations), in which meals and sleeping accommodations are offered to the foliões by different families along the route, and ritual encounters (*encontros*), which are performed when two companhias happen to meet one another en route and during which they engage in competitive riddling. The most evident differences between folias reside in the musical styles used in different parts of the country, and it is on the basis of these distinctions that foliões classify the different modalities of the tradition; the differences in ritual proceedings across groups using distinct musical styles, however, are no greater than those within any given style.

Folia Styles of the Southeast

While northeastern folias are generally instrumental ensembles, in which the melody line is performed on two reed pipes (*pifes* or *pífanos*) in parallel thirds

CHAPTER TWO

or sixths (A. Araújo 1964, 1:130), in the southeast, vocal polyphonic forms with instrumental accompaniment are the norm. Southeastern foliões classify their tradition into three major styles, which are distinguished from one another by regional referents: the *estilo paulista* (style from the state of São Paulo), the *estilo mineiro* (style from the state of Minas Gerais), and the *estilo baiano* (style from the state of Bahia).[7] For well over a century, however, these styles have coexisted side by side throughout southeastern Brazil, particularly in the coffee-growing regions of São Paulo and southern Minas Gerais; the terminology used to classify them indicates the regional origin of the people thought to have first introduced them into the southeast.

Although southeastern foliões recognize at least three distinct regional styles, all of them have a few common elements. They are all performed in polyphonic *toadas* (melodic structures) to improvised four-line verses, and most toadas can be notated in 2/4 or 4/4 time signatures. The verses are generally presented two lines at a time, and each set of two lines—a *linha* (line)—is improvised by the *embaixador,* the ritual leader of the ensemble. In order for the full verse to be presented, the musicians must perform the toada twice. During their journeys groups tend to use no more than four or five different toadas, which are repeated continuously throughout the twelve days of visitations. Folias throughout the southeast are accompanied by strings, tambourines, and caixas because it is said that these were the instruments of the Kings. There is no restriction on the number of instrumentalists who can participate in a folia, and most groups have several musicians who do not have vocal parts.

The major distinction between the various folia styles resides in their polyphonic forms, although they may also be performed at different tempos and use different rhythmic patterns. The mineiro style uses a cumulative vocal form, while the paulista style is antiphonal; the baiano style can be either cumulative or—more frequently—antiphonal, but in either case the melodies use syncopations and the instrumentation is dominated by drums. Today the mineiro style, the focus of this study, is the most common form used by folias de reis in the southeast of the country, having displaced the antiphonal styles once prevalent in the region.

Both cumulative and antiphonal styles are used in a variety of other popular Catholic traditions throughout southeastern Brazil, although the antiphonal format is by far the most prevalent. Collective recitations of the rosary are invariably performed antiphonally, as are recitations of the Lord's Prayer; many ritual events begin with a litany between lay chaplains and the rest of the participants, while sung prayers are often performed as litanies, ei-

32

ther with verse-refrain alternations or with exact repetitions of a single verse sung successively by two camps. Cumulative formats, on the other hand, rarely occur outside itinerant traditions like the folia de reis, although there are several ritual genres in which the final chord of a verse is enhanced by additional voices in the upper registers.[8] Traditional cumulative styles to be found in the paulista area, however, are usually restricted to at most four distinct vocal parts, as, for example, the *folias do divino* that collect donations for the Festival of the Divine Holy Spirit in the Paraíba Valley (Reily 1994b, 13–16).

Other musical features of southeastern folias de reis are also common to the broader musical culture of the region. First, a common distinction made throughout the region is that between toadas and *modas*. Though both of these terms could be glossed as "tunes," or melodic sequences, a particular tune tends to be called a toada if it underpins a religious text, and it is more commonly known as a moda if it is a secular song; folias de reis, therefore, perform toadas. In practically all popular Catholic traditions among the lower classes the musical leaders of the ensembles are expected to play the viola, as in folias de reis. Throughout southeastern Brazil the viola is considered a sacred instrument, and as Alceu Maynard de Araújo (1964, 2:448–49) has pointed out, in the region of the Paraíba Valley it is even held in a special, "sacred" manner—up high, close to the chin—when used during devotional rituals, a practice still prevalent when I was in that area during the 1980s. Parallel thirds are pervasive throughout the region, common to both religious and secular musical traditions; moreover, the main voice is generally in the upper register, cadencing on the mediant, as typically occurs in folia toadas. The quatrain used in all southeastern folia styles is also widespread, prevailing both in popular Catholic and secular traditions. Southeastern harmonic accompaniment is based on European chord sequences, usually restricted to I–V[7]–IV for both religious and secular music. These stylistic parallels derive from the coexistence of numerous genres within a broader social sphere marked by similar historical processes, and often the same musicians have specialist knowledge of several different musical forms, drawing on well-embodied musical habits as they move from one genre to the next.

The Paulista Style

The paulista style begins with two singers—known as the "front singers"—performing in parallel thirds, in which the embaixador presents the linha with the help of his *ajudante* (helper), also known as *segunda* (second) in

CHAPTER TWO

Musical Example 2.1

Paulista style (Folia do João Paca, Batatais, São Paulo)

some companhias. The leader can take either the upper or the lower register, but he is more likely to sing the higher of the two voices, because it is said that it can be heard more easily. As the embaixador improvises each verse, the ajudante pays attention to the text, attempting to anticipate mentally what the leader will sing in order to follow him. Thus, the second voice often lags a bit behind the embaixador, and occasionally the two singers sing slightly different texts. When the front singers finish their performance, the two "back singers"—the *resposta* (response) and his ajudante, known collectively as *respostas*—repeat as closely as possible what they have just heard.[9] After the repetition, the front singers perform the same toada again, this time with a new text to complete the verse, which is in turn repeated by the respostas. (See musical example 2.1.)

Although it is impossible to know what colonial folias sounded like, it is quite likely, given its wide diffusion, that what foliões now call the paulista style began to emerge well before the end of the colonial period. It has been the dominant style within isolated subsistence farming communities that moved steadily inland into what is now the state of São Paulo. Since the paulista style calls for only four singers continuously repeating the same eight measures, its adoption could be linked to what Antônio Cândido de Mello e Souza (1982) has called the ethos of "minimal needs" that prevailed in these small rural communities.

The Mineiro Style

The mineiro style is the most common form used in the southeast today, and it is rapidly displacing other folia styles in the region. Indeed, all the folias in São Bernardo employ some variant of the mineiro style. This style is generally slower than the paulista style, and it presents a more complex vocal structure; the most common forms use either six or eight vocal parts. Each vocal part has a name, but there is some variation in the terminology used from one group to the next. The style is recognized primarily by the "little yell" (*gritinho*) that ends each toada. The mineiro style is clearly distinguished from the antiphonal styles by the successive entrances of voices in which each vocal configuration begins performing a register above the previous singer or singers. In general, the lower the vocal part, the higher the place of the singer within the hierarchical structure of the ensemble. This cumulative process leads ultimately to a prolonged major chord, the characteristic yell. It is precisely the vocal organization of the ensemble that allows the musical structure to acquire this characteristic feature. Despite the melodic differences that distinguish one toada from another, the way of organizing the vocal parts remains essentially the same: the voices come in one after the other, and the sound becomes progressively more dense until it finally reaches a climax with the final chord.[10]

Within the mineiro style there are a number of recognized substyles, but the terminology used to classify them is far from unified. One folião distinguished between the *estilo mineiro duetado* (dueted mineiro style) and the *estilo mineiro solado* (soloed mineiro style), indicating a perceived difference between groups in which the linha is presented either as a duet or as a solo. Another folião made a distinction between the *estilo mineiro de seis* (mineiro

CHAPTER TWO

style of six [voices]) and the *estilo mineiro de oito* (mineiro style of eight). Within the dueted style foliões distinguish between the *toada ligeira* (quick toada) and the *toada lenta* (slow toada), one being quicker and less repetitive than the other, but these two styles can also be referred to as the *toada velha* (old toada) and the *toada nova* (new toada), respectively. In some areas the same folia employs two different styles during visitations, one of which is used during blessings and the other during the thanksgiving. The styles are commonly referred to as the "blessing toada" and the "thanksgiving toada," but in some ensembles the thanksgiving is performed to a syncopated melody, which some foliões call the *toada do Reis de Congo* (toada of the King of the Congo).[11]

Musical example 2.2 represents the vocal parts of a toada ligeira (or toada velha) in the dueted style, as performed by the Folia do Zé Machado, one of the companhias of São Bernardo. It begins with a duet in parallel thirds between the embaixador and the ajudante, the front singers in the ensemble (section A). Section B marks the entrance of the *meião* (big middle [voice]) and the *tipe*, while the *contra-tipe* and the *tala* come in together on the final chord of the toada to create the characteristic yell of the mineiro style (section C).[12] A very similar style is used by another folia in São Bernardo, the Folia do Seu Alcides. (See musical example A.2 in the appendix.)

Musical example 2.3 features the vocal parts of a toada performed by the São Bernardo group known as the Folia do Zé Quatorze; it is an example of the slow dueted six-part style, or the new toada. Again the two front singers are the embaixador and the ajudante, while the back singers include the *contrato*,[13] the tipe, the contra-tipe, and the tala. The toada begins with a duet between the embaixador and the ajudante (section A), and at the end of this phrase the contrato and the tipe join the ensemble to give the chord more density (section B). In the next phrase (section C), a new voice—the contra-tipe—takes the highest register, and for the final chord (section D), the group is joined by the tala, whose high, prolonged screech marks the climax of each round. In this style there are not only more vocal configurations than in the "quick" style; it is performed at a slower tempo and includes instrumental interludes within the toada itself.

Although the general norm within folias is that the lower the vocal part, the higher the place of the singer within the hierarchical structure of the ensemble, it can be noted from these examples that the embaixador sings a third above the ajudante. This practice is quite common in groups that perform in the dueted style, and I was told that this was done so that the voice of the embaixador could be heard more clearly. It is only in this case that a

Musical Example 2.2

Fast mineiro style (Folia do Zé Machado)

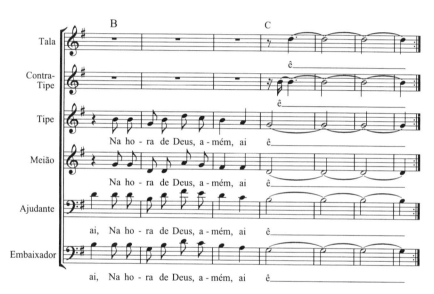

criterion other than vocal register prevails in the establishment of vocal hierarchy within these ensembles.

The solo style, the predominant form in the region of Arceburgo, Guaxupé, and Guaranésia in southern Minas Gerais, was used only by the Folia do Baeta Neves in São Bernardo, and one of the group's toadas is presented in musical example A.1 (in the appendix). It is only after the solo of the embaixador (section A), in which he presents the linha, that the resposta joins him a third above the main voice (section B). This part of the toada ends with a countermelody performed by the contrato (section C). In section D,

Musical Example 2.3

Slow mineiro style in six voices (Folia do Zé Quatorze)

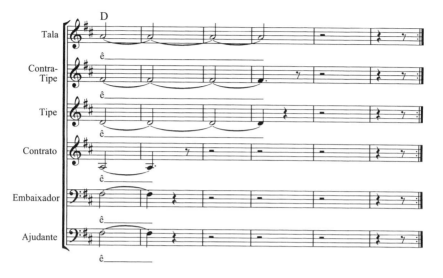

the embaixador stops singing to give himself time to think of the next linha. The vocal parts are now taken up by the resposta, which assumes the register previously performed by the embaixador, the ajudante (now performing as helper to the resposta), and the contrato. This configuration remains until three new voices—the *cacetero*,[14] the tipe, and the contra-tipe—enter the ensemble, each a register above the other (section E). For the final yell (section F), the tala comes in as it does for the dueted style. Musical example 2.4 features the thanksgiving toada used by the group. Like the toada ligeira, it is constructed around three vocal configurations, but in this ensemble it follows the "soloed" style: the embaixador presents the first couplet as a solo (section A); when he has finished, all the other singers join the ensemble in their own registers, with the exception of the tala (section B), who comes in only for the final chord (section C).

The mineiro style may also, like the paulista, have first emerged during the colonial era, but because it requires a relatively large ensemble, in which each musician performs a distinct role, it was probably most common in the highly urbanized context of the mining areas, where there were more musicians available among whom ensembles could recruit their membership. Although today it may be characterized as "modern," its initial integration into the tradition arguably could have occurred because of its resonances with the ritual process involved in folia journeys. The mineiro style is particularly well suited to the folia tradition in that the cumulative form articulates with the ritual role of the ensemble: a group of musicians who go from house to

CHAPTER TWO

Musical Example 2.4

Thanksgiving toada (Folia do Baeta Neves)

house collecting donations, progressively increasing the resources available for the promotion of the final festival. Not surprisingly, such cumulative forms are common to other itinerant popular Catholic traditions in the southeast, most notably the folia do divino, which collects donations for the Pentecost festival.

Moreover, the style articulates with the foliões conceptions about the journey of the Wise Men, in which they were told to return to the Orient singing from house to house to announce the birth of Jesus. In the mineiro style there is a sonic reenactment of the Three Kings' mission to establish the family of God on earth. The embaixador begins by proclaiming the Kings'

divine message, which is then taken up by the next voice, then by the next and so on, until the entire ensemble forms an harmonious whole in their prolonged final chord. Just as the Three Kings sang from house to house converting the pagans as they announced the birth of Jesus, each new vocal configuration of the mineiro style could be seen to represent the integration of new converts into the kingdom of God.

The Baiano Style

Although Bahia is actually in the northeast of Brazil, the southeastern baiano style is quite distinct from that of the northeastern pipe bands—the *bandas de pifes,* or *zabumbas*—that perform as folias during the Christmas season in some areas of the arid northeast. The southeastern baiano style might best be viewed in terms of its two substyles, since it can take the vocal organization of either the paulista or the mineiro prototypes, although it is most frequently performed antiphonally, a format common to numerous other African-Brazilian popular Catholic traditions, such as the congado and the moçambique. Either way, toadas in this style tend to be highly syncopated, and the accompaniment is dominated by drums and percussion instruments, which perform various rhythms based on an eight-pulse timeline (see

CHAPTER TWO

Musical Example 2.5

The eight-pulse timeline common to many African-Brazilian popular Catholic traditions

musical example 2.5).[15] The singers generally play stringed instruments, and the embaixador retains the viola. Though there were no folias performing in the baiano style in São Bernardo during the period of my research, there was a folia baiana in the neighboring municipality of Diadema.

The baiano style is probably the most recent musical style to have attached itself to the southeastern folia de reis tradition. It came to be known as the baiano style because Bahia has a strong African heritage, and throughout Brazil, African-Brazilian traditions are associated with drums and other percussion instruments. It probably developed among slaves and *forros* (freed slaves) from the northeast who were brought to work in the southeastern coffee-growing regions during the nineteenth century. In São Paulo they encountered the devotional practice in honor of the Kings, and they adopted the prototypical vocal structures of the styles prevalent in the region but retained the African-Brazilian emphasis on percussion. With the recent proliferation of the mineiro style in the region, the cumulative vocal structure has now been adapted by some groups to the syncopations of toadas baianas.

Instrumentation

Besides the singers there are various instrumentalists in the folias of southeastern Brazil. Generally each singer plays an instrument, but not all instrumentalists sing. Thus, while the genre restricts the number of singers within the ensemble, there are far fewer restrictions on the number of instrumentalists that can join the group. In effect, anyone who is able to play one of the instruments used in the genre and wishes to participate will probably be welcomed into the ensemble.

Since many foliões claim that the Three Kings played a viola, a tambourine,[16] and a caixa, most groups use three types of instruments derived from these prototypes to accompany their singing. First, there are the

42

stringed instruments, among which the viola is the most prestigious, while other stringed instruments, such as guitars (*violões*), *cavaquinhos* (instruments with four single strings similar to ukuleles), *bandolins* or *bandolas* (stringed instruments with four double courses similar to mandolins), and violins, are seen as extensions of the viola. The tambourine has also been extended in some groups to include a variety of small percussion instruments such as the *reco-reco* (scraper), the *melê* (friction rattle), the *ganzá* (cylindrical rattle), and the triangle. Finally, there are the caixas, and most folias paulistas and mineiras use only one of them.[17] If there are two, they are generally identical and perform in unison, but they may be of different sizes and perform different rhythms. Besides the principal instruments and their extensions, some groups also incorporate an accordion (*sanfona*) into the ensemble. Some foliões, such as Seu Alcides, claim that "this is against the prophecy: the Three Kings did not have an accordion on the journey they made."[18] As Seu Luizinho put it: "The right way would be just three instruments, [the Three King's] instruments; that is the right way. But if we did it that way, not everyone can play those instruments, . . . and everyone wants to follow the folia. So we have more instruments. But you have to play one of their instruments, like one of theirs. . . . And it's prettier like this, lots of instruments, lots of people. . . . Now, the accordion, that's new, but everyone likes the accordion, but only one."

The instruments are used to provide harmonic and rhythmic support for the singers, although some of the more able musicians perform countermelodies to enrich the texture of the ensemble. Most folias also have at least one instrumentalist—often the violinist or the bandolim player—to perform the *estribilho,* a melodic instrumental introduction, interlude, and/or coda which is played at specific points during performances, depending on the group's customs and aesthetic preferences. There are various ways of performing the estribilho. In some groups, particularly those that use the paulista style, the melodic instruments perform the melody of the toada, and often there are two similar instruments performing in parallel thirds, reproducing what the front singers will sing once the estribilho is over. The other instruments accompany the duo by providing harmonic and rhythmic backup.

Other groups establish a contrast between the estribilho and the toada using a technique common to various southeastern traditional dances such as the Saint Gonçalo dance and the cateretê, in which the passage from the sung melodic sections to the estribilho is marked by a more rhythmic instrumental interlude, as in the Folia do Seu Alcides. (See musical example

CHAPTER TWO

Musical Example 2.6

Estribilho with Seu Januário on the bandolim

A.2.) In the traditional dances these interludes mark the moment in which the dancers should begin to clap and stamp their feet. The instrumental interludes of the Folia do Baeta are constructed around melodic sequences that are quite distinct from the ones used in their toadas. In this group the estribilhos contrast with the toada through the use of greater note density. (See musical example 2.6, which was performed on the bandola by Seu Januário. See also plate 2.)

Journeys

Since colonial times southeastern populations have been highly mobile. São Paulo was the point of departure of the *bandeiras,* in which rugged slavers and explorers set off into the wilderness to capture Amerindians, hoping also to find gold and other precious minerals.[19] Freemen plowed their way westward into the frontier, setting up isolated subsistence homesteads deeper and deeper into Amerindian territory. Once gold was found in Minas Gerais in the late seventeenth century, movement increased dramatically in the region, as thousands of hopeful prospectors relocated to the mining areas. Mule train operators (*tropeiros*) crossed back and forth from the mines to the coastal ports, attracting other settlers, who set up rest stations (*pousos*) along the mule trails. When the gold ran out a century later, an eastward trend was set in motion, as former prospectors searched for new homes nearer to the Atlantic coast, while the westward march of coffee—particularly after 1850—dragged thousands of workers with it back into the interior. A mass eastward trend was again set in motion in the mid–twentieth century once industrialization began to supplant the coffee economy, with millions of rural migrants leaving rural areas for the industrial centers of São Paulo and Rio, where they crowded into shantytowns, or favelas, living in conditions of extreme poverty. Thus, the image of a group of travelers following a star appositely portrays the southeastern experience and the aspirations of a people caught up in the booms and busts of the regional economy.

Over the centuries, the diverse economic cycles of the region led to the development of different social configurations, each with its characteristic modes of intra- and interclass relations. The emergence of the various musical styles used in the folia de reis tradition can be understood partly in terms of the social realities that have developed in the region since the colonial era. The constant mobility of the population allowed for the dissemination of these styles, providing a fund of musical alternatives from which subsequent foliões could choose, as they re-created them to suit their changing lifestyles.

The Gold Era

The discovery of gold in the Serra do Espinhaço toward the close of the seventeenth century prompted a gold rush which attracted thousands of prospectors from all over the country as well as from Portugal. Within just a few years of their establishment, many of these settlements had achieved the official status of towns (*vilas*), though even major settlements along the coast had long struggled to sustain their population. By the mid–eighteenth century the Brazilian mines of Minas Gerais, Goiás, and Mato Grosso were producing 44 percent of the world's supply, lining the pockets of many fortunate miners.

In his representation of urban society in colonial Brazil, Emanuel Araújo (1993) highlighted the idleness and conspicuous consumption that characterized the population, and the wealth generated by gold in the mining areas significantly enhanced this orientation toward theatrical ostentation. Those who struck gold publicly exhibited their newly acquired wealth in flamboyant displays by building mansions and churches and by promoting grand religious festivals. The institutional base for these displays was lay confraternities (*irmandades*), each dedicated to a different Catholic saint and patronized by a particular "racial" group of the society: there were separate irmandades for the whites, people of mixed descent (*pardos*), and blacks. It was only during festivals that greater integration of the segregated social sectors took place, temporarily bridging the racial divides (Boxer 1969, 134).

Gold and the culture of ostentation greatly benefited the arts in the mining regions, particularly in the second half of the eighteenth century, and in several of the important mining towns of Minas Gerais there was a flowering of activity in sculpture, painting, and music. Although the music of the period has been termed *barroco mineiro* (baroque of Minas Gerais) it is more closely associated with a preclassical homophonic style, like that of C. P. E. Bach. Alongside the official liturgical repertoire of the prosperous irmandades there was a flourishing culture of lively popular music, which was performed primarily during religious festivals. While descriptive evidence of this activity abounds, I know of no transcriptions of the popular religious repertoire of the time.

Clearly, the mineiro style bears little resemblance to the barroco mineiro style of the gold era. Yet it is a fairly complex polyphonic form, particularly when compared to the "minimal" paulista style. In discussing popular religious iconography, Brazilian art historians have distinguished between paulista and mineiro styles; artifacts from colonial Minas Gerais—including those by anonymous "folk" artists—are generally more elaborate and detailed than the more rustic images common to the interior of São Paulo, the so-called *paulistinhas*. This difference has been attributed to the legacy of gold-rush culture, which instilled the "baroque" aesthetic in the population in the area (Etzel 1975).

The vocal organization of the mineiro style is remarkably similar to that of the women's polyphonic choruses still to be found in the Minho region of northern Portugal (Caufriez 1992; Oliveira 1966). It may be that colonists in the eighteenth century appropriated this familiar form in Minas Gerais because its "complexity" resonated with the aesthetics of ostentation that developed in the urban centers of these gold mining areas. Moreover, the mineiro style progressively constructs an inclusive, yet hierarchically ordered, social body, resonating with the role of the festival as a means of periodically bridging the social divides of the highly segregated colonial society.

By 1820 the gold was practically exhausted, which resulted in the decline of this equally golden era for Brazilian religious music, and the population began to disperse to more prosperous regions of the country, taking their musical traditions with them. Beef and milk production began to supplant gold in the local economy, and many mineiros moved eastward, setting up cattle ranches, while the more prosperous ones employed their newly found wealth in the establishment of coffee plantations in the Paraíba Valley; many of the poorest members of the mining societies moved into the wilderness, setting up subsistence homesteads, where they became integrated into the well-established nomadic way of life of the paulistas. When the westward march of coffee began to engulf the smaller ranches, many cattle producers moved further east, occupying the lands abandoned by the coffee barons and transforming the Paraíba Valley into a milk-producing region based around small landholdings. In this manner the mineiro style was diffused throughout the southeast.

Peasant Homesteads

Outside the gold-mining centers, the southeast was colonized predominantly by independent nuclear families of subsistence farmers.[20] The abundance of land of little economic value and the use of slash-and-burn agricultural techniques to guarantee a crop in the shortest possible time contributed to the development of a nomadic lifestyle among the southeastern peasantry (Monbeig 1984). Lack of markets limited production to the immediate needs of the family, fostering a sense of economic self-sufficiency within the nuclear unit, based on its "minimal needs." The nuclear family became the only stable corporate unit within Brazilian peasant societies, and the members of an immediate family were bound by obligations to contribute to the family's reproduction, which created a strong sense of solidarity among them.

Peasant families were organized according to the classic model of gender and age, subordinating women to men and the younger members to their elders. The ultimate figure of authority was the male head of the household, the source of his authority deriving from his control over the productive process within the family, in which the labor of his dependents was understood as "help" (*ajuda*). Tasks involved in the reproduction of the family were ideally organized according to a rigid sexual division of labor, in which the head of the household and his sons worked the family's plots and the women restricted their activities to the domestic sphere.

A fully self-sufficient household was very difficult to attain, and even large families could not perform all their agricultural tasks without the help of extrafamilial labor. Thus, economic considerations favored the aggregation of several nuclear families into small rural neighborhoods known as *bairros* or *sítios,* in which households were linked to one another through dyadic patterns of generalized reciprocity and cooperation (Johnson and Bond 1974). Each independent adult male stood as an equal to all other independent

CHAPTER TWO

males in the community (Durham 1984, 75–76), and it was through the heads of households that interhousehold reciprocal exchanges were mediated (Johnson and Bond 1974). The sense of solidarity that marked interhousehold relations within a neighborhood extended beyond its boundaries to embrace other neighboring bairros, where relatives or former neighbors may have been residing, linking neighborhoods to one another in a fluid sense of generalized solidarity. The lack of clear boundaries to define the limits separating distinct social units—other than the immediate nuclear family—allowed rural peasants to perceive the whole of their social universe in terms of the model of the family, whether or not neighbors were actually related to one another (Kottak 1967, 433).

Bairros did not develop any form of institutionalized authority, except for the forms of leadership made available in popular Catholic religious rituals (Durham 1984, 78). The authority of these leaders, however, was based on their personal qualities and ritual knowledge. Along with *mutirões* (collective work parties), popular Catholic celebrations, such as folia festivals, were among the few events available for interfamilial and interbairro sociability (Galvão 1955). Households alternated in the role of festeiro, staging festivals in their own backyards, with an attendance of anywhere from fifty to two hundred people or more. Without doubt, the ability to organize a good festival yielded the dividend of social recognition for the festeiro and his family (Willems 1961, 199–200), and in economic terms, this was the most effective way of guaranteeing the labor of one's neighbors for those annual tasks the household would have difficulty undertaking on its own.

In many respects the paulista style is well suited to the familial focus of the bairro ethos. In this style both front and back singers are subdivided into a main voice and a "helper" (*ajudante*): embaixador and ajudante do embaixador, on the one hand, and resposta and ajudante do resposta, on the other. This terminology can hardly be coincidental, given that it parallels that used to define relationships within the family unit throughout the southeastern region. It could be argued, therefore, that the relationships promoted in the paulista style of performance resonated inchoately with existing sentiments of family obligation. Each vocal unit could be viewed as a sonic representation of the nuclear family, highlighting the relationship between the head of the household and his subordinates, or "helpers."

While these ensembles manifest an overt hierarchical ordering, the front singers are explicitly identified as ambassadors; they speak with the voices of the Kings, articulating the asymmetry in the relationship between humans and the saints. This undermines any hierarchical relationship that could be associated with their *human* representatives, setting the front singers back on an equal plane with the back singers. Indeed, the front and back singers maintain a like-with-like reciprocal interaction, given that the back singers repeat word for word what has come from above.[21] This coheres with the interfamilial reciprocity of the bairro context, but the organization of the vocal group articulates these obligations in terms of a divine mandate. Quite possibly, antiphonal styles are prevalent in southeastern popular Catholic traditions because this format provides a concise means of sonically representing fundamental notions held by the peasantry regarding cosmological relationships, which places humans in a vertical relationship to the supernatural, mediated by the saints. This relationship defines the essential equality of humanity with respect to the divine, such that both familial and interfamilial solidarity and cooperation become conceived as sacred obligations, or "natural laws."

Viewed from this perspective, the paulista style emerges as a coherent reflection of an essentially egalitarian, peaceful, and cooperative society. But while it could be argued that bairros were egalitarian—at least as far as the heads of households were concerned—they were not necessarily always peaceful or cooperative. Fistfights, stabbings, and shootings were common, everyday occurrences, often leading to violent deaths. Indeed, in her classic study Maria Sylvia de Carvalho Franco (1969) has argued that it was precisely the personalized egalitarianism of the bairro context which incited men to react violently—even toward relatives and friends—at even the slightest offense to their personal integrity. Once a man had embarked on a confrontational mode of action, he felt compelled to carry it through or risk forfeiting his reputation as a man. Festivals were potentially dangerous affairs, since the presence of an audience incited some men to engage in competitive interaction as a means of publicly exhibiting their manhood.

The society envisaged in the paulista style, therefore, articulates an idealized re-creation of bairro relationships. The harmonious coexistence enchanted in performance is achieved symbolically through the introduction of hierarchical differentiation modeled on the family, which calls for the subordination of one's personhood to a higher order.[22] By emphasizing mutual obligations as a divine mandate, the tradition itself may have provided participants with a means of recognizing the contradictions inherent in their own brand of egalitarianism, better enabling them to avoid situations that could erupt in violence without compromising their personal integrity.

CHAPTER TWO

Coffee Culture

Up until the early nineteenth century, the dispersed population of southeastern Brazil was made up predominantly of subsistence farmers living in small rural bairros. This scenario was to change dramatically with the introduction of coffee, which brought a new patriarchal system and altered the distribution of land in the region.[23] Coffee could be cultivated profitably on the fertile soil of the Paraíba Valley between Rio de Janeiro and São Paulo, and the region was soon dominated by large plantations (*fazendas*) modeled on the northeastern latifundium system. Around 1860 coffee had moved westward into the regions around Campinas, and on to Ribeirão Preto, and by 1900 Brazil accounted for nearly 75 percent of the world's production. The rapid expansion of coffee production was beginning to exceed world consumption, which led to considerable fluctuations in market prices. Despite the "crash of 1929," expansion continued as depleted terrains were abandoned for new areas, and when prices soared again in the mid-1940s, northern Paraná became the locus of the new boom. Today fortunes are still being made as coffee takes over the scrublands of central Minas Gerais.

In his seminal work, *The Masters and the Slaves,* Gilberto Freyre ([1933] 1966) presented the patriarchal northeastern plantation as a large quasi-corporate group, centered around a powerful landowner surrounded by a host of dependents which constituted his patrimony. These included his wife, his concubines, his legitimate and illegitimate offspring, other "aggregates" (*agregados*), such as relatives under his protection and families of free sharecroppers on his land, and—of course—his many slaves. The patriarch mediated between his dependents and the outside world, while the enormous internal differences within the corporate body itself were mediated through a system of reciprocal exchanges which he maintained with his agregados. The patriarch, the ultimate father figure, acted as the protector and redistributor of goods for the whole corporate body, and in return he received their loyalty and labor.

The full consolidation of the northeastern ideal was never achieved on southeastern fazendas because of the constant labor shortages which plagued large landowners in the region. When the English ban on the slave trade was finally enforced in 1850, the plantocracy realized that it would be impossible to guarantee a free workforce in a country with thousands of acres of unoccupied land. Thus, the 1850 Law of the Land, which declared that all land not legally held by purchase or grant belonged to the crown, and that no land could be occupied unless it had been legally acquired, was instituted. Although prices were symbolic, few homesteaders had the necessary cash—or even the information—to gain legal rights to the land they occupied, and they were engulfed by the encroaching plantation owners as they swept across the countryside filling it with new coffee trees. Thus, forros and disenfranchised peasants had little option but to supply their labor to the plantation owners, through some sort of sharecropping arrangement.

The landholding patriarchs fostered a relationship of dependence with the sharecroppers in which their dealings were conceived as "favors" (*favores*), leaving the sharecroppers perpetually in the landowners' debt. The patriarchs' favors often involved the concession of a plot of land in exchange for a percentage of the produce, and they increased the family's income by buying any surplus at a price they stipulated; they might also have provided their dependents with a house, seeds for the next crop, and loans for other goods they could not produce on their own. In exchange for their "generosity" the patriarchs expected the loyalty of their workers, expressed through the notion of "respect," a mixture of fear and reverence (Willems 1961, 47–48).

Despite their incorporation into the plantation system, social life within the bairros underwent little change. The family patterns of the southeastern peasants remained fairly stable, and they continued to be centered on the head of the household, who mediated between the landowner and his family, which still functioned as a corporate unit of labor. He received all payments for the family's work and made the decisions on how it would be spent. Similarly, interaction across peasant households also remained relatively unaltered, and they continued to be marked by patterns of dyadic exchanges and a diffuse sense of solidarity.

While freemen were generally integrated into the plantation system as sharecroppers, often living in isolated bairros around the property, slaves were housed together in slave quarters (*senzalas*) within view of the "big house," where they could be more closely observed. During their free time they often engaged in musical activity in the vicinity of the senzala, where they developed a repertoire and musical styles of their own, based on African templates (Kazadi 1979; Stein 1990, 243–49). Thus, freemen and slaves remained fairly segregated on the plantations up to the end of the slave era, though—as they won their freedom—many former slaves were integrated into bairro culture, as many forros had been before them.

As the abolition of slavery—which was finally declared in 1888—grew imminent, even the Law of the Land was insufficient to guarantee a labor force, and a mass immigration program was set in motion to suppress the

CHAPTER TWO

demand. It is estimated that between 1881 and 1913 over one and a half million immigrants, primarily Italians, but also Germans, Spaniards, Portuguese, Poles, and Japanese, were recruited as families into the country, and most of them were destined for the cultivation of coffee, working under an indentured labor system known as the *colonato,* where they were allocated a house and the use of land to supplement their subsistence. They were paid annually on the basis of the number of trees they cared for throughout the year (about two thousand trees for men and one thousand for women and children over twelve) and for the number of bags of coffee they picked (Martins 1981, 82). Additional cash could be made by selling the surplus of their agricultural produce.

Immigrants were initially expected to repay the owner of the plantation who financed their passages, but once the state began to subsidize the immigration program, these debts were lifted. Even so, the immigrants were still tied to the plantation, since the law forbade them to squat on uncultivated land, and it has been estimated that it would take a family of *colonos* approximately twelve years to earn enough money to buy land of their own (Dean 1976, 491). Only a small handful were able to do this, and social ascent among immigrants involved moving to the cities either to work in the newly established cottage industries or to enter into commerce. José de Souza Martins (1981, 74) has argued that, from the immigrants' point of view, the colonato provided them with unknown abundance compared to the poverty they had left, and they saw their labor on the plantation as rent for the right to use the land for subsistence. The seasonal character of coffee cultivation meant that for approximately six months of the year the colono could, in fact, work for himself, acquiring a perception that he was master of his own labor. Yet, as soon as they could, the vast majority of immigrants abandoned agriculture for urban employment, and only the least fortunate dispersed into the national rural labor forces.

As the *colônias* (rows of houses inhabited by colonos) were vacated by the immigrants, the native-born labor force moved in, coming from the natural population increase in neighboring bairros as well as from internal migration chains, particularly from the arid northeast. With the depletion of the yields, the decline in profits was partially compensated through the allocation of more trees to each colono, which reduced the time the workers could dedicate to their own fields and animals (Martins 1981). The labor shortages during the coffee expansion period, however, empowered the peasantry to some degree, allowing them freedom of movement from one plantation to the next. If the head of a household felt that his position as the provider of the family was being threatened on a particular fazenda, he simply left, moving to another one where the landowner was known for his benevolence toward his workforce. Economic pressures, however, were not conducive to extreme expressions of generosity, and the notion of the "good boss" (*bom patrão*) existed more as a myth than as a reality.

In this context nomadism remained the solution for affirming personal integrity and household independence, with the nuclear family as the unit of mobility. Furthermore, sharecroppers continued to reside in bairros, following the same patterns of interhousehold exchange that had prevailed in the prefazenda era, patterns that were also transferred to horizontal relations within colônias. Sociability within these communities still centered on popular Catholic traditions, although a clear distinction began to emerge between small, bairro-based festivals with peasant festeiros and grand, patron saint festivals promoted by landowners eager to publicly demonstrate their benevolence toward their workforce (Zaluar 1983, 73). On the whole, the folia de reis tradition remained a bairro and colônia phenomenon.

Despite the fairly homogeneous ethos that developed in bairros and colônias, they were inhabited by people of very diverse backgrounds: former subsistence farmers and their descendants from various parts of the country, former miners and their descendants, former slaves and forros and their descendants, and various immigrant groups and their descendants. Each of these groups possessed a cultural legacy of its own, which through coexistence and intermarriage—a fairly frequent occurrence—contributed to the development of hybridized traditions, in which members of any of the groups could participate. Moreover, all of these groups were continuously on the move, in a constant search for better living conditions, further contributing to cultural exchange and hybridization.

I have already noted that there are no fundamental differences between folias paulistas and folias mineiras other than their polyphonic forms of musical performance. These differences, however, create distinct experiences during performance, promoting an emphasis on different aspects of the popular Catholic value system. As with the paulista style, each new configuration of the mineiro style could be understood as an independent family unit, but in this case those joining the ensemble do not repeat exactly what has been performed by the voices preceding them. The register defines the singer's position within the hierarchical structure of the ensemble, and each different vocal grouping creates a new layer of sound which distinguishes one unit from the next. When the final voice comes in, the parts conjoin to form a large, harmonious corporate body. The paulista style highlights two

CHAPTER TWO

levels of social mediation: that of the head of the household and that of the saints; the mineiro style integrates numerous hierarchically ordered groups into a single whole, distinct among themselves, but equal before God.

Just as the mineiro style probably developed within the highly segregated and stratified society of the gold rush regions before it was disseminated to other parts of the southeast, it could be seen to cohere with the patriarchal ideal of fazenda culture, which purports to integrate disparate social groupings into a large corporate whole. Yet folias paulistas did not change their performance practices, even when their members became familiar with the mineiro style. Indeed, the different styles often coexisted side by side, each ensemble performing according to its embaixador's tradition. Within the bairro context, horizontal relations remained fundamentally unaltered, such that the paulista style retained its resonance with the peasants' egalitarian ethos while continuing to restrain violent outbursts by articulating mutual obligations in divine terms. Nonetheless, the introduction of the coffee plantations required the peasants to renegotiate their livelihood with fazenda owners, and no matter how benevolent the patriarch was perceived to be, the new conditions were seen as an intrusion on their independence. In this context their musical performances may have provided them with a means of preserving the memory of the egalitarian preplantation era, in which they held full control over their own production.

Expulsion

The colonato system began to collapse in 1963 with the promulgation of the Land Labor Statute, which extended urban workers' rights to laborers in the rural areas. To avoid these new expenses, landowners expelled colonos from the land, contracting them as day laborers when they were needed, since temporary workers were not protected under the new act. Sharecropping contracts were also terminated, since landowners saw no benefit in preserving partially idle workers on land that could more profitably be used for capital-intensive agriculture. By 1965, 30 percent of agricultural labor was being contracted by the day (Pereira de Queiroz 1978, 224), and this trend was accelerated in the late 1960s, such that today only the specialized and semi-skilled agricultural workforce has secured income stability all year round.

Expelled from the plantations, hundreds of thousands of rural peasants were left destitute, since they no longer had access to land for subsistence, and their diet was drastically impoverished (Pereira de Queiroz 1978, 37). Their income was seasonal and insufficient to compensate for the new expenses required for their own reproduction. Alternative cash-yielding occupations were nonexistent in the small rural communities to which they moved in droves. A striking new phenomenon radically altered the configuration of the rural centers of the southeast: favelas suddenly sprouted around their peripheries, mimicking what had been occurring for decades in the large urban centers. Ex-colonos and ex-sharecroppers became *bóias-frias* (cold tiffins), a term which refers to the way these laborers take their lunch to the fields and eat it cold.

The dramatic decline in their standard of living and the lack of any prospect that such conditions would change led many rural workers to view a move to the city as the only viable option to guarantee their survival. In her classic study of rural-urban migration during the "expulsion," Eunice Durham (1984) focused upon the migrants' processes of adaptation to city life. Her research has shown that, despite the new surroundings, traditional rural patterns of sociability have persisted resiliently in the new context. Mobility, she argued, had long been a feature of the southeastern experience, and migrants were used to adapting to new circumstances. Like migrants from other parts of the world, southeasterners moved into neighborhoods already occupied by fellow townsmen and other migrants with similar backgrounds, reconstituting their rural communities in the urban area. This provided them with a support network upon which to count in times of need, while also serving as the basis for sociability. Moreover, the ideal of the nuclear family has remained central, and it continues to focus upon the male head of household as the primary mediator of the social unit, even though many urban families are structured according to different patterns (Mello 1995; Sarti 1995). Given the centrality of the family in the migrants' orientations, migration has been conceived as a family project of social ascent (Durham 1984).

Paralleling Durham's interviewees, the migrants with whom I worked also claimed that, on the whole, they considered themselves to be better off in the city than they had been in the country, but these comparisons were generally made in relation to their experience as seasonal day laborers, while older men often looked back to their days as agregados as an era in which food was plentiful and no one needed money, memories that have been studiously passed on to the younger generations with little experience of rural life.[24] Although migration did come to be conceived as a project of social ascent among migrants, I contend that this occurred as a means of dealing with the trauma of expulsion. Indeed, as Durham's life histories show, migrants commonly tried their lot in other agricultural areas before making the

CHAPTER TWO

definitive decision to move to the city. By articulating the move as upward mobility, they could confront their situation with optimism.

This optimistic orientation toward migration did not emerge in a vacuum; it drew upon well-established oppositions between town and country prevailing in the Brazilian imagination. The rural context was embodied in the figure of the *caipira*—the southeastern equivalent of the North American hillbilly. The caipira was characterized as rustic, backward, uneducated, ignorant, superstitious, naive, extremely timid, and awkward. In contrast the city was portrayed as the source of novelties and the locus of modernity; it was associated with the church and government—sources of power and authority—with festivals and entertainment, schools, doctors and hospitals, and fashion and stores. By drawing on these associations, migrants could articulate their move to the city as a move away from rusticity into an exciting world of modernity and sophistication; in the city they would gain access to a variety of opportunities and technological benefits that were unavailable in the rural context.

Given this opposition, an assessment of the success of migration could be measured only in terms of the achievement of some degree of upward mobility, a rather tall order in the low-paying jobs available to unskilled migrants. As is still the case today, after their arrival in the city the living conditions of the urban lower classes were extremely insecure: heavy rains were a constant threat to those living in shanty settlements; in the favelas many hundreds of people were squeezed into tiny spaces, often without running water or sewerage systems; public health facilities were far from adequate; transportation to and from work was precarious. Furthermore, urban life clashed dramatically with the rural ethos. While the metropolis may have offered migrants a better opportunity to ascend on the socioeconomic scale, the city was experienced as a place where neighbors were strangers to each other, where there was constant violence, where one did not know one's boss,[25] where one had to work odd hours at tedious or strenuous jobs for low salaries. In the city everything had to be bought with a salary which—until recently—was progressively corroded by high rates of inflation. While the rural context was characterized by a culture that valued irregular subsistence labor and centered around close-knit social and familial relations, most of the work available to migrants appeared to be incompatible with these values and was perceived as depersonalizing and disrespectful of human integrity. Thus, migrants experienced urban life as a continuous struggle to reconcile contradictory aspirations so as to achieve at least a partial realization of their ideals (Durham 1984).

While a slow transition from the paulista style to the mineiro style may have begun prior to "expulsion," it was not until well after the full collapse of the patriarchal fazenda system that folias mineiras became ubiquitous throughout former coffee regions. For foliões who previously sang in the paulista style, the adoption of the toada mineira has been seen as a means of "modernizing" the tradition. Its greater complexity resonates more closely with associations they made between technological development and aesthetic elaboration, and its adoption can be linked to their aspirations of gaining access to goods and benefits associated with modernity and city life, such as education, health facilities, electricity, and various other urban benefits.

Besides the adoption of the mineiro style, the tradition has been "modernized" in a number of other ways. Modernization has essentially entailed the rejection of traditional elements associated with an image of the rural areas as backward and rustic, such that to be modern is to be "orderly" and "organized." One of the first elements foliões highlight in defining an orderly ensemble regards clear enunciation of the linhas by the embaixador, marking the increased importance being placed on precision as an aesthetic value. Proper grammatical constructions have also become more valued in the embaixadores' improvisations in a conscious attempt to displace caipira speech mannerisms.[26] This is rather difficult to achieve, because folia verses are partly composed of traditional verbal formulas in which the proper rhyme schemes and syllabic counts have already been worked out. Furthermore, there is considerable discrepancy between what foliões and the academic world consider to be correct Portuguese, and many of their attempts to follow the standard norm end up leading to new types of grammatical "mistakes." To "put order" into folia performances also entails greater precision in the domain of the purely musical, such as care in the tuning of the instruments and a preoccupation with attacking the chords in the vocal parts simultaneously and with devising special cues for transitions so the group can execute them together; "orderly" ensembles also try to obtain instruments of the best quality the musicians can afford.

Furthermore, modernization has an extramusical dimension. Many companhias are adopting uniforms for the musicians to give them a more respectable public image, discarding the traditional headgear (*bonés*). Bonés are often made of cardboard cut in the shape of crowns to represent the Kings, and they are decorated with colored paper and plastic flowers; it must be said that to members of the upper and middle classes, these hats look rather silly. Also within the sphere of modernization, greater care in bookkeeping procedures is being introduced, and some folias have opened up bank accounts for the funds they collect.

An area receiving particular attention among foliões relates to group discipline during journeys. A major preoccupation in this sphere regards excessive alcohol consumption, and there was rarely an interview in which this issue was not raised and discussed with considerable passion. In the first place drunk musicians are not considered capable of performing properly, and they can be obnoxious and even violent. The main worry, however, is that if the foliões are drunk, people will not want them coming into their homes to perform, fearing they might break or even steal something.

Urban foliões are well aware of the changes they have been introducing into the tradition, and they are quite comfortable in claiming that they are the result of their conscious efforts to render their performances more organized and modern. The "beauty" of a folia in the urban context has come to be linked to the ensemble's ability to present itself in an orderly fashion. By adopting a modern image, contemporary southeastern companhias represent themselves through their music in terms of the processes of social ascent they perceive themselves to be undergoing. Yet, by preserving a tradition with direct associations with their rural heritage, they simultaneously affirm their desire to safeguard a social world based on the recognition of mutual obligations, which characterized their rural communities. In effect, the modernization of the folia tradition constitutes an aesthetic reconciliation of economic mobility with a noncapitalist social orientation.[27]

It is worth noting that throughout Brazil, cultural administrators tend to be attracted to those groups whom they perceive to be "organized" and "orderly," and these are the ensembles most likely to be chosen for events requiring "folkloric" representation. From these administrators' perspective, "orderly" ensembles still embody the quaintness of the rural traditions they represent, but they are not so rustic as to offend the aesthetic sensibilities of respectable urban audiences.

The Folias in São Bernardo

When I conducted my research, there were five active companhias in São Bernardo do Campo: Folia do Baeta Neves (plate 3), Folia do Zé dos Magos, Folia do Zé Quatorze, Folia do Seu Alcides (plate 4), and Folia do Zé Machado. With the exception of the Folia do Baeta, all the other ensembles in São Bernardo follow the traditional mode of naming their companhias after the "owner of the banner" (*dono da bandeira*), the administrative leader of the group, who either founded or inherited the banner carried by the group from house to house.

Each folia was made up of a relatively stable core membership of around ten people, but they also counted on several peripheral members who participated on an occasional basis. In all the folias, membership ranged in age from quite young children of five or six to elderly men of seventy or more; the young children were usually participating as bastião, but by about the age of ten children could be noted among the musicians, often as drummers. Although in most companhias the participation of women was not banned, it was also not encouraged; when present, women generally performed one of the high vocal parts, often the highest.

The members of three of the folias were closely linked by town of origin. The Folia do Baeta brought together migrants from the region of Guaranésia, Guaxupé, and Arceburgo, three neighboring municipalities in southern Minas Gerais which are located just across the border with the state of São Paulo. Both the Folia do Zé Quatorze and the Folia do Zé dos Magos were dominated by fellow townsmen from Monsenhor Paulo, which is also located in southern Minas Gerais at approximately the halfway point between São Paulo and Belo Horizonte. The Folia do Zé Machado was dominated by members of the leader's own extended family, but there were a few other core members to whom he was not related. The Folia do Seu Alcides was the most eclectic group in São Bernardo, drawing its membership from among neighbors with a wide range of regional backgrounds.

The oldest folia in São Bernardo at the time of my fieldwork was the Folia do Baeta Neves. Owaldir claimed that it had been founded originally in 1947 by João Pedro (or João Mineiro), a migrant from the town of Guaxupé, who organized the folia among fellow townsmen who had participated in the tradition before moving to Baeta. All of the original members of *finado* (the late) João Mineiro's folia had died by the time I began my research, except for Januário, who joined the ensemble when he arrived in Baeta Neves in 1949. João Pedro was responsible for the group's banner for over fifteen years, and when he died it was taken over by his brother, Vico. In 1976 Vico became a Pentecostal (*crente*), and his new religion did not permit him to continue participating in such "pagan" activities. Geraldo Reis was the group's embaixador at the time, and he took it upon himself to appropriate the banner. Three years later Geraldo Reis became ill and was no longer able to accompany the group on its journeys. He handed over the leadership of the group to Owaldir, who had come to São Bernardo from Guaxupé in

1964, but Geraldo Reis retained nominal ownership of the banner until his death in 1982, at which point Owaldir officially received it.[28]

Zé dos Magos—who is also known as Maguinho—told me that he had inherited his banner from his father, who in turn inherited it from his father. He was a young adolescent when his family migrated from Monsenhor Paulo to São Bernardo in 1969, bringing their banner with them. Since his father's cousin, Zé Chicuta, already had a companhia in Vila Nogueira in the neighboring municipality of Diadema, the cousins decided to alternate their journeys between the two banners. In 1978 Zé dos Magos's father died, but Zé dos Magos continued to represent him every other year with the group from Vila Nogueira. When Zé Chicuta died in 1981, Zé Quatorze, then the embaixador of the group, inherited Zé Chicuta's banner, which was taken over by Lázaro when Zé Quatorze died in 1992.

Zé dos Magos claimed he did not join Zé Quatorze's group because he lived too far away, and he began to go out annually on his own with his father's banner. Since Zé dos Magos did not consider himself to be a sufficiently competent musician to be an embaixador, he needed to look for someone to be the musical leader of the ensemble. During the first years Joaquim Orlando acted as the group's embaixador, and when he died in 1985, Alcides was invited to replace him. Maguinho claimed that his foliões had difficulty coping with Alcides's autocratic leadership and told him they would leave the group if he gave the embaixada to Alcides again. So Maguinho decided it best to change the embaixador, and he called Luizinho for the task. Originally from Eloi Mendes, a municipality near Monsenhor Paulo, Luizinho had been the embaixador for finado Antônio Lino's folia, a group that also sang in Vila Nogueira with fellow townsmen from around Varginha, a neighboring town of Eloi Mendes.

Alcides claimed he left Zé dos Magos's folia after just one journey because the musicians in the ensemble did not know how to sing properly. Since he had a lifelong obligation to participate in the tradition he decided to found his own banner so he would not have to depend on other companhias. While promises to the Three Kings are quite common in the folia de reis universe, Alcides's obligations are of a different order: he claimed he must always be in a folia because his "guide" (*guia*), the Caboclo Sete Estrelo, demanded it, or he would die. Caboclos, which exist in various modalities, are entities who incarnate old Amerindians, and they are associated with *umbanda,* a synchretic African-Brazilian possession cult. Alcides, however, has a unique interpretation of Sete Estrelo, seeing the deity as a personification of the star of Bethlehem. To fulfill his obligations he formed a group in 1986 from among his new neighbors in Havaí, a "deghettoization" project (*projeto de desfavelamento*) to which he was moved by the state.

Alcides was born in Muriaé, Minas Gerais, but in his youth he moved to Espírito Santo, where he encountered a folia de reis for the first time. He was brought to São Bernardo by a son in 1977 when he was nearly fifty years old, and he went to live in the distant neighborhood of Jardim do Lago. While he was based there he joined the Folia do Zé Chicuta, and he participated in it for several years without holding a leadership position.

Zé Machado arrived in São Bernardo in 1976, when he was already forty-seven, also brought by one of his sons. Though he is originally from Ponte Nova, Minas Gerais, when he was fourteen, he migrated to Espírito Santo, where he first began participating in the folia de reis tradition. For several years he sang in a folia his brother had organized in São Bernardo, but in 1983, when his brother died, he founded an ensemble of his own, drawing primarily upon his immediate family, in order to complete a "seven-year promise" (*promessa de sete anos*) made to Saint Sebastian on behalf of his eldest son, Wanderley. Since folias are not normally associated with Saint Sebastian, he also made a banner for the Three Kings to be carried from Christmas eve to Kings' Day before taking up the banner of Saint Sebastian from 7 to 20 January, the Day of Saint Sebastian. When the seven years were up he decided to continue making journeys because he felt it helped keep the family united. When I met him, he claimed he would like to "stop" his banner because he was getting too old for such a long journey; he has been prevented from doing so by the promises of some of the families on his itinerary who require an annual visitation. In 1994 he was still heading his companhia.

Zé Machado was the only folião in São Bernardo who still maintained something of a rural lifestyle in the city. He was the caretaker for a fairly large property (*sítio*) on which there was a fish-packaging company, which also provided work for two of his daughters. Most of the land was not used by the owners, and Zé Machado was allowed to develop it as he saw fit. He built his family a large—but precarious—house out of scrap plywood, and in front of the house he beat down the earth to form a yard, which was an ideal space for popular Catholic festivals! Behind the house he had planted an extensive vegetable garden, and he also built a chicken coop and a pigpen, and each year he slaughtered many of his yard animals for the festival.

As this brief overview indicates, each of the five folias in São Bernardo is unique. While a broad framework based on notions of what constitutes a folia informs the activities of each ensemble, they operate in the "real" world.

Therefore, they must take a number of factors into account in negotiating their ritual life.

One of the main differences between the groups is in the musical styles they employ. While there are marked stylistic differences between ensembles in some rural communities, it is more often the case today that all—or most—of the ensembles in a particular town use the same musical style. In São Bernardo embaixadores tend to draw on the musical heritage of their hometowns, performing in the style through which they were socialized into the tradition. To some extent one could even say that these stylistic markers have come to constitute emblems of regional identity, and some companhias have come to serve as the focal point for the organization of communities of fellow townsmen.

The perpetuation of the tradition, however, is dependent upon the existence of people who are sufficiently motivated to recruit musicians, set rehearsals, and organize journeys, and this is true in both rural and urban contexts. For those involved, the activities must be sufficiently rewarding for them to continue participating in an ensemble. While foliões often framed their participation in terms of an obligation to the saints in order to harness their protective power, they also saw it as a valued sphere of sociability. For the core members of the five companhias in São Bernardo, folia activities have been such a central part of their lives that they have actively engaged in ensuring their membership in an ensemble.

CHAPTER III

Banners

ONE DAY I WAS DRIVING AROUND in the region of Cordislândia, Minas Gerais, with several local people. As we passed a field, Seu Paulo[1] said, "Do you see that mango tree over there in the middle of the pasture? That's where the cow ate the banner."

"The cow did what?" I asked, and he proceeded to tell the story.

There had been a companhia de reis from Cordislândia that had been making visitations all night long, taking a swig of *mé* (sugarcane schnapps) at every household. By morning they were quite tipsy, so they decided to rest against the mango tree. They were so tired that they all fell asleep. While they were snoring, one of the cows in the field came over and ate their banner. When they woke up, all that was left was the flagpole.

Dona Dosinha was more shocked than amused by the story, and exclaimed, "But Seu Paulo, what did they do? What ever did they do?"

He said, "I don't know what they did, but it seems they went to the nearest house and sang:

Dá licença para o mastro	Give leave to the flagpole
De entrar no seu terreiro;	To enter your yard;
Foi a vaca que comeu	It was the cow that ate
Todos santo na bandeira.	All the saints on the banner.

He told us that after singing this verse the companhia asked the head of the household to give them pouso while they arranged for a new banner.[2]

This is a story about the hazards of excessive alcohol consumption in a companhia, but it also illustrates the central role of the banner within the folia tradition. It is common knowledge to anyone immersed in the southeastern popular Catholic universe that a companhia cannot proceed on its journey without a banner. The banner depicts the Adoration of the Wise Men, and the representations of this event on folia banners look much like Adorations one might find anywhere in the Christian world. Within the folia universe, the banner is conceived of as a material representation of the Kings, analogous to a religious icon. The banner invokes the Magi, bringing their deeds and the ideals they represent into the consciousness of the devotees. It is the banner that signals the presence of the Wise Men, and without a banner, the companhia—the spokesmen of the Kings—ceases to exist. When people say they made a banner, it is understood that they organized a companhia de reis to accompany the banner on visitations. It is to the banner that people make their donations, thereby offering them to the saints. The sacred power of the banner is made evident by the "promises" people attach to it; typically these involve tying colorful ribbons to the banner or pinning to it a photograph of the person for whose benefit the promise has been made. (See plate 5.)

It was the central role of the banner within folias that led Oneyda Alvarenga ([1950] 1982, 232) to suggest that they descended from medieval trade guilds, which emerged in procession at public festivals bearing the banners of their patrons. One sign of that central role, as Alvarenga claimed, was that some groups call themselves *bandeiras de santo reis* (banners of the Holy Kings), though I never came across this usage. The colonial explorers that roamed the interior of the country were known as bandeiras, a term that had originally applied to Portuguese militia companies (Boxer 1969, 31). This military legacy is evident in the folia de reis tradition, and foliões perceive themselves as defenders of their banners, organizing themselves into highly regimented associations. In defending their banners, companhias defend the moral principles personified in the figures of the Three Kings, but they also defend the integrity of their organizations.

BANNERS

Folia Organization

Every folia has a banner and every banner has a dono; furthermore, every journey has a festeiro to organize the final festival. The number of musicians and their roles are defined by the requirements of the musical style the folia uses, and every companhia has a few bastião, or clowns, and a banner bearer (*bandeireiro*). In the following section I shall look at each of the roles available within the folia tradition to provide the reader with a sense of how these associations are organized.

The Dono

The dono, or owner, of the banner is the person who originally had it made or the person who inherited it from its previous owner. The owner is responsible for recruiting musicians, bastião, and a bandeireiro to accompany "his" banner for each journey and for choosing a festeiro to promote the final festival. Although the dono has the last word on any issue pertaining to the group's activities, his responsibilities are predominantly associated with the general administration of the companhia. He organizes rehearsals, which are usually held in his own home; he is responsible for maintaining discipline within the group, which primarily entails regulating alcohol consumption during rehearsals and journeys; he determines the group's itinerary, making sure that there are families along the way willing to provide pousos, that is, rest stops with meals; furthermore, it is his responsibility to keep the ensemble moving, to guarantee that it sings in all the houses that have requested a visitation, and to see to it that the group arrives at their pousos without too much delay.

Although it is possible for a companhia to have a *dona* (female owner), I never encountered one. I was told that this could happen if the widow of a previous owner took on the ownership of her husband's banner, but her role would probably be nominal; more than likely she would delegate the dono's responsibilities to a close male relative, such as a son or a brother.[3]

The Festeiro

To characterize the festeiro, foliões often said he was the "owner of the festival" (*dono da festa*). As Roberto daMatta ([1979] 1991, 87) has noted, all Brazilian popular festivals—except carnival—have an owner, who serves as the focal point of the event, giving the corporate body of participants a sense

CHAPTER THREE

of unity and respectability. The festeiro's main role is to administer the funds the companhia collects during its journey, using them to promote the final festival on Kings' Day. Thus, he acts as the redistributor of the communal goods for the benefit of all. Sometimes the companhia is unable to collect sufficient funds to promote the festival to the satisfaction of the festeiro, and he and his family subsidize the event out of their own pockets. It can be, therefore, a significant financial undertaking for the festeiro and his family.

The festeiro is chosen by the dono among community members who volunteer their services, generally because they have made a promise to the Three Kings. The companhia begins its journey at his house, and it arrives back there for the festival. The festeiro's wife is known as the *festeira,* and her participation is essential to the festival. She takes responsibility for preparing the food for the event, recruiting other women among her relatives, neighbors, and friends to help her in the kitchen. Some widows do become festeiras in their own right, but they may delegate some of the public responsibilities of the position to male relatives.

The Embaixador

The most prestigious musical role in a companhia is that of the embaixador, or ambassador, and as the name implies, the embaixador is the main spokesman of the Three Kings within the ensemble. He is responsible for the *embaixada,* the improvised texts the folia sings, which contain the Kings' messages. The embaixador is expected to have extensive knowledge regarding the ritual domain of the tradition, for his abilities guarantee the symbolic efficacy of the group's performances. To become an embaixador a folião must prove publicly that he has the necessary ritual knowledge and musical competence to fulfill the obligations attached to the role. It is frequently said that the embaixador must have a special "gift" (*dom*), which manifests itself in his musical and poetic competence, in his ability to remember the correct procedures of a series of rituals associated with the tradition, and above all in his ability to confront Herods, the evil forces companhias often face on their journeys. A good embaixador, therefore, is someone who is recognized by the saints as their emissary and will respond to his summons to help the group defend its banner.

The poetic competence of the embaixador is demonstrated primarily through his verse improvisations. By drawing upon a stock of precomposed formulas, embaixadores are able to improvise long narrative sequences, in a manner reminiscent of that described by Albert Lord (1965) for Serbo-

Croatian epic singers. The improvisation of embaixada texts is often a matter of choosing the sequence of couplets that the group will sing rather than of continuous elaboration of newly composed phrases. Some verses, particularly blessings, however, are tied to the context of performance, in which case the embaixador must be capable of adapting the couplets to the specificities of the situation. The ability to improvise long sequences of verses is admired by other foliões, even though most of them are aware of the techniques involved in the process.

Some foliões claim that the toadas should also be composed by the embaixador, and the toadas he makes are considered to be his property, so that foliões speak of Owaldir's toadas or Luizinho's toadas. Alcides claimed that he knew more than eighty different toadas, of which some were his and others "belonged" to old embaixadores with whom he had sung over the years. (See plate 6.) Great embaixadores can be honored and remembered by their companions through the use of one of their toadas during a journey. For example, in remembrance of finado Zé Chicuta, the Folia do Zé dos Magos sang one of his toadas when they visited his widow during their journey in 1988/89. As soon as they began to sing it, she knelt down and began to cry. This episode was remembered several times among the foliões throughout their journey and in conversations long after it had happened.

There are also special situations in which the knowledge of the embaixador can be tested during journeys. Even though some tests are perceived as forms of entertainment, the fact that they pose a potential threat to the integrity of the embaixador and the companhia means that they are classed as Herods. The most common tests occur in the form of enigmatic inscriptions (*letreiros*) some people place at their doors to receive a folia visitation, particularly at pousos. Here the embaixador uses his verses to reveal the meaning of the inscription. For example, "TRM" means "*Três Reis Magos*" (Three Wise Kings); "GBM" means "Gaspar, Baltazar, and Melquior," the names of the Three Kings. Some households test the embaixador by "capturing" either the banner or the bastião (*prender a bandeira* or *prender os bastião*). Since the companhia cannot proceed without them, the embaixador must sing appropriate verses before the head of the household will return them to the group.

Far more demanding tests occur at folia encounters, when two companhias chance upon each other during their journeys. At encounters the two companhias "cross their banners" (*cruzar as bandeiras*) like swords, indicating that a match between them will begin. In traditional encounters the embaixador of one companhia sings a verse containing an enigma related to esoteric knowledge about the Kings' journey, to which the other embaixador

CHAPTER THREE

responds, also in verse form; if he cannot answer the question, the compa-nhia has to surrender its banner and its instruments to the other group, end-ing its journey then and there.

Foliões claimed that such events are very rare nowadays because they are considered risky undertakings, and I suspect that this has always been the case. Most foliões argued that "real" encounters are performed only by "ig-norant" embaixadores, because a ritual leader who conducts his journey as an act of faith participates only in "friendly" encounters, that is, encounters in which the two ensembles greet each other, exchange offerings, and bid farewell, without resorting to ritual confrontation. I have witnessed several "friendly" encounters over the years, but not a single "real" encounter. Even so, practically every folião was able to describe in detail the ritual process in-volved in such events. The idea that one could meet up with a competitive embaixador continued to fuel excitement, and embaixadores remained pre-pared should such an event take place.[4]

In an interview, Alcides explained that if he were to confront a "real" en-counter, he might sing the following verses:

Que encontro tão bonito	What a beautiful encounter
Que fizemo de repente:	That we made all of a sudden
Encontrou duas bandeira	Two banners have met
Que vieram do Oriente.	That came from the Orient.
Ô, meu mestre embaixador,	Oh, my master embaixador,
Queira me desculpar:	Forgive me:
Quero sua permissão	I want your permission
Para nossas bandeira encruzar.	To cross our banners.
Os Três Reis era só três	The Three Kings were only three
Que só um caminho eles seguia.	And followed only one path.
Pergunta, o mestre embaixador,	I ask the master embaixador,
Que encontro que os três fazia?	What encounter did the three make?

The other embaixador should then answer the question through improvised verses. The correct answer, according to Alcides, is that the Three Kings could not have met during their journeys, having left the Orient together. The moral here is that, since the Kings did not engage in ritual encounters, they should not occur.

Foliões diverge in their views about the protocol to be followed at encounters. Some claim that it is always the eldest embaixador who gets to ask the first question; others claim that this prerogative belongs to the folia that beats their drums first; still others claim that the privilege of beginning the bout goes to the folia whose bastião are first to draw a dividing line on the ground with their swords, which establishes a boundary between the contenders. Once the bout begins, the embaixadores take turns challenging their opponent, and the confrontation continues until one embaixador is unable to answer the question posed to him, no matter how long it takes. If after several hours—or several days—the two contenders conclude that they are evenly matched, they can declare a tie and end the bout. To signal their mutual recognition of one another's competence, the embaixadores shake hands and proceed according to the rules of a "friendly" encounter. Friendly encounters, therefore, are conceptualized as public demonstrations of the esteem in which an embaixador is held in the region in which he operates.

The competitive nature of traditional encounters makes them potentially dangerous affairs, especially—as we shall see—for the bastião, since they can challenge the personal integrity of those involved, provoking violent reactions. Even though encounters are avoided to prevent such occurrences, it is precisely their potential danger that renders them privileged topics of conversation: they are a testimony to the seriousness of the tradition. Like the various inscriptions at pousos, these events are a means of testing the knowledge and the ritual competence of an embaixador and his bastião. At pousos, however, the ritual agents are challenged by ordinary community members; at encounters they confront their peers. If an embaixador is able to leave an encounter still in possession of his banner and his instruments—even if the encounter is a friendly one—his prestige increases within the companhia. By conducting a friendly encounter, he publicly proves himself capable of negotiating his way through a threatening situation.

The Musicians

Musical roles in the folia tradition are defined by the requirements of each musical style, but all ensembles are hierarchically organized. Although a folião may join an ensemble in order to redeem a promise to the Three Kings, it would not normally be articulated in terms of a specific musical role, since what one performs depends upon one's musical competence and the specific requirements of the group one joins. On the whole it is considered more prestigious to sing than only to play an instrument, and the earlier a singer enters the toada, the higher his ritual status within the ensemble.

The instruments in the ensemble are also classed hierarchically, the most prestigious being the violas, followed by the tambourines and finally the caixas. Some foliões claimed that companhias should use only these instruments, since they were the instruments of the Kings, though I never encountered a companhia that actually restricted itself in this way. Generally speaking, the conceptual hierarchy of the primary instruments encompasses the instruments related to them, such that all stringed instruments were classed above the small percussion instruments, which in turn took precedence over the caixas. Because the accordion has only recently become prevalent within companhias, it is not included in traditional classifications, and opinions diverge considerably about its relation to the primary instruments; while many foliões argue that it should not even be used in the folia, others see it as comparable to the other melody instruments in the ensemble.

Although most singers also play instruments, not all instrumentalists sing. Because both the vocal parts and the instruments are conceived of in hierarchical terms, the singers in the most prestigious positions also tend to play the most prestigious instruments. Many foliões claimed categorically that the embaixador should play the viola. Since the guitar is gaining in popularity, one often finds the front singers playing a viola and a guitar, the viola being played by the embaixador while the resposta or ajudante plays the guitar.[5] The musicians who perform the estribilho do not usually sing, but their parts are considered the most prestigious among the instrumentalists. Since in many companhias the *caixeiros* (caixa players) do not sing either, the tambourines and other small percussion instruments will often be played by the *tipeiros,* the *contra-tipeiros,* or *taleiros* (tipe, contra-tipe, or tala singers), the last voices in the ensemble.

The hierarchical organization of the ensembles is clearly expressed in the way musicians position themselves for performance. Regardless of the style, all musicians face the banner, which at visitations is held by the head of the household. Typically, the singers line up in pairs behind one another, while the instrumentalists position themselves around them. In the dueted style there are two front singers, the embaixador and the ajudante; directly behind them stand the contrato and the tipe, and behind them the contra-tipe and the tala. The instrumentalists with strings stand toward the front, followed by the small percussionists, with the caixeiros to the rear. The estribilho players are kept quite close to the front, often directly beside the front singers. (See figure 3.1.)

Figure 3.1
Spatial organization of a folia mineira

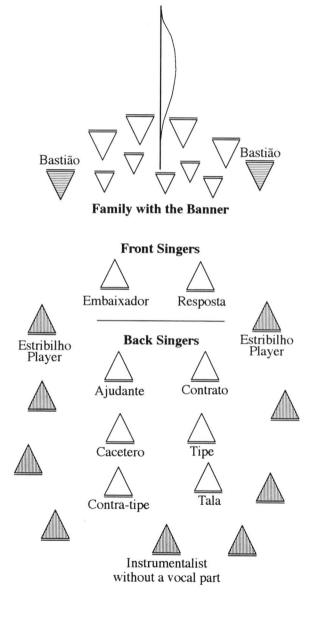

CHAPTER THREE

The layout of the ensembles during performance makes considerable musical sense, providing the group with remarkable balance. Standing in the front, the embaixador can be heard quite easily by the family receiving the visitation as well as by the musicians. The caixas, the loudest instruments in the ensemble, are kept to the back, and in many styles the drums either do not play during the embaixada or they keep their playing to a minimum, so as not to overpower the vocal parts. Since the estribilho should also stand out over the rest of the instrumental parts, it is reasonable that the musicians responsible for the instrumental solos should be positioned toward the front.

The Bastião

The origin that I have to give is that, well, the bastião are not biblical: it's a story to state a principle. I mean we didn't invent it either. We heard about it a long time ago, that the bastião were Herod's soldiers. So Herod saw that the Magi were heading off. It seems that he said, "Go after those men for me. Go see where they are going."

So they went, you see? They went, but they didn't get there, where the Kings went, but from far away they could sort of see them. But Herod wanted them to go, to say, "Look, they went to such and such a place," to teach him the way, . . . but when they arrived, they turned back.

Herod, "So, how is it? What happened?"

"Ah, it came to nothing. I didn't see anything. We went to a certain point, we didn't manage to get there. I don't know."

I mean they lied, right? But Herod, at that time, ordered—he had a lot of soldiers working for him—he ordered the killing of all children under two. At the time he killed more than two thousand children to see if he could get Jesus among them, but the divine power is great. There was no danger. Our Christ was saved, so he could come give the example, for him to fulfill his mission, just as he fulfilled it, right?

So the bastião we have today, I mean that they are blessed. The bastião are blessed. Even the soldiers that went to see, that didn't get there, were blessed, because they didn't commit any cruelty. So the bastião, the people say, "Hey, where are the bastião?" So you have to have the bastião. So today we have them, and we have them with all respect, because we have them as the guards of the banner. They arrive at the houses first, before we do, opening the way, "Hey, *patrão* [head of the household], excuse us," opening the way. (Antônio Mariano, Areceburgo, Minas Gerais)

It is very rare to encounter a southeastern companhia that does not have bastião.[6] At visitations they distribute themselves to the left and right of the banner, standing between it and the musicians, but like the family being blessed, they face the ensemble. These ritual figures stand out in the group because of the special clothes they wear, known as *fardas* (regimentals), which are generally made of a bright, red cloth or a cheap, flowery fabric (*chita*). Furthermore, they always wear grotesque masks. Often the masks have exaggerated features, such as protruding teeth, and they are frequently dark in color with shaggy beards made of unshaven animal hides, giving them a terrifying appearance. The bastião also wear pointed hats—known as *capacetes* (helmets)—which are generally decorated with colorful ribbons and artificial flowers. They carry wooden swords or whips, brandishing them about in a frightening manner, and they also have a bag (*embornal*) to keep the objects and the money they receive during the journey. In essence, the outfits of the bastião integrate elements associated with infancy and animality, constructing a figure of undomesticated subhuman characteristics. (See plates 7 and 8.)

Generally speaking, a person wears the farda as a means of fulfilling a promise to the Three Kings, and this is by far the most common—if not the normative—form of the promise within the tradition, particularly where young boys are concerned. Indeed, promises for children are extremely common in the folia tradition, since the Kings are seen as protectors of little children in opposition to King Herod, who massacred them in his attempt to annihilate the baby Jesus. When such promises are made for little girls, the family often takes on the obligation of giving pouso to a companhia for seven consecutive years; when they are for little boys, it generally involves dressing them as bastião, or "putting them in the farda." Thus, many clowns are children, some as young as five or six, and these boys are called *bastiãozinhos* (little bastião).[7] They follow the companhia along the journey, but they are not expected to perform like more experienced adult bastião.

Although some traditions prescribe two and others three bastião to a companhia, in practice, a companhia has as many bastião as there are people wanting to play the part, and I have seen groups with as many as five clowns. When communicating with one another, the bastião call each other "brother" (*irmão*), ritually marking their common status. Some foliões claimed that if a person wears the farda once, he must wear it for seven consecutive years, even if he puts it on for only a few hours during the journey; if this rule is not followed, the person could suffer grave misfortune.

As explained by Antônio Mariano, the bastião are most frequently seen

CHAPTER THREE

as Herod's spies (*espias do Herodes*) who repented of their sins when they encountered the baby Jesus. Thereafter they became the guards of the banner (*guardas da bandeira*), and followed the sacred object. This view was, however, contested by some foliões. João Paca, from Batatais, São Paulo, for example, told a different story: "There are people who say that the bastião were Herod's spies, but that's not how it was, because it was the Three Kings who dressed up as clowns to distract the Jews not to persecute Jesus. So they jumped here and there. The soldiers were entertained by them. Saint Joseph, Our Lady escaped with the child to Egypt to avoid the massacre."

As with other aspects of the tradition, the emergence of such alternative views is fueled by competition between embaixadores in their struggle over control of esoteric knowledge. Yet these theological disputes have little impact on the normative behavior of the bastião within the ritual context; in all folias their actions are marked by a series of brisk transitions: in some instances they are especially irreverent, and at others they act with extreme respect.

In their comic mode the bastião clown around and poke fun at the other foliões and the families they visit. If the head of the household requests it, they must perform the *corta-jaca* or the *chula,* fast acrobatic dances in which the bastião demonstrate their physical agility. When they enter a house, the bastião may begin to ask for things they see on the mantelpiece, or they may ask for food and drink; whatever they receive they place in their bags and keep for themselves. They also make irreverent comments about the people at the event and those they think should be there, attacking both people who can defend themselves and people who cannot. Young bastião often crawl around on the floor on all fours, getting under the furniture to pull on people's trousers and tie their shoe laces together, measuring their success on whether or not they are able to annoy people or make them trip over their own feet.

When the head of the household decides to "capture" a bastião to test the abilities of the embaixador, he must also be prepared to accept the consequences. It is when they are captured that the bastião are most inclined to get up to mischief. During a leisurely Sunday afternoon conversation in Arceburgo, a group of foliões began discussing what could happen in such situations:

> *Zezo:* [When they capture the bastião] they sometimes grab him by the arms, by the legs, three or four people together, and they lock him up in a room. . . . But if the clown wants to, he can destroy anything

that's in there. It is his right. . . . Sometimes they lock them up in a larder where there's food. . . . A few years ago they did that. These people had a small farm; on those farms those people had a lot of cheese, they killed pigs, there were sausages hanging around. There was all that, bacon, those things. And they even prepared things, sweets, those things. And when they put the bastião in there, the bastião came out with their faces all covered in food. They smeared guava paste on their faces, hung the sausages around their necks, and they came out like that.

Luiz: And if it was a young woman's room, the old man's daughter's room, all the perfumes, the rouge, the bastião destroyed everything.

Zezo: They put it on themselves. They came out white. . . .

Luiz: They even had the right to take the girl's intimate clothes, to come out showing it to everyone. . . . So when the clowns were freed, little bras were up in the air, hanging on their masks, underpants, everything; they put on everything. The girls would race to hide in the back of the yard, dying of embarrassment.

In their serious mode the bastião are seen as the assistants of the embaixador, and they may be called upon to recite verses demonstrating their knowledge at any moment during the journey. Their performances are most frequent at adorations, when the embaixador commands them to recite the prophecies, long verse sequences that narrate aspects of the journey of the Wise Men. At these events they take off their masks and helmets and kneel respectfully before the crèche; they also kneel and show their faces when the ensemble is singing for the intention of the soul of a dead member of the family. Often when the companhia encounters an inscription, the embaixador will pass the word over to his bastião, and one of them will recite a sequence of verses that reveals its meaning.

Just as the stories justifying the presence of the clowns in the folia are contested, what ritual part they should play also raises contentious issues. Indeed, Alcides claimed that the bastião should never declare the prophecies, since these sacred texts are available only to the spokesmen of the Kings; the bastião, he said, should recite only poetry, even if its content is sacred. Some foliões claimed that the bastião mediate between the musicians and the families being visited. As in Antônio Mariano's statement, in some companhias the bastião arrive at visitations before the musicians, asking the family to give them leave to perform. Similarly, according to some foliões, the bastião are supposed to ask the head of the household in what sequence he would like the group to bless the members of the family. There are foliões who argue that the clowns are the only figures in the group who are allowed to handle money during the journey, so it is up to them to receive monetary donations on behalf of the banner. Indeed, the bastião are a primary focus of discursive formulations, which, like the narratives about their emergence, are propelled by intercompanhia competition.

There is, however, a fairly universal view that the bastião play a fundamental part during encounters, since they are the "guards of the banner" and encounters are a direct challenge to the integrity of a companhia. As its guards, the bastião process immediately behind the banner, which heads the ensemble. Thus, when two companhias meet on the road, the bastião of the two ensembles confront each other. It is said that in the old days the bastião raised their swords, entering into mock battles; but often personal vendettas and rivalries would take over and serious sword fights ensued, resulting in deaths. If a bastião in one companhia fell, often his companions would be killed as well. I was shown several locations marked by three crosses, where it was said that the three bastião of a folia had met their deaths at an encounter. (See plate 9.) Like many other foliões, Matias, from Batatais, remembered a tragic incident which he witnessed when he was thirteen years old:

At a farm near Batatais there was an encounter and seven people died. The crosses are there to this day. . . . A companhia de reis came from Lagoa Seca and another was coming from Cascata, and they met. There were six clowns: two boys in each companhia and two big ones. So they carried those decorated rods. So they met. That was it.

He said, "Hey, brother, I from here and you from there." So he drew a line, made a cross there, and to one side, the two began: "Where are you coming from?" "Where are you going?" "What have you brought me?" And they went on like that.

And then the embaixador said, "How about it? Are we going to sing or not?"

"Yes, we are."

"Are we going to exchange offerings?"

"No, we're not going to exchange offerings. We're going to sing."

"No, but that's silly."

"No. We're going to sing."

"If that's what we're going to do, I'm going to sing for no one to know the answers."

The other embaixador knew a lot too, and the two were there. Each one sang a verse, and it went pa, pa, pa, and the one coming from Lagoa Seca was losing to the one from Cascata, and the two older clowns were carrying swords. They could destroy anything. They were swinging them around over each others' heads, over their helmets. When it came down, the sword would come down on the guy's stomach. The other would roll over on his back and hit the clown. Well, that went accelerating, and they began to get tired.

This guy from Cascata was called João Vitório and the other from Jatubá was called Ari Barroso. So he finally hit the boy. The other knocked Ari Barroso down and he pulled the revolver that was in his pouch and shot at João. When João fell, his companion saw his brother on the ground, and he shot at another one. There was one down from each side, and everyone started to fight. So I'm telling you that seven people died there.

Given the potential danger involved in being a bastião, quite a bit of lore surrounds their death. For example, some claimed that if a bastião dies before he has completed his seven years in the farda, someone else must take up his role for the remaining period, or his soul will not rest in peace. Others claimed that a bastião who dies while wearing his mask is damned forever, and so on.

Even though many foliões do not begin their careers within the folia tradition as bastião, the period in which a person wears the farda is explicitly perceived as a period of initiation into the tradition, after which the bastião may join the group as a musician. Indeed, many of the characteristics of a bastião are consistent with classic elements of initiates in other contexts (Turner 1974). The bastião encounter the folia from an initial state, in which they are Herod's emissaries, or sinners; they repent, entering into a liminal state, in which they assimilate the moral values of the Three Kings' message; finally, they become emissaries of the divinities when they join the ensemble as musicians, fully inverting their initial status. Throughout initiation the bastião wear a costume of inferiorization, marking them as subhuman beings, while among themselves they display a sense of camaraderie and equality. During this initiation the children learn the language of the tradition, hear the music, learn how to perform on one of the instruments, acquire knowledge about group organization, and so on. As is common to many rites of passage, the initiation takes place within a context marked by trials and tribulations and a constant threat of danger. If a child finds himself identifying with folia activities, he is already well socialized into the tradition once he takes up a musical role. Some people, however, clearly enjoy being a bastião, and a good clown can acquire considerable prestige in his community, remaining in the role for many years or even a lifetime. In fact, it is a space within the tradition that easily accommodates—and even welcomes—the practical joker.

The Bandeireiro

The bandeireiro is the person who carries the group's banner from house to house.[8] He leads the procession, bearing the sacred representation of the Three Kings. (See plate 10.) Thus, it is considered a position of great responsibility and honor. Generally it is the festeiro or one of his relatives who acts as the bandeireiro, although some groups have a specific person for the role, especially if the festeiro is one of the musicians in the ensemble. Appointed bandeireiros are often people whom the other foliões do not consider capable of performing one of the musical roles, and who are also unable to act as clowns. But unlike clowns, the bandeireiro is never a child, who might let the banner fall or let it drag along the ground if he got tired. Such disrespect could trigger the wrath of the Three Kings, bringing misfortune to the whole group. The role of bandeireiro can also be taken on as a promise, and often people promise to carry it for a limited number of houses, borrowing it from the official bandeireiro to redeem their debt.

New Roles

In 1984 the figure of group coordinator was created in the Folia do Alto do Baeta Neves and the title was bestowed on Zezo. According to Zezo, the idea of a group coordinator was first voiced by Peres, the municipal folklorist of São Bernardo at the time, who proposed it to Owaldir when Owaldir told him that the group was in crisis and on the verge of splitting up. Zezo claimed that Owaldir came to his house one evening and pleaded with him to join the companhia on a permanent basis, saying that Peres thought he would make an ideal group coordinator. His job would be to impose order upon the group and help restore pride in folia activities. He claimed he could not accept the offer, because he was still suffering form a back injury he had sustained at work. Then and there Owaldir made a promise on his behalf that if his back pains subsided, he would join the group, making it impossible for him to refuse the post. Owaldir, however, claimed that Zezo gave himself the title, but he chose not to object so as not to offend him. The resposta singer had left the group, and he needed someone with leadership qualities to help him organize group activities. Either way, on becoming group coordinator Zezo did feel he had a leadership role in the ensemble, which gave him greater incentive to join the ensemble of his fellow townsmen in São Bernardo rather than to return each Christmas season to Arceburgo to play in an ensemble there, and he remained in the group until 1990.

While he occupied the post, Zezo took his role very seriously. He saw the public image of the ensemble as his primary sphere of responsibility and set about establishing "order" within the group to make it more respectable. One of his first measures was to introduce "the notebook" (*caderneta*), in which each donation the companhia received on its visitations was to be entered by the "marker" (*marcadora*), a role he created and assigned to his wife, Conceição. In many companhias no official record is kept of the amounts raised, and this often leads to accusations that those responsible for the donations have pocketed the saints' money. With the notebook, such charges could be contested, and with everything recorded properly, the money could be kept in the bank to receive interest until it was needed for the festival of the arrival. In the beginning Conceição was fairly systematic in her bookkeeping, notating each donation meticulously. As time went on, however, her records became more lax, but sums were recorded daily or every few days. Some of the other companhias in São Bernardo also tried to institute the notebook, but none of them was quite as systematic as the Baeta group. Nonetheless, it was seen as a sign of respectability to have a marker in the ensemble, even though the job was rarely done efficiently.

Although Zezo saw his role primarily in terms of the establishment of order within the group, he acted as a key mediator between the ensemble and outside cultural administrators and other potential patrons. His experience within the labor union and the PT was crucial, for unlike most members of the lower classes, who tend to evade unnecessary contact with the upper classes to avoid the humiliation that often accompanies such encounters, Zezo was willing to persist with his demands despite successive denials. Indeed, he expected his requests to be refused, preparing himself from the start for a long battle each time he embarked on a new project.

One of his first endeavors involved securing the donation of uniforms—which the group called fardas—for all the foliões, not just for the bastião; but the musicians' outfits had to look serious, contrasting with those of the clowns. Between 1984 and 1988, Zezo managed to secure three different uniforms for his companhia, each donated by a different institution. The T-shirts they wore at first were donated by a local industry, but his vision was to see the group dressed in uniforms modeled on military bands. In 1986 he acquired them from the São Bernardo Department of Culture, after endless pilgrimages to local politicians. For the 1987/88 journey, he received new uniforms from a large food company; one of the executives of the multinational was running for town representative in São Bernardo and hoped that he could secure a few votes from the folia community by mediating on their behalf with the company, but I am unaware of any folião who voted for him.[9]

Once the group had secured the appropriate uniforms, Zezo began approaching various institutions to secure public presentations for the group, including a spot on television—later edited out—on a weekly program dedicated to folk music.[10] It was also his persistence at the Department of Culture that finally led to the production of the companhia's first LP. Once the record had been made, the Department of Culture was eager to disseminate the fact that they had produced it, and it sponsored several performances for the group. When the PT took the municipality in 1988, Zezo was able to mobilize his contacts within the party, increasing the group's public activities. After Zezo left the group their public appearances began to decline, since other members of the group were less willing to subject themselves so readily to possible public humiliation.[11]

In the contemporary context, foliões and other "folk" performers have to deal increasingly with cultural administrators, politicians, and other potential patrons. The solution negotiated within the Folia do Baeta was to hand the task over to the group member best suited to undertake it and to publicly recognize his efforts by naming his role. In most companhias this new task has simply been added to the responsibilities of the dono.

Folia Leadership

Just as there were Three Kings, the traditional structure of the folia envisages three distinct leadership roles: the dono, the festeiro, and the embaixador, each with responsibilities in a different domain. The dono recruits the members of the group, the festeiro administers the funds the group collects, and the embaixador directs the ritual proceedings. Even though it is possible for a single person to take on all three roles, they can also be distributed among three different people.

80

It is generally assumed that a person starts a banner to fulfill a promise to the Holy Kings, and this person becomes its dono. A traditional promise consists of taking the banner out on journeys for a period of seven consecutive years, and during this period the dono generally acts as the group's festeiro. Some donos are embaixadores, in which case they assume the ritual leadership of their companhias as well as the administrative role. After seven journeys the promise has been fulfilled and the banner can "stop." Then the dono can put it away in a special place in his home or take it to a pilgrimage center and offer it to the Holy Kings. Some donos make lifelong promises, while others decide not to stop their banners at the end of their promises. Others inherit their banners from deceased relatives and continue the tradition in their honor. Since the role of festeiro can be financially taxing, many donos recruit a different member of the community each year to take on the organization of the festival. This allows other people to use the ensemble to fulfill their promises to the Holy Kings without having to take on the commitments of a seven-year obligation. Some foliões argued that festeiros who organize only one festival promote the best events, since they concentrate their resources on making their festival as memorable as possible.

In São Bernardo, Alcides, Zé Machado, and Zé Quatorze took on all three leadership roles. Yet Zé Machado often transferred the embaixada to his son, Wanderley, who normally acted as his ajudante. Even though Zé Machado retained formal leadership, the members of the group relied on Wanderley for orientation, particularly when Zé Machado had had a few glasses of mé too many. As Zé Quatorze's health deteriorated during my research, he progressively handed over more and more of his responsibilities to Lázaro, who eventually took over the group when Zé Quatorze died in 1992. Alcides, on the other hand, held steadfastly to all the prerogatives of his roles, although he did rely on João, his ajudante, to send messages to the foliões whenever he decided to hold a rehearsal. For all four journeys I observed, the Folia do Baeta chose a different community member as its festeiro or festeira, but throughout Owaldir remained both its dono and embaixador while relying heavily on Zezo to help him organize the group's activities.

Even though some people take on two or all three leadership roles, the fact that the roles are conceived separately predisposes the members of these associations to think of leadership as a shared responsibility. Indeed, most companhias have at least two people who are recognized as leaders in the group. This organizational principle serves to regulate the authority of the dono, decentralizing the decision-making processes in relation to folia affairs.

CHAPTER THREE

Recruitment and Mobility

I was a boy of more or less nine years of age. . . . I was in the folia de reis to sing. My grandfather beat me. My grandfather brought me up. He even beat me with a leather strap and I would go back home. . . . I sang because I liked it. It is a gift that I have. . . . When I saw that he was snoring I would open the kitchen door and go back to the folia de reis again.

A year later I was already ten years old. . . . I went to see the folia de reis sing. It was a Sunday. They were going to depart. I was there. Then Seu Zé Juca said this to me, "Oh, but João Canico isn't coming and without him we can't depart, and without the thin voice we can't set off to sing."

Then I said, "Oh, Seu Zé, do you want me to sing?"

He said, "Do you know how to sing?"

I said, "Oh, tell them to play. We'll see if I know how to sing Seu João's voice."

When they played I came out on top. I was already used to their singing. There, quietly, I had been learning that voice. . . . When they began I was still trembling a bit, but I did it. The second time I managed it, more or less. The next time was better. Then the embaixador sped up the singing a bit. Then he stopped. He sang another toada. I sang.

"Ah, I'm going to take this boy with me."

I said, "Ah, but my grandfather won't let me go."

"No, I'll go. I'll go and talk to him."

He went to my house and said this to my grandfather: "You're going to arrange something I need badly."

My grandfather said, "Sure, whatever you want, if I can I'll arrange it."

"You are going to let this boy go with the folia de reis."

My grandfather said, "Not that! This boy doesn't know anything, and he'll only make trouble for you on the way."

He said, "No. He's going to sing just like he sang for me. . . ."

My grandfather said, "This boy is going to make trouble for you."

"No he won't, Bertolino. Leave it to me."

I really wanted to learn to play, you know, so along the way I would get the guitar from one and then from another. I would tell them to show me where to put my fingers. They started me off. Slowly I learned. . . . And I even played the guitar at the arrival of folia de reis.

Zé sent someone ahead to tell my grandfather: "Bertolino, go see the arrival of the folia de reis."

He went.

The little guitar played at the arrival. My grandfather stayed right next to me. When the folia sang, I sang. I was used to it, right? The little guitar was playing.

The old man cried. After the festival he said, "José, I'm going to buy a little guitar for you." . . .

His eyes were filled with tears.

I said, "You're crying, grandfather."

And he said, "I hit you for doing what you wanted."

I said, "No, grandfather. That's alright. It didn't hurt."

Then he bought the guitar. Then he saw what I had in mind. Then I learned to play the guitar. I learned to play the viola on my own. If I see someone playing a tune, then I pick up a guitar or a viola and play. . . .

Then I started moving toward the front [of the companhia]. . . . I've already sung all the voices. I've sung the thin one way in the back, tipe, contrato, all the voices. . . .

Then I was in José Rica Filho's folia. . . . He had a Bible, one of the best embaixadores of Monsenhor Paulo. I was one of his foliões. I sang the ajudante part. I was meticulous. He put a lot of trust in me.

He said to me, "My friend, learn to sing the embaixada."

I said, "I don't have the knowledge."

He said, "I'll lend you my book for three days, alright? If you don't learn it, nothing doing. Only three days."

He lent me the book. I took the book and copied it. . . . It's put away around here somewhere. So I copied it and I chose a part. For some two days I was repeating it, repeating it, and I put it away in my memory. . . .

My friend asked me, "Did you learn it?"

"Only a part. You gave me only three days. Only a part."

"So tell me which part?" . . .

When he saw that I knew it, he let me take the embaixada. Thank God everything went well and to this day I'm on the embaixada. (Zé Quatorze)

Like Zé Quatorze, most foliões can remember vividly when they first started singing in a folia de reis, while embaixadores also remember their first experience as ritual leaders for an ensemble. Luizinho and Zezo said they had originally entered a companhia because they had been given to the Three Kings as children in promises their mothers had made when they had become ill. Zé dos Magos had been socialized into the tradition by his father, who already belonged to his father's ensemble. As a child he had been a bastião, and at the age of five he had placed his eldest son, Luiz Carlos, in the farda; by 1994 Luiz Carlos, at the age of ten, had become one of the drummers in the group, while his six-year-old brother, Baltazar, had become a bastiãozinho. Owaldir claimed to have joined a companhia as a singer after he learned to play the cavaquinho when he was twelve years old; although none of the adults in his immediate family was a folião, he wanted to join because he liked the music folias performed. His three sons, however, have been participating in folia activities since they were very young. When I met them, the two youngest already had vocal parts—Paulinho, age seventeen at the time, sang contrato, and André, then twelve years old, sang tala—but the eldest, Careca, who was not considered to be musically gifted, continued as a bastião. Unlike Zezo's sons, who left the companhia in their late teens, all of Owaldir's sons were still in the group in 1994, and they had already begun socializing their own children into the tradition.

The process of upward mobility within the ranks of the ensemble is relatively simple, and it was explained to me by various musicians. Some foliões, however, hardly progress within the structure, while others move quite rapidly until they reach a front position. Some groups allow women to sing the highest parts, but their progression is limited because, as Paulinho put it, "Their voices don't thicken." There are some foliões who never sing, "because," as Januário said, "the voice doesn't allow it;" but if they have the gift, these musicians can participate as instrumentalists. For example, the drummers rarely sing, and this is also true of many estribilho players. Since in many companhias there are more people in the group than there are vocal parts for them, there is a considerable amount of turn taking in the distribution of parts. As the groups move from one house to the next, the configuration of the ensembles changes as musicians rotate among themselves, taking different voices. This helps guarantee the continuity of the group, since it ensures that new musicians are being trained continuously for the various positions available in the association. Moreover, it provides musicians with a welcome variation in their music making.

Competence in the musical sphere—that is, the manifestation of the gift—is a fundamental factor in determining a person's potential for mobility within the folia structure. Clearly there are people who wish to take on the front positions within the group, and they work consciously toward that end by trying to demonstrate to the rest of the ensemble that they possess a gift for music. Since at least to a certain extent musical competence can be developed over time, those people with projects of ascent within the association can attempt to find the means to achieve front positions and even become embaixadores. Other roles can be filled by almost anyone who wishes to participate in folia activities, regardless of musical competence.

Companhias in the Urban Context

When southeastern rural migrants moved to the big cities, they brought their devotional traditions with them, and often they found the means of re-creating them in the new context. Many migrant communities have been particularly successful in adapting the folia de reis tradition to city life, and this can be explained partly in terms of the organizational requirements of the genre itself. First, a companhia brings together a relatively small number of people, and it is possible for a group to conduct a journey with as few as six dedicated participants. The ensembles perform in the homes of the families they visit, so they are not dependent upon the kind of community mobilization necessary to the promotion of patron saint festivals, which take place in the streets and central squares of rural towns. Furthermore, companhias act without the interference of the institutionalized church, since there is no special event within the ritual which requires the participation of a priest. Thus, folias can circulate as autonomous organizations, depending solely on their ability to mobilize a group of lay people willing to take on the roles available in the association.

Many migrants have attempted to organize performance troupes associated with other southeastern popular Catholic traditions, such as congados and moçambiques, but they tend to come up against a series of obstacles which make it difficult for the ensembles to continue their activities in the city. One of the major problems is related to the number of people who must be continuously mobilized—twenty or more; such large numbers are hard to sustain, given that the work schedules and family obligations of potential participants are in constant flux. Furthermore, such traditions are far more dependent upon the context of a street festival, such as celebrations in honor of a patron saint, in which the inhabitants of an entire rural town are mobilized for several days. Although some neighborhood parishes in the city do promote street fairs (*quemesses*) to raise funds for the church, they have not come to substitute the traditional performance context of the dance troupes, primarily because these events do not usually honor the saints associated with popular devotional practices, such as Saint Benedict the Moor, Our Lady of the Rosary, or the Divine Holy Spirit. Moreover, many urban

CHAPTER THREE

priests view popular Catholic traditions as "folklore," or distortions of orthodox practice, and have not encouraged their appearance at quermesses.

In the rural context local parish priests tend to be quite tolerant—though often patronizing—toward the popular Catholic activities of their parishioners, and they are generally willing to perform the blessings and masses required during festivals, even though they usually disappear from the scene as soon as they have fulfilled their duties. In the urban context, however, the divide between official religious practices and popular Catholicism has widened considerably, and very few popular Catholic communities maintain links with the church as religious associations. Of the companhias in São Bernardo only the Folia do Zé dos Magos had a connection—though quite a tenuous one—with a particular parish, and every year during the Christmas season the group performed for one of the masses. The church was located in Vila Nogueira, where the parish priest sympathized with liberation theology, feeling that the church had a duty to support the spontaneous manifestations of devotion of the masses. This view, however, was not universal among priests linked to the liberation theology movement, many of whom held the traditional Marxist stance in which popular Catholic traditions are seen as forms of "false consciousness." Under current conditions, therefore, the possibility that a space could emerge within the church for urban folias and other popular Catholic performance groups seems remote, obliging groups interested in public performances to look to the state for support.

More of a nominal than an active congado existed in São Bernardo until the mid-1980s, and it was finally declared extinct when its owner died. Since then a far more successful congado has formed in the neighborhood of Parque São Bernardo, and like the Folia do Baeta it has actively engaged in processes of modernization, integrating elements from samba schools and the northeastern *blocos afro* carnival bands into the traditional congado dance steps. It was originally founded to participate in the annual Festival of Our Lady of the Rosary in Cordislândia, Minas Gerais, the hometown of the group's leadership. The possibility of an annual pilgrimage to the festival was significant in sustaining enthusiasm within the group. When I last met them in 1996 performing at the Festival of the Rosary in Turvolândia near their hometown, they claimed to have over one hundred active members. Interest was further heightened by the leadership's continuous pursuit of alternative performance contexts for the dancers and musicians, which was facilitated dramatically after Dito, one of the group's leaders, took a job as janitor in the Department of Culture in the late 1980s. Since then the group has had

86

numerous engagements to fulfill at cultural events throughout greater São Paulo. Moreover, the group has become well known throughout the Cordislândia area, and they were being invited to almost all the festivals in the region, their costs covered by the festeiros of the events. Like most other traditional performance groups I have met, the members of the congado have welcomed this outside interest in their devotional activities, as it reinforces their belief in the intrinsic value of their tradition and the ethos for which it stands.

Similar strategies have been used successfully by a few other traditional dance troupes in the greater São Paulo area as a means of sustaining enthusiasm among a large group of people for an extended period. Such a course of action, however, depends upon the groups' abilities to gain recognition among cultural administrators, which requires someone within the group to be willing to confront the appropriate authorities. While such tactics are also available to folias de reis, they are not vital. In their search for aesthetic responses to their urban experience, migrants have clearly taken pragmatic factors into account in re-creating their traditions in the urban context, and in this respect folias de reis have a definite advantage over other communal rural religious practices of the southeast.

CHAPTER IV

Rehearsals

I FIRST MET THE FOLIA DO BAETA at an event which the foliões called a rehearsal (*ensaio*), and over the years I have been to countless other rehearsals held by companhias both in São Bernardo and in various small rural towns throughout the southeast. Yet I was told by one folião after another that folias did not rehearse. They claimed that everyone knew their parts, so they did not need to rehearse; the reason they came together every now and then was so the musicians would not forget their parts.

Indeed, companhias do not rehearse, if by a rehearsal one understands the pursuit of perfection in the performance of a piece in which stress is placed on the product of the performance. In their rehearsals they do not stop in the middle of a toada to correct mistakes; they do not select out difficult transitions and perform them over and over again to get them just right; and there is no conductor attempting to draw out her personal interpretation from the musicians. In terms of the sounds of the music, there is little to distinguish their performances at rehearsals from their performances at visitations. For foliões rehearsals are seen as social events, in which they meet because of the enjoyment they get out of making music together.

Rehearsals are held at the dono's house, generally on Sunday afternoons. (See plate 11.) They are sporadic events, arranged more or less at the last minute, whenever the dono of a companhia decides to hold one. In rural areas, however, rehearsals are held less frequently than among urban companhias. Rural groups tend to concentrate their rehearsal activities in the months preceding their journeys, while the urban companhias I worked with held them throughout the year, though they increased in number during November and December to prepare for the departure. Although I do not believe my interest in their activities significantly altered their rehearsal patterns, it may have had an impact on the number of rehearsals held by some of the groups, who staged them a bit more frequently for my benefit.

For the most part, the musicians come to rehearsals on their own, but often they are accompanied by sons or nephews in the hope of encouraging them to join the group. Sometimes wives and daughters also attend, but generally they stay in the kitchen with the dono's female relatives helping them prepare coffee and snacks. In the beginning I felt quite self-conscious about the fact that I was often the only woman present among the musicians, and though my unease diminished with time, I never completely overcame it.

During rehearsals the same set of three or four toadas are repeated indefinitely for hours on end, and I could not help wondering how they did not get bored by the repetitiveness of their music. Yet, while I was among them, neither did I, even though I sometimes got tired of listening to my field recordings. After I learned various parts and began to join in the music making, I found rehearsals to be a very pleasant way to spend a Sunday afternoon, and I always looked forward to them. Many foliões openly acknowledged that their primary motivation for going to rehearsals was the pleasure they experienced while making music with other people. Zezo, for example, claimed that singing in the folia de reis was like a "bath for the brain," a comment echoed by Owaldir, who said that singing in the folia made him forget about everything else, temporarily displacing his preoccupations with everyday affairs.

With a few notable exceptions (Finnegan 1989; Koskoff 1988; Turino 1989, 1993; and others), ethnomusicologists have paid little attention to the rehearsal context, giving precedence to the study of public performances. A dominant view in Western thinking conceives of the performance context as an arena in which the musicians present a polished product to be scrutinized by a critical audience purely for its aesthetic merit. As any trained Western art musician knows, to achieve performance excellence, musicians must engage in extensive preparatory work, including a learning phase and continuous individual practicing and rehearsals with other musicians. Because rehearsals are often organized to prepare for specific performances, the procedures and processes of social interaction that take place during rehearsals articulate with the ultimate goal of presenting an acceptable final product.

Thus, along with the acquisition of performance competence, the rehearsal context is a privileged sphere for the acquisition and rearticulation of dominant concepts associated with music and the social world of its production.[1] Since many societies do not hold a product-oriented view of music making, they also have no concept of a rehearsal as such (Koskoff 1988, 59).

Foliões, however, do organize events called rehearsals, even though they hold a very different view of music making from that dominant in the Western musical universe, and in line with this difference, they orchestrate their rehearsals in terms of their own goals. Rather than emphasizing the product of their performances, foliões conceive of music making fundamentally as a space for sociability, and they organize rehearsals as social occasions. From the point of view of those involved in the music making, the "product"—the music produced—is judged in terms of the quality of the interactions the musicians set in motion to create it. During performance they strive to construct an atmosphere of camaraderie among the musicians, marking an inclusive and participatory orientation toward music making.

Blacking (1980a) argued that the performance requirements of participatory genres are likely to promote modes of interaction during the performance that articulate with the patterns of social interaction that are valued by the participants in nonmusical spheres. The concept of "performance requirements" is particularly useful to ethnomusicological analysis, in that it encompasses both the structural properties of musical sound and the performance practices employed in music making. While certain formal musical properties may be more conducive than others to generating particular interactive patterns, the musical structure of a genre does not necessarily determine the social uses to which it is put. As Thomas Turino (1993) has shown, groups performing musics that sounds almost identical can hold radically different conceptions about music, music making, and the social relations of musical production, such that their musical practices and performance experiences are also distinct. Even though a particular genre may be used in different ways, its musical structure can be explored extensively in performance in relation to the conceptual frameworks and objectives of the group making use of it. In this chapter I shall be looking at how the formal properties of the toada articulate with the conceptual orientations of the performers, in order to generate the social experience foliões strive to create during music making.

REHEARSALS

Setting Rehearsals

In the beginning it was something of a mystery to me how the foliões found out about their rehearsals, since the members of the groups did not all live in proximity to one another and none of them had telephones. I soon discovered that communication among them was maintained through word-of-mouth networks, in which the dono began by informing his closest neighbors when he intended to hold a rehearsal, and among them they decided how best to let the others know about it. Often foliões in the same companhia were employed in the same place or near the employment of other foliões, so they would take responsibility for informing them. Sometimes a folião worked with someone who lived near another member of the group, and this person would agree to take the message to his neighbor. These networks were extremely efficient, and within a matter of a few days all the members of an ensemble would find out about an upcoming rehearsal.

I was often the only person left uninformed, because I was not connected to these networks even though I had a phone. Phone calls from São Bernardo to São Paulo were quite expensive for the budgets of most foliões, but it also became clear to me that many of them did not feel comfortable talking into telephones. On the only occasion in which Alcides called me to tell me about a rehearsal, this otherwise highly articulate man became totally tongue tied. Immediately after we spoke I attempted to reconstruct our conversation in my field notebook. Admittedly my reconstruction contains a few exaggerations, but they emphasize my perception of the exchange. I have reproduced it below:

S.R.: Hello?
Alcides: Hello?
S.R.: Hello? Who's speaking?
Alcides: Hello?
S.R.: Who's speaking, please? Who would you like to speak with?
Alcides: Hello? Suzel? Is that Suzel's house?
S.R.: Yes, this is Suzel. Seu Alcides?
Alcides: Tell Suzel that Alcides, Alcides from the folia de reis, has a message.
S.R.: Oh, Seu Alcides, how are you?
Alcides: I'm fine, I'm fine.
S.R.: And how is Dona Clotilde [his wife]?

Alcides: She's fine.

S.R.: And the rest of the foliões?

Alcides: The folia, everyone's fine.

S.R.: That's good.

Alcides: Clotilde sends her regards.

S.R.: Thank you, and send my regards to her, too.

Alcides: Clotilde told me to call you.

S.R.: I see.

Alcides: She sends her regards.

S.R.: My best regards to her, too. What's the folia doing these days?

Alcides: The folia? The folia is fine.

S.R.: I'm glad to hear it. You said you had a message.

Alcides: Yes, Clotide wants to know when you are coming over here?

S.R.: Any day now. I'll come around any day now. When would it be convenient for you?

Alcides: Any time, come around any time. Are you coming on Wednesday?

S.R.: On Wednesday? Is something happening on Wednesday?

Alcides: The folia is meeting on Wednesday.

S.R.: Oh, you're having a rehearsal.

Alcides: A rehearsal.

S.R.: At what time? When should I come out?

Alcides: Come any time.

S.R.: But the foliões won't be coming around until the evening, right?

Alcides: In the evening.

S.R.: Right. I'll come around on Wednesday then. Thank you for letting me know.

Alcides: Clotilde sends her regards.

S.R.: Thank you, my regards to her, too, and tell her I'll see her on Wednesday.

Alcides: I will. Go with God.

S.R.: And you. Good-bye, and thanks for telling me about the rehearsal. I'll be there.

Alcides: OK. Good-bye, then.

S.R.: Good-bye.

The discomfort Alcides displayed in talking on the phone could be put down to his inexperience with the medium, but it also highlights the modes of interaction prevalent among members of folia communities. Alcides was far more used to face-to-face interactions, and his inability to see the person to whom he was speaking was clearly disconcerting to him. Moreover, when speaking on the telephone, the caller is required to present her intentions in a fairly direct manner; such explicit expressions of intentionality, however, cause discomfort among many foliões, as they expose them to rejection, which could be experienced as a slight to their personal integrity. Even though Alcides distanced himself from his intentions by deflecting them onto his wife—and his invitation was not rebuffed—the experience was so disquieting to him that he never called me again. To keep abreast of the groups' activities I had to be physically present among them, constantly visiting people associated with each of the groups. Their mode of communication centered on direct, face-to-face encounters, and information circulated through the networks as people met one another in their neighborhoods or at work.

Conversations

When I first established contact with Zé Quatorze, he told me that he had arranged a rehearsal with his group for that Sunday at 2:00 P.M. I arrived conscientiously at the designated time, only to find that I was the first person there. It was well over an hour before the first foliões arrived and then another two and a half hours before all the musicians were present so the ensemble could begin to sing. Among the first foliões to arrive were Lázaro, the contrato and estribilho player of the ensemble, and Quim Braz, the ajudante; the last were accompanying instrumentalists without vocal parts. Thus, the arrival of the musicians more or less replicated the group's internal hierarchy. As people arrived they sat about chatting, exchanging news, and discussing various issues related to their daily lives and folia activities. After this experience I learned to arrive a bit late for rehearsals, but I always tried to be among the first arrivals to observe the arrival patterns of the musicians and to participate in their conversations.

At one rehearsal held by the Folia do Zé Quatorze, Lázaro informed the group that he had heard that Toninho, the drummer, would be unable to make it that afternoon. Zé Quatorze said that that was too bad because Toninho was a good drummer, but they would surely be able to find someone else to play it for them for the rehearsal. Quim Braz volunteered his niece, Shirley, who had come with him to the rehearsal, and soon afterward he commented on how nice he thought folias sounded when they had two caixas. There was general agreement on this, and a discussion ensued in which the foliões began remembering ensembles they knew of that had two drums. This led into a discussion about the suitability of accordions in the folia. It was remembered that the Kings did not have an accordion, so it could not be considered a folia instrument. Another folião, however, reminded the group about how Zé dos Magos was willing to carry this heavy instrument around from house to house for his companhia, even though he was a very small, thin man; surely, he speculated, the Kings looked favorably upon this sacrifice even though none of them played the accordion. (See plate 12.) This was followed by the perennial debate about the problem of excessive alcohol consumption in the folia, and the various strategies donos can employ to regulate it.

A few days later I met up with a few members of the Folia dos Maguinho, who commented on how they had heard that Zé Quatorze was looking for a second drummer for his group. Although the ensemble never recruited another drummer while I was among them, an accordion player did join the group on their next journey. After this incident I began to view the discussions prior to rehearsals as informal committee meetings, in which the group's leaders put forward their proposals as a means of measuring their acceptance among other members of the group. Their suggestions, however, were couched as commentary on the procedures and opinions of others, rather than as direct propositions. By thus muting the authorship of intentions, the person making the proposition could maintain his distance from it in case it was not acceptable to other members of the group. The support of a proposition could be audibly measured by the number of people who entered the discussion echoing the original instance with similar examples. Likewise, an idea could slip away inadvertently through the absence of any discussion, without compromising the integrity of the person who first raised the issue. Moreover, this mode of decision making allowed for the emergence of consensus toward the leaders' proposals through nonauthoritarian means; their propositions merged with all the other examples raised after their initial comment, just as they merged into the thematic flow of the conversation, which moved continuously from one subject to another. In this manner the divide between formal decision making and informal conversation remained ambiguous, all part of the sociability of the rehearsal context.

There is a relatively restricted set of themes that emerges time after time in these discussions from one folia to the next. Without doubt the problem of excessive alcohol consumption during folia activities is the most widely discussed issue in folia communities. They also argue about what constitutes backtracking during a journey, given that folias are not supposed to pass by the same place twice, lest they encounter a Herod; they talk about the advantages of wearing uniforms on their journeys; they confirm the hazards inherent in folia encounters and so on.

The outcome of these discussions filters back into the informal communication networks, as people comment on what happened at a given rehearsal. Some issues are presented as decisions taken by the leadership, but they are often communicated as hearsay, rather than as clear-cut intentions. Indeed, the young men I met after Zé Quatorze's rehearsal claimed to have heard that he might be looking for a drummer; they did not claim to know for a fact that that was Zé Quatorze's intention. This allows for the emergence of new voices in their ongoing debates, integrating folia affairs into the social life of the community.

Music Making

Music making begins only when all the musicians that are expected to be coming to the rehearsal have arrived; to begin without someone could be taken as an offense, causing that person to abandon the group. When the dono believes everyone is present he brings in the banner and the musicians prepare themselves to start singing, tuning their instruments and taking their performance positions, all the while strumming and testing their instruments. Before taking up the estribilho, the instrumentalist responsible for this part listens to the doodling people are making on their instruments to hear if anyone is still tuning an instrument, and when he is satisfied that they are all ready, he simply begins. When the others hear the first notes of the instrumental introduction over their warm-up sounds, they begin to take up their parts. The first toada can go on for a long time, and it is followed by others which sound almost identical. Indeed, sometimes the back voices perform the exact same parts even though the front voices have different melodic lines each time. Coffee and snacks are served at some point, and after about three or four hours of singing the musicians begin to disperse.

Precisely because toadas are so repetitive, folia musicians are extremely aware of minute aesthetic details in their performances, and when questioned, many of them are able to discourse at length on the musical roles of each vocal and instrumental part. For some parts musicians are expected to incorporate variations throughout their performances; there are concepts regarding the volume appropriate to some parts; there are ideas about the personality types best suited to certain parts, and so on. This knowledge is acquired primarily through music-making experiences, and the foliões' awareness of the characteristics of the different parts is further enhanced by the changes in performance positions that often take place when the group commences a new toada.

The degree of my participation varied tremendously from one group to the next, determined primarily by the musical needs of the different groups at the rehearsals I attended. Most of the time I performed as an accompanist, playing either the viola or the caixa, but if there was an insufficient number of singers, I often filled in the missing part. Like most new foliões, I began my career as a folia singer performing the tala part, and as I gained confidence, I filled in for absences in other vocal parts as well. During one rehearsal with the Folia do Zé Machado, the group leader decided to put me to the test, since on several occasions I had sung as ajudante for him at rehearsals: I was invited to attempt the embaixada, but after a few rounds I could not think up any new verses, so I stopped and returned the role to Zé.

During their journey in 1988, Wanderley, the regular ajudante, would be arriving late one evening, but Zé Machado was anxious to keep the banner moving, so I was asked to fill in for him until he arrived. This caused quite a stir at every house we visited, and several years latter a member of the group made a point of reminding me of the night I had sung "up front." The novelty value of this was twofold: not only was it extremely rare for a woman to sing a front voice, it was altogether unheard of for a member of the upper classes to be singing in a folia at all. When I played toward the back, my presence was less conspicuous until after we had finished singing. Then, however, I was introduced as a reporter, and my reason for being there could be explained in somewhat more understandable terms.

My participation within the companhias diverged significantly from that of the wives and daughters of the foliões. The license I enjoyed clearly derived from our class differences. Patterns of interclass interactions in Brazil are marked by patronizing attitudes on the part of the upper classes toward members of the lower classes, but the relationship I established with the musicians was new for both sides, and therefore it was open to considerable negotiation. Indeed, I was caught off guard—but deeply moved—the first time a folião told me that I was different from other "rich" people: he claimed I treated the foliões as my equals. The main argument he used to substantiate his claim was the fact that I was not ashamed to sing with them.

Singers

The solo style begins with the embaixador singing on his own, clearly establishing his part as the principle voice of the ensemble (section A of musical example A.1 in the appendix). But the embaixador does not speak for himself; rather, through his improvisations he acts as spokesman of the Three Kings, which realigns him with his human companions (see Roseman 1991, 115–16). Given the sacred content of the improvisations, everyone pays close attention to the embaixada. After visitations many people could recite word for word the text of the verses used to bless them, indicating how closely they had attended to the improvisations. In particular the singers listen carefully to the embaixada because they are called upon to repeat the linha when they enter the ensemble. They also attend to it because the embaixada often includes commands which the foliões or the family being visited are expected to follow. For example, the embaixador can instruct the foliões to kiss the banner or ask the family at a pouso to put the banner away. Even in rehearsals, if the embaixador incorporates such an instruction into his verses, it is followed by the rest of the ensemble, blurring the divide between rehearsals and rituals proper.

Other folia styles begin with a duo in parallel thirds performed by the front singers. Since the text is improvised, the ajudante has to anticipate mentally what the embaixador is likely to sing, and the voice often lags slightly behind the main part. Because of its highly formulaic character the singers of the second voice in the dueted styles are able to follow the embaixador quite easily. As João, the ajudante in Alcides's companhia, put it, "As soon as he sings the first word, I already know what he is going to sing. It can change a bit, so you have to pay attention, but I always know what he is going to sing." A duo that has been singing together for many years tends to acquire a high degree of simultaneity in its performances. In fact, for someone unfamiliar with the tradition, it could be difficult to distinguish the singer of the principal voice from the ajudante.

One of the most characteristic features of southeastern traditional musics is the use of parallel thirds. Throughout the region, whenever someone begins to sing the first voice of a toada or a piece from the música sertaneja repertoire, another singer present is likely to join the soloist, placing his voice a third below—or a sixth above—the principal line.[2] The two voices are perceived as a unit, such that when one is not present, as Zé Quatorze once said, "something is missing, so two always have to sing together." In a duo of parallel thirds each part can be distinguished relatively easily, while the relationship between the voices is perceived as harmonious.[3] Parallelism involves a duplication of the melody in another register and therefore requires some of the same coordinated effort necessary to unison singing, since the text, the rhythm, the intervals, and the attacks should be enunciated simultaneously by the singers. The greater the simultaneity in the performance of the parallel lines, the more the participants must attend to one another during performance. Indeed, when singing together, the front singers often turn toward one another, which allows them to coordinate their behavior with greater precision. (See plate 13.)

Commonly the principal voice is placed in the upper register to make it easier to hear; being the more salient of the two, it is considered the most important. Yet for the last chord of the verse, the embaixador takes the mediant while the ajudante performs the tonic, creating an inversion in the musical roles of the two singers, such that the principal voice becomes harmonically subordinated to the second. By rendering the role of the first voice somewhat ambiguous, dominance becomes structurally muted, and the two voices join to form a complementary whole. Just as a high degree of simultaneity among the front singers mutes the prominence of the embaixador, the harmonic inversion in the final chord also neutralizes the musical dominance of the main voice. Far from being merely an aesthetic preference among southeasterners, as some researchers have argued, parallel thirds have conceivably been so stable throughout the region precisely because this musical element provides a sonic means of reconciling the asymmetry of social relations with notions of essential human equality.

In the mineiro styles there is a permanent game in which the prominence of one voice is subtly—and sometimes not so subtly—transferred from one register to the next up the hierarchical ladder. Members in the Folia do Baeta claimed that after the part of the embaixador, the contrato was the most demanding voice in the folia. In their performance style the contrato mediates between the front voices and the back voices; it makes its presence known in section C (musical example A.1), which is still the domain of the front voices, but it is also the lowest part in the chord sequence supporting the cacetero, the tipe, and the contra-tipe. While singing with the front voices, the contrato tends to look forward, attending to the front singers; when he begins to sing with the back voices, he generally turns toward them, identifying with the singers who have just joined the ensemble. With the entrance of the back voices (section E), the singers split into two quasi-independent vocal units, in which the four voices in the upper registers—the contrato, the cacetero, the tipe, and the contra-tipe—maintain strict vertical parallelism, in contrast to the two lower voices—the resposta and the ajudante. Consequently, the singers in each block focus their attention primarily upon those musicians with whom their parts are most closely aligned.

The contrato is in particular evidence during the period in which he sings with the front voices (sections C and D). Besides being the highest voice, which is performed with considerable gusto, a good contrato is expected to embellish his voice, purposefully deviating from an exact parallel duplication of the principal melodic line. Besides a short countermelody over the long notes of the embaixador and the resposta (section C), the contrato tends to add melodic and rhythmic ornaments through well-accented attacks. Often the ornamental variations are quite minute, such as a change in the rhythm of a melodic motif, an extra turn, or the omission of a frequent figure. Because the music is otherwise so repetitive, these minor variation stand out quite prominently, calling attention to the voice and its singer. This voice is also evident in the dueted mineiro style, where the contrato— or meião—surfaces a phrase before the final chord, as in musical example A.2. Because of the volume contratos use in their singing, their position in the upper register is especially noticeable. The foliões claimed that the contrato was well suited to "communicative" people, or those who liked to "show off." As in the Folia do Baeta, where the contrato was generally performed by Paulinho, Owaldir's second son, throughout the Guaranésia region the position was most frequently occupied by young men in their late teens or early twenties. It is seen as a trampoline to a front voice, since it is an ideal place for a promising young musician to exhibit his musical abilities.

Despite their low status in relation to the front singers, each of the back voices is valued at the level of discourse for certain characteristics attributed to it. The cacetero, the tipe, and the contra-tipe singers are meant to perform their parts with considerable volume and zest, so their entrances provoke surprise; because they are in such high registers, they are considered difficult. In several toadas the back voices come in as separate configurations, each with greater volume than the singers before them. By staggering the parts in this way, each one enjoys the limelight for a few moments during each cycle. The final voice—the tala—comes in only at the end of each toada. The low status associated with this voice is compensated by the fact that foliões claim that it is very difficult to find someone capable of performing it since it is so high and requires considerable volume. By managing to sing it, the performer demonstrates publicly that he has good lungs and would be capable of moving forward within the group when a space became vacated.

Indeed, the performance of the tala is evaluated very closely within folias, since it is this voice that guarantees the climactic effect of the final chord. The foliões' notions about the value of each of the different vocal parts in the ensemble articulate with the processes of interaction that take place during performance, causing continuous shifts in people's attention as the toada progresses. While the embaixada is being performed, attention is directed at the embaixador, but as each new vocal configuration joins the ensemble, attendance diverts toward the new singers, progressively moving from the front of the ensemble to the back. This constant cycle of successive turn taking is also implicated in blurring hierarchical distinctions, as one enters the flow of the continuous repetitions.

Instrumentalists

Just as there are discourses to neutralize the hierarchical distinctions among the singers, the space for the interpretation of musical roles in relation to the instrumental parts is just as flexible as—if not more flexible than—it is for the vocal parts. As we have seen, foliões acknowledge a clear hierarchical ordering in the instruments, in which the viola is the most prestigious folia instrument, followed by the tambourine and finally the caixa, and these notions are extended to encompass other instruments related to the primary instrument in each category. This view, however, is crosscut by numerous other discourses which relativize the importance of each of the instruments: some are valued because they are solo instruments; others are important because they provide steady accompaniment; still others enrich the texture of the music with improvisations. The prestige of an instrumental part can also be interpreted in terms of the difficulty involved in its performance, but it can be seen in terms of its function in maintaining the unity of the ensemble. Ultimately, the normative ideas about instrumental hierarchy are preserved, while the roles of each of the individuals performing them are represented in terms of their contribution to the collective effort in the music-making process.

Without doubt the most prestigious folia instrument is the viola, but usually there are several *violeiros* (viola players) in a companhia, and generally they are not all playing the same thing: some of them duplicate the toada in parallel thirds, while others strum their instruments to provide harmonic and rhythmic accompaniment for the ensemble. Because of the prestige attached to this instrument, it is often felt that the embaixador should play the viola; moreover, because it is considered more difficult to duplicate the

Musical Example 4.1

Tablature for viola in "rio abaixo" tuning (Folia do Zé Machado)

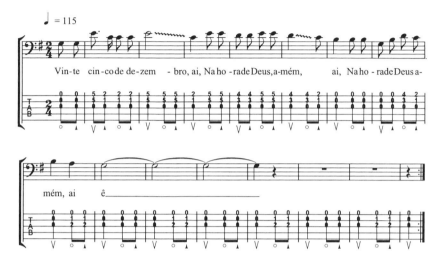

Viola tuning: d'/d' - b/b - g/g' - d/d' - G/g.
Although all the strings resonate sympathetically, only the three highest courses are strummed.

toada than simply to strum an accompaniment, many foliões claimed this too should be the role of the embaixador.

The most common tunings for the viola in southeastern Brazil—the *rio abaixo* (d^1/d^1, b/b, g/g^1, d/d^1, G/g) and the *cebolão* (e^1/e^1, c♯^{1}/c♯^{1}, a/a, e/e^1, A/a)—are particularly suitable for doing this, since a melody in thirds can be performed by sliding the fingers along the frets in two simple hand positions. The double strings give the instrument a full metallic timbre, alluding to the presence of several "voices" simultaneously. (See musical example 4.1.) Some foliões claimed that the resposta or ajudante should also play the viola, and that his part should be strummed with the "natural" tuning system (e^1/e^1, b/b, g/g^1, d/d^1, A/a). While the embaixador reproduces the two front voices, the second viola can be viewed as an instrumental representation of the back voices. The two violas, then, function as an instrumental compression of the vocal parts, and the timbral similarity of the instruments neutralizes the dominance of the embaixador's viola part. Up until quite recently an accompaniment based on two violas had been prevalent in a wide

CHAPTER FOUR

range of southeastern musical traditions of Iberian origin. Like the parallel third, it is able to articulate the value placed on the muting of recognized hierarchical relationships. Its ability to elicit this association may explain why the instrument is so favored by the saints.

Nowadays it has become more common to find companhias in which the singer of the second voice plays the guitar because of the strong influence of música sertaneja, which replaced the second viola with a guitar around the 1940s, when the style began to be recorded (Reily 1992, 346). Against a guitar accompaniment the parallel thirds of the viola remain prominent, because the timbres of the two instruments are sufficiently distinct. On several occasions foliões told me that the clarity of sound one achieves with a viola and a guitar makes the music sound more orderly. Currently, however, the prestige of the viola is declining in favor of the guitar, which is rapidly coming to be seen as a more modern instrument than the viola because of its associations with the Brazilian upper classes.[4] In the Folia do Baeta, for example, both Owaldir and Zezo played guitars, claiming the guitar is a more versatile instrument than the viola. While Owaldir strummed an accompaniment, adding picked embellishments between phrases and at harmonic transitions, Zezo performed a bass line.

The estribilho is generally performed by a high-pitched instrument, such as a violin, a bandolim, or a cavaquinho, to the accompaniment of the rest of the musicians; frequently two high-pitched instruments perform the estribilho together in parallel thirds. In companhias that have accordions, the estribilho is often played on this instrument, since it is the loudest of the melody instruments in the ensemble. The instrumentalists responsible for the estribilho general stand near the front, often directly behind or to the side of the embaixador, indicating their importance within the group. Just as toadas belong to the embaixadores who made them, estribilhos are seen as the property of the instrumentalists who play them. For example, foliões spoke of Januário's estribilho or Geraldinho's estribilho, and a competent player can have several estribilhos in his repertoire. Like toadas, estribilhos present very little melodic variation from one performance to the next, since they serve as cues to the rest of the musicians, informing them when the singing should begin or when the piece should end. According to Januário, one of the estribilho players in the Folia do Baeta, "The gang becomes accustomed to the estribilho a certain way. If you change it, it all gets messed up."

Since the estribilho often contrasts with the toada, foliões tend to think of their playing in terms of what they perform during the estribilho and what they perform during the toada. In some groups the estribilho is performed between each two renditions of the toada, but in others it is performed only at the beginning and at the end of a complete verse sequence. In such cases the musicians need to watch for a cue from the embaixador to know when to begin the coda, making the necessary adjustments to their playing. The technique Owaldir used most frequently was to sing a series of three rhyming couplets rather than just two, and when the musicians heard that a third couplet used the same ending as the previous two, they launched into the estribilho as soon as they had completed the toada. In other instances the context of the toada itself provided a clear indication that the embaixador had sung his final linha. No other outward cues or special gestures were used that would indicate his control over the group, as one would expect of a conductor. In order to move into the estribilho as an ensemble, all the musicians had to be closely tuned in to one another, and occasionally there would be someone who would not make the appropriate transition.

In many companhias a high-pitched stringed instrument is also used to provide a countermelody during the toada, and often this role is performed by the estribilho player. While the estribilho is kept stable from one interlude to the next, the instruments that play countermelodies during the singing can vary their performances, as Mário did on the cavaquinho for the Folia do Seu Alcides: "You can't always play the same thing. Like on the cavaquinho you go changing the way you play, always changing" (Mário). Since in this companhia Alcides's viola and the caixas provided a stable cue for the musicians, Mário was free to play variations even during the estribilho. (See musical example 4.2.) The chance to incorporate constant variations in his performances enhanced Mário's experience within the group, challenging him to continuously devise new alternatives. He claimed that it is because his part involved improvisation that he never got bored during performance.

Along with the countermelody, most companhias also have a guitarist to perform a bass line, which like the countermelody provides space for the musician to engage in improvisations. (See musical example 4.3.) In these examples one notes that some phrases vary from one version to the next while others remain practically identical. Indeed, the techniques used by these soloists are similar to the modes of formulaic composition used by embaixadores in verse improvisations. Over the years instrumentalists have developed a fund of musical phrases that can be inserted as alternatives for each of the sections of the toadas in their repertoire.

The remaining strings, primarily violas and guitars—but also cavaquinhos and bandolins—accompany the ensemble with strummed chords. There is no prescribed limit on the number of people allowed to play the accom-

Musical Example 4.2

Mário's performances of two different countermelodies for the cavaquinho to the same toada. They have been placed on a single system to facilitate comparison.

Cavaquinho tuning: d'' - b' - g' - d'

paniment, so anyone who can play one of these instruments and wishes to join the group can do so. This is equally true of the small percussion instruments. While some instrumental soloists have considerable scope for personal expression, the percussion instruments—the caixas and tambourines—are not so free. One of the most common patterns for the tambourine in southeastern Brazil is the one used in musical example A.2. This pattern employs a technique that is typical of folias de reis throughout the region, in which a tremolo effect is achieved by rubbing the outer rim of the skin with the thumb of the playing hand. While the tambourines can perform minor improvisations, and often very elaborate phrase endings, the caixas tend to follow much stricter rules. Generally speaking, the drummers memorize their parts and attempt to reproduce them identically from one verse to the next. (See musical example 4.4.) Sebastião, the drummer of the group, justified this practice in the following way (see plate 14): "We know when the caixa is supposed to play. If the caixa player deviates from this, if he gets mixed up, the voices also fall out. . . . So the caixa player is like the heart of the companhia: the whole ensemble depends on him. . . . The caixa player cannot make a mistake. Anyone else can make a mistake, but the caixa player cannot make a mistake."

In Alcides's companhia the drums are known as the caixa and the *repico*,

Musical Example 4.3

Geraldinho's performance of three different bass lines for the guitar to the same toada. They have been placed on a single system to facilitate comparison.

and the caixa is considered more important than the smaller repico because it plays on the beat. (See the caixa and repico parts in musical example A.2.) Yet the foliões were quick to point out that even though it is more important because it keeps the group together, the repico is more difficult to play, and Alcides claimed that "you can't let just anyone take it or the group will turn into anarchy." To some extent as it is for the tala, the low status of the caixa is compensated by its importance in maintaining the unity of the group. If the caixa is the heart of the ensemble—the instrument that gives it life—the tala is the voice that guarantees that the group achieves a climax at the end of each toada. Just as this is generally the first voice a young folião performs before progressing forward in the vocal ensemble, it is often through the caixa that young instrumentalists are initiated into the ensemble.

Although the vocal parts are considered more prestigious within the ensemble, some instrumentalists insisted that it is more fun to play among the accompanists, and I would be inclined to agree with them. Instrumentalists with the same instrument generally cluster together, entering into private musical dialogues with one another. For example, an instrumentalist with a rhythmic part can introduce a different pattern or a new way of marking a

CHAPTER FOUR

Musical Example 4.4

Toada and percussion parts (Folia do Baeta Neves)

harmonic transition into his performances. If those around him notice the new motif and find it appealing, they can take it up on the next round. As others take notice, they too often adjust to the new musical suggestion. Over the years, instrumentalists have built up a series of accompaniment motifs and transitional passages, and they attend to one another in order to introduce them simultaneously. When these transitions are achieved successfully, broad grins appear on the faces of all involved.

Throughout the toada most of the instrumentalists are continuously engaged in performance, and this sustains their attention to the group, marking its participatory and inclusive orientation. This continuous engagement emphasizes the communal nature of the music making (Sugarman 1988, 26), neutralizing the hierarchical distinctions embedded in the structure of folia organization. The diversity of roles performed by the instrumentalists requires them to coordinate their parts with the rest of the musicians in a variety of ways. Some musicians perform in unison with other participants, and often these musicians stand together to facilitate the simultaneity of their actions. Others have unique parts which have to be coordinated rhythmically and harmonically with the rest of the ensemble, requiring them to attend to their colleagues according to a series of individual strategies, depending upon what part they play and where they are positioned within the ensemble. The percussionists and the accompanying strings are primarily responsible for maintaining the pulse for the group, which they establish in negotiation with the estribilho player. All other parts coordinate with this tempo by tuning in to one another in a complex network of mutual attendance to achieve musical consensus. As the group gains momentum, they tend to slowly increase the tempo of their performances, which also increases the tension in their mutual attendance.

Social Relations of Musical Production

Among foliões the social relations of musical production are conceived in terms of the musicians' ability to act in consort to produce a coherent performance within an atmosphere of camaraderie. During performance foliões tune in to one another, listening carefully to how those around them interpret their parts. The performance requirements of the music are such that they lend themselves to a diversity of interactive patterns among participants, promoting constant shifts in the focus of their attention, organizing them and reorganizing them into various groupings. At particular moments in the toada the performances of specific individuals are put in relief, drawing the attention of the other participants to what they are doing. At the same time, each musician is coordinating his behavior with the others, synchronizing it with some while entering into contrastive musical relationships with others, generating fluid and shifting patterns of mutual attendance. Such processes of group coordination are, of course, common to ensembles everywhere, but among foliões they are overtly expressed through body language: the musicians turn toward one another to indicate their identification with their peers, and they look at one another and smile to acknowledge the contributions of others. Given their emphasis upon the sociability of music making, foliões actively play up the processes of social interactions they engage in during performance, openly expressing their enjoyment in the group activity.

All the musicians attend to the cues of the estribilho player, since his performances begin and end each toada, although the estribilho player attends to the cues given him by the embaixador so he will know when to begin playing his solo. The singers pay special attention to the texts of the embaixador's improvisations, since they have to repeat them once they enter the ensemble. Special attendance is given to the entrances of the different vocal configurations, since positive evaluations of the group's performances are closely linked to their ability to create a powerful crescendo effect. The different vocal blocs listen carefully to one another in order to achieve a high degree of simultaneity. At times some musicians focus upon the contrato's variations, evaluating his musical ability, just as they pay special attention to the subtle variations in an instrumental solo. The instrumental accompanists attend to one another, often synchronizing their rhythmic patterns to give greater coherence to the ensemble. The specific musical interests of particular individuals draw their attention to the performances of particular foliões, especially if they are trying to learn their parts. Thus, the musicians' attention is in a constant state of flux, shifting from one coparticipant to the next, and in the act of performing together they assimilate and re-create their repertoire. It is precisely the absence of a clearly defined musical leader to centralize the group's attention which heightens the participants' experience of the interactive diversity they generate in their performances.

It is in performance and with the musical support of the rest of the group that individuals engage in experimentation, presenting new contributions to their companions. All of them use rehearsals to try out new musical alternatives: the embaixador experiments with new verses; the contrato tries out new accents; the instrumental soloists attempt to create new ways of performing their countermelodies; accompanists devise new patterns and passages. If the musicians are not satisfied with the outcome the first time around, they have another chance when the toada begins again. The repetitiveness of the music allows them to elaborate and perfect their ideas, and once they have arrived at a satisfactory alternative, they can consolidate it in the next repetitions. While they are experimenting they also attend to the reactions of their coparticipants to see how others view the suitability of the proposed alternatives; others express their approval of new musical suggestions through overt body language as well as by taking them up in the next rounds.[5] In this way musicians build up a stock of shared musical ideas which can be introduced at different times to add variety to their performances.

Since foliões conceive of music making in terms of the social relations involved in musical production, they orchestrate their performances in a manner which highlights their musical interactions. They explore the interactive possibilities embedded in their repertoire, such that the musical structure articulates dialectically with their conceptions about music and music making to enhance the experience of sociability during their musical activities. The respect foliões have for the embaixador's ritual knowledge and improvisational skills is expressed in their attention to the embaixada, the notion that the contrato part provides a privileged space for a young musician to demonstrate his musical potential directs attention toward his performance, expectations heighten toward the end of each cycle as the ensemble awaits the climactic entrance of the tala, and so on, each performer in turn becoming the focus of group attention. Their enjoyment in making music together does not derive from an ability to reproduce their parts in perfect concordance with a predetermined model, but from the interactive processes they set in motion during performance. Within folia communities it is the quality of the social interactions that take place during performance that informs the evaluations participants make of their music-making experiences.

The foliões' notions about rehearsals are consistent with a participatory and inclusive orientation toward music making, leading them to engage in extraordinary conceptual acrobatics to downplay the hierarchical distinctions that are structurally embedded in their organizations. Because all are constantly engaged throughout the performance, guided by their own individual interests—rather than those of a conductor—they create an atmosphere of camaraderie and egalitarianism which marks their music making as a collective achievement. Like countless other genres of participatory music, the repertoire of the folia de reis is highly repetitive and adheres to a strict formal structure, features which allow participants to learn their parts with relative ease and enter the performance arena without requiring extensive prior training. Furthermore, the folia can accommodate people with varying levels of musical competence, from beginners to experienced musicians, creating spaces for anyone interested in participating. The clear framework of the style allows for controlled variation, in which each participant leaves his imprint upon the whole while simultaneously acquiring an awareness of the contributions of others. During performance foliões maintain a continuous dialogue with one another, balancing their search for novelty with their attempts to achieve musical consensus based upon a well-embodied musical scaffolding.

The kind of negotiation foliões achieve is possible only because all the musicians know their parts very well. Instead of having to focus their attention primarily on what they are performing, they can gear their attention toward each other. Their familiarity with the music allows them to alter their parts and perceive minor alterations and cues proposed by others. It is precisely the formalization and repetitiveness of the folia repertoire that allows participants to become so familiar with the music they are performing that they are able to divert their attention away from what they are doing to focus upon one another, increasing their awareness of their relationships with others.[6] The intensity of interpersonal interaction among the participants promotes a recognition of the presence and contributions of their peers.[7]

Given the social emphasis foliões place upon music making, they sing only when they are experiencing a sense of well-being. When a musician is in mourning, for example, he temporarily leaves the group until he has overcome his sorrow; when the companhia arrives at a house where someone has died recently, the household often asks the companhia not to sing, taking only the banner into the house to bless it. The association between singing and well-being means that foliões generally stop singing when they feel ill at ease with their colleagues, often abandoning the group on a permanent basis.

Folias are voluntary associations, and to maintain their numbers they depend upon preserving a sense of camaraderie among their members, but this is not always easily achieved. It is most commonly the leader of the group who is accused of having offended a member by abusing his position or by manifesting an attitude of superiority toward other foliões. Zé dos Magos's foliões refused to continue singing under Alcides because of his autocratic leadership style; Longa, Zé dos Magos's sister, left her brother's companhia to join the Folia do Zé Machado because she felt that, in her presence, Maguinho had intimated that he did not approve of women in a companhia; Tonico left a companhia that is now extinct to join the Folia do Baeta because the dono commented that he sang too softly. Just as mobility was the peasant solution for affirming personal integrity, folia membership is extremely volatile, with musicians moving about from one group to another each time they feel the least bit slighted.

To an outside observer, foliões appear to be extremely sensitive to offense. This is not surprising, given the constant humiliations they experience on a day-to-day basis as members of the lower classes in the worst-paid and most demeaning jobs available in a highly class-conscious society. While they must put up with much of this humiliation in the workplace, the idea of tolerating it among their peers is out of the question. Even the slightest affront can be taken as an insult, such that leave taking is accompanied by the saying "excuse anything" (*desculpe qualquer coisa*), in the hope that some unintended disrespectful action will be overlooked. Living on the margins of society, they have all experienced humiliating situations in their encounters with the upper classes, and within their own communities they strive to shield themselves from further belittlement.

The preoccupation with offending colleagues becomes particularly touchy when a folião is systematically making a mistake. A common way of dealing with such problems is the use of positive reinforcement. I experienced this in 1994 during my first performance with a folia do divino in Campanha, Minas Gerais, where I was given the tambourine.[8] The group played in a style that was slower than any group I had performed with up until then, and I was obviously speeding everyone up, even though I was doing my best to hold back. After a few cycles I finally assimilated their tempo and was able to keep my part fairly steady. Soon afterwards a few of the musicians turned and smiled at me in approval; until I was able to play it to their satisfaction I was basically ignored. A feeling of acceptance into the group persisted from then on, in that eye contact and smiles continuously linked me to other musicians in the group for the rest of the day.

While musical integrity is ultimately the responsibility of the embaixador, musical practices are learned more through imitation than direct instruction. Verbal disapproval of someone's performance may be voiced on occasion in relation to children, but it is avoided where adults are concerned, at least in their presence. To come right out and tell someone that he is performing incorrectly could offend him, and a folião who feels he has been slighted will almost certainly abandon the group. Since sociability is the ultimate aim of the activity, camaraderie outweighs considerations regarding the aesthetic quality of a performance as a product. Thus, "incorrect" performances are generally tolerated, while the rest of the group remains hopeful that eventually a musician playing inappropriately will note where he errs and align his performance more closely to that of the rest of the group. This is not to say that foliões do not make aesthetic judgements about musical sounds; rather, the sound quality of one's own group's performances is perceived first in light of the quality of the social interactions musicians engage in to generate the musical sounds. The coherence of a performance is seen as a result of the degree to which the participants are able to coordinate their behavior with one another to achieve musical consensus. The quality of the sound is a measure of the quality of the social integration within the group. The ultimate goal is to achieve an aesthetically pleasing product in which the harmonious sounds of the music reflect harmonious social relations among the performers.

In participatory genres like the folia de reis, the reification of music—that is, the divorcing of music from the social relations of its production—is hindered, since participants experience a direct involvement in the creation of the final product. With reification, music comes to be conceived in terms of fixed structures, which once composed take on an existence as real entities. Thus divorced from the processes involved in their production, musical structures become available for evaluation purely in terms of their aesthetic merits as objects. In a reified orientation to music—like that dominant in Western thinking—the focus of attention is placed upon the integrity of the sounds, to which the music makers become subservient. In nonreified orientations to music it is the sounds that reflect the integrity of the social relations of the music makers. Among foliões the sounds heard as music are perceived as an outcome of the negotiations of those involved in producing them, allowing the musicians to acquire consciousness of how they have contributed to the music that emerges out of their encounters with other people, just as they note the role of others in the final production. Thus, what appear to be "conceptual acrobatics" may in fact reflect quite accurately the way in which many foliões experience their music making; they are, therefore, far more than rhetorical discourses formulated to comfort musicians in the ensembles' lower ranks.

Competing Frameworks

If the foliões' social ideal during music making emphasizes egalitarianism and camaraderie, why, one might ask, do they repeatedly mark the hierarchical organization of their associations in such explicit terms? Although a particular conceptual framework may be dominant in a given context, people rarely operate according to a single set of coherent ideas, and these conceptualizations can be—and usually are—contradictory and conflictual (Boon 1986; Watson 1991). Indeed, folia activities are informed by both hierarchical and egalitarian orientations. On the one hand, companhias are highly structured and rule-governed associations, but on the other, they are extremely fluid; just as their membership is in constant flux, people's roles within the organization are constantly changing. For every "norm" there are countless exceptions, which accommodate the pragmatic circumstances of the moment.

For companhias to exist as associations they require some form of leadership, and as we have seen, they envisage three leadership positions as a means of decentralizing the decision-making process. Thus, the hierarchical organization of the folia is itself relativized, and any folião who is interested in par-

CHAPTER FOUR

ticipating in internal decision making need only arrive at rehearsals early enough to participate in the discussions before the music begins. Furthermore, companhias must contend with other factors: first, the style is structured around a variety of distinct musical parts, and second, their membership is continuously changing. Because folias are voluntary associations, the norms must be continuously negotiated to accommodate the people participating in them without threatening their personal integrity. By defining each of the roles within the organization in hierarchical terms and by establishing a clear framework for the internal mobility of their membership, participants—particularly newcomers—are able to assess fairly rapidly what roles might be available to them, accommodating their individual projects to the requirements of the tradition in accordance with the makeup of the group at any given time. The norms provide a backdrop against which negotiations can take place, constituting a shared understanding of the degree of elasticity the organizations can tolerate without requiring overt explications that could be taken as offenses; to join the group, newcomers will have to perform toward the back, unless none of the former members of the group is interested in occupying an opening in one of the more prestigious parts.[9]

In effect, then, the internal hierarchy of the companhia provides a mechanism for dealing with the negotiation of musical roles within a style marked by heterogeneous parts in which participants hold a nonreified orientation toward music making. Thus, foliões are emphatic in representing their associations in terms of their internal hierarchy, while they simultaneously engage in downplaying it. Yet in negotiating the weight each conceptual framework is to receive, there is considerable scope for variation. While Alcides's authoritarian leadership procedures were considered unacceptable to the members of the Folia do Zé dos Magos, the members of his own companhia are willing to accede to them; his centralized mode of leadership is legitimated by the fact that his foliões considered him to be the most knowledgeable embaixador in São Bernardo.

The competition among companhias brings to the fore its own set of conceptual frameworks. When assessing the performances of other companhias, foliões do not only evaluate the extent of the embaixador's esoteric and ritual knowledge, they also become highly critical observers of the aesthetic merits of their musical performances, even though such evaluations are downplayed in relation to their own groups. Since these exercises are generally geared to pointing out the shortcomings in the performances of others, one's own companhia supposedly emerges as aesthetically superior, and one's own embaixador as more knowledgeable. Thus, the construction of the integrity of one's own companhia is predicated upon an ability to extract the performances of other groups from the social relations of their production.

The modernization of the folia tradition that is currently taking place, particularly in the urban context, however, has increased the space given to aesthetic considerations in assessing one's own group's performances. This often conflicts with the social orientation toward music making, by placing greater stress on the quality of the music and on the public image of the group during performance than previously occurred in such groups. In São Bernardo this was most noticeable in the Folia do Baeta Neves, where there was the greatest number of entrances and exits of musicians during my research period. Just before I began working with them, the group had lost a drummer; I was told by other members that this had happened because one of the leaders of the group had called his attention to the fact that he was late one day, even though people were still milling around when he arrived; allegedly he handed the caixa back there and then and never returned again. The new caixeiro stayed in the group only for a short period. He left, it was said, because he occasionally missed a beat; one time this happened during a visitation, and someone looked at him with a frown on his face, publicly humiliating him. Two elderly brothers left in 1988 because they felt some of the young musicians in the group had ridiculed their style of singing; they said they saw them imitating it to their peers, calling it old fashioned. These are but a few examples of the ten or so foliões who have abandoned the group since Owaldir took the banner; the vast majority left because they felt slighted by another member of the group.

The Folia do Baeta is also the only companhia I ever encountered that had actually expelled any foliões from its ranks. It is a point of honor among folia leaders to claim that they do not tolerate disorderly behavior in their ensembles, but very rarely are direct measures taken to expel anyone. One dono in Batatais, São Paulo, once told me that he allowed only respectful people to join his group, but he had never had to exclude anyone from his companhia, because only orderly people ever wanted to join it; anyone who is devoted to the Three Kings, he claimed, would know how to respect the tradition. In the Folia do Baeta three musicians were turned out of the group for excessive alcohol consumption. While their drinking had long been considered problematic within the group, things came to a head when they arrived besotted to a public presentation organized by the São Bernardo Department of Culture. It was decided that to allow them to join the group on the stage could ruin the group's reputation, and after some loud and strong exchanges between the three and the leadership, they finally agreed to leave the premises. Two of the excluded musicians were allowed to rejoin the companhia several months later, having promised to moderate their drinking during folia activities.

On the one hand, the imposition of order in a companhia resonates positively within folia communities, since it is seen to reflect the modern urban lifestyles of its membership, marking them off from the backward and rustic aesthetic of their rural past; on the other, it entails a greater preoccupation with the product of performance, constituting a move toward a more reified conception of music making. Finding the means of reconciling these radically opposing forces constitutes a major challenge for the leaders of urban companhias, which they achieve to a greater or lesser degree. Throughout my research the Folia do Baeta had little difficulty replacing the musicians who abandoned the group, since new members were easily attracted by the "orderly" image of the folia, with its various uniforms and "modern" sound, but especially by the opportunities afforded within this group to make records and to participate in public presentations in São Bernardo and other places, sources of considerable pride among the group's membership. For the sake of these opportunities some foliões were willing to swallow their pride when slighted, remaining in the group for longer than they might have done under similar circumstances in another folia.

Negotiations

In São Caetano one year I had to teach Owaldir a lesson, and the next day he didn't sing; he spent the whole day without singing. I had to take the embaixada all day. . . .

The banner was at Geraldinho's house, and we went to get it. . . . When we were leaving, I said, "Look, let's see if we sing all the way to Belê's house and we'll leave the banner there . . . and we'll go home to rest. Tomorrow is Saturday and we can sing the whole day." . . . I even asked the group if everyone agreed. They all agreed. . . .

When we got to Belê's it was around 10:15. . . . I was going to sing to ask the family to put the banner away, . . . but before I could begin [Owaldir] talked . . . to his son, Paulinho, to Juarez, to Jacaré. He said, "Look, let's sing through the night?" . . . But I was the coordinator, and we had decided we were going to stop there and return on Saturday. He was responsible for the banner, but I was coordinating the group. . . .

Then I said, "Listen, are you serious or are you joking?"

"No, I'm serious. Let's sing all night?"

I said, "What did I say at Geraldinho's? Didn't I say that when we got here we would stop to come back tomorrow morning, that we would rest, and that tomorrow we would sing all day?"

"Right, but we've decided to sing all night."

"All right then, but I end my part here. Tomorrow I'm off to Arceburgo, because when you invited me to coordinate this, I intended to coordinate it. If I am to coordinate it, the responsibility is mine; if it's not mine, then it's yours." I said, "Look here, the notebook is here. . . . From now on you follow on with the banner without me."

"Ah, but, Zezo."

"No, either I decide or you decide. If you think you have the right, fine. I made my decision back there. If you want to disregard my decision, go ahead." . . .

He said, "Alright, but we're going to sing." . . .

So I moved aside, and he said, "Ah, but you have to sing the resposta for me."

I said, "No, from now on you make do. Don't you make the decisions? If you're going to continue all night long, then you can sing the embaixada and then 'respond' to yourself as well. You think you can do both things at the same time, so do both of them; sing both voices. I'm not going to sing," and I didn't sing.

Then his son, Paulinho, did the second voice. Paulinho was singing the contrato. He would leave that voice and respond to the embaixada, . . . and on the return he would sing the contrato.

In his verse he called me . . . twice to come sing, . . . and he started to cry. . . . With tears flowing he pleaded with me to sing; I didn't go. Then he sang another verse apologizing for what he had done; I didn't go. . . . When he reached the last verse, he asked the family to put the banner and the instruments away. Then I went and responded for him, because that was what we had decided. . . .

The next day he didn't sing. He was so upset, he was so ashamed, . . . that he stayed the whole day following the banner without singing. (Zezo)

Zezo's account of his confrontation with Owaldir represents more than a mere struggle over authority within the group; it was played out amid tensions between "traditionalist" and "modernist" orientations toward folia practices in the ongoing negotiations of the group's public image. In the days in which companhias made "direct journeys" (*giros diretos*), remaining en route for the full twelve days of the Christmas season, the groups often performed all night long; some foliões even claimed that companhias should perform only at night, since the Kings traveled only when the stars were out. Musicians often spoke of their nightlong peregrinations with fondness, remembering them as contexts which consolidated the sense of camaraderie they strove to create during performance. But they also claimed that nocturnal visitations commonly led many foliões to overindulgence in alcohol consumption. In fact, in rhetorical fashion Owaldir himself once asked me, "Nowadays who would like to be woken up at four in the morning to let a motley band of drunkards into their house? . . . What would we do if some family refused the banner?"

Obviously I wanted to know whether this had ever happened. Owaldir claimed that the companhia had never been openly rejected, but some families had pretended to be away or not to have woken up when the companhia came around; others had given them an offering, but had asked them to wait outside while they took the banner around the house to bless it. But, he said, "Sooner or later someone was bound to offend the Three Kings"; it was just a matter of time. In their drive toward "modernization," the foliões had been negotiating an end to late-night visitations, to restore their respectability within the local community. By the time I began my research there was general consensus in the group that they should stop singing around ten in the evening.[10]

While the victor here seems to have been the "civilizing process" (Elias 1978–82), the responses to the conflicting frames of reference continued to be triggered by deeply rooted commonsense notions of personal integrity and the role of singing as an expression of social well-being. In marking the boundaries of his authority, Zezo explicitly invoked the structure of the music as an icon of the mutual dependence and complementarity of the roles of the leaders. Furthermore, he claimed his decision had not been imposed autocratically; before taking it he had sought—and received—the (harmonious) consent of the whole group. However "modern" the Folia do Baeta may have appeared to its members, the dominant conceptual framework informing their musical activities continued to articulate a social orientation toward musical production.

From the time a folião enters an ensemble, he becomes immersed in the interactive web that characterizes folia music making, in which the exchange of overt facial and bodily expressions among musicians acknowledges their contributions to the collective achievement. To perform together the musicians coordinate their actions with one another, and in the sounds they produce, their links to one another reverberate throughout the body, heightening their sense of social integration. These are powerful bodily experiences, which are not easily debased by competing conceptual frames, particularly when they are also resonant with everyday patterns of sociability.

The sociability of music making, particularly in the rehearsal context, is integrated into a complex network of face-to-face interactions linking musicians, their families, neighbors, and work colleagues on a day-to-day basis. Rehearsals are special events which break with the everyday to highlight nonverbal means of sociability, but they are also familiar, resonating with valued patterns of social interaction outside the immediate musical sphere. These patterns are rearticulated, organizing social exchanges throughout the rehearsal. Just as the vocal parts have staggered entrances, arrivals at rehearsals more or less replicate these entrance patterns, such that those with the most prestigious parts arrive first. This provides the leadership with an opportunity to discuss group affairs while they wait for the rest of the musicians. Suggestions are put forward as commentary on the procedures of others, and they are endorsed through successive repetitions of analogous situations. The crescendo effect of the successive vocal entrances in performance replicates this mode of collective decision making; in performance the embaixador improvises a text which is then taken up by the successive vocal configurations, in a manner which repeatedly endorses the initial proposition. Furthermore, because improvisations have a formulaic quality, similar themes emerge time and time again in different guises, just as foliões discuss a set of stock themes over and over again in a different order and with a different emphasis each time they meet.

By transporting familiar modes of social interaction into the performance arena, foliões add new dimensions to the way they experience their social relations. While on a day-to-day basis face-to-face interactions emerge primarily in the form of dyadic relations across households, group music making re-creates these complex webs in a single event, allowing them to be experienced as the basis of a community. During performance musicians engage in a diversity of interactive patterns, articulating links with all the other musicians simultaneously, links which can be—and are—extended conceptually to encompass their families and neighbors into a fluid social network.

Plates

1. Seu João Isaias, from Monsenhor Paulo, one of the greatest storytellers I have ever met.

2. Seu Januário performing an estribilho on his bandola during a visitation by the Folia do Baeta Neves. The man on the right, playing the guitar, is Seu Owaldir.

3. The Folia do Baeta Neves posing for a photograph during their three-day excusion to Arceburgo in January 1988.

4. The Folia do Seu Alcides posing for a photograph during their journey in 1988.

5. The banner of a folia in Monsenhor Paulo. The man holding the banner is Zé dos Magos's brother, Lourenço, who still lives in Monsenhor Paulo, and the man on the left is Zé Quatorze. The picture was taken when I accompanied Zé Quatorze to his hometown to visit a daughter living there.

6. Seu Alcides leading his ensemble with an embaixada.

7. A bastião imitating the musicians, using his whip like a guitar, during a folia encounter in Batatais organized by the municipal government.

8. The three bastião of the Folia do Zé dos Magos posing for a photograph. The bastiãozinho is Zé dos Mago's eldest son when he was five years old.

9. Three crosses in the municipality of Arceburgo marking the spot where it is said that three bastião lost their lives during a folia encounter.

10. A folia in Arceburgo processing down the street, making its way to the next visitation. Note that the banner leads the procession and the bastião, the guards of the banner, march on either side of it.

11. The Folia do Seu Matias, in Batatais, São Paulo, meeting for a rehearsal on a Sunday afternoon.

12. Zé dos Magos playing the accordion during a visitation.

13. The two front singers in the Folia do Zé dos Magos, Luizinho (*right*) and Pedro (*left*), facing one another as they bless a family during a visitation. Note how Zé dos Magos, the accordion player, attends to Luizinho's performance.

14. Seu Sebastião, a member of the Folia do Baeta Neves, playing the caixa.

15. A manger scene in a family home in Arceburgo.

16. A folia in Monsenhor Paulo arriving to sing at a family home. The head of the household is holding the banner as the group sings a few verses before entering the house.

17. The Folia do Baeta performing for the festival of the arrival at Geraldinho's. Note the bamboo arch in the entranceway, from which hangs the inscription, "L G Z." Zezo is the front singer facing the camera. In his embaixada he tells the audience that the *L* stands for *lembrança* (memory), which reminds the faithful of the Three Kings; the *G* stands for Galiléia (Gallilee), where Jesus was born; and the *Z* stands for *zombando* (mocking), invoking King Herod's thwarted attempt to kill the baby Jesus.

18. A couple dancing at a folia festival in Monsenhor Paulo.

19. A group of men in conversation during the festival of the arrival of the Folia do Zé Machado.

CHAPTER V

Departures

THE DEPARTURE IS THE RITUAL that launches the annual journey of each folia de reis. Departures are held at the festeiro's house, and at the end of the journey the ensemble returns there to celebrate the festival of the arrival. Although central to the tradition, departures are fairly low-key and intimate events, involving the foliões, the festeiro and his immediate family, and a few other close relatives and neighbors. They are, however, set apart form ordinary visitations, in that they involve a few ritual acts that are specific to this context. First, departures begin with an obligatory rosary—more precisely, a shortened version of the rosary known as the *terço*. The terço is also performed at the arrival, but at visitations it is not customary unless the foliões have been asked to sing for the soul of a dead relative.[1] Another common ritual act at departures is the performance of the "mission verses" (*versos da missão*), in which the foliões state the purpose of the journey. There are also a number of protection rites to ward off any Herods, and the thanksgiving verses are omitted, as the festeiro makes no donation to his own festival. Traditionally departures take place at midnight between 24 and 25 December, but such norms can always be stretched to accommodate group requirements, and in São Bernardo only three of the five companhias began their journeys in the "traditional" manner while I was among them. The Folia do Zé Quatorze departed on Christmas morning so the foliões in his group could attend midnight mass; the Folia do Baeta departed several days before Christmas, claiming that it was only by starting their journeys early that the group was able to visit all the households that had asked for the blessing of the Kings.[2]

The departure marks the end of an intense, offstage preparatory phase, in which participants have mobilized their resources to guarantee a successful journey. If the banner has become faded, a new one has to be provided; the companhia will have established its itinerary, making sure there are families prepared to provide pouso along the way; the musicians will have prepared their instruments, adorning them with colorful ribbons and plastic flowers, replacing old ones that may have fallen off or become faded over the years; in some companhias new strings for the instruments are distributed during the final rehearsals so they will sound their best for the journey; some companhias wear crowns, and these have to be prepared and distributed to the musicians; other groups have special uniforms which set the musicians apart, and they have to be made ready, as do the outfits, or fardas, of the bastião.

These preparations constitute major expenses for the foliões, and lengthy discussions take place each year to negotiate how they will be met. Often the festeiro takes on part of the expenses, but foliões and their families also cover some of the costs, particularly those pertaining to their personal needs. Occasionally the municipal government of São Bernardo helps each of the groups confront some of its initial expenses: in 1987 they each received a small check to use as they pleased, but the year before that they were each presented with a new instrument of their choice and several sets of new strings. Sometimes companhias are able to secure uniforms for the musicians and other donations by enlisting politicians to mediate on their behalf. Even though some financial help may come from outside the community, it is the foliões and the families they visit who cover the bulk of the journeys' expenses.

On the day of the departure the festeiro and his family focus their attention on preparing their house to receive the folia and any other guests who might happen to show up. The women prepare coffee and snacks for everyone, mobilizing relatives and neighbors to help out in the kitchen and to lend cups and other utensils if necessary. The family has to set up an altar for the banner of the Kings in the front room. Some festeiros place a manger scene on the altar and others surround the banner with flowers and images of saints, such as Our Lady, Saint Anthony, Saint John, Saint George, Saint Gonçalo, and other figures of popular devotion. Many of the ornaments placed on the altar are borrowed from relatives and neighbors for the occasion. This intense activity is geared toward setting the stage for the journey, creating a space distinct from the everyday world. Countless members of the community participate in one way or another in this preparatory process, enhancing their sense of involvement in the project even before the actual journey has begun. Their expectations and commitment toward the upcoming journey are thus heightened, predisposing them to a positive evaluation of the event.

Dona Mariinha's Departure

In 1987 the Folia do Baeta held the departure on a Saturday afternoon, six days before Christmas. The journey was being sponsored by a festeira, Dona Mariinha, whose family had made a promise on her behalf to sponsor three folia journeys to help her recover from a severe back problem. For two years running in the early 1980s the family had taken the banner, but the third sponsorship had had to be postponed when her husband died. The family was now in a position to fulfill the final stage of their obligation.

I arrived at her house with some of the members of the companhia at around 3:30 in the afternoon, and quite a few people were already there, mostly close relatives and a few neighbors of the festeira. The house, a precarious construction of plywood, was set at the far end of a long, narrow plot. Along one side of the plot there were several other smaller constructions, equally precariously built, which were inhabited by the families of a son and a brother, forming an extended family compound, and one other house was occupied by a tenant family. The houses shared a fairly large front patio that had been cemented over, and this provided an ideal space for people to mingle with one another while they waited for the departure to begin.

Soon after I arrived, most of the other foliões arrived as well, and some of them were accompanied by a few members of their immediate families. On arrival people greeted everyone, and the foliões took their instruments into the house to store them in a bedroom until the singing began. On their way through the front room, most people stopped at the altar for a short moment of individual devotion. A woman who arrived with a few children lifted up the youngest and placed the cloth of the banner over his head and instructed the others to kiss it; she told me this was to protect them against illness during the year. The altar was set on a small table covered with a white cloth, and along with the banner there were a few statues of popular saints, a large framed print of the Sacred Heart of Jesus, and two vases of plastic flowers.

The women congregated in the kitchen, while the men remained out on the patio. Some of the musicians were distributing bits of rue that had been rubbed against the banner, and I was informed of its beneficial properties for protecting the companhia against Herods during the journey. Occasionally a woman would emerge with a tray of coffee and sandwiches for the guests. The musicians were dressed in everyday clothing, since their uniforms were reserved for special occasions, which meant public presentations and the arrival ceremony; that year, however, they also wore them during the three days they spent making visitations in Arceburgo from 31 December to 2 January.

At around 4:00 P.M. Dona Mariinha's son emerged with a bottle of mé and a few glasses to serve the musicians a swig or two, which in small medicinal doses was considered necessary to open their throats and help them sing with loud voices. Throughout the departure her son took on all the responsibilities of the festeiro considered inappropriate for a woman, so he set off the fireworks at around 4:30 P.M., calling everyone to the rosary. Once everyone had settled into the small front room, approximately thirty people in all, Owaldir took the role of chaplain (*capelão* or *rezador*) and led the collective prayer, as everyone faced the altar. He recited his own version of the joyful mysteries, which contemplated the Nativity, the journey and Adoration of the Wise Men, the Annunciation, and the Presentation in the Temple. As is customary, the prayer was recited responsorially, involving everyone in attendance. When they had completed the rosary, the foliões formed a queue and each in turn knelt at the altar, where they touched the banner before crossing themselves. Some foliões took this opportunity to perform very elaborate expressions of personal devotion, communicating to the Kings—and to others—that, for them, participation in the companhia was an act of deep religious commitment. After the foliões had blessed themselves, other attendants took their turn at the altar.

After the rosary there was a short break for the festeira and the foliões to prepare for the musical performance. The festeira removed the banner from the altar and took it to the bedroom, where it stayed until called for in the embaixada. The two clowns, the guards of the banner, remained there with it. The foliões went to the get their instruments, and they tuned them in the bedroom before returning to the altar. Once everyone was back in the front room, the foliões positioned themselves to begin their musical performance. When Januário, the estribilho player, felt sure that all the musicians were ready, he launched into the instrumental introduction. Owaldir began the embaixada with the mission verses:

CHAPTER FIVE

1

Louvado seja meu Deus,	Praise be to my God,
Pra sempre seja louvado.	May He always be praised.
Já rezamo o santo terço,	We have already prayed the holy rosary,
Já estamos preparado	We are now prepared

2

Pra seguir nossa jornada	To follow our journey
Com amor e alegria,	With love and joy,
Pra cumprir nossa missão	To fulfill our mission
E a promessa da família.	And the family's promise.

3

Vou pedir para a festeira	I will ask the festeira
Pra trazer nossa bandeira,	To bring our banner
Pra seguir nossa viagem,	To follow our trip,
Nossa guia verdadeira.	Our true guide.[3]

As the foliões sang the third verse, Dona Mariinha emerged carrying the banner, and she was followed by the bastião, who came out making piercing whoops and howls to accompany the energetic prancing steps they performed on each side of the banner. As the foliões sang, one of the bastião took the banner from the festeira and dragged it over the attendants' heads to bless them, and then he returned it to her. The foliões played the estribilho, and the music stopped. In the pause Owaldir struck up a short conversation with one of the bastião, asking him who he was. He responded by saying that he and his brother were the guards of the banner, and they followed it wherever it went. To provoke the embaixador he asked him if he had any objection to their presence, to which Owaldir responded that they could stay, as long as they behaved themselves. This the bastião rebuffed by warning the embaixador that if he wanted them to behave he should not turn his back on them. This elicited the laughs the bastião was after, and his short performance was over.

Januário struck up the estribilho once again, and Owaldir introduced the family verses (*versos da família*), which contained the blessings of the Kings. To receive her blessings Dona Mariinha stood beside the altar tightly hugging the banner as tears welled in her eyes. Her daughter-in-law stood close beside her holding her young son, whom she instructed to clutch the banner as well. Though there would be no thanksgiving verses, the *foliões* expressed their gratitude to the *festeira* and her family by extending the blessing to five verses, which took them nearly twenty minutes to perform:

4

Este verso é pra festeira	This verse is for the festeira
Com toda a sua família.	With all her family.
Está sendo abençoada	They are being blessed
Dos Três Reis de nossa guia.	By the Three Kings on our guide.

5

Santos Reis 'tá despedindo	The Holy Kings are saying good-bye
Pra terra do Oriente.	To the land of the Orient.
Pra festeira e a família	To the festeira and the family
Deixa a bênção de presente.	They leave the blessing as a present.

6

Santos Reis já vai embora;	The Holy Kings are leaving;
Quem quiser pode beijar.	Those who wish to may kiss [the banner].
Dia nove de janeiro	On the ninth of January[4]
Santos Reis tornam a voltar;	The Holy Kings will return;
Deixa a bênção e os milagre;	They leave the blessing and their miracles;
Eles deseja um bom Natal.	We wish you a good Christmas.

7

Se despede da festeira	Saying good-bye to the festeira
E a família da senhora.	And your family.
Vocês vão ficar com Deus;	You will stay with God;
Nós vai com os Reis da Glória.	We go with the Kings of Glory.

8

Leve a bandeira na porta	Take the banner to the door
Foliões vamos beijar.	We, the foliões, will kiss it.
Ela é a proteção	It is the protection
Pra livrar de todo mal.	To free us from all evil.

CHAPTER FIVE

At this point Dona Mariinha's son took the banner from his mother and held it over the passage of the front door. The foliões began their exit by kissing the banner before passing under it. In this way they received a holy blessing protecting the group against the potential dangers of the journey. Once outside the house, the banner had departed, and the ensemble began its visitations in the neighborhood to collect the offerings for the festival of the arrival. The first house they visited was Dona Mariinha's son's, which was right next door in the same compound.

The Sacred Frame

Folia rituals are staged affairs that construct a sacred space in which the faithful renew their links with the Three Kings, heightening their awareness of the continuous presence of the Magi among them. This is achieved through the framed enactments of an encounter between humans and saints that gives their presence tangibility. The departure demarcates the onset of this symbolic space by introducing the voices of the Magi into the realm of humanity. The performances of the folia redefine the social sphere, effecting a fusion of the divine and terrestrial domains that places humans in direct contact with the saints. Just as the faithful find pleasure in their encounters with the Kings, it is thought that the Kings appreciate the opportunity to commune with humans. Indeed, the journey is conducted in their honor; it is a gift offered by the faithful to the Kings in fulfillment of their promises, but also as an expression of gratitude for their ongoing protection. Embodied in the banner, the Magi lead the foliões from house to house, such that through humans they acquire the means of reliving their mythic journey. Through the mediation of the musicians, humans and saints participate in face-to-face interactions with one another, entering into reciprocal exchanges of blessings and gifts. It is through the foliões that the Magi are enchanted into the presence of the faithful, and a heightened sense of their protective power is sustained through to the arrival.

To orchestrate the encounter of the divine and terrestrial domains, folia rituals mark the distinctions between the two spheres (Bell 1992, 74) through the use of performative devices that set the ritual space apart from the pragmatic world of everyday life (Bauman 1975, 1992). For the departure, the physical space of the home is prepared, and a number of saints are set on the altar together with the banner. The ritual is conducted through a series of formalized modes of communication, such as memorized prayers and musical performances, media that contrast with the speech mode of daily interaction. The participants take on special roles which are defined by their ritual functions, and each role is clearly identified and named; some of the participants—the bastião in particular—wear special outfits, which articulate with their ritual roles. The whole event is organized by a recognized script that provides directionality (Parkin 1992) to the movements of people and objects throughout the journey.

The departure is central to the journey as a whole, as it is in this event that the transformation of the social space is effected. When the foliões and other guests arrive at the festeiro's house, they engage in ordinary social activity with one another as they await the rosary. Coffee and sandwiches are served, and they discuss the upcoming journey as well as a series of mundane themes pertaining to their jobs and family life. That a break from the quotidian world is soon to take place is loudly announced when the fireworks begin to explode, calling everyone into the front room for the rosary. During the rosary the faithful face the altar; it is adorned with the banner of the Three Kings and several other iconographic representations of Catholic saints, forming two separate camps of social beings: humans and divinities. Though in the departure described above the attendants remained standing during the rosary, in many folia communities everyone kneels throughout the prayer, confirring to bodily memory a sense of the divide separating humans from the saints (see Connerton 1989). By thus enacting the distance between the two realms, folia communities safeguard the sacred ahistoric and immutable truths of their religious tenets from the ever-changing and corruptible world of humanity.

Sanctified and removed from the everyday world, the stage is set for the Kings to come to earth to commune with the faithful. Their introduction into the ritual frame is prefaced by the mission verses, in which the foliões make "performatives" (Austin 1975, 4–7), declaring themselves spokesmen of the Kings. When the group begins to sing, the embaixada proclaims the group's mission, and this declaration mechanizes the symbolic transformation of the ensemble, turning the musicians into representatives of the Magi; by claiming to be their spokesmen, they become their spokesmen. By becoming the voices of the Magi, they can proceed with the distribution of the blessings. For the blessings the banner is taken from the altar, placing the Kings in the midst of the faithful; the voices of the singers—now those of the Kings—transmit the saints' blessings directly to the devotees, who respond through their donations to the festival.

Once the foliões begin to sing, the embaixada becomes central to the en-

CHAPTER FIVE

actment of the ritual script. This is made especially evident in the various commands that emerge in the verses, as in verse 3, above, in which the embaixador asks the festeira to bring in the banner, or in the final verse, in which he orders the banner to be taken to the door. But it is through the performatives in the embaixada that much of the ritual action takes place: as the embaixada declares that the Kings are blessing the family, the family is blessed (verse 4); in stating that the Kings are bidding farewell, they take their leave (verses 5, 6, and 7); and so on. Furthermore, the ritual sequence is organized in terms of the sets of verses that are performed in the various ritual acts of the tradition, which include mission verses, adoration verses, family or blessing verses, thanksgiving verses, encounter verses, and so on. For different types of verse sequences a particular ordering of the attendants is required: for the mission verses, for example, all face the altar, directing their collective gaze toward the saints; for the blessings, the family stand facing the musicians, altering the positionality of the attendants; while the musicians and other guests may have their gaze directed at the family, the family members focus upon the musicians and their message. The roles of the bastião are also organized through the embaixada, in that their actions coordinate with the type of verse being performed: for adorations and verses for the souls of dead relatives (*versos de intenção*) they kneel on the floor and remove their masks; on other occasions they dance around the banner facing the musicians; their recitations and verbal banter are inserted in the pauses between the singing, but the level of their reverence—or irreverence, as the case may be—articulates with the mood of the occasion as defined by the ritual script.

While the embaixada serves as the primary medium for sustaining the progression of the ritual enactment, the skeletal framework it constructs is elaborated upon—or thickened—through the use of various communicative media, giving symbolic density to the ritual experience of the participants. Throughout folia rituals numerous expressive forms, both verbal and nonverbal, are brought into play, and they promote an experience of the extraordinary among participants. Song texts, gestures, ritual objects, food and drink, spatial organization, musical performance, and so on bombard them, stimulating their aural, visual, tactile, and olfactory senses and provide participants with the sense of being immersed in a whirlpool of disparate motifs (Fernandez 1986).

Plunged into this sea of sensory stimuli, the participants become predisposed to read associations into the motifs, linking them into even larger webs of meaning. These associations emerge from many sources: some motifs resonate with the ritual script, providing a sense of unity to the collective drama; others are constructed in relation to a shared narrative repertoire, particularly the stories connected with the Nativity and with the miraculous power of the Three Kings; others refer to the social universe of the participants: their commonsense notions and aspirations as well as their extraritual experiences of day-to-day interactions; and still others resonate on a very personal level, eliciting private memories, hopes, and fears. The participants are differentially involved in the proceedings, and they bring their distinct biographies with them, such that they experience the ritual from different vantage points. Thus, the associations each participant makes are unique, and the meanings individuals give to their ritual experiences are constructed around the motifs they find personally meaningful. While the ritual script provides the directionality of the event, the complexity of motifs used in padding it out provides a wide fund of resources for the construction of personal meaning through the shared repertoire.

Ritual Resonances

While the multiplicity of media within the ritual context creates the potential for a never-ending proliferation of associations, the clear framework of the ritual script provides a means of periodically refocusing collective attention upon the proceedings. At each stage of the ritual, particular motifs are presented in the form of clusters that articulate with the ritual script. The concept of motif clusters would suggest that a motif is the smallest unit of symbolic significance within the ritual context. However, I do not intend for the term to be taken this literally: since the significance of a motif derives from the associations it invokes, motifs never emerge in consciousness as isolated units; once a motif is recognized it is already a representation. Furthermore, motifs articulate with ritual action, placing the participants within the webs of association they evoke; meaning is constructed through involvement, enhancing the personal significance of the shared heritage.

The density of ritual clusters varies, as some are more prominent during particular ritual acts, foregrounding restricted webs of association, while others evoke more extended associative webs, giving unity to the tradition by linking the restricted webs into larger wholes. Associations elicited by motif clusters that are built into the ritual enactment could be viewed as "scripted resonances," some of which have an integrative effect, in that they transcend specific ritual acts, and others articulate more closely with specific

CHAPTER FIVE

moments of the journey. Yet, it is possible for motifs of restricted prominence to have considerable associative density for particular individuals. Thus, "personal resonances" engage specific motif clusters that articulate with individual biographies. Within the folia tradition there are scripted resonances that are specifically designed to promote personal resonances, linking personal memory to the collective memory of the community.

Singing for the Kings

In the folia ritual context, song emerges as the embodiment of the voices of the Magi. According to the ritual script, the first set of verses a companhia should sing in setting off on the journey is known as the mission verses; in performing them, the foliões announce their obligation to sing on behalf of the Kings. Even if this is not stated explicitly in the embaixada, as in Dona Mariinha's departure, it is implied by the ritual script. The very use of the medium of song in the act that transforms the foliões into mouthpieces of the Kings establishes musical performance as their medium of communication, and what is sung in their repertoire is taken for a divine message.

As a mode of communication, music contrasts dramatically with the speech mode of everyday interaction. Its highly formalized structure imposes restrictions upon the performers which create the illusion of stability, referring the sung messages to the timeless domain of the saints. The use of rhetorical mythic imagery in the improvised couplets allows participants to locate and recognize the realm being represented, while the use of verbal formulas gives the embaixada a timeless and immutable character. All folia styles involve the repetition of the embaixada by the back singers: in the paulista style it is repeated once as it was originally performed by the front singers; in the mineiro styles it is repeated several times, as the various voices join the ensemble. Through these repetitions the content of the embaixada is endorsed; what is proclaimed in the embaixada is acknowledged in the echoes of the back singers.[5]

Today the mineiro style is the dominant form used in southeastern Brazil, and without doubt, the single most striking feature of this style is the final chord of the toada, the moment at which all the vocal parts join to form a prolonged harmonious whole; indeed, it is this chord—the *gritinho* (little yell), as they call it—that foliões highlight when characterizing the style. In Dona Mariinha's departure the ensemble burst into the final chord of the toada no fewer than seventeen times in the twenty-five minutes they spent singing, and as the journey progresses it is this chord which continuously punctuates folia performances. On numerous occasions I have noted that when the ensemble reaches this point in the toada, other participants, even small children, join the chorus. The long chord seems to invite one to thicken it, and an almost involuntary reaction overtakes many people, compelling them to add their voices to the ensemble. When, for some reason, I am reminded of the folia tradition, the final chord of the toada seems to begin reverberating in my head. A few years ago I met a man in Campinas, São Paulo, who had grown up in a small town in Minas Gerais; when I asked him if he was familiar with the folia de reis tradition, his response was simply, "Êêêêêêêêiiiii!," invoking the tala of the final chord of the toada mineira.[6]

When the Kings arrived at the manger, they were given musical instruments in exchange for their gifts. The Magi's legacy to humanity, then, is the music they received, and it constitutes the primary means of instating God's vision on earth. The embaixada proclaims the truths of the saints; these truths are disseminated across the world through the successive endorsements they receive by the back singers; when they finally prevail, the world becomes dominated by the social order epitomized by the final chord: to produce it, the individual notes of each of the singers resonate sympathetically with one another, creating a thick harmonious whole.

As discussed in the previous chapter, music making within folia communities is understood both as an expression of well-being and as a means of constructing an atmosphere of social harmony. The integrity of a performance is measured in terms of the quality of the social interactions that take place during performance; in a successful performance, the foliões achieve a sense of camaraderie that neutralizes the hierarchical structure of their organizations, and the harmonious sounds of the music resonate with the harmonious social relations they ideally set in motion through music making. To sing in the folia, then, is to experience the social ideal of the saints. In joining the chorus at the end of the toada one joins in the construction of this vision.

Guarding the Banner

The bastião—the guards of the banner—make their entrance when the banner is called forth, placing the Kings in the midst of humanity. The immense discursive interest folia communities display in the bastião indicates that their emergence sparks multiple associations during ritual performances. Indeed, their entrance is dramatic, given their colorful outfits and terrifying masks as well as the loud yells and howls they often make to attract atten-

CHAPTER FIVE

tion. As we have seen, their costumes integrate elements associated with infancy and animality, creating an image of undomesticated subhumanity. Their behavior is marked by brisk transitions, fluctuating between expressions of extreme irreverence and extreme deference. This juxtaposition of the comic and the serious is common—if not a defining feature—of ritual clowning the world over;[7] it is prescribed by their ritual role, rendering them ambiguous figures.

The dominant view of the bastião within folia communities ascribes to them the role of Herod's spies. As emissaries of the evil King Herod, they stand in direct opposition to the musicians, the emissaries of the benevolent Kings. This opposition articulates with other oppositions evident in the roles of these two types of ritual figure, enhancing the associations evinced by each category. First, while the musicians sing, the bastião only speak. Singing, as noted above, is the communicative mode of the saints, which by implication renders speech the human medium. While singing—a mode of coordinated collective activity—articulates social harmony and well-being, speech—the medium for argument (Bloch 1974) and for the expression of personal concerns (Sugarman 1988)—creates the potential for social discord and the fragmentation of collective interests. Song—a medium which unites—is, therefore, sacred, while speech—a medium which divides—belongs to the realm of humanity.[8]

Similarly, the musicians and the bastião display contrasting attitudes toward the donations they receive during visitations. The donations collected by the musicians are given to the banner in return for the blessings, and they are redistributed to the whole community during the festival; the bastião, on the other hand, arrive at visitations and begin asking for things without offering anything in return; moreover, what they receive they keep for themselves. Thus, the reciprocity embodied in the exchanges between the Kings and the faithful are distinctly absent in the willful and nonreciprocal accumulation of goods by the bastião.

The bastião are the focus of attention at several moments during visitations, particularly at pousos; yet their comic behavior disqualifies them from being taken seriously. Their self-interested actions, their continuous demands for objects, their manifestations of vanity, and their insulting remarks do not threaten established values; rather, one could say that they elicit the self-satisfied condescension that Arthur Koestler (1964) saw as typically felt toward humorous characters, convincing the audience of its own moral superiority. Because they are unambiguously clowns—or inferior beings—they can act in the realm of the forbidden with impunity. In this context, the actions of the bastião allow for a ritualized experience of transgression without threatening the rules of proper social conduct (Eco 1984, 1–3). According to Mary Douglas (1975), however, jokes—or clowning—always have a subversive effect upon the dominant structure of ideas, revealing its conceptual antithesis. Clearly the actions of the bastião are undignified; but they also strip those they target of their dignity. Through their clowning, the bastião reveal the frailty and the private and the hidden dimensions of people's lives, shattering their self-righteousness. In effect, folia clowns reveal the humanity of their victims; behind their public façades lie individuals with the same self-centered urges prominently displayed in the behavior of the bastião.

A fundamental aspect of their role, however, is that they repented of their self-indulgent ways on encountering the baby Jesus; thus, their irreverent behavior is juxtaposed to expressions of extreme piety during moments of direct contact with the sacred. At such occasions the clowns remove their masks and kneel humbly in an expression of intense humility. Through these demonstrations of reverence during particularly solemn moments, they appear to state that petty, clownlike behavior is a predicament of the alienated human condition; the transcendence of the self-interested orientation of humankind can be achieved only by allowing oneself to be subjugated by the superior morality of the saints. To domesticate one's infantile and animalistic tendencies and become a moral human being, one must subordinate one's urges to the divinities and the truths they represent. Thus, while entertaining, the clowning of the bastião articulates matters of extreme gravity.

Within the ritual context the bastião—the embodiment of the human predicament—emerge when the banner is brought into the midst of the faithful. Taking their positions on either side of the banner, they assume their role as its primary defenders. Their emergence with the banner gives dramatic impact to the associations attached to them, while also serving to remind everyone that the moral principles embodied in the figures of the Kings need to be carefully and continuously guarded against human instinct.

While the bastião draw forth dense, scripted resonances, their presence can also spark associations among participants that derive from their personal involvement with these figures. Close relatives of foliões dressed as bastião take a special interest in the performances of their relations; foliões who have themselves once worn the farda may be reminded of these past experiences when the bastião emerge; mothers who made promises on behalf of their sons may remember the miracle the Kings bestowed upon their families; and so on. During a visitation I witnessed in Arceburgo one of the

CHAPTER FIVE

bastião was taunting some children sitting on the sofa; he would race toward them, head first, mockingly frightening them with his mask, as the children squealed with delight. I was standing nearby with a few other foliões and the head of the household, who seemed particularly absorbed by this playful banter. Noting his interest, one of the foliões told me that the man's son made bastião masks, and a lengthy discussion ensued, in which I was told about how his son's masks were so widely appreciated in the region that even companhias from other municipalities would order them. Then the man produced a stack of photographs of companhias, and he proceeded to methodically point out each of the bastião wearing a mask his son had made.

Closing the Folia

Foliões are highly fearful of forces that might upset the harmony of their associations, and considerable energy is expended to ward them off. The threats requiring protective measures are typically represented through such concepts as Herods, demolitions (*desmanches*), works of magic (*trabalhos*), persecutions (*perseguições*), and the evil eye (*mau-olhado*), and the ensemble can be isolated from them through any number of techniques. These rituals are often referred to as *fechamentos* (closures), and they are meant to shield the group against threats to group integrity during the journey. While rituals of closure may occur at any time, they are particularly evident at departures. By performing them in this context, the group embarks upon the journey insulated by a protective armor.

Closures can involve the distribution of amulets of various kinds to the ensemble members, such as ribbons taken from the banner, bits of rue plant, or other small sacred objects, which the foliões attach to their instruments or put in their pockets. Some rituals involve direct contact with the banner; examples of this occurred at Dona Mariinha's departure, as when the bastião waved the banner over the musicians at the end of the mission verses, or when the foliões left the house by passing under it. Some embaixadores perform special verses at the departure, which are intended to ward off dangers. At a departure I observed in Arceburgo, Minas Gerais, for example, Antônio Mariano, the ritual leader, began his embaixada by mumbling a few verses that I was unable to make out. I asked a few of the foliões if they had understood them, but no one seemed able to decipher them for me. I was told that only the embaixador knew what he had sung, because he had performed *versos de fechamento* (closure verses) with special magical powers; if the verses were to become public, they could lose their potency.

Rituals of closure are of particular interest to embaixadores, since their prestige is closely linked to their ability to protect their companhias against destructive forces. Thus, for them, they may be the source of dense personal resonances. In mumbling the closure verses, Antônio Mariano drew attention to the breadth of his esoteric knowledge, heightening awareness of his reputation among the members of his group.

The Herods one can encounter during journeys are discussed frequently, and these discussion often elicit extended narratives of how a particular situation was negotiated. Luizinho, for example, once explained to me how he had dealt with a desmanche:

> For example, we arrive at a house where someone wants to do something to us, because at the time of the Kings there was a lot of persecution, wasn't there? There are many foliões in the world who are persecuting others, doing evil, these things, right? The person sometimes says something, or just by looking at them, you already lose your note; the strings begin to break; the instruments start going out of tune. One person sings this way, the other that way, and everything goes wrong. So when we feel it is that thing, we sing three or four verses of the Prayer of Calvary (*Oração do Carvário*), and nothing sticks to us. . . .
>
> Once this happened here in Diadema. I arrived at a house in Eldourado. There was a colored man there who had gone out in a folia de reis, but it wasn't very together, it wasn't good. . . . When we arrived at that house I began to sing. Not a single voice in back came out. The musician tried hard, but nothing came out. And after that everything went out of tune. Even the caixa missed the beat.
>
> I said, "Our Lady!" Then we stopped, tuned all the instruments. When I finished tuning the instruments, we started to sing again. Then I pleaded, "Oh, my good Jesus of Calvary, help me."
>
> Then I began to sing four verses of the Prayer of Calvary. Then the instruments stayed in tune. Then I sang for him there.
>
> He said, "You have an incredible protection, so you do. You were supposed to leave here all out of tune."
>
> Then I said, "The Prayer of Calvary helped me."
>
> Then he showed me everything he had written, all the verses that he was going to destroy me with. He wanted to write them all down for me, but I didn't want them.
>
> "I don't want to destroy anything," I said, "especially of the folia de reis. I belong to the Holy Kings. Who am I going to destroy?" That's what I

CHAPTER FIVE

said to him. "I don't want it. You can keep it. You can destroy someone else, but you can't destroy me."

"But I wanted to separate you all so you'd never sing Kings again."

You know how it is: bad people, right? You know how it is with bad people, people who are envious of this, who can't do what we were doing. His folia de reis was no good.

During closure rituals, foliões are reminded of stories such as this one, and they enhance the group's self-image, giving the members added confidence to confront threats to the group's integrity.

Though it is generally claimed that the evil forces that affect an ensemble are caused by the envy of outsiders, especially foliões who belong to "disorganized" companhias, foliões are keenly aware that they can be equally—if not primarily—the outcome of internal strife. Stories abound within folia communities of musicians who abandoned their ensembles for having felt slighted by another member of the group. Foliões also tell of companhias that dissolved acrimoniously because of internal discord, but such cases are rather rare, since foliões tend to avoid open conflict by simply removing themselves from humiliating situations.

However hard companhias may strive to preserve a sense of camaraderie within their associations, there is always the possibility that human pettiness will surface at any moment. This danger is particularly acute during journeys, when the foliões remain in close company with one another for long hours over a period of several days. Through the multiplicity of rites and practices in their repertoire, foliões heighten their awareness of the potential conflicts that can emerge in their midst in an attempt to minimize the risks of disintegration. In closing the group they warn themselves to be on guard against their own "bastião-nesses" in order to uphold the harmonious moral ideal of the Magi.

Expressing Devotion

As I stated earlier, departures are rather intimate, low-key events; they are staged for the benefit of the festeiro's family, but the foliões also stage them for themselves. Although the household may be blessed, the departure is not understood as an ordinary visitation, and to demarcate its distinction, it has its own name. The main ritual acts specifically associated with the departure are the rosary and the mission verses, both of which are understood as communal expressions of devotion to the Wise Men. Furthermore, the departure is marked by a number of individual expressions of devotion: when the foliões arrive at the festeiro's house they usually go to the altar to kiss the banner before engaging in conversation with their peers. At Dona Mariinha's departure the embaixador scripted in a moment for the expression of individual devotion, which took place between the rosary and the mission verses, and in verse 6 he invited the attendants to kiss the banner.

In popular Catholic communities devotion is understood as a declaration of one's subservience to the moral superiority of the saints, and it affirms one's commitment to uphold their divine truths. In reciprocation for their loyalty, folia communities hope to harness the protective power of the saint. Foliões generally claim that they participate in folia activities because of their devotion to the Kings, and the journey as a whole is conceived of as an act of devotion. The embaixada proclaims their moral order, such that participation in folia activities constitutes a public expression of adherence to these truths. While singing for the Magi is an expression of devotion, it is also a gift to reciprocate for their protective power and to ensure its continued presence in the world. Indeed, many of the foliões participate in a companhia to redeem a promise to the Magi, just as journeys are commonly sponsored to redeem promises.

In performing acts of devotion, the faithful are reminded of their personal experiences of the miraculous power of the Kings, particularly if they are present in the companhia because of a promise. Throughout the journey there are moments for the expression of devotion, but the devotional orientation of the tradition is given special emphasis at departures, as the foliões prepare themselves to confront the journey. By performing a series of devotional acts at this moment in the ritual script, the foliões depart with a heightened sense of spiritual strength to help them safeguard the social ideal of the Kings while en route. While closures may remind the foliões of the types of behavior which can disrupt social harmony, acts of devotion evoke a sense of the ideal toward which they need to strive.

Holding the Banner

Folia communities see the banner as the embodiment of the Three Kings. It depicts the Adoration of the Magi, and foliões refer to it explicitly in their embaixadas as the Three Kings. It is kept on the altar together with other iconic representations of popular saints, and it is held and touched during the blessings to give them greater efficacy. Moreover, it is taken on the journey, the gift of the faithful to the saints, allowing the Magi to relive their mythic journey. In folia journeys the banner leads the procession from house to house, serving as a guide to the musicians, just as the star of Bethlehem once led the Wise Men to the Christ Child. To hold the banner is to enter into direct physical contact with the sacred. As an object it is quite heavy, and it seems to get heavier the longer one holds it, continuously reminding one of the weight of the saints—and of the tradition—one is upholding.

The person holding the banner stands facing the companhia, becoming a focal point of the ritual act. Blessings are conducted through the improvised couplets of the embaixada, and the fact that they are improvised allows the embaixador to link their content to the immediate circumstances of the performance context. Thus, they can be taken as personalized messages, and after visitations many people can recite the verses the companhia has sung to them during the blessing. During Dona Mariinha's departure, she was systematically referred to as the festeira, which marked her relationship to the ensemble. In the second verse, reference was made to her promise, highlighting an episode in her life which her family considered sufficiently serious to warrant three folia sponsorships. Blessings, then, are a means of integrating significant aspects of people's personal biographies into the collective memory of the community.

Just as these telegraphic references spark dense resonances for the person receiving the blessing, they also elicit associations among other participants based on their knowledge of the person's life history. Even though Dona Mariinha had told me about her promise before the rosary had been said, as the musicians moved to the next house one of the foliões told me about the pain she had been suffering when the promise was made. Through the blessings different members of the community, each in turn, attract the gaze of the participants, and as they stand before the group bringing back memories of their personal lives, their individuality is publicly recognized and their personhood collectively acknowledged.

It is worth noting that almost every time the festeira is mentioned in the embaixada, there is also a reference to her family, as in verses 2, 4, and 7. In the folia universe, one's personal identity is defined in terms of one's primary family relations, and the verse sequences through which blessings are transmitted are referred to as both blessing verses and family verses. During blessings people experience a heightened awareness of the place of the family in their social world, and they are reminded of significant family relations in their own lives. To receive the blessing, the family stands as a unit around the banner. By defining the individual in familial terms within the wider social context of ritual interaction, participants are oriented toward an experience of resonance between family relations and other social relationships, extending their notions of the family to encompass a broader social sphere. Indeed, folia communities perceive themselves in terms of the metaphor of the family, both implicitly and explicitly; through their shared devotion they are integrated into the "family of God." By defining the community in terms of the extended family, people experience a heightened sense of belonging within the wider social network, which reinforces sentiments of mutual obligation and solidarity.

Through the blessings the members of the household are integrated musically into the ritual drama. As they face the companhia, they are embraced by the sounds of the music. In the cramped spaces in which folia performances commonly take place, the vibrations of the music generate bodily sensations that heighten the sense of a heavenly presence. These sensations grow as the successive voices enter the ensemble, culminating in the final chord, in which one can feel as though one is resonating sympathetically with the world. The person being blessed carries the weight of the banner while being engulfed by a torrent of sound in which the words refer to the self in terms of collective values. For many people this promotes a powerful emotional experience, and they often cry when they receive the Kings' blessings. Indeed, tears welled up in Dona Mariinha's eyes as she hugged the banner to receive her verses.[9]

Enchanted Webs

Folia journeys are highly scripted traditions, and they are divided into a series of recognized ritual acts and events, each of which is identified by a specific name. To mark the distinctions between the sections, each one is constructed around a specific cluster of motifs that draws attention to a particular aspect of human experience. The departure opens the journey by demarcating a sacred space where humans encounter the Wise Men. As the event that launches the journey, it is geared toward preparing the foliões for the days ahead. They assert their devotion to the Kings, and clothed in their will to uphold their moral truths, they acquire the authority to speak on behalf of the saints. However true to their convictions, humans remain humans, and folia rituals remain within a human social space. It is to this truth that foliões direct their attention at departures. By reminding themselves of their own humanity, they are made aware of the realities of sociality: if on the one hand it can be the source of rewarding moments of camaraderie, it can

CHAPTER FIVE

also result in discord, particularly when people remain in proximity to others for extended periods. In highlighting the dangers of the journey, the foliões attempt to reduce the threat of group disintegration and preserve within it an atmosphere of mutual respect and cordiality.

The various motif clusters that emerge during the ritual address specific domains of experience, such as illness, envy, pettiness, generosity, family relations, camaraderie, and so on, each generating its own web of associations. As the associations expand within each web, they start to overlap with one another, and as redundancy sets in, the webs become linked into larger webs, unified by a diminishing set of core motifs. Within the folia tradition the three motif clusters with the densest scripted resonances are unquestionably those that emerge around the banner, the bastião, and the musical repertoire. While the banner is the embodiment of the Three Kings, the bastião refer to the human condition; the music is the means of bridging the divide between humans and saints. The folia repertoire was given to humans by the Kings as a way of domesticating their natural tendencies. Indeed, one could say that the unifying trope of the tradition as a whole is embodied in the final chord of the toada, the ultimate expression of social harmony. It is this chord that punctuates each message from the Magi, and each time it erupts, their vision for humanity is momentarily enchanted into the world.

CHAPTER VI

Adorations

DURING THEIR JOURNEY OF 1987/88 the Folia do Baeta arrived at a house one evening, and as usual the drummers began beating their instruments to let the family know they were outside. However, instead of allowing the ensemble to enter, the head of the household took the banner but remained standing in the doorway with his wife at his side. She held a lit candle, which served as a sign (*sinal*) that there was a manger scene (*presépio*)[1] in the front room. It meant that the visitation would be special, since the companhia would have to "adore" the Holy Family, as the Kings had done on their arrival at the crib, before they could perform the blessings. Acknowledging the signal, Owaldir began the embaixada at the doorstep with the following verses:

Santo Reis veio chegando,	Holy Kings were arriving,
A estrela clariou,	The star brightened,
Avisando nesta casa	Warning that in this house
Nasceu Jesus Salvador.	Jesus the Savior was born.
Dá licença pra bandeira,	Give leave to the banner,
Pro bastião e a companhia.	To the bastião and the companhia
Vou louvar o seu presépio,	I shall praise your crib,
Jesus, Filho de Maria.	Jesus, Son of Mary.

CHAPTER SIX

As this verse was being sung, the couple moved into the house, and the companhia followed them in, without interrupting their musical performance. The bastião made their way to the crèche, where they knelt down and removed their masks and hats to show their respect to the sacred figures. The musicians stood behind them and continued their singing.

The crib was arranged in front of a small Christmas tree, and it had been placed on a side table, covered with a white cloth, which gave it the appearance of an altar. Much like manger scenes throughout the Christian world, this one had as its central figure the baby Jesus lying in the straw, and to the right and left immediately behind him were Mary and Joseph, both kneeling with their faces turned toward the child. An angel had been placed immediately behind the baby, and a cow, a mule, and a rooster were also present. These figures were housed within a grotto, and a shooting star was placed at the highest point on the structure, just above the Christ Child. All the other figures of the crèche were placed outside this frame. To one side there was a shepherd with a few sheep, and to the other were the Three Kings. Each of the Kings was made to look different from the others: two were white and one was black; their garments were of different colors; the presents they carried were distinct; and each of them wore a different type of crown. The crèche was further decorated with flowers, candles, images of other saints, and a few small toys.

Positioned before the altar, the embaixada proceeded with verses that rekindled memories of the Nativity:

O presépio é a lembrança	The crib is the memory
Que ficou no coração.	That stayed in the heart.
Os Três Reis chegou contente,	The Three Kings arrived with joy,
Ganhou o seu perdão.	Received their forgiveness.
Pra lembrar da profecia,	To remember the prophecy,
Vou deixar pro meu bastião.	I will leave it to my bastião

At this point one of the bastião stood up and faced the couple being visited. He recited a prophecy, as he had been instructed to do by the embaixador, and this was followed by yet another prophecy by the other bastião. Because the prophecies in the repertoire of the Folia do Baeta are quite long, only the second recitation has been transcribed below:

Cesar Augusto assinou	Augustus Caesar signed
O decreto para se alistar.	A decree to enlist.

ADORATIONS

Todo povo, neste tempo,	All people at that time
Tinha que se apresentar.	Had to present themselves.
Porque era lei do Criador,	Since it was the law of the Creator,
Ninguém podia faltar.	No one could be absent.
Quando a lei foi decretada,	When the law was decreed
Foi todo o povo intimado	All the people were called
Para apresentar na cidade	To present themselves at the city
Dentro do prazo marcado.	Within the stated period.
E todo povo reuniu	And all the people united
Na cidade de Belém.	At the city of Bethlehem.
José e Maria foram	Joseph and Mary went
E se apresentaram também.	And presented themselves also.
Os hotéis e as pensões	The hotels and the inns
Estavam super lotado.	Were overfull.
Não havia hospedaria	There was no accommodation
Para poder descansar.	To be able to rest.
Avistaram a cabana,	They saw a cottage
Cobertura de sapé,	Covered with straw,
Onde foram descansar,	Where they went to rest,
Maria com São José.	Mary with Saint Joseph.
A cabana estava escura,	The cottage was dark
Sem luz, sem claridade.	Without light, without clarity.
José ascendeu a vela	Joseph lit a candle
Pra ficar mais à vontade.	To feel more at ease.
E Maria já esperava	Mary was waiting
E seu esposo também	And her husband also
Que a cabana transformasse	For the cottage to be transformed
Numa lapa de Belém.	Into a grotto of Bethlehem.
E foi meia-noite em ponto	And it was exactly midnight
Quando o anjo anunciou;	When the angel announced;
Surgiu um claro no céu	A light emerged in the sky
E os anjos todos cantou.	And all the angels sang.

Os Reis Magos do Oriente,	The Wise Kings of the Orient
Pelo anjo foi avisado	Were told by the angel
Que nascia em Belém	That being born in Bethlehem was
Nosso Jesus esperado.	Our awaited Jesus.
Arriaram seus camelos,	They saddled their camels,
Seguiram caminho afora,	They followed the path,
Seguindo a santa estrela	Following the holy star
Que apareceu nesta hora.	That appeared at that moment.
E seguindo a santa estrela,	And following the holy star,
Os Três Reis Santos contentes,	The Three Holy Kings were happy
Para ver nosso Jesus Menino,	To see our Baby Jesus,
Nosso Rei Onipotente.	Our Omnipotent King.
A estrela foi abaixando,	The star started to descend,
Diminuindo o resplendor:	Losing its brilliance;
Foi até chegar na lapa	It went until it arrived at the grotto
Onde estava o Salvador.	Where the Savior was.
Eles chegaram na santa lapa	They arrived at the holy grotto
E Simião encontrou.	And found Simon.
Foi a primeira visita	It was the first visit
Em nome do Salvador.	In the name of the Savior.
E tomou Jesus nos braços	And he took Jesus in his arms
E no templo apresentou,	And presented him at the temple,
Dizendo as santas palavras	Saying the holy words
Quando assim pronunciou:	When he thus pronounced:
"Glória a Deus no alto céu!	"Glory to God in the highest!
Pai Eterno que enviou	Eternal Father who sent
Jesus Cristo aqui na terra	Jesus Christ here to earth
Para ser o Salvador!"	To be the Savior!"
E estas santas palavras	And these holy words
No livro ficou gravado.	Were engraved in the book.
Quem estuda, sempre aprende:	Who studies always learns:
Está na escritura sagrada.	It is in the Holy Scriptures.

Já cumpri minha missão	I have completed my mission
Nesta lapa de Belém.	At this grotto of Bethlehem.
Pai, Filho, Espírito Santo,	Father, Son, Holy Ghost,
Seja para sempre, amém.	Be forever, amen.

After the prophecies, the bastião called out the "vivas" to end the adoration.

Bastião: Viva os Três Reis Santo! [Long live the Three Kings!]
Everyone: Viva!
Bastião: Viva toda a companhia! [Long live all the companhia!]
Everyone: Viva!
Bastião: Viva o dono da casa e toda sua família! [Long live the head of
the household and all his family!]
Everyone: Viva!
Bastião: Viva agora com emoção! Um viva meu e do meu irmão! [Now
an emotional "viva"! One for me and one for my brother]

The audience laughed, and some people answered ironic "vivas" to the clowns. After the adoration the clowns put their masks back on, while the group prepared to begin the family verses.

Encounters with Crèches

Adorations occur only when there is a crib in the home being visited. Since most families do not have manger scenes, the ritual of the adoration is relatively rare. During the journey a companhia might encounter only one or two manger scenes a day, and they are often in the homes of people providing pouso for the ensemble. In fact, crèches are most common in the homes of families with a special devotion to the Three Kings; by setting up a manger scene the family enhances the ritual script of the visitation at their home. The effort foliões put into their performance of the adoration is duly reciprocated through the meals they are offered by their hosts. If the crib is not at a pouso the hosts will probably serve them coffee and mé as well as some sort of snack, such as sandwiches, cake, or biscuits, to show their appreciation for the special treatment their household has received from the group.

Adorations, then, mark a special relationship between the companhia and the household with a crib, based on their common devotion to the Three Kings. Indeed, adorations set up a complex dialogue between the foliões and the family, which is articulated through the symbolic repertoire of the tradition, marking a mutual acknowledgement among the parties regarding their special relationships with the Magi. In the example above, the companhia arrived at the house, and the couple opened the door holding a lit candle, which the foliões immediately recognized as a sign that the house had a crib.[2] Since the couple remained in the doorway, Owaldir realized they expected the companhia to begin their performance outside the house, and in his verse he made reference to the candle, relating it to the star that led the Wise Men to the manger, demonstrating his recognition of their signal. He then asked leave for the group to enter the house, to which the couple responded, and the head of the household took the banner inside, making way for the companhia. He stood with his wife next to the crib, banner in hand, while the group proceeded with the adoration.

Through their actions, the couple indicated their familiarity with the motifs and the procedural repertoire of the tradition, and the companhia acknowledged this by performing a particularly extensive adoration, graced with not one, but two prophecy recitations. Foliões perceive their encounters with crèches as moments in which their ritual and mythic knowledge is put to the test. For this reason many foliões—embaixadores and bastião in particular—see adorations as privileged spaces for the public exhibition of the extent of their sacred repertoire, especially when they realize their efforts will be fully recognized by the household. In such cases they often indulge in extending their performances, taking full advantage of the theatricality they afford. In this way, the foliões and the families they visit are coparticipants in the negotiation of each adoration, mutually confirming their common devotion to the Kings through their recognition of one another's ritual competence.[3]

Because foliões view adorations as tests of their ritual knowledge, there is considerable controversy regarding the way these events should be conducted. Some embaixadores say that the verse sequences must consist of twenty-five verses, while others claim that one verse should be dedicated to each "animal"—that is, each figure—the family has put in its manger scene, constructing the narrative around the role each character played in the Nativity story. Despite these claims, I never observed a companhia that followed either of these prescriptions. Another point of contention centers on the role of the bastião during adorations. Some groups bar their entrance into a house with a manger scene, arguing that they desacralize the ritual context, as in Alcides's companhia. In others their presence is fundamental, since their manifestations of humility enhance the atmosphere of sacredness of the adoration. Some groups even allow the clowns to "speak the manger scene" (*falar o presépio*), that is, recite the "prophecies," hastening the ritual process, as in the Folia do Baeta. Owaldir claimed that if all the necessary verses were to be sung, the adoration alone could last up to two hours. Regardless of whether or not "proper" procedures are followed, it remains a point of honor among foliões that they are aware of how adorations should be conducted; in fact, it appears that embaixadores are more concerned with indicating their knowledge of proper ritual procedure than they are with actually following it.

In practice, adorations—like all aspects of the folia tradition—are highly fluid events, but the foliões' preoccupation with proper procedure marks their attempts to give them stability; after all, their adorations are understood as reenactments of the Adoration of the Wise Men in Bethlehem, and the Magi could have conducted it in only one particular way. Furthermore, the whole adoration is structured around a set of relatively stable elements. The verse sequences used at these occasions, for example, are fairly fixed: the prophecies of the bastião are memorized, and the performances of each clown display little variation from one recitation to the next; most embaixadores have a repertoire of three or four adoration verse sequences, which they repeat with only slight variations from one manger scene to the next. These verses encapsulate the foliões' interpretations of the Nativity and the journey of the Wise Men, articulating their concepts about the immutable realm of the saints, and their relative stability heightens the sense of timelessness and sanctity of their content.

The adoration verses are performed before the manger scene, and this visual representation is also fairly standardized. Indeed, the arrangement of crèches in southeastern Brazil is reminiscent of manger scenes throughout the Christian world, even though they often include a few uncommon motifs, such as a rooster, toys, holy water, an offering plate, and other decorations. The rooster is present because it is commonly said that a rooster crowed when Jesus was born;[4] the toys, such as soldiers, superheroes and action figures, cartoon characters, plastic animals, dolls, and cars, are emblems of childhood which are thought to amuse the baby Jesus; the holy water enhances the sanctity of the altar; and the offerings collected at the manger scene are either donated to the parish church or to a companhia to help finance the festival of the arrival. (See plate 15.)

The figures on the altar are balanced more or less symmetrically on either side of the crib, and all of them are usually arranged so that they face the Christ Child. The baby Jesus, however, appears to be looking into space, at

CHAPTER SIX

no one in particular. This arrangement draws attention to the central figure, and it creates the impression that all the figures around the baby are paying homage to him. The frame around the Holy Family, however, sets this nucleus apart from the other figures in the complex, marking its significance as a model for the family unit. All the figures, then, become integrated into this unit, forming a symbolic family, through their acknowledgement of the sovereignty of the baby Jesus.

In folia adorations, all participants in the ritual become integrated into the mythic sphere of the crèche, joining the figures on the altar in their act of deference.[5] Like many of the images in the manger scene, the bastião kneel in humility before the crib, while the musicians stand reverently before it. The household is also integrated into this act of homage, as they stand alongside the altar holding the sacred banner. As they reenact the scene of the adoration, the foliões recount the events of the Nativity in song and recitations, fusing the past with the present, thus affirming its relevance to their contemporary lives. In effect, the set procedures, the fixed texts of embaixadas and prophecies, the repetitive musical mode of the folia tradition, and the fairly stable structure of the manger scene coalesce at adorations to create a sacred sphere of everlasting truth.

The performance of the adoration is a privileged moment within the folia tradition, constituting a unique ritual sphere in which the motif clusters objectify the foliões' vision of the immutable realm of the saints. This objectification is embodied primarily in the fixed texts of adoration verses and in the visual representation of the manger scene, which mutually enhance one another. Through these media the foliões articulate their interpretations of the Nativity and the journey of the Magi, and in paying homage to the crèche, they acknowledge the ultimate authority of the mythic repertoire that informs their ritual practices.

The Canon

As the bastião in the Folia do Baeta proclaimed in the conclusion of his prophecy, his words reiterated what had been inscribed in the Holy Scriptures; therein resided its authoritative canonical status. Indeed, the ritual journey of the folia de reis tradition is based on the biblical passage in Saint Matthew 2:1–12, which narrates the visit of the Magi to the Christ Child, and numerous aspects of the tradition echo motifs of wide diffusion throughout the Christian world, even though they may not be entirely canonical. The

Bible, for example, speaks of "some magi," which Christian tradition has transformed into "three kings."[6] Theologians often claim that this occurred because the Bible refers to three presents, and in biblical times these articles were associated with royalty. Furthermore, in Psalm 74 there is a passage stating that the Messiah would be visited by kings who would bow before him to offer their gifts. Already in the fifth century various apocryphal texts had emerged which referred to "three kings."[7] By the late sixth century they had acquired the names by which they became commonly known in many parts of the Christian world: Melkon, Caspar, and Balthasar (James 1926, 83). Throughout Brazil, for example, the Three Kings are generally known as Melquior (or Belquior, Blechió, or Brechó, among other variants), Gaspar, and Baltazar.

Many of the episodes of the Nativity narrated in folia adoration verses are clearly rooted in Christian tradition, as in the prophecy recited by the bastião, above. The text begins by announcing the census which brought Joseph and Mary to Bethlehem. It proceeds by saying that the inns were all booked, which forced the holy couple to seek refuge in a "dark cottage," or stable, where the Christ Child was born. It tells of an angel who summoned the Wise Men, and they followed the star until they reached the crib. This prophecy also includes the Presentation in the Temple.

Other verse sequences concentrate on other episodes and motifs related to the Nativity. Some begin with a reference to the miraculous conception, calling attention to its importance in Christian doctrine. The Kings' encounter with Herod receives considerable attention, and the verses tell how the Magi promised to return to tell the villain where the baby could be found. The verses are quick to remind the audience of Herod's true intention—to kill the baby—and this often leads into accounts of the massacre of the innocents. Adorations also tell of how the Kings were told to return by a different route to avoid encountering Herod again, but even so, some versions tell of a second encounter with Herod, going on to narrate how the Kings manage to escape his grasp. There are also verse sequences that enter into considerable detail in their descriptions of the Magi: they are cited each by name; their origins are given, highlighting that one of them was black; reference is made to their gifts; and sometimes it is mentioned that one of them had a white beard, indicating that he was older than the others.

Alongside these more or less orthodox motifs, foliões have elaborated upon the Nativity story, creating what are at times quite fanciful narratives with only marginal links to officially accepted canons. While some of these motifs have become widely diffused throughout the southeast, such as the

CHAPTER SIX

representation of the Kings as musicians, others are best viewed as the result of a particularly original individual's imagination. Many fanciful versions of the Nativity are likely to have emerged in the relative isolation of bairro culture, where foliões may have indulged in the continuous elaboration of the world to enhance their social environment far from the control of the clergy. With the expansion of the church into even the most remote areas of the country, however, official Roman Catholic symbolism has been reestablishing its hegemony. But even when folia prophecies appear to be constructed around a set of motifs of wide acceptance in the Christian world, the foliões' localized understandings of the texts are often quite idiosyncratic. Consider, for example, the following adoration performed in an embaixada by Luizinho:

Os Três Reis dormiram sono,	The Three Kings slept,
Tiveram sonho profundo.	They had a deep dream.
O anjo anunciou:	The angel announced:
Já era nascido o Rei do Mundo.	The King of the World had been born.
Assim seguiram os Três Reis Magos,	Thus, the Three Wise Kings departed,
Todos três um só destino.	All three with a single destiny.
Partiram pro Oriente	They left for the Orient
Pr'adorar Jesus Menino.	To adore the Baby Jesus.
Seguiram os Três Reis Santos,	The Three Holy Kings departed,
De longe terra vieram.	From a distant land they came.
A viagem era de um ano	The trip took one year,
Mas com doze dia fizeram.	But they did it in twelve days.

I was given an explanation for this text by Zé dos Magos, who claimed that these verses tell why the Three Kings are also known as the Three Magi, or *Magos*. To grasp his explanation, one must be aware that in the caipira dialect *r*s are often omitted in the pronunciation of words, such that "magos" is understood as "*mag[r]os*" (thin people). This is what he said: "É que a viagem era de um ano, mas em doze dias eles fizeram. Nessa viagem, eles sofreram bastante. Passaram fome. Emagreceram, né? Ficaram Três Reis Magos." [It is because the trip would have taken a year, but they did it in twelve days. On this trip they suffered a lot. They went hungry. They lost weight, didn't they? They became Three Thin Kings.]

The formulaic character of the verses in which the narratives are preserved gives them a certain degree of mnemonic stability over time. Moreover, they are performed with considerable frequency year after year, so foliões are generally quite familiar with the episodes and motifs they embody. Because they are presented in verse form, however, the narrative motifs emerge in telegraphic encapsulations, and entire episodes are compressed into a few lines, which requires the audience to fill in the blanks to make sense of them. An audience that knows the stories is able to fill in the gaps of information and follow the narration without any difficulty. As Rosaldo (1986, 104–9) has shown in his discussion of Ilongot hunting stories, telegraphic narrations can communicate a rich body of narrative detail through allusions to a shared repertoire. Thus, the various motifs in the verse sequences function as "metonyms of narrative" (Smith 1975, 97–100); the compressed episodes invoke associations which refer the audience to a wider collective narrative repertoire.

Telegraphic presentation, however, also creates ambiguity, serving as fertile ground for the emergence and diffusion of quite idiosyncratic interpretations. In his attempt to make sense of the traditional verse, Zé dos Magos humanized the Wise Men.[8] By presenting them as characters who experienced suffering and hunger during their lifetime, he made them more sympathetic to the human condition. Having themselves undergone moments of anguish, they are better placed to intercede with God on behalf of those who call upon them in times of need. Thus, while his interpretation is amusing to people with an orthodox understanding of what a magus is, it articulates with the wider Catholic ethos in which it has emerged. In fact, I was soon to discover that Zé dos Magos was not alone in his deductions; throughout southeastern Brazil I encountered similar understandings of why the Three Kings are also known as the Magi.

While the primary ritual context for the performance of this repertoire occurs during adorations, the episodes and motifs they encapsulate are continuously drawn upon during informal conversations among foliões, and this integrates them into the processes of folia sociability. In their discussions about the use of the accordion in the folia, for example, foliões often remind one another that this was not one of the instruments used by the Kings. In negotiating the itinerary of their journeys, a folião might argue that a particular route is inappropriate, because it would require the group

CHAPTER SIX

to backtrack; it is remembered that the Kings returned by a different route to avoid reencountering Herod on their way back. In many instances no more than an allusion is made to a well-known episode of the Nativity, but in other cases—particularly when children are about or when there is a "reporter" eager to document their tradition—narrations with elaborate story lines often emerge.

For foliões, discussions relating to folia issues are perceived as social events. For this reason many of the "formal" interviews I conducted took place in the presence of several foliões, replicating to some extent the conversational mode before rehearsals discussed earlier. Often the conversation moved into the realm of the folia Nativity repertoire, and the foliões engaged in exchanging stories. Frequently their theological discussions were aimed at contesting versions of particular episodes they had heard from other foliões, which transformed the storytelling arena into a context of intense debate and negotiation over the truth—or canonical status—of particular versions. These debates have the effect both of generating ever more fanciful stories, as narrators lay claim to highly specialized knowledge which lesser foliões do not possess, and of realigning the narrative repertoire to more global orthodox interpretations, often backed by information obtained from such authoritative sources as old embaixadores, priests, books, television programs, and other visual representations.

A folião from Cordislândia, Minas Gerais, for example, once told me that the Kings had traveled on animals called camels; they were not on horses, as an old embaixador had told him in his youth. He backed his assertion by affirming that these were the animals in the crib at the parish church, and he assured me they still exist, since he had seen them on television. While his reassessment of the mode of transport of the Magi may have aligned his representation with the dominant image within the Christian world, where the Kings are commonly depicted with camels, to this man the strange image seemed to have enhanced the mythical value of the Kings. By placing them on quasi-mythic beings, rather than on such ordinary animals as horses, their otherworldliness —and sanctity—increased substantially.

Paralleling myth among the Kachins, as observed by Leach ([1954] 1970, 278), the Nativity repertoire of southeastern folia communities is hardly a "chorus of harmony," but for it to be taken as an effective "language of argument" it must also be accepted that there is an authoritative canon. Indeed, foliões do not question the existence of such a canon. This permits individual foliões to lay claim to canonical status for their versions, or it allows them to reassess them in light of new evidence and new deductions. The mnemonic encapsulations contained in adoration verses generate narrative elaborations of the telegraphic forms in prose styles, just as these reinterpretations reemerge back in verse, in a continuous process of canonical re-creation.

This cacophony—or that which Gramsci (1985) called the "mosaic of tradition," the "confused agglomerate of fragments" drawn from an infinite fund of conceptual resources—is, however, compiled through processes of selectivity, as successive narrators choose among the motifs available to them in terms of how they conform to their commonsense categories and aspirations. While at the surface level the motifs may be quite different, they evince a series of common themes that embody a more or less coherent moral discourse based on the foliões' notions of "natural law." Within these discourses, there are also "hidden transcripts" of symbolic inversions of the world, articulating fantasies of revenge against the persistent assaults the narrators experience against their dignity (Scott 1990). Thus, as foliões debate the truths of their canons, they also forge interpretations of their social universe, constructing visions of the world in which they would like to live.

Kings

The Three Kings are central figures in the folia tradition, and the foliões' understandings of these characters objectify core themes in their moral values and social aspirations. While kings are generally represented as sovereigns and hereditary rulers over hierarchical states, this notion seems to be quite muted within the folia tradition. Although echoes of common usage have persisted, it appears that the dominant view within the folia universe does not conceive of the Three Kings as rulers at all. In fact, it is common for foliões to refer to each specific king as a *reis*, employing the plural form of the term in the singular mode: thus, there is Kings Blechó, Kings Gaspar, and Kings Baltazar, which suggests that a "kings" designates a particular type of supernatural being, or a particular species of saint, so to speak. Far from being sovereigns, these beings are commonly depicted as dispossessed: in João Isaias's story, which opens chapter 2, for example, the Three Kings are represented as Herod's slaves, who are routinely beaten; in numerous accounts they become thin as a result of their sacrifice and suffering. Zé Canhanga, a folião from Campanha, Minas Gerais, claimed that "[the Three Kings] were not kings of a mandate; . . . they were kings of faith. It was their faith that turned them into kings," echoing Zezo's claim that "the Magi were the first pagans to become religious." According to Pedro Cigano, also from Campanha, it was Jesus who crowned them during the Adoration; they became kings only after acknowledging Christ's sovereignty over them. Beyond the mere humanization of the Kings, the folia tradition has established an identity between the Magi and the faithful based on their shared experience of poverty and exploitation. Through their recognition of the moral superiority of the baby Jesus, the Kings were ennobled and redeemed from their pagan status.

While foliões do not think of the Kings as rulers in the conventional sense, they are "kings" insofar as they each represent recognized collectivities, defined by such categories as age, race, and nationality, but also musical talent and productive activity. João Isaias from Monsenhor Paulo, for example, claimed that Gaspar—who played the viola and brought the incense—was African; Baltazar—who brought myrrh—was Portuguese; and Blechió—who brought the gold—was German. According to Owaldir, "The one from Africa was black; there was a German, and one from Italy." For João Paca from Batatais, Melquior was Spanish, Baltazar was African, and Gaspar was Chinese. Antônio Mariano from Arceburgo used a verse to say that:

Blechió era africano;	Blechió was African;
Baltazar era alemão;	Baltazar was German;
Gaspar era turco,	Gaspar was Turkish,
Na cidade de Adão.	In the city of Adam.

Commonly the Kings are represented as an African, a European, and a Middle Easterner, with the occasional mention of a Far Easterner. Thus, the ethnic origins attributed to the Wise Men among southeastern rural workers draw on their experience of interethnic contact: the African presence is, of course, a legacy of the slave era, while Europeans, Middle Easterners, and Far Easterners became especially visible in southeastern Brazil with the mass immigration program in the late nineteenth and early twentieth centuries.[9]

While recognizing differences between the Kings, foliões also represent them as a solitary unit, thus defining them as essentially equal. In fact, there are also narratives which depict the Three Kings as brothers, a view vigorously defended by Alcides. João Isaias attributed distinct ethnic origins to each of the Magi while also claiming that they had the same mother. Though the Wise Men came from different places, looked different, played different instruments, brought different gifts, and were of different ages, they became brothers—or equals—through their common recognition of the sovereignty of the baby Jesus. Thus, in Dumontian (1980) fashion, the Kings are encompassed by the Christ Child and join the "family of God"; in turn, the Wise Men, as representatives of human collectivities, encompass the whole of humanity. Like the Kings, humans can become integrated into this "family" by proclaiming their subservience to the Christ Child through their devotion to the Wise Men.

The act of the Adoration of the Magi — the act which asserts the Kings' recognition of Christ's sovereignty — was performed through the donation of gifts: gold, frankincense, and myrrh; in return for their presents the Kings received their musical instruments, the means of orchestrating social harmony on earth. In offering their voices to the Kings in adoration during their journeys, folia communities are rewarded with an experience of this social reality. By participating in this moral sphere of reciprocal exchange, humans can also be ennobled and redeemed from their human condition.

The folia narrative repertoire is quite explicit about the debased human condition from which people need to be redeemed: it is embodied in the figure of Herod, the central character in the repertoire of hidden transcripts in the folia tradition. Herod, however, is represented in two contrasting ways: first in a plural form, as the petty Herods foliões encounter along their journeys, and second as a particular individual, the evil King Herod who massacred the innocents. In the plural form, Herods are closely linked to the figures of the bastião: they embody the trivial everyday expressions of envy and misplaced superiority, that is, the petty "Herod-ness" in everyone. One confronts such Herods primarily among one's peers, and these encounters are the main causes of strife within folia communities. By drawing attention to mundane antisocial behavior, foliões construct a critique of the primary sources of discord within their own social circles. This intragroup critique allows people to project their own behavior onto Herod, gaining a glimpse of how trivial some of their social dramas might appear to others.

King Herod, on the other hand, is conceived of in conventional regal terms: he ruled over a distinct territory, he lived in a castle, he commanded an army and had spies, he owned slaves, and he was very rich. While the Three Kings submitted to the moral superiority of the baby Jesus, King Herod tried to destroy the child to guarantee his earthly kingdom. While he claimed that he wished to adore the baby, his gift — or antigift — was to be the child's death. So preoccupied was he with the threat to his power that he was capable of murdering thousands of children in his attempt to stamp out his enemy.[10] Indeed, the massacre of the innocents receives considerable attention within the folia tradition, highlighting the helplessness of the victims

CHAPTER SIX

and their families, with particular reflection upon the sorrow of the mothers at the loss of their babies. Consider, for example, a set of adoration verses performed by Luizinho with the Folia do Zé dos Magos:

Os Três Reis saiu andando,	The Three Kings were walking,
Pisando pelas pedrinha,	Stepping on the little stones,
Pra visitar Menino Deus	To visit the God Child
Deitado em suas palhinha.	Lying on his straw.
O Herode perguntou	Herod asked
Os Três Reis aonde vem.	The Three Kings where they go.
"Vou visitar o Menino Deus	"I'm going to visit the God Child
Que nasceu pro nosso bem."	Who was born for our good."
O anjo do Senhor	The angel of the Lord
Avisando os pelegrino:	Warning the pilgrims:
"O Herode quer saber	"Herod wants to know
Pra ir matar o Deus Menino."	To go kill the God Child."
Herode vendo isso—	Herod seeing this—
E os Três Reis não voltava—	And the Three Kings did not return—
Mandou matar todas criança	Had all the children killed
Que em Belém ele encontrava.	That he could find in Bethlehem.
Foi a maior tristeza	It was the greatest sadness
Que em Belém foi receber:	That Bethlehem was to receive:
Acabar tantas criança	End so many children
Sem ninguém poder valer.	Without anyone able to stop it.
Coitada daquelas mãe	Pity for those poor mothers
Que criava seus filhinho,	Who raised their children,
Vendo o povo matar	Watching the people kill
Todo aqueles 'nocentinho.	All those innocent ones.

In his greed for both material wealth and worldly power, King Herod stopped at nothing to achieve his goals; he did not even show mercy toward defenseless little children, setting his powerful army against them. This Herod is not in everyone, for unlike the bastião, he did not repent of his evil ways. He represents single willful individuals who through deceit and deviousness appropriate wealth and power at the expense of others.

Just as foliões are always able to maneuver their way out of their encounters with Herods during their journeys by invoking the superior power of the saints, divine justice prevails over the will of the evil King Herod, and Jesus is saved. Moreover, in many folia narratives Herod is punished by God for his evil acts, and he dies prematurely. Consider, for example, the following verses performed during an adoration by Zé Machado:

O Herode, como perverso,	Herod, as perverse,
E de longe apercebeu,	From a distance noted [the star],
Aperseguindo o Menino,	Persecuted the Baby
Dizendo que era seu.	Saying [he] was his.
Sabendo que a estrela guia	Knowing that the guiding star
É do tempo dos judeu.	Was from the time of the Jews.
Clariava todos canto,	It brightened all places,
O Herode faleceu.	Herod died.

Paralleling the denunciations of the injustices of a class society, other hidden transcripts within the folia repertoire comment on the unjust experience of racial prejudice, which affects many—if not most—members of folia communities. This commentary emerges primarily in the special attention bestowed upon the African King, who is often contrasted with the white Kings. In a story told by Zé Quatorze, for example, the black King receives special protection from the baby Jesus against humiliation from his companions.

A star gave the signal that the baby Jesus was born. . . . Two whites and a colored person set off and took the route, and the star guiding them, the Three Kings.

Then they came to a crossroads. The two whites said to the colored King, "You go this way and we'll go this way. Whoever arrives first can pass the vision to the others."

The two light Kings were near Bethlehem and the star was pointing that way, and they sent the colored one along the dark path. . . . The two light ones kept going. After they had walked a few meters, the beam came down for the colored one, who arrived in Bethlehem first.

He received the two white Kings and became the baby's guard. He received the other two Kings, that arrived after the colored King. It was Baltazar: the King of the Congo.[11]

The black King is also singled out for special attention in a story narrated by Matias from Batatais, São Paulo.

> They are Kings Baltazar, . . . who is dark, and then Kings de Água and Kings Gaspar are white. . . . And so they went to visit the baby Jesus, and there were a lot of people there. . . . Kings Baltazar, he was ashamed, all those people, and he being dark, he didn't want to arrive there first. So they arrived, Kings de Água and Kings Gaspar, adoring the baby Jesus. And so . . . he stayed away, adoring from afar. And so the baby Jesus raised his sacred hand, called him to him. So . . . he was the last to arrive. . . .
>
> Kings de Águas took gold; Kings Gaspars took incense; and he took myrrh. . . . And then Jesus said, "Ah, I'm sorry, I can't accept gold. I accept incense and myrrh. Put it there. It's to embalm the dead."
>
> So Kings de Água, feeling badly done by, got up, took his knee off the ground, and returned to his homeland.[12]

In Matias's story the African King has internalized a sense of racial inferiority and is ashamed to approach the baby in front of so many people because of his color. But the Christ Child calls him forward, publicly affirming his equality in relation to the other Kings. In contrast, it is the gold brought by a white King which is rejected—an allusion to the racial dimension of the class divide in Brazilian society.[13]

Subaltern Morality

The "mosaic of tradition" of the folia narrative universe has been constructed out of symbolic motifs of wide diffusion within the Christian world, and undoubtedly many readers will be familiar with them. Yet they have been substantially reshaped, such that the stories are not only unorthodox in content, but often are also understood in ways that contrast with orthodox interpretations. In appropriating Christian themes, the foliões have been highly selective, muting certain elements while emphasizing others, reconfiguring the material in a manner which resonates with their experiences of life as members of the Brazilian lower classes. It is by viewing the narratives in relation to the lives of the foliões that one is able to glimpse the special significance global themes might have for them.

The folia narrative tradition constructs a world based on how the foliões' imagine God envisages it: drawing on their notion of the Three Kings as representatives of all humanity, in the ideal world the essential equality of all would be recognized, regardless of age, ethnic identity, race, class affiliation, musical talent, or any other socially constructed distinction. The foliões' everyday experiences, however, stand in direct contrast to this vision. In accordance with orthodox interpretations, folia communities account for this disparity by contrasting the Three Kings to King Herod: while the Magi acknowledged the moral superiority of the Christ Child and were redeemed from their human inclinations, King Herod did not, giving free rein to his sinful predisposition.

In the dominant Christian tradition, the Magi are represented as gift bearers; there is no representation of a direct exchange between the Kings and the Holy Family; as representatives of humanity, they receive the promise of salvation. In the folia tradition, however, direct reciprocal exchanges are given special prominence: in return for their gifts the Three Kings received their musical instruments. They may have been poor, but they were ennobled and sanctified through this exchange. In contrast, King Herod enters into a (thwarted) relationship of negative reciprocity with the baby: he sets out to kill the child, but is himself ultimately punished by God with a premature death. This opposition presents two contrasting scenarios: life through participation in a system of reciprocal exchanges or death through the accumulation of material wealth. Thus, reciprocity is presented as an equalizing force, while accumulation leads to social stratification, as it can occur only because some people take more from others than they give in return. Ultimately, the asymmetry in such exchanges leaves vast numbers of people with nothing to exchange in order to secure their livelihood. In this moral economy, accumulation is denounced as evil, and it is presented as the source of social deprivation and death.[14]

Thus, in the folia worldview God's law—or "natural law"—is the law of reciprocity; to violate this law is to commit an offense against God, and it is through divine intervention that justice is served. Indeed, it is God who punishes Herod for his evil deeds, just as he rearranges the social order to reinstate racial equality. God's intervention stands as proof of the everlasting truths of "natural law," marking a clear distinction between God's laws—which are always good and just—and human laws—which are not always so.

CHAPTER SIX

While such stories of symbolic inversion articulate fantasies of revenge, they also serve to remind people that the prevailing social order is far from monolithic; they proclaim that it is a constructed order (Scott 1990, 168), and therefore it can be reconstructed. By invoking divine justice in their narratives foliões maintain that the implementation of God's "natural laws" on earth would guarantee an equal and just society among humans.

From this perspective Herod's horrific act of violence is all the more shocking, as it presents a limit case of the extremes to which power holders might go to enforce their will. The daily lives of foliões are marked by arbitrary acts of violence and impositions from others, and the figure of King Herod gives voice to the feelings evoked by such experiences. Folia narratives underline two complementary perspectives on the massacre of the innocents: first, they articulate a sense of indignation at the experience of the helplessness of the population to stop the murders, and second, they single out the pitiful suffering of the mothers over the loss of their children. Since the experience of the mothers is explicitly qualified, by implication one can take the experience of helpless indignation as the embodiment of fundamentally male sentiments. One could say, then, that these feelings articulate (male) commonsense notions about the division of emotional labor within the family, in which women—or mothers—are allocated the "emotion work" (Hochshild 1979), while men—or heads of households—are responsible for the material well-being of their dependents, and the inability to fulfill this role generates feelings of profound impotence and resentment.

Maternal love as personified in the Virgin Mary is an ever-present image throughout Brazil, and a dominant discourse portrays her as the *mater dolorosa,* the sorrowful mother of the dead Christ. Among the Brazilian lower classes people coexist with death, particularly infant mortality, which heightens women's identification with the Virgin (Scheper-Hughes 1992, 357). Soon after I began fieldwork among popular Catholic communities, particularly in rural areas, I learned to brace myself every time I asked a woman—especially if she was over the age of forty—how many children she had, because it is customary for mothers to respond by saying how many pregnancies they have had, followed by the number of children that survived. It was very rare for a woman to be able to claim that all her children had lived, and often far more had died in early childhood than had survived. In many cases women would proceed by outlining the circumstances of each death, particularly if the child was not stillborn. The image of Herod massacring thousands of babies, then, resonates deeply with their experiences of loss. In the urban context, the levels of infant mortality have fallen dramatically, but the experience of violence and the premature death of loved ones has remained a part of everyday life.

The folia tradition is, however, fundamentally a male domain, and therefore I had far more access to the ways in which the foliões' interpretations of the massacre of the innocents frames their experiences of everyday violence. Among foliões King Herod is most frequently invoked to articulate encounters with members of the upper classes—particularly employers—which were experienced as exploitative and humiliating, giving voice to their outrage at systematically having to submit themselves to asymmetrical interactions. Zé Machado, for example, once told me that he had encountered many fazenda owners in his lifetime who acted like Herod. One of the most frequent reasons men gave for their constant moves from one large landholding to another during the fazenda era was that the landlord was stingy, and the conditions he imposed did not allow them to support their families. To exemplify this stinginess Zé singled out a specific instance in which he had been employed by such a Herod. Zé was a colono in Espírito Santo when his young son became very ill and needed to see the doctor. Several hours later the landlord finally came to the house and drove them into town, where the doctor prescribed an expensive medication. Although food, grown on the family plot, was plentiful, cash was a rare commodity, since the colonos were paid annually at the end of the harvest. In order to buy the medicine Zé had to borrow the money from his boss. When the harvest was over, Zé discovered that the landlord had docked the cost of the medication from his pay, leaving him with hardly enough cash to get through the following year. Zé's indignation was such that he immediately packed the family's belongings and left in search of a new fazenda. He concluded the story by saying, "I'm the head of the household. I have responsibilities. How could I stay on that fazenda? If something were to happen with someone in my family I have to know the boss will help me. . . . That man was greedy. All bosses are greedy, but he was worse than others. . . . This one would have let my son die."

Zezo also invoked King Herod to frame an experience of interclass contact, which occurred when I accompanied him to Arceburgo on a short holiday. We were walking around in the town square when we met a local landowner. Zezo had recently purchased a small plot adjacent to the man's property, where Zezo intended to build a house for his retirement. The man offered to drive us out to see the property the next day, reciprocating for his use of the plot to graze a few horses until the construction began. We arranged to meet him in the afternoon at his house, and when we arrived we were served drinks and tidbits before setting off. Once at the plot the man indicated that he would be interested in buying it from Zezo. He went on to suggest that Zezo should consider buying a ready-built house in Arceburgo, rather than try to construct one on his own, particularly since it would be difficult for him to supervise the construction from São Bernardo. In fact, the man had just finished a house on the outskirts of the town, which he intended to put on the market in the next few days. If Zezo was interested he would consider the plot a down-payment. He then took us to see the house before dropping us back off in the town square. As soon as the man drove off, Zezo said, "Did you see how he treated us? All that drink and all the food, and then the big car and all? That's how Herod treated the Three Kings when he was trying to fool them into thinking that he was sincere about wanting to adore the baby Jesus." Zezo was convinced the man intended to exploit him if he agreed to the exchange. The situation was experienced as all the more humiliating because it was conducted with cunning and deception. Although he did not invoke Herod directly, it is also worth remembering that it was the experience of his daughter's death in the hospital that moved Zezo into political militancy. His anger was directed at the factory, which he claimed had deliberately withheld the news of her death from him, indicating that the bosses felt no responsibility toward the well-being of his family.

Through the figure of King Herod, the foliões' articulate their ambiguous stance toward patronage. Although patron-client relations were far more explicit during the fazenda era, they continue to color interclass relations even in the highly industrialized complexes of greater São Paulo. In their encounters with members of the upper classes foliões expect asymmetry, but the degree of imbalance in the exchange is always an open issue, allowing myths of the "good boss" (*bom patrão*) and the "bad boss" (*mau patrão*) to remain unchallenged. As in the examples discussed above, analogies with King Herod, whether explicit or implicit, are always directed at particular individuals or—in the urban industrial context—at specific organizations; foliões are careful not to generalize the figure of Herod to embrace "the rich" as a unified category. This would eradicate the myth of the "good boss," which, as Scheper-Hughes (1992, 108) notes, would be "to admit that there is no structural safety net at all and that the poor are adrift within an amoral social and economic system that is utterly indifferent to their well-being and survival." Herods, then, can be cordoned off as aberrations—those bosses who are greedier than most—while the hidden transcript remains available as a frame for interpreting experiences of humiliation in interclass encounters, just as it provides a means of voicing subaltern indignation toward their dependence upon asymmetrical relations with the dominant classes.

The lower classes protect themselves from the perversity of interclass relations as best they can by barricading themselves within the confines of their own neighborhoods, leaving them only to go to work. Similarly, the upper classes avoid entering "dangerous" areas, fearing the assaults and violence that have become associated with poor neighborhoods. Thus, in their segregated niches the cultural divide between the rich and the poor progressively widens. As the rich mark their social superiority through ostentatious displays of material wealth, the poor lay claim to moral superiority, ennobled by their adherence to the noncompetitive reciprocal ideal of the saints.

The motif clusters used in adorations articulate with one another to create an atmosphere of stability which marks the enduring truths of God's natural laws. When the foliões stand before the crèche for their performances, they join the figures on the altar to proclaim their acknowledgement of these truths. Through their adorations, the foliões and the families they visit enchant themselves into the "family of God," grounded in their mutual acknowledgement of the moral superiority of the Christ Child. Their ritualized dialogues with one another are guided by the ideal of reciprocity, based on the expectation that among their peers their efforts will be mutually recognized and recompensed.

CHAPTER VII

Visitations

ALTHOUGH THERE ARE CRIBS in some homes, most visitations involve only two ritual moments: the distribution of the blessings and the thanksgiving. According to foliões their principle "mission" is the distribution of blessings, and the main reason people invite a companhia into their homes is to receive the blessings of the Magi, bringing the saints' protective power into their households for another year. (See plate 16.)

In both the rural and the urban contexts, companhias are selective about the homes they visit, performing only for families that have requested a visitation. Their reasons for doing this, however, are distinct. In the rural context, at least in the peripheral lower-class neighborhoods of rural towns, few families would reject the banner if a companhia were to approach them, so rural foliões claim they would never be able to complete their circuits if they knocked at every door; if a family has made a point of informing the dono that they wish to receive the ensemble, the group feels obliged to visit them. Even so, rural companhias often find they are unable to move very rapidly along the route they have established, because a family may hear that the companhia is nearby, and quickly send a message, saying they want the musicians to bless their household. Since most foliões claim that all requests must be honored, even such last minute invitations, the companhia endeavors to find the time to stop at the home.

In the urban context, on the other hand, foliões are selective about where they make their visitations for fear of having their banners rejected. Unlike the rural context, where, as the saying goes, "everyone knows everyone else," the urban space is far more anonymous, and foliões are aware that many people fear the thought of allowing a group of strangers into their homes. Furthermore, urban migrants have very different regional backgrounds, and not all of them are familiar with the folia tradition. There is also a greater diversity of religious backgrounds in the urban context; while members of African-Brazilian cults tend to be syncretic in their religious orientation—like many foliões themselves—Pentecostals in particular are likely to reject the banner, and some foliões have heard stories in which they had openly blasphemed it as idol worship. Thus, urban companhias construct their circuits around their personal social networks, and their visitations tend to focus upon families from their hometowns as well as other close neighbors who have come to respect the tradition through their contact with the foliões. It is not uncommon, however, for an urban companhia to be invited into the home of total strangers who have heard the group performing for a neighbor, just as anonymous passersby often stop the companhia in the street to request a blessing. These unexpected events are greatly valued, as they serve to confirm that the merits of the tradition are recognized even outside their own communities. During their 1988/89 journey, the members of the Folia do Zé dos Magos were particularly gratified by an invitation they received to sing in the home of a Pentecostal family; in their discussions with the family and among themselves, they repeatedly confirmed that they were all devoted to the same—and only—God.

A Few Visitations

Sunday, 3 January 1987: The Folia do Baeta had been conducting visitation since 10:30 in the morning. At around 3:30 P.M. they made their fifth visitation of the day at the home of one of Januário's brothers, where they would receive their (late) lunch. When the head of the household heard the companhia was outside his home, he came out to meet the group at the front gate. Before taking the banner he kissed it and then led the ensemble into the house. The musicians entered the front room, and Owaldir began the embaixada to bless the family with the following verses:

Vou cantar para o senhor,	I will sing for you, sir,
Pra sua esposa também.	To your wife also.
Santo Reis lhe abençoa	May the Holy Kings bless you
Na hora de Deus, amém.	At God's hour, amen.

Vou cantar pra sua irmã,	I will sing for your sister,
É da mesma religião.	She's of the same religion:
Santo Reis do Oriente	The Holy Kings of the Orient
Te recubra de bênção.	Cover you with blessings.

Outro irmão tá na bandeira,	Another brother is at the banner,
Tá sorrindo de contente:	He is smiling with joy:
Tá recebendo a bênção	He is receiving the blessing
Dos Três Reis que está presente.	From the Three Kings who are present.

Vou cantar para a senhora	I will sing for you, madam,
Nesta hora verdadeira	At this true hour
E tá sendo abençoada	And you are being blessed
Desta sagrada bandeira.	By this sacred banner.

At this point the foliões stopped singing. Throughout their performance the banner had been passed from one person to another; as the embaixador noted who took it he adjusted the content of his verses accordingly. When they stopped, the head of the household approached one of the bastião, asking him to inform the embaixador that he would like the companhia to bless his daughter-in-law and his five grandchildren, which he had called in from the back yard. He arranged the children around the banner, instructing them all to take hold of an edge of the cloth. As they prepared themselves to receive their blessings, the companhia struck up the estribilho, and continued to sing the following verses:

Rodiou todas criança,	The children surrounded [the banner],
Todos anjos inocentes.	All innocent angels.
Santo Reis está benzendo	The Holy Kings are blessing [them]
Para não ficar doente.	So they won't become ill.
A bênção do Santo Reis	The blessing of the Holy Kings
Pros seus neto é um presente.	To your grandchildren is a present.

Vou cantar pra sua nora,	I will sing for your daughter-in-law,
Atendendo o seu pedido.	Responding to your request.
Santo Reis abençoando	The Holy Kings are blessing [her]
No momento concebido.	At this conceived moment.

Having completed the blessings, the head of the household took the banner to a room in the back of the house, where it would stay until the companhia sang again, asking him to return it to them so they could continue their journey. During the pause the foliões were served a hearty meat-and-vegetable stew together with bread and various drinks. When they had finished eating, the musicians returned to the front room to perform the thanksgiving, using, of course, the fast thanksgiving toada.

Meu senhor, dono da casa,	Sir, head of the household,
Santo Reis mandou dizer:	The Holy Kings have had me say:
Faz favor, traz a bandeira,	Please, bring the banner,
Eu quero agradecer.	I want to thank [you].
Agradeço a boa oferta	I thank the good offering
Do senhor e sua senhora:	From you, sir, and your wife:
Seja tudo abençoado	May all be blessed
Do meu Santo Reis da Glória.	By my Holy Kings of Glory.
A oferta de sua irmã,	The offering from your sister
Santo Reis agradecendo:	The Holy Kings are thanking:
Toda a família dela	All her family
Santo Reis está benzendo.	The Holy Kings are blessing.
Agradeço a sua nora	I thank your daughter-in-law
E pros seu filho também:	And her children also:
Santo Reis abençoando	The Holy Kings are blessing [them]
Na hora de Deus, amém.	At the hour of God, amen.
Santo Reis te agradecendo	The Holy Kings are thanking you
A oferta dos seus netinhos:	[For] the offering of your grandchildren:
Santo Reis te abençoando	The Holy Kings are blessing [them]
No lugar dos seus padrinhos.	In place of their godparents.
Sua esposa tem promessa	Your wife has a promise
De cumprir com essa bandeira:	To fulfill with this banner:
Pegue nela e dê um beijo	Take it and give a kiss
Nesta guia verdadeira.	To this true guide.

Santo Reis te abençoou	The Holy Kings have blessed you
E a promessa está completa:	And the promise is complete:
Santo Reis está levando	The Holy Kings are taking [it]
Lá pras terra do Oriente.	To the lands of the Orient.
Agradeço a comida	I thank you for the food
Que ofertou pros folião:	That you offered to the foliões:
Santo Reis te abença	May the Holy Kings bless
Esta sua devoção.	This, your devotion.
Agradeço a bebida	I thank you for the drinks
Que ofertou pra nós tomar;	That you offered for us to drink;
Santo Reis vai lhe dar outra	The Holy Kings will replace it
Na mesa de refeição.	On the dinner table.
Nossa Senhora pergunta,	Our Lady asks,
"Quem tratou dos folião?"	"Who cared for the foliões?"
Santo Reis tá respondendo,	The Holy Kings are answering,
"Foi o filho da bênção."	"It was the son of the blessing."
Já tá tudo agradecido,	Thanks have been given for everything,
Santo Reis tá despedindo:	The Holy Kings are bidding farewell:
Santo Reis já vai embora,	The Holy Kings are leaving,
Pra cumprir nosso destino.	To fulfill our destiny.
Dá um beijo na bandeira,	Kiss the banner,
Manda a família beijar.	Tell the family to kiss [it].
A bandeira vai embora,	The banner is leaving.
Os milagre vão ficar.	The miracles will stay.

After this verse the foliões thought they had finished their musical performance, but the head of the household asked them to sing for the soul of his sister-in-law before they left. As soon as the bastião realized the group would be singing for one who had died, they removed their masks and knelt on the floor before the banner, remaining in that position until all rituals relating to the dead woman had been completed. The ensemble reverted to the extended style and performed the following verse:

Alembrou de sua cunhada	You remembered your sister-in-law
Que na glória está morando:	Who is living in glory:
A terceira oração	The third prayer
Foliões está rezando.	The foliões are praying.[1]

After this verse there was the performance of an Our Father followed by a Hail Mary, and then the musicians struck up the toada once again with one more intention verse:

Intenção de quem morreu,	For the intention [of the soul of] one who died,
Tá morando lá na glória	She is living in glory
Com Deus Pai, o criador,	With God the Father, the creator,
No lugar que mereceu.	In the place she deserved.

When the companhia stopped singing, the bandeireiro took the banner from the head of the household, and the foliões followed it out of the house. Their next visitation occurred in the home of an elderly couple with no special links to any of the members of the ensemble, so it was conducted quite rapidly. As the husband held the banner, the companhia performed one six-line verse for the blessing followed by two verses of thanksgiving, each in the appropriate musical style:

Recebeu nossa bandeira	You received our banner
Nessa hora abençoada.	At this blessed hour.
Santo Reis tá visitando	The Holy Kings are visiting
A família e a morada.	The family and the dwelling.
Pede oferta de presente	They ask for an offering as a present
Pra bandeira consagrada.	For the consecrated banner.

Agradeço pro senhor	I thank you, sir,
E também para a senhora.	And also you, madam.
Santo Reis te abençoa	May the Holy Kings bless you
E também Nossa Senhora.	And also Our Lady.

Já tá tudo agradecido.	Thanks have been given for everything.
Santo Reis já vai embora.	The Holy Kings are leaving.

CHAPTER SEVEN

Deixando um ano feliz,	Leaving a good year,
Muita paz cheio de glória.	Much peace full of glory.

As the musicians were making their way to their next visitation a middle-aged man unknown to any of the musicians approached the group to say that he had been a folião in his home town of Araraquara, São Paulo. He asked if the companhia would kindly sing a verse to bless his family, and the bandeireiro handed him the banner as the companhia began their performance in the street.

O senhor é folião,	You, sir, are a folião,
Recebeu nossa bandeira	You received our banner
E pediu pra nois cantar	And you asked us to sing
Pra toda a família inteira.	For your whole family.
Dá oferta e ganha a bênção	Give an offering and receive a blessing
Nesta hora verdadeira.	At this true hour.

Agradeço meu colega,	I thank my colleague,
É devoto verdadeiro:	He is a true devotee:
Santo Reis abençoando	The Holy Kings are blessing [him]
No dia três de janeiro.	On the third of January.

Before stopping for the night at around 11:00 P.M. the companhia had sung at six more houses, and for two other anonymous people in the street. Among the twelve houses visited on that day there were three containing manger scenes, calling for the performance of the adoration.

Blessings and Thanksgivings

As these examples indicate, each visitation is distinct, constructed in terms of the specificities of the situation. But there is also a definite ritual script to be followed, whether the foliões spend several hours or only a few minutes at a visitation: they begin by distributing the blessings which are exchanged for a donation, and then they thank the family for their contribution.

Some companhias distinguish between these two acts by performing in two distinct musical styles: one for the blessings, the other for the thanksgiving. The Folia do Bacta normally used their extended style for the family verses and moved to the compressed style for the thanksgiving verses at the ends of their visitations. The extended repetitious style was used for the solemn sections of their performances, and having fulfilled these divine obligations, the foliões could depart, but in accordance with proper social conduct they still had to thank and bid farewell to their hosts, and this could be done with less theatricality. One companhia in Monsenhor Paulo marked this transition by beginning with a slow toada, similar to the one used by the Folia do Zé Quatorze, and ending with a fast toada, like the one used by the Folia do Zé dos Magos. In the Folia do Zé Quatorze, performances often ended with farewell verses sung to the toada of the King of the Congo. One folião from São Sebastião do Paraíso, Minas Gerais, claimed that visitations should end with the toada of the black King because the African was ashamed to go all the way to the manger, adoring the baby Jesus from afar. It seems that he used the marginalized condition of blacks in Brazilian society as a metaphor for marking the relative formality in these two sections of the ritual script.

The use of such stylistic markers promotes associations that attach one of the styles to the sacred realm of the Magi, which by implication defines the other as a human style. Viewed in terms of their succession within the ritual drama, they articulate an embedded message: through the blessings humans are touched by the Kings, thus gaining a momentary glimpse of the holy realm; in their attempt to re-create this realm on earth, they are hindered by their human limitations and achieve only a partial transposition of the heavenly order on earth; their toadas, then, emerge as humanized versions of the music of the Magi.

While the transition in the musical styles used at visitations can elicit inchoate resonances, each of the ritual acts is constructed around a unique set of motif clusters of its own, adding further density to the ritual experience of relatedness.

Family Verses

Before the foliões begin to sing at visitations, it is usual for one of the bastião to ask the head of the household how he would like the group to sing: that is, does he require a verse for each member of the family or can the family unit be addressed in a single verse? As soon as the embaixador has been informed of the family's wishes, the music begins. Those receiving the verse take hold of the banner, and in an act that combines text, music, and physical contact with the material manifestation of the divinities, the Three Kings

CHAPTER SEVEN

bless the faithful through the companhia's performance. While the companhia pauses to move into the thanksgiving toada, the family makes its donation.

It is generally presumed that unless there are special circumstances relating to the visitation, the companhia will perform one or at most two verses,
addressing the family members jointly; for example, the husband and the
wife may be blessed together in one couplet and their children in the other.
Very rarely, however, does a companhia visit a home in which there are no
special circumstances, since foliões generally visit families with links to their
membership. Thus, they are aware of the family's history and current conditions, and this information is used by the embaixador to personalize the content of the blessings. There are numerous circumstances which might call for
special attention: for example, the family may be fulfilling a promise to the
Three Kings; someone may be ill, requiring a special blessing; a member of
the family may have died recently, and the family has asked for a special
prayer for the person's soul; the family may intend to serve a meal or a snack
to the ensemble, and an extended performance serves to indicate the foliões'
gratitude toward their generosity; in previous years the family may have
made a generous contribution to the festival, and in anticipation that they
will do so again, the musicians may extend their performance.

As the examples above indicate, family verses are mediated through the
head of the household, and since families within folia communities are conceived of in patriarchal terms, the head of the household is typically male.
Furthermore, the order in which the members of the family are addressed often identifies their relationship to the head of the household unit (e.g., "your
wife," "your sister," "another brother" and so on). Most foliões consider it to
be self-evident that the companhia should sing first to the head of the household, followed by his wife and children, but then it is up to the patriarch to
determine the order in which other relatives and neighbors present at the
time receive their verses. Zezo, however, claimed that there is a prescribed
order in which the family verses should be sung when there are either relatives of the nuclear family living in the household or visitors present at the
home when the companhia arrives. He provided the following sequence,
based on notions of the proximity of family relations within an extended
family network:

1. The head of the household
2. His wife
3. His unmarried children, beginning with the eldest

4. His consanguineous relatives and their families (e.g., his father and mother and their unmarried children; his grandparents; his brothers and sisters, their spouses, and their unmarried children; his sons and daughters, their spouses, and their unmarried children)
5. His wife's consanguineous relatives
6. Neighbors and friends and their families
7. Deceased kin

This sequence is a fairly accurate reflection of the way in which many low-income southeastern migrants reckon their proximity to relatives, restricting significant bonds almost exclusively to those that derive from the immediate nuclear family. Depth rarely exceeds three generations, and parallel reckoning does not tend to transcend one degree beyond a direct bond. There is, however, considerable flexibility in the order in which people are blessed, and the head of the household makes his decisions according to his own criteria. For example, one of the houses Zé Machado visits each year has an obligation to receive the companhia because of a promise they made when their daughter needed to undergo a serious heart operation; she is, therefore, always the first to take the banner when the companhia arrives for its visitation. Similarly, the Folia do Zé dos Magos once arrived at a house in which the seven-year-old grandson of the head of the household had fallen and broken a leg; to help speed his recovery the ensemble was asked to begin by blessing the boy. When the Folia do Baeta went to visit a migrant family from Guaranésia, one of the daughters had recently died in an automobile accident, and the head of the household asked the companhia to begin by singing for the intention of her soul; to receive the verses, the head of the household knelt before the companhia, and throughout their singing he sobbed uncontrollably.

Despite the fluidity in the ordering of blessings, a typical performance of family verses is informed by commonsense notions regarding family organization and the role of the head of the household in mediating interhousehold relations. First, nuclear families are generally blessed as a unit and addressed through the head of their household; other nuclear families are equally corporatized, and they are related as units through the heads of their households to the head of the household being visited. Indeed, the ideal household structure among southeastern migrants is the nuclear family composed of a male head of the household, his wife, and their unmarried children. Foliões recognize, of course, that not all families follow this ideal, and the improvisatory nature of the embaixada allows them to adjust their

CHAPTER SEVEN

verses to account for the peculiarities of each situation they confront along the journey.[2]

Given the familial focus of blessings, the performance of family verses reminds people of their departed relatives. When visiting the home of a deceased embaixador, the Folia do Zé dos Magos purposefully used a toada formerly associated with him; when his wife heard it she was reminded of her husband and burst into tears. The ritual script of the folia tradition recognizes the place of dead relatives within the family, and a special category of verses and practices are performed when a family asks the foliões to sing for the soul of a dead relation. In such cases the banner is often placed on an empty chair, the place formerly occupied by the person in life. The souls of the dead are associated with the sacred; in bringing the Holy Kings to earth for their ritual journey, the dead also return temporarily to the realm of humanity through the memories they invoke among their relatives and friends. By singing to the dead, they can bring them back into the midst of their loved ones, reviving memories of experiences shared with them in life.[3]

Thanksgiving

After the blessings, the companhia marks the reciprocal nature of the relationship linking the family to the Three Kings through their performance of the thanksgiving verses. Although embaixadores sometimes make open requests for an offering during the blessings, this is not necessary, since reciprocity is an implicit imperative within this social universe. After blessing the family, many companhias simply stop singing for a moment to collect the family's donation to the banner, and then they proceed with their acknowledgement of the offering.

In his description of a folia visitation in the region around Caldas, Minas Gerais, Brandão (1981, 23–25) noted that the bastião publicly announced each donation as it was made. Throughout my research, however, I never came across this practice, even though donations were not considered to be particularly secretive. A donation seems to elicit commentary among the foliões only if it is thought to be either very generous or especially stingy. In the urban context, including areas within the boundaries of small towns, offerings are made almost exclusively in the form of money; in rural areas, however, people often donate chickens, pigs, calves, or produce from their gardens that could be used to feed the community at the festival or be sold at auction to help cover its costs. There was general agreement among foliões that they received the most generous donations in the countryside.

More recently, however, monetary donations have become more common there also.

It is assumed that the attention the foliões give to the family in the form of independent verses should match the generosity of their offering. They repeatedly claimed, however, that they did not measure generosity in absolute terms; rather, it was to be gauged in terms of the relative financial security of the family at the time of the visitation. In somewhat rhetorical fashion, foliões commonly claimed that the better off a family was, the less truly generous they tended to be, even though in absolute terms their donations were often greater than those of poor families.

The obligation of reciprocity requires the foliões to express their gratitude for every token of generosity shown by the family, and as with blessings, the thanksgiving is mediated through the head of the household. The musicians begin by thanking him for his family's donations to the Kings, and this is followed by an itemized acknowledgement of their hospitality toward the musicians. If the companhia was offered coffee, the embaixador thanks the family for the coffee; if they gave them something to eat, food is mentioned in the verses; if the banner and the instruments stayed in the house overnight, the embaixada will thank the family for caring for them, and so on. In general, homes that receive extended performances during the blessings are also graced with lengthy thanksgivings. As they give thanks, the foliões reiterate the Kings' blessings, linking them directly to the gift. In the folia worldview, God and the Three Kings are witness to the donor's generosity. Though it is humans who benefit from it, the return payment is represented as coming from the saints—with interest (e. g., "The Holy Kings will replace [the drinks] on the dinner table"). It is implied that those who offer the foliões something to eat will always have food in their homes.

Ritual Exchanges

One of the few anthropological studies of folias de reis was conducted by Carlos Rodrigues Brandão (1981), who focused upon the system of ritual exchanges in the tradition. It is, in fact, in terms of these exchanges that he defines the ensemble: "The Folia de Reis is a symbolically constructed peasant space within an equally ritualized time-frame, for the purpose of circulating gifts—goods and services—between a mendicant group and the dwellers of a particular region" (Brandão 1981, 36). He argues, that unlike the classic cases presented by Marcel Mauss ([1950] 1997), "in the Folia the two groups of transactors are unequal partners: one of the parties [the family] gives material goods and receives symbolic-religious goods; the other [the foliões] receives material goods and gives symbolic-religious goods. But the [family] *gives to others* (. . . the festive community) and *receives on their own behalf*. . . . In turn, the [foliões] *give to others* (return gifts [blessings] to the givers) and *receive* on their own behalf (food and hospitality) and for others (. . . the Festival of the Three Kings). . . . Spiritual goods coming from God, mediated by the Three Holy Kings and then by the verses of the foliões, are given to those who gave material goods to [the festive community], in whose name the requests are made on behalf of the Kings and God, mediated by the verses of the very same foliões" (Brandão 1981, 47–48; italics in the original). Brandão goes on to note that the material gifts in the ritual exchange never have symbolic value in themselves, so they cannot be easily identified with the household that gave them: they come in the form of either money or marketable goods that can be transformed into money. Thus, he claims, the family's donation can be used to produce a "symbolic situation," that is, a communal festival.

By pointing to the centrality of gift exchange within the folia tradition, Brandão has made a major contribution to the understanding of popular Catholicism among the Brazilian subaltern classes. Yet his model is constructed around two groups of transactors: the household and the foliões. From the devotees' perspective, however, there are three categories in the transaction: the household, the foliões, and the divinities. During folia visitations there are exchanges of gifts between humans and the saints, which are mediated by folia performances, and exchanges between two sets of humans, the foliões and the members of the household. It is only by making this distinction that it becomes possible to understand the nature of the ritual exchanges at visitations and their relation to the festival. To show why this is so, I shall begin by looking at another context of reciprocal exchange within popular Catholicism which is central to the folia tradition: the promise.

Divine Reciprocity

When I was eight years old my father had to go to Eloi Mendes, because we lived in the country. . . . So he told me to go get a horse for him out in the pasture so he could go, because he went on horseback.

So I went to get the horse, and I got on the horse . . . and set off galloping. And then the horse stepped into an armadillo hole and threw me forward, and in this I hit my mouth on the trunk of a corn stalk. The reed entered my throat this much [he indicates about one inch]. And then until about the age of twenty I couldn't speak.

Then a folia de reis came by our house. My mother took a ribbon off the banner and put it around my neck, she tied it to my neck, and asked the Holy Kings that if I freed my speech and sang normally, just like I was just singing here, I would belong to the Holy Kings in body and soul. She gave me to the Holy Kings from that moment onward.

And I freed my speech and started to sing for the Kings again. Then in '46 I started as embaixador of the Kings here in São Paulo. But when I came here, I didn't speak yet. I only started freeing my voice when I was twenty-one. I didn't speak at all, and she gave me to the Holy Kings in body and soul. After that day, I belonged to the Holy Kings.

I had to go out each year at least to one house, if I freed my speech, if I got well, singing like I was just doing. After I freed [my voice], I sang *requinta*.[4] (Luizinho)

Luizinho's narration recounts the promise that his mother made on his behalf when he was a child. As anthropologists have repeatedly noted, promises are reciprocal contracts made between a devotee and a saint, who is asked to intercede before God on behalf of the promisor (Brandão 1981, 84–92; Maués 1995; 352–57; Zaluar 1980; 1983, 80–106, among others). The Three Kings are often summoned to cure sick children, since it is thought that they can counteract the evil done by King Herod in the massacre of the innocents. The miraculous power of the Magi, however, is not thought to be restricted to childhood illnesses, and promises to the Three Kings are often made for sick adults as well as for other types of misfortune, especially perilous trips, unemployment, and alcoholism. Given the precarious condition in which the lower classes live, there are very few devout Catholics among them who go through life without ever participating in such a contract.

Many promises, particularly those to Our Lady, involve some sort of physical sacrifice, such as a long walk—possibly even on one's knees or in bare feet—to a major pilgrimage center. This is because Our Lady is closely associated with the archetypal *mater dolorosa,* and the kinds of sacrifices thought to move her involve physical pain. Promises in the form of *ex-voto* votive offerings are also common throughout Brazil. The ex-voto is an iconic representation of the miracle received, such as a photograph of the person who benefited from the promise, a sculpture of the body part that

CHAPTER SEVEN

was cured by the saints, or a representation of the circumstances that called for the miracle. Often the ex-voto is taken in a ritual pilgrimage to a center associated with the saint to whom the promise was made, and many pilgrimage sites have a special "miracle room" (*sala dos milagres*) to house the ex-votos.

Promises to saints who are associated with collective ritual traditions such as the folia de reis, however, typically involve payment through a "sacrifice" that contributes to the saint's celebration. Thus, as in Luizinho's case (and Zezo's and that of countless other foliões), the promise can involve payment through direct participation in the companhia itself. Indeed, it is commonly assumed that the child-clown bastiãozinhos are in a companhia to fulfill their part in such contracts. But there are many other ways of contributing to the tradition without joining an ensemble; the contracts are as numerous and creative as the people who make them, and the level of the "sacrifice" depends, to some extent, on the magnitude of the miracle requested of the saints and the resources available within the family. For example, one can promise to act as festeiro, one can serve a meal to the musicians, one can kneel during the visitation, one can carry the banner during the journey, one can make a generous donation to the festival, one can put a photograph or a ribbon on the banner, and so on, and any one of these contracts can be made for a limited period of time or for life.[5]

Several foliões emphasized that miracles were actually the work of God the Father, and the saints act only as intermediaries between humans and the inaccessible Almighty God. It is precisely because the saints have human characteristics that they are in a privileged position to act on behalf of humans; having themselves once walked the earth, they are thought to be more acutely aware of the human condition. Even though their intermediary status is frequently verbalized, the concept of mediation represents an abstraction that is rarely integrated into people's accounts of the "graces" they received; in everyday discourse the miraculous power experienced in promises is attributed directly to the saints, and in many cases to a particular iconographic representation of them. Saints associated with performative ritual practices are thought to have a vested interested in the continuity of the devotional traditions in their honor. As Raymundo Heraldo Maués (1995, 355–56) points out, however, the saints do not act purely out of self-interest; by defending their own traditions they create the conditions that keep their miraculous power at the disposal of their devotees.

Luizinho's account of the promise that restored his voice follows a pat-

VISITATIONS

tern that is typical of promises within the southeastern folia tradition. Note, in particular, that it was made on his behalf by a third party—his mother—but it was up to him to redeem it. Though it is said that people can make promises for themselves, very few people claimed to have done so; by comparison countless foliões told of promises made on their behalf by other people. Promises made on one's own behalf are not to be taken seriously, and when they are made they are generally directed to saints associated with match-making (*santos casamenteiros*) or, alternatively, they are made to request luck in gambling or other trivial matters.[6] Some foliões openly claimed that to make a promise on one's own behalf would be to act with self-interest, whereas if the promise is made by someone else it is because another person has noted one's needs, so that the promise expresses that person's care and concern for one's well-being.

By structuring the promise in this way a set of relationships is created among all three parties involved in the contract: the divinities, the promisor, and the recipient of the grace, and these links articulate mutual obligations on both vertical and horizontal axes. Vertically, the obligations of the contract link humans to the saints, in that both the promisor and the recipient of the grace become indebted to the saints for answering the prayer. Horizontally, the contract mutually obligates the recipient and the petitioner: the recipient is obligated to the promisor in gratitude for the grace requested on her behalf, while the promisor becomes obligated to the recipient for agreeing to fulfill the divine obligations of the contract. Though rare, there are instances in which recipients refuse to fulfill their obligations: this can happen, for example, if a person converts to Pentecostalism before the obligation has been met or if the recipient has come to view such contracts as outmoded forms of rural superstition. The debt, then, falls upon the petitioner, who must find a way of fulfilling it.

To refuse to fulfill one's obligation to the saints can have perilous consequences, for the saints are thought to be vindictive. Indeed, stories of divine punishments (*castigos divinos*) abound to confirm this, as in the one below:

This happened in [the bairro called] Servo. The man had lots of horses. The folia arrived there one night. The clowns knew he had pigs, horses, chickens.

"Hey, mister, would you give us a sow? We're hungry. If she's alive, we'll take it and kill it. Tomorrow we'll eat it."

He said, "No, all my pigs died. There are no pigs."

CHAPTER SEVEN

"Well, then give us a little chicken, just a little chicken."

"But I'm not raising chickens any more. The skunks, the animals got to them."

They sang. The man gave them coffee there, and the folia went away, you know. . . . The next day the man got up: five pigs were dead.[7] (Zé Quatorze)

When—as Brandão (1981, 88–89) notes—the promise is associated with a ritual tradition, it can be redeemed only when—and if—the ritual is staged, and the promisor becomes dependent upon a community of devotees to fulfill her obligation. Luizinho, for example, can pay back his lifelong debt to the Three Kings only with the support of other foliões willing to form an ensemble with his participation. The institution of the promise is, therefore, a fundamental factor in ensuring the continuity of the folia tradition, since the payment of a person's promise becomes the responsibility of the whole community. As long as someone has a promise to participate in the ritual in some capacity, foliões claim they cannot stop their journeys. Several elder foliões in positions of leadership often complained of being too old and tired to keep the companhia going, but they claimed they could not stop the group because they could not leave someone's promise unredeemed. If the companhia folded, how would a young bastiãozinho complete his seven years in the farda? If the child suffered a misfortune for leaving his promise unfulfilled, the foliões who prevented him from redeeming it would have to answer for their irresponsibility before God. By the same token, a folião could find himself with an outstanding debt in the future which he would become dependent upon others to redeem. Thus, the principle of reciprocity that links the faithful and the divinities provides the basis for conceptualizing mutual obligations among humans as a divine mandate, such that one person's debt to the Holy Kings becomes the obligation of the whole community. Thus, promises articulate social networks which link devotees into a system of mutual obligations to one another through their own individual obligations toward the Holy Kings.

The promise, however, marks an explicit reciprocal contract related to a particular situation of misfortune, and such contracts are made only when circumstance call for them. On a day-to-day basis, devotees perceive themselves to be in an ongoing—but diffuse—relationship of reciprocity with the divinities. Thus, promises mark moments of special urgency within the ongoing experience of life and its necessities, and participation in the folia tradition in any form provides a means of ritually renewing one's relationship with the saints to guarantee their continuous protective power. Since one's obligations to the saints are articulated through one's obligations to one's peers, the preservation of the saints' protection obligates one to engage in perpetual exchanges with other people.

This would suggest that the concept of reciprocity within folia communities — and other popular Catholic communities — is far more diffuse than anthropological literature would lead one to believe. Since the community studies of the 1950s, researchers have argued that interhousehold reciprocity among the Brazilian peasantry is constructed around dyadic interactions. Although each household within the folia communities of São Bernardo did have a set of preferential households of relatives and neighbors with whom it maintained fairly systematic dyadic relations, the kind of diffuse interhousehold reciprocity Scheper-Hughes (1992, 99–108) described in relation to a poor northeastern community was equally operative, and I observed many instances in which the companhia served as the focal point of community mobilization in cases of misfortune.

One evening the adolescent niece of a family who received an annual visitation from the Folia do Zé Machado did not come home, and someone was quickly sent to tell the leader of the companhia. He, in turn, informed Zé dos Magos, and within a few hours the two foliões had spread the word through their visitation networks. Zé Macahdo claimed that over one hundred men spent the night searching for the girl, but despite their efforts, she was never found. When in late January of 1989 a torrential rain dragged the precarious shack of a home on Zé dos Mago's circuit down the hill upon which it was perched, several members of the companhia along with some of their relatives turned up the next day to rebuild it. The family claimed that donations to replace their lost belongings emerged from nowhere. Jacaré, a member of the Folia do Baeta Neves, had a similar experience when his house burned down just before the ensemble's journey in 1990. The companhia organized a campaign within the community on his behalf, and he received almost all the construction materials he needed to rebuild the house with the help of friends and relatives. Moreover, he said people whom he did not even know turned up with household goods and clothing to help the family rebuild their lives.

The folia, then, particularly within the urban context, provides a framework for organizing independent nuclear families into a larger interfamilial network of relatives and friends, bound to one another by patterns of reciprocal exchange across households and by a diffuse sense of collective solidarity. The examples given above, however, represent only the more visible

CHAPTER SEVEN

expressions of communal solidarity. Alongside these moments there is a continuous flow of goods across households to assist people in times of need. When Zé Quatorze became ill, his foliões and neighbors often sent groceries to his house so he could use his meager pension to buy the expensive medicines he needed. Alcides, whose pension was but one-half the minimum wage, would have had great difficulty surviving without the support of his children, friends, and neighbors. Moreover, he was known in the neighborhood for the curative power of his prayers (*benzimentos*); though he would not accept money for his services, most clients arrived with a bag of food to express their gratitude for his time.

As several researchers have noted (Kottak 1967; Sarti 1995),[8] the strong pressures of communal obligations within low-income communities in Brazil engender ambiguous sentiments, since the better placed one is financially, the more one is expected to contribute to the well-being of others. Social ascent within one's own community, then, is seen to be systematically blocked by the demands of one's kin and neighbors; to free oneself of these obligations it becomes necessary to move away, and as migrants achieve a better standard of living, many of them do move into new neighborhoods where the majority of the inhabitants have incomes comparable to their own. By taking this option, however, one also loses one's support network within a wider social context in which there is no other reliable system of social security. Thus, even if one moves away, there is rarely a complete break with the original community, and one may become the link through which other kin relations and former neighbors make their move into "better" neighborhoods, repeating the patterns documented for migration chains in the processes of urban upward mobility. Collective efforts of social ascent, however, need not always lead to dislocation; one can help pull one's kin and neighbors up the financial ladder—and thus reduce one's own obligations toward them—by helping them find employment in one's own company, just as Zezo served as an "employment agent" (Durham 1984, 211) for several relatives and friends after he got the job at Mercedes-Benz.

Folia Exchanges

The original exchange upon which the ritual exchanges in the folia tradition are based took place with the Adoration of the Magi. The Kings arrived at the manger with their presents—gold, frankincense, and myrrh—and in return they received a viola, a tambourine, and a caixa. These are the means of making music, and it is through music making that social harmony can be constructed and experienced. By participating in the exchange, the Magi were ennobled and sanctified, becoming mediators between humans and the Almighty God. Thus, what pleases God is to see his vision implemented on earth, and he gave music to the Three Kings so that they could set about instating it. Their legacy to humankind was the music God gave them, the music of the folia de reis. By performing this music in their annual visitations, humans can reenact the mythic journey of the Wise Men, temporarily reenchanting God's vision among humans. While family verses highlight the obligations involved in family relations, reciprocity with the Three Kings extends these obligations to encompass a greater "family" of devotees. The community of devotees becomes a "symbolic family," united through their faith in the power of the saints, and this link binds them into a network of mutual obligations. By perceiving themselves as a "family," the devotees give continuity to the task God placed before the Kings.

The foliões, acting as emissaries of the Kings, distribute their blessings to the faithful, and in return the family makes a donation to the festival. Thus, the exchange articulated here is between humans and the saints, in which material goods are exchanged for "symbolic-religious" goods. The material goods, however, are destined for consumption by the community during the festival, so the family's offering to the saints is simultaneously an offering to the community. Paralleling these exchanges there are exchanges between the foliões as humans and the family they visit: while the family offers them food and hospitality, in return the foliões offer their services as mediators—their time and their talents, that is, their musical performances. Yet, these services are also gifts to the Three Kings, in return for promises they answered. To give to the saints and to give to others, then, constitute one and the same act.

Why? Because what is offered by humans was once itself a gift from God: the gift of life. What the family gives, God replaces, so they will be able to make another offering the following year; similarly, the divine music of the folia reached humanity through the Kings, so it can be performed every year during folia journeys. Through the folia tradition these gifts are circulated and redistributed among humans in a symbolic enactment of God's vision for the world, where peace and harmony can be achieved only through adherence to the divine "natural laws" of reciprocity. The festival, a "symbolic situation," is the culmination of the ritual exchanges that take place at each visitation. In their singing, companhias make use of the Kings' gift to humanity, and in so doing they offer the saints their enchanted vision of the

CHAPTER SEVEN

world, which, because it is an offering to the Kings, is a gift to other humans. Through their visitations the foliões weave their way through a network of households, linking them to one another to form God's "family" on earth, the existence of which is confirmed with the final festival. The blessings of the Magi transubstantiate into material donations, that is, food, the source of human livelihood, which is consumed collectively at the festival. The enchanted vision constructed in the music making is preserved in the temporal and material world of humanity through the distribution of food, the sustenance of terrestrial life.

Enchanted Obligations

The moral imperative of reciprocity is ritually enacted during folia visitations through two major acts, which are contained in the ritual script: the distribution of the blessings and the thanksgiving. Without doubt, it is during blessings that devotees have the most highly charged affective experiences within the folia tradition, and foliões even assess the success of their performances at visitations in terms of their ability to provoke tears in the eyes of the person holding the banner. Foliões themselves often cried when they were being sung to, even though the music did not have this effect upon them while they performed within the ensemble. At a pouso, I was in the kitchen with the women when they began discussing the powers of the banner. Taking advantage of the opportunity, I commented on how I had noticed that people often shed tears during blessings. One woman responded, "It's the devotion of the person." Another continued, "When we hold the banner it seems like the saint is right next to us, and it fills us with emotion." The first woman spoke again, "When the person is devout, she is overcome with emotion."

The blessings are orchestrated in order to generate intense bodily sensations, and this intensity of experience demands interpretation. Interpretations of experience are informed by the resonances they invoke in the consciousness of the individual, and these resonances emerge out of the articulation of past personal experience with a shared cultural heritage. Thus, what is experienced and how it is experienced are culturally informed, but it is through experience that cultural representations become meaningful at a personal level. Intense personal experiences built around the shared representational repertoire create spaces for the revelation of meaning, giving substance to religious discourse: it is in the act of being blessed that the singing of the foliões emerges as the voices of the Magi; it is through holding the banner during a visitation that it comes to be experienced as the presence of the Three Kings.

The potential impact of ritual experience within the folia tradition was brought home to me the first time I held the banner in a formal context. This occurred in January of 1987 toward the end of the journey of the Folia do Baeta. By this time I had acquired some sense of the dominant motif clusters operating in the folia universe, and even though I was not fully conscious of it at the time, my inchoate familiarity with the folia ethos was sufficient to promote resonances that gave me a sense of the intensity of experience the blessing could evoke in the devotees of the Kings. The ensemble was singing at the home of one of the folia members, and after the group had finished blessing his family, Owaldir asked the head of the household to give the banner to me, saying that I had followed the musicians around for so long that the Kings wanted to bless me. Though I had already heard countless folia performances, this had not prepared me for the experience of standing face to face, banner in hand, before the musicians as they sang directly at me. I was honored with two full blessing verses:

Vou cantar pr'essa senhora,	I will sing for this woman,
Reportando os folião.	Reporting on the foliões.
Vem seguindo essa bandeira	She's been following this banner
Em sinal de devoção.	As a sign of devotion.
Vou cantar para os seu pais.	I will sing for her parents.
Eles tá pra viajar;	They are about to travel;
Guarde eles pela ida	Be with them on their way
E não deixa demorar.	And don't let them delay [their return].

In the first verse the embaixador defined my relationship to the ensemble in terms of a relationship with the Three Kings I was seen to share with the foliões; in the second verse members of my immediate family were integrated into the folia community through my relationship to the group. Since my family was an extension of my person, and I was now seen to belong to the folia community, my family was readily accepted into their social circle as well. What was especially touching was that Owaldir referred to particulars of my life, defining their significance in terms of the social relationships they circumscribed, and I experienced a momentary sense of belonging which was indeed overwhelming. I was moved by the fact that Owaldir had even come to know about the trip my parents would be making the next day, since I had commented on it with a different folião. The reason the issue had come up at all was that I needed to alert the foliões I generally gave rides to that I would be unable to take them home that evening; I had agreed to take my parents to the airport early the next morning, so I would need to leave the companhia earlier than usual that day. Clearly, my family obligations had been considered sufficiently significant to become an issue for commentary among the musicians, and from their own experiences of the hazards of travel, they believed that a bit of supernatural protection would not go amiss. Moreover, it seemed self-evident to them that my siblings and I would miss our parents and that we would be worried about them while they were away: thus, the final line of Owaldir's embaixada asks the Kings to bring them home safely as soon as possible.

While the texts of the verses made explicit a recognition of my membership in a social network defined in such strong, affective relational terms as those associated with the family—which was in itself a moving experience—it was the *way* in which the words were transmitted that magnified these sentiments and conferred upon them special meaning. Standing before the group I felt myself the center of attention, and I imagined people conjuring memories of our shared experiences during the journey, just as I had found that I had been reminded of the snippets of information I had accumulated about different people I had seen take the banner. Moreover, standing directly in front of the companhia I experienced their music as a massive waterfall cascading down upon me in successive waves, which gained momentum as the toada progressed. My whole being was embraced, as though the sound had material substance. While the text referred to aspects of my life, the successive repetitions and the progressive increase in the volume of the music as the back voices joined the ensemble made me feel as though I was being encompassed by a world in which I was fully accepted and appreciated: I felt truly blessed. Just as other members of folia communities, I felt the desire to reciprocate for the gift of this rare experience, and I made my donation to the festival.

After the emotional impact of the blessing I felt a sense of deep relief as the thanksgiving verses were performed. Shorter and lighter in character, they seemed to soften my return back to earth and "normality."

Clearly, my experience differed from that of the faithful—and indeed their blessing experiences are not uniform—but lacking a representational model through which to interpret it, I drew upon theirs and considered myself blessed. Even though my experience was distinct from that of the devotees, it provided me with a means of better understanding the intensity of experience blessings can generate, paralleling Renato Rosaldo's (1984) account of how the loss of his wife in the field enhanced his understanding of the rage caused by death among the Ilongot.

Devotees experience their blessings as gifts from the Magi. While I too experienced the blessing as a gift, I saw it as a public recognition on the part of the foliões of my appreciation of their aesthetic world, which was profoundly enhanced after this personal experience. Regardless of their provenance, gifts—as Mauss has stressed—demand reciprocation. The gift of the blessing originates from the saints, but it is through the performances of humans that the tangible experience of the blessing is orchestrated—or enchanted. Visitations, then, construct enactments in which the foliões' obligations to sing on behalf of the Kings articulate a sense of obligation among the devotees that encompasses both the saints, from whom the blessings come, and the foliões, the mediators of the blessings. The cultural response to the gift of the blessing is to reciprocate with a gift that embraces both divinities and mortals simultaneously: a donation to the festival. The festival is staged in honor of the Magi to the benefit of their devotees. Through the highly charged enactment of a complex exchange system, blessings enchant experiences that promote a sense of commitment to the divine "natural laws" of reciprocity, the very source of the Kings' protective power to preserve life.

CHAPTER VIII

Arrivals

IN THE FOLIA DO BAETA IT IS CUSTOMARY for the festeiro to serve a lunch to the musicians on the day of the arrival, before they conduct their final ritual ceremonies in the late afternoon. In 1988 the foliões, their families, and other community members with close ties to the musicians or to the festeira met for lunch at the dining pavilion of the ceramics company where Dona Mariinha worked. The meal would be a larger affair than usual, because, instead of being offered by the festeira, it was financed by a local industrialist who was running for a seat on the town council. In fact, he had taken a special interest in the companhia that year. It was through his mediation that the musicians had acquired a new uniform before the journey, which had been donated by the multinational food company for which he worked. The new farda—their third one—had been designed by Owaldir and Zezo and consisted of a white long-sleeved shirt and "elegant" dark green trousers. Furthermore, the industrialist had been instrumental in helping the companhia secure a bus from the local Department of Culture to take them to Arceburgo for three days during their journey. Through this patronage he hoped to secure votes from the foliões and their community; though he may have received some, no one openly admitted to having voted for him, and he was not elected. The lunch menu was similar to other meals the foliões had received along their journey: rice, beans, chicken, potatoes, spaghetti, and salad. Around fifty people were served at a long table.

After lunch the foliões changed into their new uniforms and set off to sing at three more houses before arriving at Dona Mariinha's front gate, by which time it had started pouring rain. Because of this the outdoor sections of the arrival ritual were conducted hastily under umbrellas. To give the reader a better sense of how the foliões envisage their arrivals, I will describe the event of the preceding year, when Geraldinho, the violinist of the companhia, acted as festeiro. Because he lived in São Caetano, which is quite a distance away from the neighborhood in which the group normally circulates, the audience was far smaller than usual, but the ceremony was performed in full, all the musicians attired in the shiny red uniforms they had just received from the Department of Culture. The full performance of the arrival lasted over two hours.

To begin their performance the foliões congregated at the crossroads of the block where Geraldinho's house was situated and began playing the estribilho. As they repeated the instrumental section several times, they slowly processed down the road toward the house, stopping at intervals along the way to perform "half-moons" (*meia-luas*). "Half-moons" are choreographic formations performed in the street, in which the two queues of musicians move in a circle, one going clockwise while the other moves counterclockwise.[1] The singing began when the group finally stopped at the front gate of Geraldinho's house, which had been adorned with a bamboo arch containing an inscription with the letters *T* and *R*. There were three more arches with inscriptions leading into the front room, where the crèche had been set up. Furthermore, Geraldinho had hung a star on a string that connected the arches to the crib. When one arch was knocked down, the string was pulled, and the star moved to the next arch. In this way the companhia literally followed the star to the manger scene he had set up in the front room of his house.

Owaldir began his embaixada, revealing the meaning of the first inscription:

A folia está chegando	The folia is arriving
Na cidade do Oriente.	At the city of the Orient.
Encontrou o que está escrito	They found what is written
Dos Três Reis que está presente.	About the Three Kings [Três Reis] who are present.
Na chegada do Oriente,	At the arrival of the Orient,
Os Três Reis que vêm chegando	The Three Kings who are arriving

CHAPTER EIGHT

| Louvar o arco primeiro | To praise the first arch |
| Na chegada deste ano. | At this year's arrival. |

Meus Três Reis pede licença	My Three Kings ask leave
Nesta hora aqui presente:	At this present hour:
Pede licença ao festeiro	They ask leave of the festeiro
Pra você passar pra frente.	For you to move forward.

Though there was no interruption in the singing, the festeiro moved forward to allow the bastião to pull down the arch, and he took the banner to the next one. In his verses Owaldir made reference to the star guiding the group to the next arch. Hanging from this arch were the letters *M* and *S* followed by the full alphabet.

A estrela está seguindo:	The star is moving forward:
No segundo arco parou.	It stopped at the second arch.
Tá guiando os Três Reis Santos	It is guiding the Three Holy Kings
Com seu lindo resplendor.	With its lovely splendor.

O M é de Moisés,	The M is for Moses,
O profeta que escreveu	The prophet who wrote
A sagrada profecia	The sacred prophecy
De Jesus, filho de Deus.	Of Jesus, son of God.

S quer dizer o santo	S means the saint
Baltazar que está chegando.	Balthazar who is arriving.
Pra falar do *ABC,*	To speak of the *ABC,*
Meu bastião vai estudando.	My bastião is studying.

At this point the music stopped and one of the bastião came forward and began his recitation, dedicating a verse to each of the letters of the alphabet. Only the first three letters have been transcribed below, followed by his concluding verse:

Com *A* eu anuncio	With *A* I announce
O nascimento de Jesus.	The birth of Jesus.
Ele nasceu para nos salvar,	He was born to save us,
Depois ele morreu na cruz.	Then he died on the cross.

O *B* é de Belém,	The *B* is for Bethlehem,
Cidade de Nazaré,	City of Nazareth,
Onde o Reis foi visitar	Where the Kings went to visit
Jesus de Maria e José.	Jesus of Mary and Joseph.
O *C* é a caminhada	The *C* is the trek [caminhada]
Dos Magos do Oriente.	Of the Magi of the Orient.
Visitaram Deus Menino,	They visited the God-Child,
Nosso Rei Onipotente.	Our Omnipotent King.
. . . .	. . . .
Já cumpri minha missão	I have completed my mission
Neste momento presente.	At this present moment.
Maestro, agora canta	Maestro, now sing
Pra passar pro arco da frente.	To move to the next arch.

The bastião was applauded enthusiastically for his performance. The arch was torn down, and the musicians moved forward to the next one. The estribilho began again, and Owaldir resumed the embaixada with three more verses. When he had completed his performance, he changed places with Zezo, who then took over the ritual leadership. Zezo performed five verses, and as the arch was demolished, the two front singers changed places once again, and Owaldir continued the embaixada at the final arch with a further five verses. Then he handed the limelight over to the other bastião, who proceeded to recite a prophecy, and the final arch was demolished. (See plate 17.)

The companhia then moved into the house, where a further four verses were performed, before the attendants proceeded with the terço. As soon as they finished the prayer, one of the bastião called out the traditional vivas, and everyone clapped. Then the foliões started hugging each other, wishing one another a happy Kings' Day. This moment was reminiscent of what one expects when the clock strikes midnight at a New Year's Eve party among close friends. For foliões the annual cycle begins and ends with the last "amen" of the rosary at the arrival. Normally, the end of the rosary would signal the start of the festival, but because it was known that it would be difficult for the community to go to São Caetano, there would be no festival that year, and the proceeds of the companhia's journey were to be given to a local children's play group.

CHAPTER EIGHT

Dona Mariinha's journey, however, did culminate in a festival, which was held in a large hall at her workplace in Baeta Neves. Thus, it is this festival which I shall now describe.

At around 7:00 P.M. the foliões began congregating at the hall, but it was still locked, and someone had to be sent to find the key, which took nearly an hour. As more and more people arrived, there were many who had not received the companhia in their homes because they lived in distant neighborhoods, and they had come with the hope that the foliões would sing for them during the festival, as was their custom. To fulfill these obligations—and to keep themselves busy—the foliões began to sing for one community member after another. Once inside the building, the blessings continued until around 9:30 P.M. They stopped only when the northeastern *forró* ensemble that had been contracted to provide the music for the social dancing had set up and was ready to play.[2] The dance (*baile*) lasted until around 2:30 A.M., when the musicians packed up their instruments to leave. By that time the number of people in the hall had dwindled, but it was not until around 4:00 A.M. that the hall was finally locked up again.

Throughout the dance the lights were left on, and though there was couple dancing, most dancers maintained a respectable distance from their partners. Moreover, during a good part of the evening the "hat game" was played. In the hat game, one partnerless man begins by roaming about among the dancing couples wearing a hat. When he finds a woman with whom he would like to dance, he places the hat on the head of the man dancing with her, and takes his place as the woman's new partner. Then this man sets off to pass the hat to another dancer, so that dancing partners continuously shift. Whoever had the hat tended to search out established couples; a man dancing with his wife or—even better—a young man dancing with his girlfriend were the favored targets. This encouraged people to dance with many different partners, and even couples who had not been broken up by the hat frequently exchanged partners with other couples they met on the dance floor. This generated considerable interaction among the dancers, integrating people of all ages into the game, while giving the event a familial atmosphere of respectability.

At the far end of the hall there were sandwiches and other snacks as well as soft drinks and beer. The amount of food available was astounding, and Dona Mariinha said she and her female relatives and neighbors had been preparing it all week. All around the hall groups of people engaged in conversation. Among the foliões, the privileged topic was the highlight of their journey—the three days they spent in Arceburgo—and they discussed it thoroughly among themselves and recounted details of the trip to other community members. People with connections to Arceburgo inquired about the well-being of relatives and friends there, and together they reminisced about their former rural life. Throughout the evening people assessed the journey and the festival, which were judged a great success. The leadership of the group claimed that there had been around five hundred people at the festival, the largest event the companhia had ever staged.

Performance and Festivity

The arrival of the banner is the high point of the journey, and considerable time and energy are expended by the festeiro and his family to make their festival memorable. Similarly, the companhia goes to great lengths to present a good show. Indeed, the arrival is divided into two distinct sections: one focuses upon the companhia as a performance group and the other upon the generosity of the festeiro. The companhia begins with a ritual performance in front of the festeiro's house, that is, in full view of the community; then the festival proper begins, in which the goods accumulated by the companhia are consumed collectively. Although, as we have seen, some companhias conduct the two sections in different venues, they are conceived of jointly, and most companhias continue to hold them in succession at the festeiro's home; immediately after the ritual performance the festival begins, in which there should be an abundance of food and drink, and possibly music for social dancing. (See plate 18.) Although this binary structure was evident in every arrival I observed, no two events were the same, nor could they be, given the fluidity of social life. Indeed, different companhias follow different norms, their members and constituencies live under different conditions, and they have different levels of resources at their disposal.

The festivals promoted by the Folia do Zé Machado, for example, were known in the neighborhood for their generosity, since the group's owner spent the whole year fattening up a pig to feed his guests. It was, therefore, always very well attended. Of all the festivals in São Bernardo, his had the most "rural" feel about them, since his house was set in a large yard surrounded by woods (*mato*), a vegetable garden, and yard animals. Moreover, the house was large, which allowed people to congregate in several different settings, each with a distinct atmosphere. As is common to many rural festivals, the arrival ceremonies for this group began with the "raising of the flagpoles" (*levantamento dos mastros*) for the Three Kings and Saint Sebast-

CHAPTER EIGHT

ian in his front yard. Then the companhia sang in front of each of the flag-poles to honor the saints. When they completed their performance, the festival began.

Women congregated in the kitchen, where the food was being prepared, and the men engaged in conversation, scattered about the property in small groups, while children ran about the house and yard as they pleased. (See plate 19.) Once the food was ready, the women started serving it, and people ate as plates and cutlery became available. At the festival in 1988 there were several different musical activities going on simultaneously: in the front room Wanderley had set up a record player for people to dance, in the front yard two young men engaged in a musical duel accompanying themselves on tambourines, and in one of the bedrooms members of the Folia do Zé dos Magos were performing música sertaneja. By around 1:00 A.M. people had dispersed and the festival was over.

For the Folia do Seu Alcides in 1988 the festival centered on the ritual performance, which was conducted with considerable attention to detail and dramatic effect. As in the arrival described previously, there were several bamboo arches to be "sung," and each of them was decorated with a paper chain, which also called for special verses. When the companhia finally arrived at the crib, the embaixador led the ensemble in an extensive adoration. The performance attracted many people from the neighborhood, which indicated Alcides's prestige as a ritual healer. After the rosary one cup of coffee and half a sandwich were offered to everyone in attendance. After receiving their food, most people left the scene, and no festival as such took place. The contrast between the display of ritual savoir faire during the arrival and the material poverty that followed was striking. Alcides was the poorest of the ritual leaders in São Bernardo, and he also circulated in an area of very limited economic wealth, so his companhia collected only small donations at each visitation. Two weeks after the arrival, however, he offered a lunch to the foliões (but not their families), which included a plate full of rice, a few beans, manioc flour, and a very small piece of meat.

The binary structure of the arrival divides the event into two complementary halves: in the first there is a celebration of the community's "symbolic capital" (after Bourdieu 1977), and this is followed by the redistribution of their material potential. Because it is public, foliões conduct their arrivals as elaborate displays of ritual know-how, which exploit to the full the pageantry and theatricality of the tradition. For the arrival of the Folia do Baeta in 1987, Geraldinho had prepared his front yard to receive the ensemble, erecting bamboo arches decorated with inscriptions, and he had devised an ingenious way of pulling a star from one arch to the next for the Kings to follow in reaching the crib in the front room. The companhia had put on their bright new uniforms for the occasion, the only time during that journey in which they had worn them. The versatility of the group's membership was displayed, in that two embaixadores performed in succession, and each of the bastião was given space to demonstrate his art.

In displaying their ability to defend their banner through a public performance at the arrival, the foliões also proclaim their adherence to the moral principles for which it stands. By extension, the audience in attendance marks their identification with the Kings' moral order, which is embodied in the companhia's performance. Thus, through the display of their "symbolic capital," the faithful mark their membership in the moral community circumscribed by the ritual journey. The festival, the event that unites all the families visited by the banner, celebrates the transubstantiation of the blessings into displays of generosity, and it is the collective consumption of these donations that defines the community as a familial congregation of humans. In other words, the festival is the celebration of a moral order, which permits the preservation of human life.

While ritual journeys in the city are essentially the same as those in the rural areas, the "family" united at arrivals emphasizes the origin of the members of the ensemble and that of the households they visit. As we have seen, urban companhias tend to be made up of fellow townsmen and other migrants from neighboring regions. The members of the Folia do Baeta, for example, come predominantly from Guaranésia, Guaxupé, and Arceburgo, three neighboring towns in the south of Minas Gerais, and the Folia do Zé dos Magos congregates fellow townsmen from the regions surrounding Monsenhor Paulo. Likewise, urban companhias tend to visit families who also migrated from their towns of origin, though they also visit other families, such as neighbors or people they met at work, who come from other places. On the whole, though, these people also tend to be migrants who participated in folia rituals or other popular Catholic traditions in their hometowns. Indeed, the very notion of fellow townsmanship can be extremely elastic, progressively encompassing an ever-expanding territory, moving from town to region to state and, finally, to "the interior"; even this category can be transcended to encompass any member of the lower classes who claims to honor the Kings.[3]

Urban journeys, then, constitute privileged contexts for the construction of a sense of subaltern identity, articulated through a regional tradition with rural associations. What unites the participants transcends geographically defined locations; rather, it is a shared ethos based on the widely diffused moral tenets of popular Catholicism. The festival congregates a community of urban poor whose shared worldview allows them to see themselves as a moral community wedged within a greater urban society marked by impersonal and asymmetrical social relations and class and racial discrimination. The annual reunion celebrates personalized bonds of solidarity, which migrants and the urban poor alike have come to associate with the rural context. These bonds are articulated through the metaphor of the family, which implies a commitment to the mutual obligations entailed in family relations.

Most companhias restrict their ritual activities to their own neighborhoods, and therefore they have little visibility outside their immediate social spheres. Even in small rural communities, where generally the existence of folias is known to the local elites, few of them have a sense of how these groups operate. In large urban centers, on the other hand, it is very rare for members of the upper and middle classes ever consciously to have heard one of these ensembles, and most are surprised to hear that they can be found anywhere within the metropolitan areas, imagining them to be folkloric relics on the verge of extinction. Since they are associated with folklore, the idea of folias de reis elicits nostalgic sentiments among the upper classes, and this glosses them with a veneer of naive caipira innocence. In James Scott's (1990) terms, then, one could say that the folklorization of the tradition has given it an effective disguise for infrapolitical activity. Classed as quaint and innocuous, companhias are not seen to pose a threat to the status quo, and they can be left unattended by both state and church; their perceived innocence safeguards their autonomy.

In his study of the "weapons of the weak," Scott (1985, 1990) has emphasized such covert activities as foot-dragging, sabotage, fantasies of revenge, and other forms of negative resistance. The infrapolitical realm, however, is also marked by positive strategies aimed at reclaiming self-esteem, and this is particularly marked in such popular Catholic traditions as the folia de reis. As we have seen, companhias circulate in peripheral neighborhoods on the margins of a wider society marked by class and racial prejudice, and the daily lives of their constituencies are punctuated by constant assaults upon their dignity. While folias de reis may not provide platforms for open political action, in the infrapolitical realm of everyday forms of resistance they do carve out spaces for the reassertion of self-worth among their participants, giving them greater confidence to confront society from the condition of subalternity. Through their tradition, the embodiment of their "moral capital," folia communities reconstitute themselves as moral communities amid the perversity of their social exclusion. By fueling their sense of moral integrity, they become better equipped to confront—head high—the daily humiliations that punctuate their lives. Shielded behind the veil of harmlessness of their traditions, they are free to conduct their performances, continuously rekindling their sense of self-esteem.

Visibility

Like most folias de reis, the Folia do Baeta pursues its musical activities primarily within the confines of its own neighborhood, far from the view of the dominant classes. During the 1980s, however, the companhia gained numerous opportunities for public presentations which gave them greater visibility within the municipality of São Bernardo. This projection generated greater interest in the activity among the members of the group, giving them a renewed sense of pride in their cultural heritage; it increased their prestige within their own community; and it attracted many young second- and third-generations migrants back into the group, particularly during the period in which the LP was being recorded.

Their sense of achievement was at its height during their 1987/88 journey, giving them much to celebrate that year. Even though their presentation outside Dona Mariinha's house was thwarted by the forces of nature, it did not affect their festival, which was still being remembered when I last encountered members of the group in 1994. The ensemble had accumulated more funds than usual, much of it a consequence of the production of their first LP. Extra funds had been generated through sales of the record; to promote the LP the Department of Culture had arranged a number of public presentations for the group, and for most of them they had received a small check; as their visibility within the municipality increased, they also attracted patronage, particularly from local politicians, who took it upon themselves to cover different aspects of the group's expenses. Besides the production of the LP, the foliões had spent three days during the journey circulating in Arceburgo, finally fulfilling their dream of returning to their hometown as an ensemble. These achievements created an atmosphere of euphoria and an enhanced sense of self-esteem within the ensemble, which marked the event as special for the whole community.

According to the foliões, their projection into the wider community began when the local government created the Centre for Folklore Research in 1980, under the coordination of Antônio Perez. Soon after its foundation

CHAPTER EIGHT

Perez proceeded to contact all the "folkloric groups" (*grupos folclóricos*) that existed in São Bernardo, collecting artifacts of all sorts for a permanent exhibition of local folklore, which opened in 1984 in the Casarão da Chácara Silvestre, a lovely old mansion in an isolated neighborhood. Perez also set about reorganizing the municipal Christmas celebrations to include a "folk" participation and arranged to have all the local companhias perform before the municipal crèche in the town plaza. For their efforts each group received an instrument of their choice and strings for some of the instruments they already had. From then on their participation in the event was institutionalized, and instead of payment in kind, they began to receive a small check to use as they saw fit.

From the very beginning Perez took a special interest in the Folia do Baeta, and he convinced the local newspaper, *Diário do Grande ABC,* to send someone to write a story about their activities. The reporter interviewed the leadership of the ensemble and followed the companhia on a few visitations. In early January 1984, one whole page in the cultural section of the newspaper was dedicated to the companhia, including pictures of the ensemble and the members' names. From then on Perez began arranging presentations for them around town, at such venues as schools and clubs. Zezo told his colleagues in the Metalworkers' Union about the companhia's activities, and when a group of Germans came to visit asking to see some local culture, the union leaders invited the companhia to perform for them. This was the event the foliões remembered as the time they had been filmed; moreover, the film would be taken abroad, giving them international recognition—even though not everyone knew for sure where Germany was. In time, the Folia do Baeta was being invited to perform for all major street events promoted by the municipal government in which it was felt that a "folkloric" presentation was appropriate, such as the annual St. Christopher's cart-and-buggy procession, the celebrations for the anniversary of the town, or neighborhood "sertanejo festivals" (*festivais sertanejos*), dedicated primarily to the performance of música sertaneja.

Emboldened by the visibility they were achieving within the municipality, the group's leadership began to openly seek out politicians and others who they thought might be interested in promoting the group. It was from within the group itself that the idea of the LP emerged, probably influenced by the generalized notion among *duplas sertanejas* (duos that perform música sertaneja) that one's popularity is guaranteed once one has made a record (see Martins 1975, 121). Having decided to embark upon this project, toward the end of 1985 Owaldir and Zezo made their way to the Department of Culture for the first time to see if they could gain their support. Finally, after several such visits, the secretary of culture suggested they make a demonstration tape to be studied by a committee, which would assess its viability. After countless visits to various offices in the Department of Culture and to several town representatives who were thought to be sympathetic to their cause, the LP was finally approved, recorded, and produced just before Christmas of 1987. It was launched during the official municipal Christmas ceremony in front of the town hall with the presence and participation of all the local companhias.

Eager to publicize their production, local government officials arranged to have the ensemble perform on a folklore program produced by TV Cultura, the government-sponsored television station. In the end their contribution was edited out of the final broadcast because the producers decided the sound quality of the recording had not been of a high enough standard to be put on the air. The problem was that there had not been enough microphones for all the voices and instruments to achieve proper balance, a problem that has affected every staged presentation of a folia de reis I have ever observed. Even though the sound technicians had arranged around ten microphones for the performance, they probably would have needed around twenty-five or more to get an adequate recording. The foliões, however, were baffled by their exclusion from the program, since normally they were lucky if they had four or five microphones for their public presentations.

By this time organized folia gatherings known as *encontros* (encounters) had become popular throughout southeastern Brazil. Unlike traditional folia encounters these gatherings were being promoted annually as cultural events by the municipal governments of small interior towns and consisted of numerous ensembles of the same type, such as processional bands, school marching bands (*fanfarras*), or choirs, each representing its own municipality, and they performed in turn for all the others. While generally such encounters have been geared toward the musical expressions of rural polite society (i.e., processional bands, fanfarras, and choirs), some municipalities have begun turning to the cultural manifestations of the lower classes, particularly the folia de reis tradition, in which thirty or more companhias are brought to perform successively upon a stage. As soon as the leaders of the Folia do Baeta found out where such an event was going to be held, they set off to the Department of Culture in an attempt to secure a municipal bus to take the folia there. By the early 1990s they were participating in two or three such gatherings each year. The municipality agreed to fund these trips, since

CHAPTER EIGHT

local officials saw them as an ideal way of promoting the LP. Indeed, the foliões set off on their trips with several copies of the record, and they rarely had problems selling them. When they returned from one such trip in 1992 they were elated when they told me how a bastião in one of the companhias had recited word for word the prophecy from their LP during their stage performance. This was seen as an indication of how widely known the group had become.

Patronage

Several researchers, such as Brandão (1981, 117–24), Marcos Ayala (1987), and Rowe and Schelling (1991, 83–84), have noted that state institutions and politicians are playing an increasingly central role in the promotion of what are called "folk groups" in the country. With the decline in the old-style patriarchal landowners, and with them their patronage in large parish-wide patron saint festivals, the performance space for popular Catholic ensembles, particularly congados and moçambiques, was becoming ever more restricted.[4] The concept of folklore as a repository of national and regional heritage has been quite well established in Brazil since the early twentieth century (see Reily 1994a; Rowe and Schelling 1991, 3–6), making these traditions worth preserving, if only as tourist attractions and sources for museum artifacts and compositional elements for the artistic world. When defined in national and regional terms, their conservation becomes a state affair, and indeed the state, in its various permutations from the local to the national levels, has set about "inventing traditions" (after Hobsbawm and Ranger 1983), such as folklore festivals and gatherings, through which the country's rich cultural heritage is to be safeguarded. These inventions, however, often also serve populist objectives, by creating safe frames for politically incorporating—and controlling—the lower sectors of society.

It should come as no surprise, therefore, that generally social scientists have taken ambiguous stances toward the state's patronage of "folklore," or, in their terms, popular culture. Besides objecting to the political capital thought to be made off the presumed innocence of the popular groups, they often argue that events organized by state cultural administrators interfere with the "authenticity" of the performances, as those responsible for organizing them do so in accordance with their own criteria, disregarding the religious and symbolic content of the presentations. Be that as it may, it is highly unlikely that under the current conditions within Brazilian society a "folk group" emerging from the subaltern classes could achieve a degree of visibility without patrons in influential positions. Moreover, the degree and character of the so-called interferences vary considerably from one context to the next, as do the dynamics of the groups subjected—and who subject themselves—to them. And finally, patronage is in no way a one-way street; after all, the Folia do Baeta made no objection to accepting the mediation of a local candidate, but once in the ballot box they followed their own political inclinations.

Foliões make clear distinctions between their journeys—ritual events that are undertaken as an expression of their devotion to the Three Kings—and their public presentations (*apresentações*), in which they demonstrate the tradition to a wider public in a somewhat more secular context. On the whole, they welcome the attention they receive from cultural sponsors as confirmation of the intrinsic value of their tradition, and receiving invitations for public presentations enhances the groups' prestige within their own communities. While program organizers may distort the symbolic meanings of folia performances by placing them on a stage (with far too few microphones to go around), the foliões often find the means of resignifying these event in terms of their own value systems.

In Batatais, São Paulo, in 1989, for example, I attended my first folia gathering, which was held in a large, open rodeo enclosure. In turn each companhia made its way to the stage to perform to the thinnest of audiences. But this was not the only singing going on: all around the venue there were clusters of people surrounding other companhias, waiting their turn to take the banner and be blessed. There were at least as many people surrounding each of these groups as there were people in the audience for the "official" presentations.[5]

According to Brandão (1981, 119), the dilemma facing popular Catholic religious groups is finding ways to preserve sufficient autonomy to safeguard the sacredness of their tradition while also accepting a degree of external control to guarantee their survival. This being the case, it would appear that the foliões at the gathering described above managed to accomplish a reconciliation of this dilemma quite successfully. In fact, it could be argued that their success was predicated upon a *partial* subversion of the structure established by the organizers: even though they were well aware of the lack of audience interest in their stage performances, none of the ensembles refused to take their turns as instructed. According to one embaixador at the event, "We had to sing. It was our obligation. The man invited us here, so we had to sing for him." Thus, for this folião—and probably

CHAPTER EIGHT

many others—the stage performance was interpreted as reciprocation for the opportunity to travel to the gathering. It is worth noting, however, that this stance also ensured that the organizers would not feel antagonized. After fulfilling their "obligations" toward the officials, the foliões and their audience proceeded to redefine the event, transforming it into a ritual space, over which they maintained considerable control.

Foliões, therefore, are hardly passive and innocent bystanders in the hands of powerful administrators. Indeed, once they had been "discovered," so to speak, the Folia do Baeta no longer sat back waiting to be "invited" by local officials for presentations; rather, they began to actively seek them out, demanding public space to present their cultural capital. And more, they began accompanying their demands with stipulations. For example, the group members requested and designed two of the uniforms that were donated to them. During the negotiations over the LP, the Department of Culture tried to get them to accept an EP, which would have been much cheaper to produce. The group leaders said this would be unacceptable and continued demanding the LP that had already been approved by the council anyway, and even then they felt they had to cut down their performance quite a bit so it would fit in the allotted forty-two minutes.

In 1987 the Folia do Baeta spearheaded a campaign among the companhias in the municipality to boycott the annual Christmas ceremony at the town hall. Even though the other groups had also resented what had occurred the previous year, they were at first uneasy about participating in the boycott, because this was one of the few events they could count on being invited to each year, and they looked forward to the public recognition it conferred upon them. In 1986 the groups had been scheduled to sing at the manger scene at the same time at which, at the other end of the square, there was jazz dancing going on to the accompaniment of blaring music, which was not only considered disrespectful toward the Kings, but also drowned out the companhias' performances. Moreover, while the last group was still singing, Santa Claus arrived in a helicopter, and it was too much to expect a folia de reis to be able to compete with that. As a result of their mobilization, they were scheduled to be the first attraction at the ceremony, and the event was also used to launch the new LP. Thus, as the Folia do Baeta achieved greater visibility within the municipality, its leaders gained in confidence, which better enabled them to negotiate the contours of their projection.

When Zezo left the group in 1990, the companhia's public appearances began to decline. In comparison with his peers, Zezo was far less intimidated by the threat of a slight from government representatives. Though less assertive than Zezo in dealing with state officials, Owaldir continued to maintain contacts with the Department of Culture, and when I last met with members of the group, the Folia do Baeta was still the most visible of the local companhias, actively participating in folia gatherings throughout the state. Owaldir had, therefore, acquired new negotiating skills over the years and remained committed to preserving the privileged position of the Folia do Baeta within the local cultural scene.

Previously I argued that the folklorization of the folia de reis tradition provides foliões with a safe cover, protecting them from external surveillance. But actually its impact has been even greater than this: with the folklorization of their tradition, foliões have been afforded a means of expanding their performance spheres outside their immediate communities. Now that they have been defined as folklore—that is, as a national and regional heritage—the preservation of such popular Catholic traditions as the folia de reis has been placed squarely upon the shoulders of the state. If the state is to do its job, its representatives have to negotiate the terms of their "invented traditions" with "folk" performers, even though their position gives them the upper hand in these negotiations.

Given the stark asymmetry in the power relations between state representatives and "folk" performers, foliões and their peers in other popular Catholic traditions wishing to integrate the "invented folk traditions" circuit must adopt strategies which preserve their nonthreatening air of innocence, a cover which the state itself has helped to create: it is from the safety provided by the folklorization of their traditions that foliões and the members of other popular Catholic communities have been able to participate in defining the contours of the public events in which they participate. The perceived harmlessness of the traditions gives the practitioners greater scope to assert their demands, be it indirectly through their actions, or more boldly, through direct verbal requisitions. In fact, veiled by common Catholic motifs articulated through "simple," "rustic" expressive forms, during their public performances foliões and their peers are even able to give voice to their critiques of the immorality of a system which marginalizes them in full view of the very seat of power. Indeed, annually all five companhias in São Bernardo perform their adorations before the manger scene in front of the town hall.

During their journey of 1987/88 the Folia do Baeta was even able to negotiate state sponsorship for their ritual activity, bypassing altogether a state-organized event. Indeed, from the foliões' point of view the absolute high point in the golden age of the ensemble occurred during the three days

CHAPTER EIGHT

they spent as a companhia in their hometown. After extensive negotiations, their trip was jointly sponsored by the municipalities of São Bernado and Arceburgo.

Arceburgo

The bus provided by the Department of Culture to take the Folia do Baeta Neves to Arceburgo parked in front of Owaldir's house at around 10:00 A.M. on 31 December 1987, and about an hour later it was ready to depart carrying the foliões and as many of their relatives as possible. They also took a stack of copies of their first album, which was hot off the press. The five-hour drive was broken by two stops: the first one for a snack at the halfway point; the second at the last garage before reaching the town. Here the foliões changed into their new uniforms to make their grand entrance.

Back on the bus Zezo made a short speech; it was formulated as a message to the children and adolescents, but many of the foliões perceived its primary target to be those members in the group who might have been thinking about spending time in the local bars. He told the children that the companhia was representing São Bernardo, and it was important for everyone to show how "orderly" their group was. People in the interior, he said, often see the violence of São Paulo on television, and they think that people in the city lose their religion; they were there to show that this was not the case. Anyone who misbehaved, he warned them, would be letting the whole group down.

It was late afternoon by the time they reached the roundabout leading into Arceburgo. It was here that the bus stopped to let everyone out. The mayor and a few other local authorities were there to meet them, as were relatives and other members of the community. After the greetings everyone moved in procession to the central plaza, and the companhia began to sing, making its way to the municipal crèche in front of the church. Owaldir performed an extended adoration followed by prophecies from the two bastião. Then the group went to the local school for a dinner sponsored by the Arceburgo prefecture, and the rest of the evening was free, to allow the foliões to visit their relatives and friends. That very evening all the LPs they had brought sold out, and Zezo started taking names of people who wanted the album, which he promised to bring on his next trip.

The next day the foliões wore their red uniforms to conduct their visitations in the town. Pousos had been arranged at the homes of relatives, and the foliões outwardly marveled at the reception they were given. The highlight of the day, however, was their "friendly encounter" with a local companhia, which attracted a large audience. In song the two embaixadores openly congratulated one another on the "beauty" of their companhias, affirming they were both on the same journey with the same devotion. Jointly they negotiated the event so as to extract the maximum in manifestations of mutual deference. In the embaixada Owaldir instructed his foliões to kiss their rival's banner, which they did, one by one, and after that they each greeted the group's embaixador by shaking his hand; the other embaixador then called upon his foliões to reciprocate the gesture. When they had completed the "kissing," they resumed their singing, reiterating their common mission and their mutual obligations to the Three Kings. Then they thanked each other and wished one another good journeys. When the singing finally stopped, the foliões from both groups engaged in conversation for a while before continuing their visitations.

On their last day the foliões were back in their white and green uniforms to proceeded with visitations until lunchtime, and immediately after the pouso they packed up their belongings to make their trip home. There seemed to be little doubt in any of their minds that theirs was the best companhia in Arceburgo that year. First, they agreed that none of the local companhias had nice uniforms like theirs; there was one companhia in which the musicians did wear the same shirt, but it was made out of a cheap, flowery material that was thought better suited to the clowns. Their "orderly" presentation extended to their musical performances, which were shown to be clearly enunciated (after all, no one could understand what the rival embaixador at the encounter had said); it was obvious to them that their instruments were of better quality; and they also considered it self-evident that their singing was the best, since too many of the local musicians were visibly drunk. The fact that "everyone" in Arceburgo wanted a copy of their LP was taken as proof of their superior performances. Although they saw their performances as more orderly and organized than those of the companhias in Arceburgo, they praised the local community for their great respect for the folia tradition, lamenting that in São Bernardo they could not expect to be received in every household and did not experience the same level of generosity at visitations.

By comparing their own ensemble to those of their hometown, the members of the Folia do Baeta engaged in assessing the success of their migration, their style of performance serving as the yardstick. The exercise permitted them to forge a positive image of themselves, which, like their music, combined the "best of both worlds." Insofar as their performances had become more organized and "cleaner" than those of the rural groups, so had they; similarly, since the language in their verses has become more grammatical and sophisticated, it reflected upon them, allowing them to see themselves as more "cultured" and better educated. These elements, then, stood as evidence of the process of social ascent they viewed themselves undergoing, or at least toward which they aspired, as a consequence of migration. Yet by maintaining a rural tradition grounded in a moral system that focuses on generosity and mutual obligations, they could also make a parallel statement about themselves: despite their social ascent, they could claim to have evaded contamination by the individualism, greed, and selfishness prevailing in the metropolitan context. Their performances, then, allowed them to aesthetically reconcile their aspirations of social ascent with their popular Catholic ethos, proudly constituting themselves as both morally sound and modern, reasserting their self-esteem in their continuous struggle to preserve their dignity.

While the results of the modernizing efforts of the Folia do Baeta enhanced the self-esteem of its members, they were implicated also in the group's success outside their own community. As we have seen, soon after Perez took up his post as municipal folklorist he singled out the Folia do Baeta for special attention from among the five companhias in São Bernardo. In all likelihood he was attracted by the "orderliness" of the group and the greater "complexity" of their musical style in relation to the other companhias: they employed eight voices rather than just six. Furthermore, their adorations and prophesies were longer and more elaborate than those of other groups, which the folklorist took as a sign of the group's greater authenticity, assuming it meant that less of the "original" script had been lost over time. Moreover, the majority of the members of the Folia do Baeta were somewhat better off financially than their peers in the other ensembles, and their neighborhood was far more domesticated, and thus less threatening, than the favelas in which some of the other groups lived and circulated. Likewise, alcohol consumption was curbed more effectively among its members, they dressed more tidily, and they were more experienced in relating to members of the upper and middle classes. All in all, then, they seemed to have been further along on the continuum of the "civilizing process." From the state representatives' perspective, this facilitated their negotiations with the ensemble, while their "product"—in opposition to that of their peers—could be more easily transposed to a stage setting: it was still sufficiently quaint to parade as folklore, yet sufficiently "orderly" not to offend urban aesthetic values. Just as the Folia do Baeta attracted the attention of state cultural administrators in São Bernardo, the ensembles commonly invited to participate in gatherings and folk festivals are those that have invested most heavily in their own "modernization." Indeed, the "modern folk" groups have become the hallmark of the state's "invented traditions" throughout southeastern Brazil.

During the journey of 1987/88 enthusiasm within the Folia do Baeta was at a height. In celebrating their arrival that year, their sense of achievement was hardly disguised. That year the members of the group suddenly had seen themselves as more than just gardeners, janitors, or watchmen for some big company, more than bricklayers at a construction site, more than one in thousands of other machine operators at one of the municipality's large multinationals. They had become performers who had almost appeared on television; they had made a record; they were being invited to perform at various events, even outside of São Bernardo; they were being interviewed by people from the university who were writing books about them (myself); the same owners of the companies for which they worked were giving them uniforms and financing ceremonial dinners for them. For a few moments they were being pulled out of the anonymity of their daily lives to be placed under the spotlight of the whole municipality, where they were being recognized publicly for their special abilities. Moreover, the foliões felt they were being valued not only by people of their own community, but also by certain members of the upper classes, that is, by people of the classes who usually just ignored them, if they did not humiliate them outright. For once they were being recognized for that which they valued, and they were being contacted for what they could show those who generally set themselves up as the instructors. This inversion in the "normal" relational structure boosted their self-esteem, increasing their success in negotiations with state officials. Indeed, that year the Folia do Baeta had much to celebrate.

CHAPTER IX

Visions

J UST AS THE KINGS RETURNED from Bethlehem singing from house
to house to enchant God's vision into the world, several thousand companhias de reis throughout southeastern Brazil continue this mission each
year. Even though there are differences in the mythic material and the ritual
practices of the companhias, certain elements of the journey have remained
stable throughout the region: when a folia confronts a manger scene, the
musicians pay homage to the sacred figures; during visitations they distribute the blessings of the Three Kings to the members of the household in exchange for donations; all folias end their journeys by redistributing the
goods they have collected along the way through a communal celebration or
by donating them to charity. Through their visitations, folias de reis weave
their way through the community, stringing together the various families in
their neighborhoods to create a greater family, the existence of which is confirmed annually at the festival of the arrival.

If the ritual process of the journey is viewed as a whole, one could say that
folias sing first to the Holy Family represented in the manger scene; then
they sing to the components of the nuclear family, the human representation
of the sacred unit; to complete the cycle, the journey culminates in a large
festival uniting all the faithful in a celebration of the family of God on earth.
Thus, the journey itself echoes the crescendo of the mineiro style: as each
nuclear family is linked to the Holy Family, it simultaneously becomes integrated into the community of the faithful; like the final chord of the toada,

the community joins to form a harmonious whole for the festival, united by its collective devotion to the saints.

Catholicisms

Catholicism is constituted as a moral religious system with a legal orientation: natural law—or God's law—is defined in ethical terms, and a world governed by this order is represented as a just world; heaven, the sphere of the sacred, is detached from the domain of humanity, which protects the divine moral tenets from the temporality and unpredictability of the human world. To lay claim to the universality of its "truths," "official" Catholicism has striven to codify and standardize its dogmas and ritual practices into a prescribed global "orthodoxy." Yet, as Goody (1986) has noted, the inscription of standardized doctrine often produces an ever-widening gap between the orthodox and people's daily lives, and this frequently leads activities within the official religious institution to elide into unenthusiastic rote enactments of prescribed liturgies (Bell 1992, 137; Whitehouse 1995). Alongside the official church, however, countless vernacular permutations of Catholicism have proliferated over the centuries, resignifying the orthodox precepts in terms of localized conditions.

In Brazil, popular Catholic traditions probably emerged with the first Portuguese settlers. On arriving in the New World, they often found themselves far from any priests to celebrate mass and dispense the sacraments. To fulfill their religious needs, they drew upon their own resources, constructing lay communities organized around the devotion to particular popular saints. Although the church expanded during the colonial era, affecting popular Catholic traditions to a greater or lesser extent, depending upon their proximity to urban centers, it was only in the late nineteenth century that the church was separated from the state, acquiring sufficient independence to embark upon the Romanization of the institution. Since the primary targets of this program were the members of polite society, the urban poor and the peasantry remained marginal to the church's civilizing onslaught, and they continued to organize their day-to-day religious activities in lay associations on the fringes of society, limiting their employment of church officials almost exclusively to such fundamental sacraments as baptisms, marriages, and funerals. Within their own organizations, these lay communities could negotiate their sense of morality and their ritual practices in face-to-face interactions with one another, drawing on the immediacy of their everyday experiences. By continuously re-creating and resignifying the motifs of their tradition, they kept the gap between daily life and religious doctrine narrow, hindering the reification of popular Catholic worldviews into standardized scripts. Thus, the construction of ritual spaces accompanied the devotees' ever-changing notions of the moral integrity of the sacred, and ritual participation could be constituted as a means of experiencing a world governed by God's natural laws.

At a fundamental level, however, the doctrinal basis of popular Catholicism is in consonance with that of the orthodox church. Although the notion of "original sin" is rarely integrated into popular Catholic religious discourse, humanity is represented as being "naturally" oriented toward self-centeredness and nonreciprocation. But the popular Catholic understanding of this conceptual framework is predicated upon the experience of subalternity in a highly segregated class society. In the folia tradition, the consequences of unbridled human tendencies are vividly portrayed in the figure of King Herod, whose nonreciprocal orientation promotes social asymmetry and, ultimately, the end of life. The Three Kings, however, embody the supreme value of reciprocity: by exchanging material goods for music they created a context for reenchanting essential human equality and social harmony into the world. Thus, the continuity of life requires the subjugation of one's human orientations to the moral order of the saints. The bastião, however, demonstrate that human imperfection limits the degree to which human urges can be domesticated; at most one can strive to become a moral human being by affirming one's commitment to uphold the divine truths. However orthodox folia narratives may be in their representation of human nature, the stories themselves diverge from official versions. Furthermore, many popular Catholic rituals are conducted with little or no interference from the clergy. In their own autonomous spaces, popular Catholic communities carve out hidden niches in which they reclaim a sense of dignity by affirming their moral integrity, placing themselves in opposition to the privileged sectors of society.

Anthropological literature on religion has typically represented religious systems in terms of dichotomies: on the one hand, the official, inscribed, and rationalized religions that articulate with the prevailing power structures; on the other, the vernacular, oral, and fluid systems of peripheral resistance.[1] According to Harvey Whitehouse (1995, 193–99), these oppositions might be more fruitfully viewed in terms of the cognitive impact different religious systems have upon their followers, and he distinguishes between two basic modes of religiosity: the standardized and routinized "doctrinal mode," typical of centralized institutions, that strives to persuade through intellectual argument; and the episodic and highly flexible "imagistic mode," common to localized vernacular traditions, that is predicated upon the promotion of sensual stimulation and loosely qualified affective experiences.

Brazilian popular Catholic religiosity, however, does not sit comfortably at either of these poles; rather, it draws fairly equally from the characteristics of both paradigms: having been in existence for centuries, popular Catholic traditions are hardly episodic, but they are also not routinized, since their performances are generally concentrated at regular intervals on a annual basis; while popular Catholicism stands in opposition to the centralized official church, it is also conversant with it; furthermore, within each devotional tradition there is a certain uniformity to the ritual practices of localized communities across large geographical regions of the country, and the ethos of popular Catholicism articulates a subaltern moral code that is almost universal among the Brazilian lower classes throughout the country; many popular Catholic traditions have an elaborate doctrinal base, which is articulated through a fairly stable representational repertoire in both narrative and "imagistic" media, but they also build in significant spaces for the continuous incremental elaboration of sensual motifs that enhance their experiential value. This is hardly a case of two parallel modes of religiosity operating simultaneously: rather, popular Catholic traditions strive to promote experiences of cosmic wholeness that bridge the gap between intellectual imagination and bodily sensations.

That popular Catholic religiosity in Brazil escapes Whitehouse's model should come as no surprise; after all, it is rarely possible to fit "reality" into "ideal types," since "realities" are constructed by engaged social actors within historically constituted cultural spaces. It is also worth remembering that religious discourse is itself "imagistic," as it is typically constructed through allusive metaphorical language, or entextualizations, and this ambiguity is one of its major defenses against temporality, which is true both for the inscribed and highly rationalized religious systems and for vernacular forms of religiosity. Furthermore, human beings have bodies with sensory capacities; even if a religious system strives to emphasize its doctrinal rhetoric, the bodily sensations of the devotees accompany them wherever they are, regardless of how conscious they may be of them in any given situation. Indeed, the very attempt to neutralize bodily sensations creates its own type of bodily experience.

In effect, Whitehouse's perspective attempts to objectify and quantify the highly subjective experience of cognitive impact on the basis of the researcher's assessment of the balance between sensory stimulation and verbal exegesis employed in ritual performance. Yet what rings hollow to one person may be densely resonant to another. Therefore, any assessment of the cognitive impact of religious experience can be measured only contextually; although a particular ritual may be designed to promote certain types of experience, there is no guarantee that it will succeed, since the predisposition of the participants is directly implicated in ritual efficacy (Blacking 1985a).

Whitehouse's ethnographic data, however, make a significant contribution to the understanding of religiosity by pointing to the crucial role of affective experience in promoting commitment to religious truths. In his discussion of the Pomio Kivung movement of Papua New Guinea, he observed that the mainstream doctrinal organization relied on localized, episodic, and highly charged imagistic revival movements to reinvigorate religious sentiment among its followers. Having undergone powerful revelatory experiences during an episodic ritual setting, the faithful could continuously reinvoke the memory of these experiences during their routine religious activities, suffusing the doctrinal codes with dense personal resonances. In this way, the metaphorical language of the doctrinal representations became meaningful to the faithful, rekindling their religious fervor each time the revelatory experience was evinced.[2] Thus, Whitehouse's own ethnography demonstrates that what might appear to be a doctrinal mode of religiosity to the researcher can be experienced "imagistically" by the devotees. But this raises crucial questions: Where is one to locate the productive moment of religious persuasion? To what extent is the doctrinal mode dependent upon the imagistic mode, and vice versa?

Clearly, what is at issue is not a dichotomy between distinct modes of religiosity, but the role of affective experience in the construction of religious consciousness. Experience is intensely personal (see Bruner 1986), and it is constructed and interpreted by the individual through the associative resonances evinced in consciousness within a given situation, regardless of whether the ritual context is heavily oriented toward rhetorical discourse or loosely strung sensory motifs. The persuasive power of any religious doctrine is predicated upon its ability to provide a meaningful representational framework for the interpretation of experience. Just as doctrinal religions rely upon affective experiences to generate a sense of personal engagement with their rhetoric among their followers, imagistic movements that are unable to generate adequate representational frames for the interpretation of the sensory experiences they promote have little chance of long-term survival.

Every religious systems, then, must contend with the dialectic interaction between doctrinal representation and the life experiences of the followers, and this tension is crucial to placing a check upon struggles over the control of religious discourses and practices among ritual specialists. While official standardized religious systems with strong institutional bases may find it necessary to reinvigorate religious sentiment through occasional revival movements, even though they pose a potential threat to the authority of the clergy, established vernacular religious systems, like popular Catholicism in Brazil and other Latin American countries, owe their resilience to their ability to continuously renegotiate the ritual space, maintaining a degree of coherence between the representational repertoire of the traditions, the ritual experiences they promote, and the daily lives of the devotees.

Representations and Experience

As with other popular Catholic traditions in Brazil, in the folia de reis, centuries of sedimentation have produced a fairly widespread and stable ritual script to organize the collective drama, but this skeletal framework is continuously thickened through creative elaboration, as aesthetic motifs and practices drawn from various domains of experience are integrated into the archaeological mosaic of each performance. Just as the ritual space is constantly being pruned of extraneous motifs that detract from its coherence, new motifs are introduced in accordance with the changing lives and aspirations of the faithful. In this way the fit between the representational repertoire of the tradition and the experiential world of the faithful is readjusted within the ritual context, which enhances the density of associations invoked among the devotees during ritual performances.

This negotiation is conducted communally. Although popular Catholic communities depend upon leaders to organize collective activity, their recognition is predicated upon their ability to involve the faithful in the community's religious life. With the leaders' control of the religious space thus hindered, the ongoing discussion of religious representations and practices embraces a wide social sphere. In the folia de reis, everyone present has a role to play during ritual enactments. The foliões are, of course, the central agents of the tradition: the musicians are engaged in the music making, while the bastião have scripted parts that are often performed between musical performances, but during the music making they are kept busy by their dancing. The families visited by an ensemble also play an active role in ritual performance, and they are integrated directly into the ritual drama. The embaixador draws on his knowledge of the household to construct the verses of his embaixadas, integrating the family's story into the collective memory of the community. Throughout their journeys foliões and the families they visit maintain a continuous dialogue, collectively negotiating each situation in terms of the immediacy of the moment. When a household has made a special investment to receive the banner, the musicians respond by acknowledging their efforts, and together the parties engage in mutually confirming their devotion to the Kings. There are also less visible dimensions to the community's involvement in folia activities: the festival is produced with their donations; many families serve meals and snacks to the musicians along the way; large numbers of volunteers are mobilized by the festeiro to help organize the departure and the arrival ceremonies. By the end of a journey several hundred people will have contributed in one way or another toward its success, heightening their sense of involvement in the community's religious affairs.

The multiplicity of voices engaged in the negotiation of the tradition gives it considerable fluidity, and this conceals the potential impact the introduction of a new motif might come to have upon ritual performance. While isolated acts can be absorbed into the flow of the moment, over time the cumulative effect of the repetition of similar acts becomes apparent. Though it was once prevalent in the southeast, the paulista style is now almost obsolete, overhauled in favor of the more "modern" mineiro style. With urbanization, the move toward "orderliness" has become increasingly evident, articulating with changes in the aesthetic values and aspirations of migrant communities. Similarly, changes in the instrumentation have been taking place to accommodate current trends in musical tastes. Although donations in the form of goods to be consumed at the festival were once the norm, in urban areas today donations are made almost exclusively in the form of money, and this is also becoming more common in rural areas. To adapt to the work schedules of their constituencies under wage labor, very few companhias now engage in continuous journeys; most groups restrict their performances to evenings and weekends, returning home each night to sleep. This has made it more acceptable for women to participate in an ensemble, and their presence is becoming more visible.

As innovations acquire visibility, they often become the source of intense debate and contestation within folia communities. In time, however, their resonances with changing values and lifestyles begin to increase, and the tensions they once evoked start subsiding. Ultimately, the new trends find their place within the tradition, becoming integrated into its repertoire of motifs and practices. Folia narratives claim that the Kings received three instruments—a viola, a tambourine, and a caixa—suggesting that there was a time in which only these instruments were used within the tradition. With the emergence of such urban musical street traditions as *serestas* and choros in the eighteenth and nineteenth centuries, cavaquinhos, bandolins, and guitars became popular, and it was probably during this period that these instruments started to be incorporated into the ensemble. Given their secular associations, this is likely to have caused considerable controversy, but eventually they were resignified and came to be seen as extensions of the divine instruments, losing their former associations. Today debate centers around the incorporation of the accordion into the ensemble. Although this instrument carries close links with the forró and other secular genres of couple dancing, its associations are being renegotiated to align them with the folia ethos: its potential religious connotations are being forged in terms of the sacrifice its player makes on behalf of the Kings in demonstrating a willingness to carry such a heavy instrument about on the journey.

A problem that emerges in such diffuse contexts as folia communities is that of finding the means of coordinating collective action. Like many other community-based traditions throughout the world, the solution in the folia de reis is to center the ritual around continuous participatory musical performance. Communal music making provides a means of filling the ritual time frame in a manner that engages the participants in structured activities that funnel the collective gaze toward common focal points while preserving strict limits upon the leaders' control over the ritual space. More important, participatory music making is particularly well suited to bridging the gap between religious representations and affective experience. Although musically directed communal rituals are quite prevalent cross-culturally, in each context the music making is employed in a specific manner, in accordance with the particularities of the historical and social setting. Yet, some generalizations are possible, which derive from the structural properties of the medium.

Since music lacks a semantic base, musical meanings can be expressed only through metaphors, and the most immediate associations available within a religious ritual context are those evinced by the ritual motifs, referring the music to religious ideals. But metaphorical associations can be highly allusive, remaining open to multiple interpretations and continuous resignification. This polysemy allows the music to resonate with a multiplicity of motifs, drawing them together into ever-expanding webs of association. In the folia de reis—and probably in many other contexts—the musical sounds are continuous throughout the ritual performance, providing a thread for linking the multiplicity of associations generated during the ritual enactment; it is, therefore, central to the promotion of the experience of cosmic wholeness. Throughout this book I have identified numerous associations that can be invoked by the mineiro style, and these encompass a wide diversity of experiential domains: it can be linked to the mythic repertoire of the tradition, reproducing the Kings' mission to convert the pagans; it articulates with the accumulation of donations along the journey; it resonates with the ritual script at visitations as well as with the ritual process of the journey as a whole; it can invoke associations with social experience, echoing the patterns of decision making within folia communities as well as their patterns of interhousehold exchange; and it can also refer to the wider structure of society. Ultimately, this vast range of resonances is compressed into a unified ideal of social harmony, epitomized by the final chord of the toada.

While the constant presence of sounds may be implicated in promoting cross- categorical linkages, the experience of associative resonance is greatly enhanced by direct participation in the performance, and, as noted above, folia rituals are marked by a strong participatory ethos. By becoming engaged in the performance, the attendants are encompassed within the associative webs they construct, which better enables them to find personal relevance in the cultural heritage. Although the household members at visitations are not directly involved in the music making, blessings are the most highly charged experiences to be orchestrated within the folia tradition. During such performances the devotees are embraced by a powerful torrent of sound, its impact enhanced by the cumulative form of the mineiro style. The bodily sensations produced by the vibrations of the music heighten their awareness of the presence of the Magi, giving substance to the concept of the blessing. Standing before the ensemble with the Kings in hand, the household becomes the focus of communal attention, and through the public acknowledgement of their personhood, a sense of recognition and acceptance is generated. Furthermore, during blessings identity is constructed through family relations, the strongest affective bonds within folia communities, and the communal context of the ritual extends these bonds to encompass the wider community. Their links to one another become defined by their common devotion to the Magi, whose voices temporarily fill the gaps between them, and for a fleeting moment devotees can feel as though they are resonating in sympathy with a perfectly tuned universe.

For the musicians the musical experience is far more subdued, as indeed it would have to be, given the length of time they sustain their performances. For them music making promotes a diffuse sense of well-being that emerges from the flow of the activity. Foliões generally become involved in a companhia of their own volition, so they tend to be predisposed to find satisfaction in the music making, and this enhances the atmosphere of sociability within the performance space. To perform in consort the musicians must attend to one another, and this constructs a unique world of social interaction in which personal concerns are put aside in favor of the collective undertaking. Because music is produced through the aural medium of sound, within a split second they are able to tune in to one another, continuously adjusting their behavior in a quasi-instantaneous fashion in response to their peers. Among foliões, music making is conceived as a space for sociability, and they explore its interactive possibilities to the full, continuously acknowledging each others' contributions to the communal project. The atmosphere of camaraderie they construct during performance neutralizes the internal hierarchy of the association. The quality of the sounds they produce is understood in terms of the quality of their interactions during music making, the goal being to achieve a harmonious performance that reflects the harmonious context of sociability they set in motion to produce it.

One could say, then, that experiences of participatory music making typically promote an encounter with social ideals. To make music together is to enchant that ideal into the world. Within a religious context, the potential for an enchanted reality to be experienced as an encounter with the moral order of the divinities is greatly enhanced. In such a context, the webs of association constructed during ritual participation are momentarily linked, and religious discourse and ritual experience become tightly intertwined. The persuasive power of enchantment rests on its ability to allow the participants to visualize themselves within the moral order of their religious tenets. Through direct participation in the coordinated activity of music making, ritual participants construct and place themselves within an alternative reality, which allows them to acquire a fleeting glimpse of a world governed by their vision of God's natural laws.

Enchanted Visions

"As an anthropologist and as a music-maker and devotee of the performing arts, I find myself constantly torn between concern for the world as it is and

CHAPTER NINE

as it might be. . . . I am appalled by the contrast between our technical ingenuity and our inability to organize peaceful, co-operative societies, harmonious families, and equitable political systems, and to develop the full intellectual potential and sensibilities of every individual human being. And yet, when I perform or listen to music, I often enter a world of sensuous beauty that is noble and uplifting and which compels people to be gentle and loving, as long as they are involved" (Blacking 1980b, 8).

Since musical performance in a group setting involves coordinated interaction among the participants, John Blacking saw all communal music making as inherently political, even when the music being performed is not explicitly articulated in political terms. He held a broad conception of "the political," seeing it as the "relationships between [humans] and fellow [humans]" (1973b, 7). For Blacking, the relevance of ethnomusicological inquiry did not reside in demonstrating the parallels between musical behavior and extramusical spheres, but in its potential to indicate the ways in which musical activity heightens people's awareness of their position within the wider context of relationships affecting their lives. By constructing temporary utopian universes, experiences of participatory music making highlight the contrasts between relationships within the performance context and relationships outside it, and this could have an impact on the participants' attitudes and actions in extramusical arenas.

Since colonial times, the performance requirements of the musical styles used in the folia tradition have articulated idealized visions of social integration derived from the characteristic modes of intra- and interclass relations prevailing at different periods within the southeastern context. In the mining regions, where the mineiro style first developed, the cumulative form resonated with the ostentatious aesthetic orientation of the colonial society, but it also provided a model for the integration of the various social sectors of this highly segregated setting. Within the egalitarian context of bairro culture, the paulista style emphasized mutual obligations as a divine mandate in order to inhibit public confrontational displays which could disrupt the harmonious coexistence of the community. Although the patriarchal fazenda created a new class with which peasants needed to negotiate their livelihood, this did not disrupt the egalitarian ethos operating within peasant communities. So long as their integrity and livelihood were not unduly threatened, performance practices remained essentially unchanged. Indeed, they provided a means of safeguarding an egalitarian orientation within a stratified social context.

Fundamental structural transformations in folia performance practices occurred only after expulsion, which turned the peasantry into a marginal and dispossessed proletariat. Confronted with the impersonal capitalist modes of interclass relations, their perspective on fazenda patriarchy was renegotiated in terms of their familial discourse of obligations and reciprocity. What was previously a reality—but never assimilated as an ideal—came to be reelaborated into a vision. This was not out of a wistful desire to return to fazenda life—no one I encountered wished that—but despite their asymmetries, the mutual obligations mandated by the personalized character of fazenda relations provided the rural workforce with a safety net in times of crisis. In the absence of direct access to their bosses within a greater social context lacking any other effective form of social welfare, the old myth of the "good boss" found space to resurface.

Rather than constituting iconic representations of social structure, the social formations envisaged in each musical style of the folia repertoire have spoken to the ways in which the devotees conceived of the threats to their livelihood and their social integrity, and they have constructed their ritual motifs and practices in relation to their lived experiences of the wider social order. In fact, the ensemble itself is constituted as a group of travelers following a star in search of dignified living conditions, and this image can be seen to resonate with the constant mobility of southeastern populations in their continuous pursuit of their aspirations.

Foliões are acutely aware of their precarious position in the current Brazilian social order, and they use their musical performances as a means of symbolically re-creating a world in which their livelihood might be guaranteed. The systematic violations of their natural laws have not eradicated their vision of a world in which people recognize their obligations toward one another. On the contrary, it has reinforced their conviction of its truths: those who—like the Three Kings—give freely of their wealth promote life; those who strive to accumulate it will ultimately subject everyone to Herod's fate, death; humans can be redeemed and ennobled only by subjugating their will to the moral superiority of the saints.

When the foliões begin to sing, the voices of the Magi reverberate on earth, enchanting a space in which the heavenly ideals of the Kings are temporarily instated in the world. Through the divine power of enchantment, a transformation is effected that lasts for the duration of the journey: the world becomes more colorful, adorned with flowers, ribbons, and shiny paper; it becomes more poetic and more musical through the performances of the folia; there is also space for clowning and joking, which enhance the atmosphere of sociability within the ritual frame; food and drink for all be-

CHAPTER NINE

come abundant. People are transformed by their direct contact with the Magi: they become more joyful and predisposed to give of their time, their talents, and their limited possessions in order to heighten the experience of communion with the saints.

This is a space "betwixt and between," to borrow Victor Turner's (1967) representation of the ritual context. It is neither totally human nor totally divine, but a sphere for the expression of the humanity of the saints and the divinity of humanity. Within this sphere, humans and saints engage with one another, entering into reciprocal exchanges of messages and gifts. By embodying the Three Kings during their journeys, foliões enchant the harmonious ideal of the saints into their social lives, transforming the ritual context into an experience of this visionary reality. The truths of this enchanted vision are confirmed when the presence of the Kings among humans articulates exchanges which promote acts of generosity and experiences of social harmony. Although this vision can be sustained only temporarily, its reenchantment at regular intervals keeps it alive, providing devotees with a means of affirming their moral integrity. Within the restricted realm of marginality, folia journeys allow the Brazilian subaltern classes to express their aspirations and articulate their moral codes, forging a positive self-image of themselves the better to confront the daily humiliations that punctuate their lives. By reclaiming their self-esteem in this infrapolitical realm, they equip themselves for their constant struggle to preserve their dignity within a wider social sphere marked by tenacious class boundaries and thinly veiled forms of racial discrimination.

APPENDIX

Musical Examples

Musical Example A.1

Slow mineiro style in eight voices (Folia do Baeta Neves)

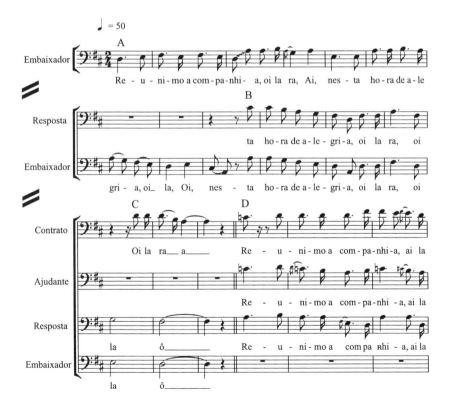

APPENDIX

APPENDIX

APPENDIX

Musical Example A.2

Toada mineira: full score (Folia do Seu Alcides)

APPENDIX

APPENDIX

APPENDIX

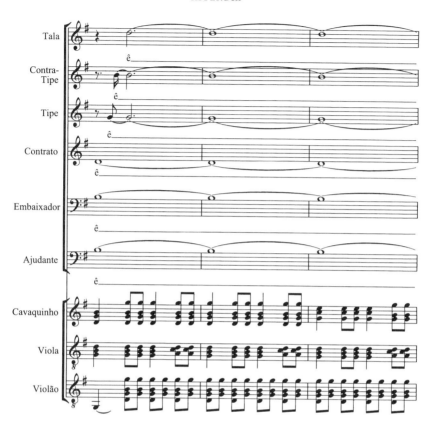

APPENDIX

Notes

Preface

1. *Seu* is a colloquial form of *senhor* (mister); it is commonly used as a sign of respect.

2. In the dialect of southeastern Brazil, the plural form of a noun is generally provided by the article, such that the noun itself is maintained in the singular. Thus, here, the plural of *bastião* is *bastião,* rather than *bastiões.*

Chapter One

1. I acknowledge the influence of Anthony Seeger's (1987) book, *Why Suyá Sing,* which draws on the mouse ceremony as its organizing trope.

2. There are numerous studies of the construction of networks of mutual support among migrant communities throughout the world. See, for example, Epstein (1975), Mayer (1963), and J. C. Mitchell (1956). Ethnomusicologists, such as Erlmann (1990), Koetting (1975), and Turino (1993, 169–90), have also noted that musical associations among migrant communities are commonly used for similar purposes.

3. Although the term "enchantment" has been used in an ethnomusicological context (see Sullivan 1997; Zuhur 1998), it has not undergone systematic conceptualization within the discipline. In this book I refer to enchantment as a specific way of orchestrating religious ritual enactment through musical performance.

4. There are numerous studies relating the development of the church in Brazil to the emergence and resilience of popular Catholic beliefs and practices. See, for example, Azzi (1977), Brandão (1985, 129–61), Hoornaert (1979), and Maués (1995).

5. The CEB movement was established by the progressive wing of the Brazilian Catholic Church linked to liberation theology. It is predicated on belief in the value of life, and its mission is to strive to ensure that this sacred, God-given gift is preserved in a dignified manner for all. The movement is organized all the way up to national level, but its base is the many small lay associations of Catholics in low-income areas of both urban and rural setting. The members of the associations meet regularly to discuss the issues that affect their lives, particularly the forces that threaten their livelihood. Based on their discussions, decisions are taken at various levels of the organization as to what actions might be best suited to overcome these forces.

6. A survey of the representation of popular Catholicism in some of this literature was conducted by Zaluar (1983).

7. I note that Fernandez speaks of "images," but, as an ethnomusicologist, I prefer to use a metaphor with more ambiguous sensory associations.

8. The use of musical metaphors to represent the unity of the universe has a long history in Western thinking, dating at least as far back as the high Middle Ages (see Sullivan 1997). Furthermore, in *The Raw and the Cooked,* Lévi-Strauss (1969) made use of musical metaphors to il-

NOTES TO PAGES 16–30

lustrate the structural relationships in myths. It appears, therefore, that throughout history thinkers have drawn on their own inchoate perceptions of resonances between music and cross-categorical linkages in formulating their theoretical models.

9. Similarly, the state of *muabet,* an atmosphere of intimacy and openness, among Prespa Albanians is achieved through highly structured social events, involving a well-defined sequence for the presentation of musical styles as the evening progresses (Sugarman 1988).

10. Around 13 percent of the Brazilian workforce earn only a "minimum salary" per month or less. The minimum wage is meant to represent the sum needed to sustain a family of four at a minimum level of subsistence, and it fluctuated between US$50 and US$75 a month from 1980 to 1995. Moreover, only 16 percent of the labor force earns at least US$2,000 a month (Marcos Sá Corrêa 1994, 34).

11. ABC stands for Santo André, São Bernardo, and São Caetano, three neighboring municipalities of greater São Paulo. This region, which also includes Diadema, Mauá, and Ribeirão Pires, is the industrial heartland of the country.

12. While these conditions obtained during my research, the dramatic decline in inflation rates since the institution of the "Real Plan" in 1994 have begun to reverse this trend (Nascimento 1996). It remains to be seen whether this stability can be maintained.

13. It is worth noting that on numerous occasions Zezo made a point of informing me that José Cicoti of the PT, the vice-mayor of Santo André between 1988 and 1992, had been a *folião* in his youth.

14. A dominant trend in Brazilian anthropology focuses upon the search for the essence of Brazilian-ness. This is particularly marked in the work of daMatta ([1979] 1991, 1985), who has developed a model of the Brazilian "double ethic," framed as a conceptual dichotomy between the "house" and the "street." DaMatta argues that this dichotomy permeates the whole of Brazilian society, giving cultural unity to the nation.

15. Given the continuity between the rural and the urban within migrant communities in the large cities of Brazil, Eunice Durham (1986) has suggested that it may be more appropriate to think in terms of an "anthropology in the city" than an "anthropology of the city" when dealing with the Brazilian urban context.

Chapter Two

1. The cateretê—also known as *catira*—is a social dance genre found throughout the rural areas of central and southeastern Brazil as well as in some regions of the northeast, and it is quintessentially linked to the rural peasantry. In some areas it is considered the secular counterpart of the Saint Gonçalo dance, and the choreography of the dances is very similar. It is performed in two rows by pairs of dancers, often only men, to the accompaniment of two violas heading the lines. The dance consists of an alternation between two separate phases: those in which there is singing and those with dance movements, primarily clapping and the stamping of feet to the intricate rhythm of the instrumental interlude between the verses.

2. The original Portuguese version of this story can be found in Reily (1996, 214–17). See plate 1 for a photograph of the narrator.

3. For an extended study of the pastoril in northeastern Brazil, see Pinto (1997).

4. This and all other translations from Portuguese throughout the book are my own, unless otherwise stated.

5. Further inventories of historiographic descriptions of itinerant ensembles in honor of

the Three Kings can be found in Mario de Andrade (1989, 229–31). It is worth noting, however, that early references to the pastoril are far more prevalent than are references to groups dedicated to the Three Kings. This is probably because such groups were—and continue to be—more popular in the northeast than folias de reis. For much of the colonial era the northeast dominated the colonial economy, so documentation pertaining to that region is more pervasive than material on southeastern traditions. A historical perspective on folia traditions viewed in terms of the relationship between the church and popular Catholic communities can be found in Brandão (1985, 129–61).

6. Alceu Maynard de Araújo (1964, 1:129–61), for example, described the folias that perform in the Paraíba Valley in the state of São Paulo, comparing them with similar ensembles in Minas Gerais, Rio de Janeiro, Espírito Santo, Bahia, and Rio Grande do Sul. Other researchers have documented the tradition in Minas Gerais (Brandão 1981, 19–55; Bruffatto 1948; Porto 1977), in the state of Rio de Janeiro (Castro and Couto 1977), on the northern coast of the state of São Paulo (Setti 1985), and in the state of Goiás (Brandão 1977, 1983b). See also Brandão (1985, 129–61; 1983a, 11–110) for futher descriptions of the folia tradition.

7. For the Vale do Paraíba, São Paulo, Alceu Maynard de Araújo (1964, 1:141–61) documented a distinction between *folias de reis de caixa* and *folias de reis de música;* the *caixas* were said to perform in rural areas while *músicas* kept within city limits. Among foliões in Goiás, Brandão (1983a, 103) also noted classification systems of musical styles based on perceived regional differences. According to the leader of one group, "the system of the Folia is *goiano, maranhense,* and mineiro; it is all almost the same rhythm. Now, paulista, *cuiabano* is different." I came across numerous other terms to designate perceived stylistic differences within the tradition, but it is not my intention to provide an exhaustive survey of folia terminology. It is significant, however, that foliões seem highly preoccupied with classifying the various styles with which they are familiar.

8. For examples of such traditions, see Setti (1985, 182, 189, 218–19). This practice is also common in Portugal, where the high, shrill voice is typically called the *guincho.*

9. In some ensembles the front singers perform in parallel thirds and the response of the back singers is performed in parallel sixths.

10. For a recording of the mineiro style, see track 11 of the CD in Olsen and Sheehy (1998).

11. Foliões commonly use the plural form of the word *rei*—*reis*—when speaking of only one King, indicating that they perceive it as the singular form, plurals being constructed in their vernacular through the use of the article or qualifier preceding the noun.

12. These terms probably derive from medieval terms used to designate various musical registers. For example, *tipe* may well have come from *triple* and *tala* was probably derived from *taille.*

13. *Contrato* is probably a corrupted version of *contralto.*

14. The term *cacetero* may have developed out of *caccia,* a canonic form of the fourteenth century in which the second voice ran after—or hunted—the one before it.

15. In Atibaia, São Paulo, groups that call themselves *ternos de congos* perform during the Christmas season and include a repertoire associated with the devotion of the Three Kings. Their performances, however, are not conducted in the form of visitations. Like many dance troupes associated with patron saint festivals, they perform primarily in the church square (Girardelli 1981).

16. According to Alcides the Kings used an *adufo,* which he described as a tambourine without a skin. More frequently, however, *adufo* refers to a small hand drum of Arabic origin (Cas-

NOTES TO PAGES 42–64

cudo 1969, 54). It is generally a square-shaped, double-headed frame drum which contains small pebbles that rattle when the instrument is played.

17. Folias baianas may have as many as ten or more different drums, but there are rarely fewer than four.

18. When Alcides made this statement he did not have an accordion player (*sanfoneiro*) in his companhia. Only a few months later an accordion player offered his services to the ensemble, and Alcides did not object to his participation in the group.

19. A bandeira is a banner, and this was the term originally applied to Portuguese militia companies (Boxer 1969, 31).

20. Although literature on the family in Brazil has emphasized the extended patriarchal family, a concept first introduced into Brazilian sociology by Gilberto Freyre ([1933] 1966), among the peasantry the nuclear family prevailed. This has been widely documented in historiographic surveys and community studies, such as A. Araújo (1955), Metcalf (1992), Mello e Souza (1982), and Willems (1961). See also A. Almeida (1987), Mariza Corrêa (1993), and Samara (1987).

21. Marina Roseman (1991, 115–16) made a similar observation in relation to antiphonal repetitions in the healing rituals of the Temiar in Malaysia.

22. According to Raymond Kelly (1974, 268–73) equality, as in the equality among siblings or the members of a culturally constituted "sisterhood," can only be conceived in terms of "equivalent transitive relations," that is, in terms of relations defined through a mediating figure of a higher order, in which the relationship of each of the "sisters" to the mediator is identical. Thus, a conception of equality implicates a recognition of hierarchy. By referring the figure of mediation to the realm of the supernatural, it becomes possible to preserve human equality, linking equals through their common links to the divine.

23. Life in the coffee-growing regions has been extensively investigated by Martins (1975; 1981), Monbeig (1984), Stein (1990), and Stolcke (1993), among others, and it is from these and other authors that I have derived the discussion that follows.

24. In the late 1970s Verena Stolcke's (1993, 87) informants distinguished the plantation era from the postplantation era as "the time of abundance" and "the time of money," a distinction I still encountered with remarkable frequency well into the 1990s.

25. Although clientelism is one of the mechanisms the rural elites have used to sustain their positions, it does involve face-to-face (or personalized) relations between landowners and laborers (on clientilism in Brazil, see Cubitt 1988, 97–101; Forman and Riegelhaupt 1979; Schepper-Hughes 1992; and Wagley 1971). On numerous occasions, workers in big industries told me of their resentment toward the lack of direct contact they had with their employers.

26. Similar tendencies have been noted in the development of *música sertaneja,* a genre of popular music based on southeastern styles of Iberian origin (Caldas 1979; Reily 1992, 351).

27. Other southeastern styles have been viewed from a similar perspective, particularly música sertaneja (Reily 1992).

28. When Geraldo Reis became ill, the folia split into two groups, but two years before I began my research, the other group dissolved, and many of its members joined Owaldir's folia.

Chapter Three

1. *Seu* is a colloquial form of *senhor* (mister); it is commonly used as a sign of respect.

2. It seems that banner-eating cows are fairly common in southeastern Brazil. A folia that lost its banner to an ox in Arceburgo arrived at a house and sang the following verse:

234

NOTES TO PAGES 64–102

Senhor, dono da casa,	Mister, head of the household,
Veja só o que aconteceu:	Look at what happened:
Dá oferta pro bambu	Give an offering to the bamboo
Que a bandeira o boi comeu.	Because the banner was eaten by an ox.

3. While donas are practically nonexistent in the folia de reis universe, they are not so uncommon to congados and other African-Brazilian Catholic traditions. This may be because a matriarchal orientation is more evident in the Brazilian African heritage than in the Portuguese legacy. Indeed, female leaders in such African-Brazilian possession cults as candomblé and umbanda are common (see Brown 1986; Landes 1947; and Silverstein 1979, among others).

4. A similar distinction between friendly and competitive encounters exists among *cantadores,* the performers of sung duels in northeast Brazil. Elizabeth Travassos (2000) argues that the contemporary code of ethics within the tradition is predicated upon this distinction.

5. This instrumental configuration—viola and guitar—has become especially common with the rise in popularity of música sertaneja, where it is often referred to as "the couple": the viola represents the husband and the guitar, the wife (Reily 1992, 346).

6. From one region to the next there are differences in the terms used to designate these ritual figures. The most frequent designations in southeastern Brazil are *bastião*—the term most commonly used in São Bernardo—*palhaço, marungo,* and *alferes,* among many others. See A. Araújo (1964, 1:129) for other terms used in Brazil to designate the clowns.

7. I was told that sometimes little girls become bastiãozinhos, but I never saw one.

8. In some folias the bandeireiro is known as the alferes.

9. The only other folia in São Bernardo that had a uniform during my research was Zé Machado's. He received his T-shirts from the furniture company where his son and nephew worked.

10. The producers claimed that the sound quality of their contribution had been below standard because there had not been a sufficient number of microphones to cover all the vocal and instrumental parts.

11. In her study of a northeastern urban community, Nancy Scheper-Hughes (1992, 109–11) provides several vivid descriptions of the humiliating experiences her informants had when they found themselves obliged to make requests to their employers and local officials. It is the memory of similar experiences that accounts for the foliões' hesitation in confronting members of the upper classes with their demands.

Chapter Four

1. The role of the musicians' conceptual framework in the orchestration of overt musical behavior was pivotal to Alan Merriam's (1964, 32–33) "model" for ethnomusicology. Although the functionalist perspective under which he operated has been questioned (Rice 1987), the articulation between people's conceptions about music and their musical activities has remained central to the discipline. See, for example, Feld (1982, 1994), Nettl (1989, 1992), and Turino (1993).

2. In contemporary styles of música sertaneja, parallel sixths have become the norm.

3. In European early music theory the third was classified as a consonant interval, although it did not possess the perfect consonance of the octave, the fifth, or the fourth. Thus, it was considered to be "harmonic" while still allowing for a clear perception of each of the notes performed simultaneously. The Brazilian use of the third seems to draw upon this feature of the interval.

4. While the guitar had long been used in Brazilian urban popular musical styles, particu-

NOTES TO PAGES 102–122

larly the *choro*, where it provided the bass line, it was with the emergence of bossa nova in the late 1950s that a clear association between the guitar and the upper classes was consolidated (Schreiner [1977] 1993, 65–66). The adoption of the guitar by the upper classes also reinforced the association of the viola with the Brazilian lower classes.

5. This mode of experimentation is reminiscent of the cooperative composition of the Peruvian Aymara described by Turino (1993, 76–78).

6. According to Maurice Bloch (1974), the formalization and repetitiveness of ritual singing and dancing constitute features of articulation that restrict creativity because such redundancy does not permit the construction of logical arguments, as is possible in speech. Thus, he posited, participation in group dancing and music making implies a complete acceptance of the proceedings, locking people's consciousness into a meaningless repertoire which engulfs their senses. For Bloch the music making context anesthetizes people's critical faculties while it simultaneously mutes dissident voices. Since their initial presentation his propositions have received considerable criticism from ethnomusicologists and anthropologists, such as Blacking (1980a, 1987), Irvine (1979), Parkes (1994, 182), Parkin (1984), and Tambiah (1985). These critiques tend to point out the relativity in the degree of formalization in ritual dancing and music making, showing that within its structure there is considerable scope for individual expression and the negotiation of meaning, such that far from meaningless personal statements and arguments can indeed be made, even in highly formalized contexts. The preoccupation with refuting Bloch's extremist propositions, however, has meant that alternative readings of the role of formalization and repetitiveness have remained unexplored. I contend that it is precisely the formalization and repetitiveness of many participatory styles that allow people to become so familiar with the music they are performing that they are able to divert their attention from what they are doing to focus upon one another, thus allowing them to gain *greater* awareness of their relationships with others.

7. Charles Keil (1987, 1995) draws attention to what he calls "participatory discrepancies," those out-of-time and out-of-tune features of many participatory styles which lift people up onto the dance floor. Yet he seems to have missed a very potent dimension of his concept: the fundamental role of participatory discrepancies in sustaining tension among music makers. Indeed, it is precisely during those moments in which coordination falters, when musicians perceive they are out of time or out of tune, that they renew their awareness of one another as co-sound-producers, quickly readjusting their actions, acknowledging that the activity is a collective undertaking.

8. In this region the folias de reis and the folias do divino use the same musical style: the toada lenta, which is very close to the style used by the Folia do Zé Quatorze. Zé Quatorze came from Monsenhor Paulo, which is twenty kilometers away from Campanha.

9. When Sebastião formed a folia with his son and other young men in Arceburgo, as the eldest participant and the group's disciplinarian, he could have taken a prestigious musical role within the ensemble. Instead, he opted for the drum, the part with which he has always felt most comfortable.

10. Other folias in São Bernardo, however, routinely sang through the night, particularly on weekends.

Chapter Five

1. It is not, however, the full terço that is normally performed in such a context: sometimes the prayer for the dead is restricted to one Our Father followed by one Hail Mary.

236

NOTES TO PAGES 123–151

2. In some regions it is customary for the departure to take place on New Year's Day. Because of these differences in group practices, in the 1987/88 journey I was able to attend the departure of four different companhias.

3. It is common for foliões to speak of the banner as their guide, since it leads the procession when the ensembles are on the road moving from one house to the next. Insofar as it represents the Three Kings, the banner is also conceived of as a moral guide for daily life.

4. Although traditionally the arrival occurs on 6 January, many groups now hold their festivals on the first Saturday or Sunday after Kings' Day, when more people are free to attend them. The Folia do Baeta was planning its arrival for the ninth for this reason.

5. Similar uses of repetition in musical performance within ritual contexts have been noted by Parkes (1994, 171) and Sugarman (1988, 26).

6. Frequently I have asked people familiar with the tradition what they consider to be its most characteristic feature, and by far the most common responses make reference to the final chord; the second most common response refers to the bastião.

7. The ritual clown has received considerable anthropological attention, and the juxtaposition of the comic and the serious in contexts of ritual clowning has been noted repeatedly. See, for example, Handelman (1981), Hieb (1979), Makarius (1970), and W. Mitchell (1992).

8. Since Bloch's (1974) controversial dichotomization of speech and song, in which speech is presented as the medium of argument while song is seen as an impoverished form of communication, other researchers have shown that some social groups construct oppositions between speech and song which herald the integrative potential of musical activity in a manner similar to that of folia communities. See, for example, Sugarman (1988) and Stewart (1989).

9. It may be that the mineiro style has become the dominant form in the southeast because of the effects it can have during blessings; similarly, dueted toadas seem to have been slowing down over the years, and this too may have happened to enhance bodily experiences during blessings.

Chapter Six

1. In São Bernardo the foliões usually referred to the crib as "presépio," but it was also called *lapa* (grotto) or *lapinha* (little grotto).

2. Other families warn the ensemble by placing a star or an inscription on the door.

3. See Brandão (1981, 21–32) for another description of a folia visitation that highlights the ritualized dialogue between foliões and their hosts.

4. Throughout Brazil, midnight mass on Christmas Eve is known as "*missa do galo*" (mass of the rooster).

5. Morphy and Banks (1997, 16) note that the Jains of Gujarat, India, "consider the worshippers to be as much a part of the adornment and decoration of a temple as the more permanent paintings, carvings and other ritual objects."

6. In the early Latin tradition four magi were common, while the Syriacs represented them as twelve (Otero 1979, 362).

7. The most well-known apocryphal texts that refer to the Wise Men are *The Gospel of Thomas, The Arab Gospel of the Infancy, The Story of Joseph the Carpenter,* and *The Armenian Gospel of the Infancy* (Otero 1979, 280). Chapter 10 of the Armenian text provides a detailed description of the journey of the Wise Men, their entourage, and their arrival in Bethlehem (Peeters 1914, 131–50). For discussions of these and other apocryphal texts that contributed to the representation of the Wise Men as the Three Kings, see James (1926), and Hennecke (1963), among others.

NOTES TO PAGES 151–160

For Edmund Leach (1983, 46), what led to the transformation of the magi into three kings "lies within a convention which seems to derive from classical sources whereby the witnesses to a miraculous birth should be three gift-bearing Graces." A similar argument is made by Goodenough (1964, 203–24).

8. Zé's whole family is known as the Maguinhos (Little Magos) not because they are closely associated with the tradition in honor of the *magos* (magi), but because of their physical stature; like the Kings, they too are very thin (*magros*).

9. The prevalence of the African king can also be explained by the fact that there is a long-standing tradition within Christianity that one of the kings was black. This is based on an identification between the Three Kings and the three sons of Noah—Shem, Japheth, and Canaan—who populated the world after the great flood. According to Christian tradition, each of the brothers occupied a different part of the world: Japeth went to the north and to the west; Shem moved to the east; and Canaan populated the south. His son, Ham, damned by Noah for having seen his nudity, moved further south and became black (Enslin 1962). Through an extension of Inineus's theology of recapitulation, the black King redeems the Hamites, creating the possibility for their return to Christendom (see Otero 1979).

By far the largest immigrant group that came to Brazil during the early colonato era was made up of Italians, and their presence throughout the southeast is still highly visible. It comes as no surprise, therefore, that one of the Kings should be represented as an Italian with considerable frequency. Although German immigration was concentrated in the southern part of the country, the coffee expansion into Paraná in the 1940s would have allowed numerous southeasterners to enter into contact with them. The fairly common presence of a Middle Eastern King could be a legacy of their association with the Orient. Moreover, numerous Syrians and Lebanese—colloquially known as "Turks"—immigrated to Brazil in the early twentieth century, occupying themselves primarily with trade (Holloway 1989, 155). The Far Eastern King, on the other hand, is probably related to the Japanese immigration, which was also quite prevalent during the expansion of the coffee economy; their presence in rural areas is still quite evident, where they are involved primarily with truck farming. The distinction between the Japanese and the Chinese is not always clear to many southeasterners.

It is worth noting, however, that none of the Wise Men ever seems to be portrayed as a native Brazilian, though in a painting of the "Adoration of the Magi" by the sixteenth-century Portuguese artist, Vasco Fernandes, there is such a representation. It seems reasonable to assume that this absence is due to the almost complete annihilation of the indigenous populations in the area by the late seventeenth century.

10. Some folia texts are explicit about the number of children Herod sacrificed, as can be noted in the following verse performed by a bastião in the Folia do Baeta in confronting the letter z in an inscription:

Com *z* escrevo "zombando";	With *z* I write "mocking";
Herodes me vem na lembrança.	Herod comes to my mind.
Pra zombar de Jesus Cristo	To mock Jesus Christ
Matou 4,000 criança.	He killed 4,000 children.

11. For the original Portuguese version of this narrative, see Reily (1996, 214). A Portuguese document dating from the early eighteenth century relates the participation of African slaves in

a Nativity play, in which they enact their identification with the black King Balthazar. Based on the text of one of the songs they performed in honor of the black king, José Ramos Tinhorão (1994, 33) claims that "blacks could finally live a moment of equality in the shadow of the glory of someone who, similar in figure, deserved the dignity of being addressed as Your Mercy and was slave to no one."

12. For the original Portuguese version of this narrative, see Reily (1996, 213).

13. The study of racial discrimination and race relations in Brazil has been fraught with controversy ever since Gilberto Freyre (especially [1933] 1966 and 1959) published his representation of the country as a "racial democracy," claiming that slavery in Brazil had been more benign than in other parts of the New World, because the Portuguese held a tolerant attitude toward racial mixture, freely interbreeding with their female slaves. This created a racial continuum which precluded the possibility for racial polarization, minimizing the emergence of racial prejudice in the country. Freyre's ideas were quickly taken up by the nationalist intelligentsia at the time, who propagated his vision of Brazil as a "race relations paradise." Propelled by the patriotic wave that engulfed the country during the Vargas era (1937–54), this vision was soon to become a commonsense discourse throughout Brazilian society. Brazilians—particularly those belonging to the urban white middle and upper classes—embraced the image of themselves as a unique, racism-free society, transforming it into a hallmark of national identity (Ortiz 1986, 36–44). Yet, while vehemently contesting the existence of racial prejudice in the country, Brazilians felt free to acknowledge class discrimination, constructing a complex ideological discourse which excused class prejudice by juxtaposing it to the greater evil of racism; while class boundaries can be crossed, it is argued, race is imprinted upon the body, marking one's racial category for life.

This discourse has remained entrenched despite extensive academic challenges, starting in the 1950s with the series of studies on race relations in Brazil sponsored by UNESCO. These and countless other subsequent investigations have consistently shown that the concentration of blacks increases, the lower one moves down the socioeconomic scale. Thus, it has been shown that for blacks, class boundaries are very difficult to transcend in Brazil, and this difficulty cannot be put down simply to the fact that blacks, emerging out of slavery, began the process of upward mobility for a disadvantaged position in relation to other racial and ethnic groups in the country. While opportunities for upward social mobility are limited for all members of the lower classes, they are particularly so for blacks, poor mulattos fairing little better (see Lovell 1994; Skidmore 1993, among others). If Brazil is a racial democracy, it is so only among the poorest social classes; among the privileged classes, those who control the means of production and the job opportunities, racial prejudice is rife, systematically blocking the social ascent of nonwhites. For overviews of the literature on race relations in Brazil, see Skidmore (1993), Wade (1997), and Winant (1992), among others.

14. The foliões' notions of King Herod parallel the devil beliefs Michael Taussig (1980) encountered in other parts of South America. For Taussig devil beliefs embody the peasants' understanding of capitalist accumulation as an essentially nonreciprocal exchange system: it is the exchange that ends all exchanges.

Chapter Seven

1. Here the embaixador indicates that this is the third time that day that the folia would be singing for the intention of a dead soul.

NOTES TO PAGES 176–203

2. At different stages in the developmental cycle of the household this ideal may not be realized. Actual households often incorporate other relatives on a permanent or temporary basis, and the female head of household is becoming increasingly common (Fonseca 1987; Mello 1995; Sarti 1995). A household my also consist of a widowed parent, a son or daughter-in-law soon after their marriage, a relative or fellow townsman who recently arrived in the city, and so on.

3. In his research on the Saint Gonçalo dance, a tradition in which ritual dances are frequently staged in honor of dead relatives, Carlos Rodrigues Brandão (1981, 92; 1989, 187–219) makes a similar observation, arguing that the dance is a privileged sphere for reviving memories of the deceased.

4. The requinta is another name for the tala, the highest vocal part in a folia ensemble.

5. The number seven features prominently in folia promises. For example, a person can promise to act as festeiro for seven years, to carry the banner to seven houses,and so on.

6. A whole community, however, can make a collective promise to the saints, particularly during a drought or some other form of natural disaster.

7. An inversion of the promise, divine punishments are forms of negative divine reciprocity. If to give to the saints increases the return to the donor, to refuse a donation increases one's loss; for the one pig the man refused the folia in Zé Quatorze's story, he lost five animals.

8. See also Lomnitz (1988) for similar observations in a Mexican shantytown.

Chapter Eight

1. Half-moons are often performed in front of houses offering pousos as well. This choreographic formation is common to many popular Catholic traditions in southeastern Brazil, such as congados, moçambiques, and Saint Gonçalo dances. When it is performed, the dancers in the two queues continuously meet face to face with their companions in the other queue as they pass by, which enhances the interactive experience of performance (see Reily 2001, 25).

2. It is commonly said that forró is a corruption of the English "for all" (Cleary 1994, 563); allegedly the announcements for social dances which British companies organized for their employees in Recife during the nineteenth century stated that they were "for all." In southeastern Brazil the northeastern forró was popularized by Luiz Gonzaga during the late 1940s, and today it is associated with northeastern migrants, but its popularity extends to other migrant communities as well. The classic instrumentation for the forró, and that which was used by the ensemble at the festival, includes an accordion, a triangle, and a bass drum (zabumba), and the most common musical genre of the forró is the baião, which is structured around an eight-pulse timeline: 3 + 5.

3. The concept of "the interior" emerged during the colonial era to designate the country's vast wetsern hinterland. Today it refers to rural areas that are removed from the major urban areas along the coast.

4. It is worth noting, however, that processional bands have also been hit hard by the demise of such festivals. Many towns that in their heyday boasted two or even three bands now struggle to maintain just one.

5. This was not the only instance in which I noted such practices. After their performance at a mass in Diadema, the Folia do Zé dos Magos was surrounded by devotees outside the church, and they remained there for nearly two hours distributing blessings. Similarly the Folia do Baeta often blessed the faithful after their public performances.

NOTES TO PAGES 212–214

Chapter Nine

1. Such dichotomous representations have been discussed in Benedict (1935), Gellner (1969), Goody (1986), I. M. Lewis (1971), Turner (1974), and Weber ([1922] 1963), among others.

2. Within the various denominations of mainstream Christianity, revival movements have also emerged from time to time with similar aims, and one could argue that the current surge in charismatic movements throughout the Christian world, including the Catholic Church in Brazil, are aimed at rekindling religious sentiment.

Glossary

adufo—a double-headed frame drum containing rattles

agregado—aggregate; a person connected to a plantation or a household who does not belong to the immediate nuclear family

ajudante—helper; commonly the second voice in a folia de reis and other southeastern musical genres

alferes—second lieutenant; in some folia de reis, designates the clowns, and in others the bearer of the banner

apresentação (pl. *apresentações*)—presentation; in the folia de reis designates the public presentations of an ensemble in a nonreligious context

baião—a northeastern musical style commonly used in forrós

baile—ball; a dance event

bairro—neighborhood; a small, rural community as well as an urban neighborhood

banda de pifes—a northeastern instrumental ensemble structured around two transverse reed flutes

bandeira—banner; also a group of colonial frontiersmen who set off into the wilderness to capture Amerindians and search for gold and other precious minerals; in some regions designates a popular Catholic musical ensemble organized around the banner of a particular saint

bandeira de/dos santos reis—the banner of the Three Kings

bandeireiro—the bearer of the banner in a folia de reis and other popular Catholic traditions

bandolim (pl. *bandolins*), also *bandola*—an instrument with four courses of double strings similar to a mandolin

barroco mineiro—baroque of Minas Gerais

bastião—a clown or clowns in a folia de reis

bastiãozinho—little bastião; a child dressed as a clown in a folia

benzimento—blessing or prayer

bloco afro—a northeastern carnival percussion ensemble

bóia-fria—cold tiffin; a rural day laborer, because he or she takes food to the fields and eats it cold

bom patrão—good boss; commonly used in relation to an ideal patriarchal plantation owner

boné—cap; the headgear worn by some folias de reis, often shaped like a crown

cacetero—one of the voices in the mineiro style of the folia de reis; it is often the fourth-lowest voice in the ensemble

GLOSSARY

caderneta—notebook; in the folia de reis designates the notebook in which a record of the donations is kept

caipira—a person from the interior of São Paulo; the term carries connotations similar to "hillbilly"

caixa—a double-headed cylindrical drum

caixeiro—caixa player

camarada—hired agricultural laborer

candomblé—an African-Brazilian possession cult

cantadores—singers; in the northeast designates the singers of improvised musical duels known as *repente* or *cantoria*

capacete—helmet; the headgear worn by the clowns in folias de reis

capelão—chaplain; in Brazilian popular Catholicism the leader of a communal prayer session

castigo divino—divine punishment

cateretê—a men's double-line dance commonly performed in southeastern rural festivals

cavaquinho—an instrument with four courses of single strings similar to a ukulele

chita—a cheap, flowery fabric

choro—an instrumental musical style that emerged in Rio de Janeiro in the later part of the nineteenth century

chula—one of the acrobatic dances of the clowns

colonato—a labor system during the plantation era set up to accommodate foreign immigrants on southeastern coffee plantations

colônia—colony; in southeastern Brazil designates the rows of houses inhabited by rural laborers working under the colonato system

colono—colonist; in southeast Brazil designates a rural laborer working under the colonato system

companhia de reis—a musical ensemble that performs in honor of the Three Kings during the Christmas season in various regions of Brazil

congada or *congado*—an African-Brazilian dance troupe that performs for festivals of Our Lady of the Rosary, Saint Benedict the Moor, and other Catholic saints associated with blacks in Brazil

contra-tipe—the next voice up from the tipe in the mineiro style of the folia de reis

contra-tipeiro—the singer of the contra-tipe

contrato—one of the voices in the mineiro style of the folia de reis; it is often the third-lowest voice in the ensemble

corta-jaca—one of the acrobatic dances of the clowns

crente—believer; commonly denotes Pentecostals

dança de São Gonçalo—Saint Gonçalo dance; a devotional double-line dance in honor of Saint Gonçalo

desmanches—a work of magic aimed at destroying something

dom—gift or talent

dono—owner; in the folia de reis designates the administrator of an ensemble

embaixada—the improvised verse sequences of the embaixador

embaixador (pl. *embaixadores*)—the ritual leader of a folia de reis

embornal—bag

encontro—encounter; a chance meeting of two folias de reis during their journeys; nowadays

GLOSSARY

the large gatherings of musical ensembles promoted by cultural administrators throughout the southeast

ensaio—rehearsal

estilo baiano—style from Bahia; in the folia de reis it refers to a musical style with numerous drums

estilo mineiro—style from Minas Gerais; in the folia de reis it refers to a cumulative musical style that leads up to a long, prolonged major chord

estilo paulista—style from the São Paulo region; in the folia de reis it refers to an antiphonal musical style in which the back singers repeat the performance of the front singers

estribilho—an instrumental interlude in the repertoire of numerous southeastern musical genres

ex-voto—an iconic representation of a miracle

fanfarra—marching band

farda—regimentals; the outfit worn by the clowns, the guards of the banner; can also denote the uniform of a popular Catholic ensemble or dance troupe

favela—shantytown

favor—favor; articulates patron-dependent relations between landowners and their workers

fazenda—plantation

fechamento—closure; in the popular domain refers to a ritual of protection against works of magic

festa da chegada—festival of the arrival; the festival at the end of a ritual journey

festeira—the festeiro's wife

festeiro—the patron of a festival

festival sertanejo—a song festival featuring música sertaneja

finado—deceased, or "the late"; term of address for a dead person

folia de reis—a musical ensemble that performs in honor of the Three Kings during the Christmas season in various regions of Brazil

folia de reis de caixa—a term used in the Vale do Paraíba region to refer to a folia de reis that performs in rural areas

folia de reis de música—a term used in the Vale do Paraíba region to refer to a folia de reis that performs in urban areas

folia do divino—a folia that sings in honor of the Divine Holy Spirit

folião (pl. *foliões*)—a member of a folia de reis; can also refer to the member of any popular musical or dance ensemble

forro—freed slave

forró—a northeastern dance event

ganzá—cylindrical rattle

giro—circular movement; another term for the ritual journey

grupo folclórico—folk group; term used by cultural administrators

guarda da bandeira—guard of the banner; in the folia de reis designates the clowns

guia—guide; commonly denotes the banner of the folia de reis

guincho—a term used in Portugal to refer to a high voice that adds a long note at the end of a musical phrase or short melody

irmandade—lay confraternity

irmão—brother

janeiras—groups similar to mummers in Portugal

GLOSSARY

jornada—journey; denotes the ritual journey of a popular Catholic itinerant ensemble, particularly the folia de reis

lapa or *lapinha*—grotto; designates a manger scene

letreiro—inscription; in the folia de reis tradition, an enigmatic inscription

levantamento do mastro—the raising of the flagpole; this is often the first ritual at a popular Catholic festival in Brazil

linha—line; in the folia de reis tradition, denotes a single couplet of two lines performed to each round of the toada

mago—magus

marcador (fem. *marcadora*)—marker; the person who keeps a note of the donations made to the ensemble along the journey

marungo—clown

mau patrão—evil boss; commonly used in relation to an exploitative plantation owner

mau-olhado—evil eye

mé—sugar cane schnapps; can also be referred to as *cachaça*

meia-lua—half-moon; in popular Catholic traditions, a choreographic formation in which the two queues of participants move in a circle in opposite directions

meião—big middle; the third-lowest vocal part of some folias de reis

melê—friction rattle

moçambique—an African-Brazilian dance troupe that performs for festivals of Our Lady of the Rosary, Saint Benedict the Moor, and other Catholic saints associated with blacks in Brazil

moda—melody or tune; usually used for secular music

música sertaneja—a genre of popular music based on southeastern styles of Iberian origin

mutirão (pl. *mutirões*)—a communal labor system for special tasks

palhaço—clown

pandeiro—tambourine

pardo—grey; colonial term for a person of mixed descent

Partido dos Trabalhadores (PT)—Workers' Party

pastoril—a musical shepherds play

patrão—boss; can refer to the male head of a household

paulistinha—denotes a "simple" iconographic representation of a saint in the São Paulo region

persequição (pl. *persequições*)—persecution; in the Brazilian popular domain designates a work of magic

pífano—reed pipe

pife—reed pipe

pouso—rest station; denotes a household that serves a meal and provides accommodation for the folia along the journey

presépio—manger scene

profecia—prophecy

promessa—promise; a contract between a devotee and a saint

quermesse—street fair; these events are often promoted to raise funds for a nonprofit organization, such as a parish church or a school

reco-reco—percussive scraper

reis—kings; though in standard Portuguese the term is in the plural form, it is often understood to be in the singular among foliões, suggesting that it designates a particular species of divine entity

GLOSSARY

Reis Magos—the Magi (lit. Wise Kings)

repico—a small, double-headed cylindrical drum used in some folias de reis

requinta—another term for tala, the highest voice in the mineiro style of the folia de reis

resposta—response; in the folia de reis it refers to the first voice to repeat the embaixada during the performance of a toada

rezador—someone who prays; in Brazilian popular Catholicism the leader of a communal prayer session

saída da bandeira—departure of the banner; the event that marks the beginning of a ritual journey

sala dos milagres—a room in a pilgrimage center that houses ex-votos

sanfona—accordion

sanfoneiro—accordion player

santo casamenteiro—saint associated with matchmaking

segunda—second; commonly denotes the second voice in a folia de reis and other southeastern musical traditions

senzala—slave quarters

seresta—serenade; can also refer to an ensemble that performs serenades

sítio—small rural property

tala—the highest voice in the mineiro style of the folia de reis; this voice usually enters the ensemble only for the final chord

taleiro—the singer of the tala

terço—a shortened version of the rosary

terno de congo—the same as congado

tipe—one of the voices in the mineiro style of the folia de reis; it is often the fourth- or the fifth-lowest voice in the ensemble

tipeiro—the singer of the tipe

toada—melody or tune; usually used in relation to religious music

toada do Reis de Congo—toada of the King of the Congo, a toada that evinces African-Brazilian rhythmic elements

toada lenta—slow toada; a form of the mineiro style with more than three vocal configurations; in this style the toada is often broken up by instrumental interludes

toada ligeira—quick toada; a form of the mineiro style with three vocal configurations

toada nova—new toada; a form of the mineiro style with more than three vocal configurations; in this style the toada is often broken up by instrumental interludes

toada velha—old toada; a form of the mineiro style with three vocal configurations

trabalho—work; commonly denotes a work of magic

Três Reis Santo—the Three Holy Kings

tropeiro—a colonial mule train operator

umbanda—a syncretic African-Brazilian possession cult

verso—verse; the combination of two rhyming couplets in the folia de reis tradition

viola—an instrument with five courses of double strings slightly smaller than a guitar

violão (pl. *violões*)—guitar

violeiro—viola player

zabumba—the bass drum in a northeastern banda de pifes; in some regions the banda de pifes is known as a zabumba

Bibliography

Almeida, Angela Mendes de. 1987. "Notas sobre a família no Brasil." In *Pensando a família no Brasil: Da colônia à modernidade,* ed. Angela Mendes de Almeida, Maria José Carneiro, and Silvana Gonçalves de Paula, 53–66. Rio de Janeiro: Espaço e Tempo and Ed. da UFRRJ.

Almeida, Renato. 1942. *História da música brasileira.* Rio de Janeiro: F. Briguiet.

Alvarenga, Oneyda. [1950] 1982. *Música popular brasileira.* São Paulo: Duas Cidades.

Andrade, Mario de. 1976. *O turista aprendiz.* São Paulo: Duas Cidades.

———. 1989. *Dicionário musical brasileiro.* São Paulo: EDUSP.

Araújo, Alceu Maynard de. 1949. "Folias de reis de Cunha." *Separata da revista do Museu Paulista* 3:413–64.

———. 1955. "A família numa comunidade alagoana." *Sociologia* 17 (2): 113–31.

———. 1964. *Folclore nacional.* 3 vols. São Paulo: Melhoramentos.

Araújo, Emanuel. 1993. *O teatro dos vícios.* Rio de Janeiro: José Olympio.

Austin, J. 1975. *How to Do Things with Words.* Cambridge, Mass: Harvard University Press.

Ayala, Marcos. 1987. "O samba-lenço de Mauá (organização e práticas culturais de um grupo de dança religiosa)." M.A. diss., University of São Paulo.

Azzi, Riolando. 1977. *O episcopado brasileiro frente ao catolicismo popular.* Petrópolis: Vozes.

———. 1978. *O catolicismo popular no Brasil.* Petrópolis: Vozes.

Bauman, Richard. 1975. "Verbal Art as Performance." *American Anthropologist* 77:290–311.

———. 1992. "Performance." In *Folklore, Cultural Performance, and Entertainment,* ed. Richard Bauman, 41–49. New York: Oxford University Press.

Bauman, Richard, and Charles L. Briggs. 1990. "Poetics and Performance as Critical Perspectives on Language and Social Life." *Annual Review of Anthropology* 19:59–88.

Béhague, Gerard. 1979. *Music in Latin America.* Englewood Cliffs, N.J.: Prentice-Hall.

———. 1982. "Ecuadorian, Peruvian, and Brazilian Ethnomusicology." *Latin American Music Review* 3 (1): 17–35.

———. 1991. "Reflections on the Ideological History of Latin American Ethnomusicology." In *Comparative Musicology and Anthropology of Music: Essays on the History of Ethnomusicology,* ed. Bruno Nettl and Philip V. Bohlman, 56–68. Chicago: University of Chicago Press.

Bell, Catherine. 1992. *Ritual Theory, Ritual Practice.* New York: Oxford University Press.

Benedict, Ruth. 1935. *Patterns of Culture.* London: Routledge and Kegan Paul.

Blacking, John. 1973a. *How Musical Is Man?* Seattle: University of Washington Press.

BIBLIOGRAPHY

———. 1973b. "The Political Role of Music in Social and Technological Development." Paper presented at the Third International Congress of Africanists, Addis Ababa.

———. 1977. "Some Problems of Theory and Method in the Study of Musical Change." *Yearbook of the International Folk Music Council* 9:1–26.

———. 1980a. "Political and Musical Freedom in the Music of Some Black South African Churches." In *The Structure of Folk Models,* ed. Ladislav Holy and Milan Stuchlik, 35–62. London: Academic Press.

———. 1980b. "Purpose, Theory and Practice for the Next Twenty-five Years in Ethnomusicology." Paper presented at the annual meeting of the Society for Ethnomusicology, Bloomington, Ind.

———. 1985a. "The Context of Venda Possession Music: Reflections on the Effectiveness of Symbols." *Yearbook for Traditiona Music* 17:64–87.

———. 1985b. "Movement, Dance, Music, and the Venda Girls' Initiation Cycle." In *Society and the Dance: The Social Anthropology of Process and Performance,* ed. Paul Spencer, 64–91. Cambridge: Cambridge University Press.

———. 1987. *"A Commonsense View of All Music": Reflections on Percy Granger's Contribution to Etnomusicology and Music Education.* Cambridge: Cambridge University Press.

Bloch, Maurice. 1974. "Symbols, Song, Dance and Features of Articulation: Is Religion an Extreme Form of Traditional Authority?" *Archives européennes sociologiques* 15:55–81.

Bohlman, Philip V. 1997. "World Musics and World Religions: *Whose World?*" In *Enchanting Powers: Music in the World's Religions,* ed. Lawrence E. Sullivan, 61–90. Cambridge, Mass.: Harvard University Press.

Boon, James A. 1986. "Symbols, Sylphs, and Siwa: Allegorical Machineries in the Text of Balinese Culture." In *The Anthropology of Experience,* ed. Victor Turner and Edward M. Bruner, 239–60. Urbana: University of Illinois Press.

Bourdieu, Pierre. 1977. *Outline of a Theory of Practice.* Cambridge: Cambridge University Press.

Boxer, Charles R. 1969. *The Golden Age of Brazil: 1695–1750.* Berkeley: University of California Press.

Brandão, Carlos Rodrigues. 1977. *A folia de reis de Mossâmedes.* Rio de Janeiro: FUNARTE.

———. 1981. *Sacerdotes da viola.* Petrópolis: Vozes.

———. 1983a. *Casa de escola: Cultura camponesa e educação rural.* Campinas: Papirus.

———. 1983b. "A folia de reis de Mossâmedes: Etnografia de um ritual camponês." *Revista goiânia de artes* 4 (1): 1–57.

———. 1985. *Memória do sagrado: Estudos de religião e ritual.* São Paulo: Paulinas.

———. 1989. *A cultura na rua.* Campinas: Papirus.

Brato, José Carlos Aguiar. 1983. *A tomada da Ford.* Petrópolis: Vozes.

Bresser Pereira, Luiz Carlos. 1985. *Desenvolvimento e crise no Brasil, 1930–1983.* São Paulo: Brasiliense.

Brown, Diana. 1986. *Umbanda: Religion and Politics in Urban Brazil.* Ann Arbor: UMI Research Press.

Bruffatto, Wanny. 1948. "Festa do santo rei ou dos três reis magos." *Revista de arquivo do município de São Paulo* 15 (119): 45–50.

Bruneau, Thomas C. 1974. *The Political Transformation of the Brazilian Catholic Church.* Cambridge: Cambridge University Press.

BIBLIOGRAPHY

Bruner, Edward M. 1986. "Experience and Its Expressions." In *The Anthropology of Experience*, ed. Victor Turner and Edward M. Bruner, 3–30. Urbana: University of Illinois Press.

Caldas, Waldenyr. 1979. *Acorde na aurora*. São Paulo: Nacional.

Cardoso, Fernando Henrique. 1981. "A crisma de São Bernardo." In *Album memória de São Bernardo*, ed. Fernando Henrique Cardoso, 11–25. São Bernardo do Campo: Prefeitura Municipal.

Cascudo, Câmara. 1969. *Dicionário do folclore brasileiro*. 2 vols. Rio de Janeiro: Edições de Ouro.

Castro, Zaíde Maciel de, and Aracy do Prado Couto. 1977. *Folias de reis*. Rio de Janeiro: FUNARTE.

Caufriez, Anne. 1992. "Les polyphonies du nord du Portugal." In *SEEM a València: Encontres del Mediterrani*, 61–75. València: Generalitat Valenciana.

Chernoff, John Miller. 1979. *African Rhythm and African Sensibility: Aesthetics and Social Action in African Musical Idioms*. Chicago: University of Chicago Press.

Cleary, David. 1994. "Meu Brasil Brasileiro." In *World Music: The Rough Guide*, ed. Simon Broughton, 557–69. London: Rough Guides.

Clifford, James. 1986. "Introduction: Partial Truths." In *Writing Culture: The Poetics and Politics of Ethnography*, ed. James Clifford and George Marcus, 1–26. Berkeley and Los Angeles: University of California Press.

Connerton, Paul. 1989. *How Societies Remember*. Cambridge: Cambridge University Press.

Corrêa, Marcos Sá. 1994. "Eles têm o país na ponta da língua." *Veja* 1360:32–40.

Corrêa, Mariza. 1993. "Repensando a família patriarcal brasileira." In *Colcha de retalhos: Estudos sobre a família no Brasil*, ed. Antonio Augusto Arantes, Bela Feldmann-Bianco, Carlos Rodrigues Brandão, et al., 15–42. Campinas: Ed. da UNICAMP.

Correia de Azevedo, Luiz Heitor. 1956. *150 anos de música no Brasil (1800–1950)*. Rio de Janeiro: José Olympio.

Cubitt, Tessa. 1988. *Latin American Society*. Harlow, Essex: Longman Scientific and Technical.

daMatta, Roberto. [1979] 1991. *Carnival, Rogues and Heroes: An Interpretation of the Brazilian Dilemma*. Notre Dame, Ind.: University of Notre Dame Press.

———. 1985. *A casa e a rua: Espaço, cidadania, mulher e morte no Brasil*. São Paulo: Brasiliense.

———. 1994. "Some Biased Remarks on Interpretivism: A View from Brazil. " In *Assessing Cultural Anthropology*, ed. Robert Borofsky, 119–32. New York: McGraw-Hill.

Dean, Warren. 1976. "A pequena propriedade dentro do complexo cafeeiro: Sitiantes no município de Rio Claro (1870–1920)." *Revista de história* 53 (106).

Douglas, Mary. 1975. "Jokes." In *Implicit Meanings: Essays in Anthropology*, ed. Mary Douglas, 90–114. London: Routledge and Kegan Paul.

Dumont, Louis. 1980. *Homo Hierarchicus: The Caste System and Its Implications*. Chicago: University of Chicago Press.

Durham, Eunice R. 1984. *A caminho da cidade: A vida rural e a migração para São Paulo*. São Paulo: Perspectiva.

———. 1986. "A pesquisa antropológica com populações urbanas: Problemas e perspectivas." In *A aventura antropológica: Teoria e pesquisa*, ed. Ruth Cardoso, 17–37. Rio de Janeiro: Paz e Terra.

Eco, Umberto. 1984. "The Frames of Comic 'Freedom.'" In *Carnival*, ed. Thomas A. Sebeok, 1–9. Amsterdam: Mouton.

BIBLIOGRAPHY

Elias, Norbert. 1978–82. *The Civilizing Process*. 2 vols. New York: Pantheon Books.

Enslin, M. S. 1962. "Melkon." In *Interpreter's Dictionary of the Bible*. New York: Abingdon.

Epstein, A. L. 1975. *Kinship and Urbanization*. London: Academic Press.

Erlmann, Veit. 1990. "Migration and Performance: Zulu Migrant Workers' *Isicathamiya* Performance in South Africa, 1850–1950." *Ethomusicology* 34 (2): 199–220.

Etzel, Eduardo. 1975. *Arte sacra popular brasileira: Conceito—exemplo—evolução*. São Paulo: EDUSP.

Feld, Steven. 1982. *Sound and Sentiment: Birds, Weeping, Poetics and Song in Kaluli Expression*. Philidelphia: University of Pennsylvania Press.

———. 1994. "Aesthetics as Iconicity of Style (Uptown Title); or (Downtown Title) 'Lift-Up-Over-Sounding': Getting into the Kaluli Groove." In *Music Grooves: Essays and Dialogues*, ed. Charles Keil and Steven Feld, 109–50. Chicago: University of Chicago Press.

Fernandes, Ruben Cesar. 1982. *Os cavaleiros do Bom Jesus*. São Paulo: Brasiliense.

Fernandez, James W. 1986. "The Argument of Images and the Experience of Returning to the Whole." In *The Anthropology of Experience*, ed. Victor Turner and Edward M. Bruner, 159–87. Urbana: University of Illinois Press.

Finnegan, Ruth. 1989. *The Hidden Musicians: Music-Making in an English Town*. Cambridge: Cambridge University Press.

Fonseca, Claudia. 1987. "Mulher: Chefe da família?" *Revista de ciências sociais* 1 (2): 261–68.

Forman, Shepard, and Joyce F. Riegelhaupt. 1979. "The Political Economy of Patron-Clientship: Brazil and Portugal Compared." In *Brazil: Anthropological Perspectives*, ed. Maxine Margolis and William E. Carter, 379–400. New York: Columbia University Press.

Franco, Maria Sylvia de Carvalho. 1969. *Homens livres an ordem escravocrata*. São Paulo: Instituto de Estudos Brasileiros.

French, John D. 1992. *The Brazilian Workers' ABC: Class Conflict and Alliances in Modern São Paulo*. Chapel Hill: University of North Carolina Press.

Freyre, Gilberto. [1933] 1966. *The Masters and the Slaves*. Trans. S. Putman. Abridged, 2d ed. New York: Alfred A Knopf.

———. 1959. *New World in the Tropics: The Culture of Modern Brazil*. New York: Alfred Knopf.

Galvão, Eduardo. 1955. *Santos e visagens: Um estudo da vida religiosa de Itá, Amazonas*. São Paulo: Editora Nacional.

Gellner, Ernst. 1969. "A Pendulum Swing Theory of Islam." In *Sociology of Religion: Selected Readings*, ed. Roland Robertson, 127–38. Harmondsworth, England: Penguin Education.

Gerholm, T. 1988. "On Ritual: A Post-modern View." *Ethnos* 3–4:190–203.

Girardelli, Élsie da Costa. 1981. *Ternos de congos, Atibaia*. Rio de Janeiro: FUNARTE.

Goodenough, E. R. 1964. *Jewish Symbols in the Greco-Roman Period*. New York: Pantheon Books.

Goody, Jack. 1986. *The Logic of Writing and the Organization of Society*. Cambridge: Cambridge University Press.

Gramsci, Antonio. 1985. *Selections from Cultural Writings*. Edited by David Forgacs and Geoffrey Nowell-Smith. London: Lawrence and Wishart.

Handelman, Don. 1981. "The Ritual-Clown: Attributes and Affinities." *Anthropos* 76:321–70.

Hennecke, E. 1963. *Gospels and Related Writings*. Vol. 1 of *New Testament Apocrypha*. London: Lutherworth Press.

BIBLIOGRAPHY

Hewitt, W. E. 1991. *Base Christian Communities and Social Change in Brazil*. Lincoln: University of Nebraska Press.

Hieb, Louis A. 1979. "The Ritual Clown: Humour and Ethics." In *Forms of Play of Native American Indians*, ed. Edward Norbeck and Clare R. Farrer, 171–88. St. Paul, Minn.: West Publishing.

Hobsbawm, Eric, and Terence Ranger, eds. 1983. *The Invention of Tradition*. Cambridge: Cambridge University Press.

Hochshild, Arlie. 1979. "Emotion Work, Feeling Rules, and Social Structure." *American Journal of Sociology* 85:551–75.

Holloway, Thomas H. 1989. "Immigration in the Rural South." In *Modern Brazil*, ed. Michael L. Conniff and Frank D. McCann, 140–60. Lincoln: University of Nebraska Press.

Hoornaert, Eduardo. 1979. *História da igreja no Brasil*. Vol. 2 of *História geral da igreja na América Latina*. Petrópolis: Vozes.

Humphrey, John. 1982. *Capitalist Control and the Workers' Struggle in the Brazilian Auto Industry*. Princeton, N.J.: Princeton University Press.

Irvine, Judith T. 1979. "Formality and Informality in Communicative Events." *American Anthropologist* 81:773–90.

Iulianelli, Jorge Atilio Silva. 1999. "'Pega ele Jesus': RCC e CEBs no Brasil, política e modernidade." *REB* 233:67–87.

James, M. R. 1926. *The Apocryphal New Testament*. Oxford: Oxford University Press.

Johnson, Allen, and George C. Bond. 1974. "Kinship, Friendship, and Exchange in Two Communities: A Comparative Analysis of Norms and Behavior." *Journal of Anthropological Research* 30:55–68.

Kadt, Emanuel de. 1970. *Catholic Radicals in Brazil*. Oxford: Oxford University Press.

Kazadi wa Mukuna. 1979. *Contribuição bantu na música popular brasileira*. São Paulo: Globo.

Keck, Margaret E. 1992. *The Workers' Party and Democratization in Brazil*. New Haven, Conn.: Yale University Press.

Keil, Charles. 1987. "Participatory Discrepancies and the Power of Music." *Cultural Anthropology* 2 (3): 275–83.

———. 1995. "The Theory of Participatory Discrepancies: A Progress Report." *Ethnomusicology* 39 (1): 1–19.

Kelly, Raymond. 1974. *Etoro Social Structure: A Study of Structural Contradiction*. Ann Arbor: University of Michigan Press.

Koestler, Arthur. 1964. *The Act of Creation*. London: Hutchinson.

Koetting, James. 1975. "The Effects of Urbanization: The Music of the Kasena of Ghana." *World of Music* 17 (4): 23–31.

Koskoff, Ellen. 1988. "Cognitive Strategies in Rehearsals." *Selected Reports in Ethnomusicology* 7:59–68.

Kottak, Conrad Philip. 1967. "Kinship and Class in Brazil." *Ethnology* 6:427–43.

Kowarik, Lucio. 1987. "The Logic of Disorder." In *Sociology of Development Studies: Latin America*, ed. Eduardo P. Archetti, Paul Cammack, and Bryan Roberts, 221–28. Basingstoke: MacMillan Education.

Krumholz, Micaela. 1982. "A dinâmica populacional do Grande ABC." In *O Grande ABC: Memória em movimento*. São Bernardo do Campo: Instituto Metodista de Ensino Superior.

BIBLIOGRAPHY

Kuipers, Joel C. 1990. *Power in Performance: Creation of Textual Authority in Weyewa Ritual Speech.* Philadelphia: University of Pennsylvania Press.

Landes, Ruth. 1947. *The City of Women.* New York: Macmillan.

Leach, Edmund. [1954] 1970. *The Political Systems of Highland Burma.* London: Athone Press.

———. 1983. "Why Did Moses Have Sisters?" In *Structuralist Interpretations of Biblical Myth,* ed. Edmund Leach and Alan Aycock, 33–66. Cambridge: Cambridge University Press.

Leite, Serafim. 1938–50. *História da Companhia de Jesus no Brasil.* 10 vols. Lisbon: Livraria Portuguesa.

Lévi-Strauss, Claude. 1969. *The Raw and the Cooked.* New York: Harper Torchbooks.

Lewis, Gilbert. 1980. *Day of Shining Red: An Essay in Understanding Ritual.* Cambridge: Cambridge University Press.

Lewis, I. M. 1971. *Ecstatic Religion: A Study of Shamanism and Spirit Possession.* London: Routledge.

Livermore, Ann. 1972. *A Short History of Spanish Music.* London: Duckworth.

Lomnitz, Larissa. 1988. "The Social and Economic Organization of a Mexican Shanty Town." In *The Urbanization of the Third World,* ed. Josef Gugler, 242–63. Oxford: Oxford University Press.

Lord, Albert. 1965. *The Singer of Tales.* New York: Atheneum.

Lovell, Peggy A. 1994. "Race, Gender, and Development in Brazil." *Latin American Research Review* 29 (3): 7–34.

Macedo, Carmem Cinira. 1986. *Tempo de gênesis: O povo das comunidades eclesiais de base.* São Paulo: Brasiliense.

MacKinnon, Niall. 1994. *The British Folk Scene: Musical Performance and Social Identity.* Buckingham, England: Open University Press.

Makarius, Laura. 1970. "Ritual Clowns and Symbolic Behaviour." *Diogenes* 69:45–73.

Mariz, Cecília Loreto. 1994. *Coping with Poverty: Pentecostals and Christian Base Communities in Brazil.* Philadelphia: Temple University Press.

Mariz, Vasco. 1983. *História da música no Brasil.* Rio de Janeiro: Civilização Brasileira.

Martins, José de Souza. 1975. *Capitalismo e tradicionalismo.* São Paulo: Pioneira.

———. 1981. *O cativeiro da terra.* São Paulo: Livraria Editora Ciências Humanas.

Maués, Raymundo Heraldo. 1995. *Padres, pajés, santos e festas: Catolicismo popular e controle eclesiástico: Um estudo antropológico numa área do interior da Amazônia.* Belém: Cejup.

Mauss, Marcel. [1950] 1997. *The Gift: The Form and Reason for Exchange in Archaic Societies.* London: Routledge.

Mayer, P. 1963. *Townsmen and Tribesmen.* Cape Town: Oxford University Press.

Mello, Sylvia Leser de. 1995. "Família: Perspectiva teórica e observação factual." In *A família contemporânea em debate,* ed. Maria do Carmo Brant de Carvalho, 51–60. São Paulo: EDUC and Cortez.

Mello e Souza, Antônio Cândido. 1982. *Os parceiros do Rio Bonito.* São Paulo: Duas Cidades.

Merriam, Alan P. 1964. *The Anthropology of Music.* Evanston, Ill: Northwestern University Press.

Metcalf, Alida. 1992. *Family and Frontier in Colonial Brazil: Santana de Parnaíba, 1580–1822.* Berkeley: University of California Press.

Mitchell, J. Clyde. 1956. *The Kalela Dance.* Rhodes-Livingston Papers, no. 27. Manchester: Manchester University Press.

BIBLIOGRAPHY

Mitchell, William E. 1992. "Introduction: Mother Folly in the Islands." In *Clowning as Critical Practice: Performance Humor in the South Pacific,* ed. William E. Mitchell, 3–57. Pittsburgh: University of Pittsburgh Press.

Monbeig, Pierre. 1984. *Pioneiros e fazendeiros de São Paulo.* São Paulo: Hucitec.

Morais Filho, Alexandre José de Melo. [1901] 1967. *Festas e tradições populares do Brasil.* Rio de Janeiro: Ed. de Ouro.

Morphy, Howard, and Marcus Banks. 1997. "Introduction: Rethinking Visual Anthropology." In *Rethinking Visual Anthropology,* ed. Marcus Banks and Howard Morphy, 1–35. New Haven, Conn.: Yale University Press.

Morris, Brian. 1987. *Anthropological Studies of Religion: An Introductory Text.* Cambridge: Cambridge University Press.

Nascimento, Antenor. 1996. "Dinheiro no bolso do pobre." *Veja* 29 (51): 48–55.

Nettl, Bruno. 1989. *Blackfoot Musical Thought: Comparative Perspectives.* Kent, Ohio: Kent State University Press.

———. 1992. "Mozart and the Ethnomusicological Study of Western Culture." In *Disciplining Music: Musicology and Its Canons,* ed. Katherine Bergerson and Philip V. Bohlman, 137–55. Chicago: University of Chicago Press.

Oliveira, Ernesto Veiga de, Leonardo Boff, João Batista Libânio, and Estevão Bettencourt. 1966. *Instrumentos musicais populares portugueses.* Lisbon: Fundação Calouste Gulbenkian.

Oliveira, Pedro A. Ribeiro de, et al. 1978. *Renovação carismática católica: Uma análise sociológica, interpretações teológicas.* Petrópolis: Vozes.

Olsen, Dale A., and Daniel E. Sheehy, eds. 1998. *South America, Mexico, Central America, and the Carribbean.* Vol. 2 of *Garland Encyclopedia of World Music.* New York: Garland Publishing.

Ortiz, Renato. 1986. *Cultura brasileira e identidade nacional.* São Paulo: Brasiliense.

Otero, Aurelio de Santos. 1979. *Los evangélios apócrifos.* Madrid: Biblioteca de Autores Cristianos.

Parkes, Peter. 1994. "Personal and Collective Identity in Kalasha Song Performance: The Significance of Music-Making in a Minority Enclave." In *Ethnicity, Identity and Music: The Musical Construction of Place,* ed. Martin Stokes, 157–85. Oxford: Berg.

Parkin, David. 1984. "Political Language." *Annual Review of Anthropology* 13:345–65.

———. 1992. "Ritual as Spatial and Bodily Division." In *Understanding Ritual,* ed. Daniel de Coppet, 11–25. London: Routledge.

Peeters, P. 1914. *Evangiles apocryphes.* Paris: Hemmer et Lejay.

Pereira de Queiroz, Maria Isaura. 1978. *Cultura, sociedade rural, sociedade urbana no Brasil.* São Paulo: EDUSP.

Petrini, João Carlos. 1984. *CEBs: Um novo sujeito popular.* Rio de Janeiro: Paz e Terra.

Pierson, Donald. 1966. *Cruz das Almas.* Rio de Janeiro: José Olympio.

"Pingente da economia." 1993. *Veja* 1297:22–25.

Pinto, Mércia de Vasconcelos. 1997. "The Brazilian Pastoril: A History of a Popular Musical Genre." Ph.D. diss., Liverpool Univerity.

Porto, Guilherme. 1977. *As folias de reis do sul de Minas.* Rio de Janeiro: FUNARTE.

Rainho, Luiz Flávio, and Osvaldo Martines Bargas. 1983. *As lutas operárias e sindicais dos metalúrgicos em São Bernardo, 1977–1979.* São Bernardo do Campo: Fundo de Greve.

Reily, Suzel Ana. 1992. "*Música Sertaneja* and Migrant Identity: The Stylistic Development of a Brazilian Genre." *Popular Music* 11 (3): 337–58.

BIBLIOGRAPHY

————. 1994a. "Macunaíma's Music: National Identity and Ethnomusicological Research in Brazil." In *Ethnicity, Identity and Music: The Musical Construction of Place*, ed. Martin Stokes, 71–96. Oxford: Berg.

————. 1994b. "Musical Performance at a Brazilian Festival." *British Journal of Ethnomusicology* 3:1–34.

————. 1996. "The Three Kings: Inter-ethnic relations in Brazilian oral narratives." In *Gender, Ethnicity and Class in Modern Portuguese-Speaking Culture*, ed. Hilary Owen, 185–224. Lewiston, N.Y.: Edwin Mellen Press.

————. 2001. "To Remember Captivity: The Congados of Southeastern Brazil." *Latin American Music Review* 22 (1): 4–30.

Rice, Timothy. 1987. "Toward a Remodelling of Ethnomusicology." *Ethnomusicology* 31 (3): 468–88.

Rolim, Fancisco. 1980. *Religião e classes sociais*. Petrópolis: Vozes.

Rosaldo, Renato. 1984. "Grief and a Headhunter's Rage: On the Cultural Force of Emotions." In *Text, Play and Story: The Construction and Reconstruction of Self and Society*, ed. Edward M. Bruner, 178–95. Washington, D.C.: American Anthropological Association.

————. 1986. "Ilongot Hunting as Story and Experience." In *The Anthropology of Experience*, ed. Victor Turner and Edward M. Bruner, 97–138. Urbana: University of Illinois Press.

Roseman, Marina. 1991. *Healing Sounds from the Malaysian Rainforest: Temiar Music and Medicine*. Berkeley: University of California Press.

Rowe, William, and Vivian Schelling. 1991. *Memory and Modernity: Popular Culture in Latin America*. London: Verso.

Samara, Eni de Mesquita. 1987. "Tendências atuais da história da família no Brasil." In *Pensando a família no Brasil: Da colônia à modernidade*, ed. Angela Mendes de Almeida, Maria José Carneiro, and Silvana Gonçalves de Paula, 25–36. Rio de Janeiro: Espaço e Tempo and Ed. da UFRRJ.

Santos, Milton. 1993. *A urbanização brasileira*. São Paulo: Hucitec.

Sarti, Cynthia. 1995. "Morality and Transgression among Brazilian Poor Families: Exploring Ambiguities." In *The Brazilian Puzzle: Culture on the Borderlands of the Western World*, ed. David J. Hess and Robert A. daMatta, 114–33. New York: Columbia University Press.

Scheper-Hughes, Nancy. 1992. *Death without Weeping: The Violence of Everyday Life in Brazil*. Berkeley: University of California Press.

Schreiner, Claus. [1977] 1993. *Música Brasileira: A History of Popular Music and the People of Brazil*. New York: Marion Boyars.

Schutz, Alfred. [1951] 1977. "Making Music Together: A Study in Social Relationship." In *Symbolic Anthropology: A Reader in the Study of Symbols and Meaning*, ed. Jane L. Dolgin, David S. Kemnitzer, and David Scheider, 106–19. New York: Columbia University Press.

Scott, James C. 1985. *Weapons of the Weak: Everyday Forms of Peasant Resistance*. New Haven, Conn.: Yale University Press.

————. 1990. *Domination and the Arts of Resistance: Hidden Transcripts*. New Haven, Conn.: Yale University Press.

Seeger, Anthony. 1987. *Why Suyá Sing: A Musical Anthropology of an Amazonian People*. Cambridge: Cambridge University Press.

Setti, Kilza. 1985. *Ubatuba nos cantos das praias*. São Paulo: Atica.

Silverstein, Leni M. 1979. "Mãe de todo mundo: Modos de sobrevivência nas comunidades de candomblé da Bahia." *Religião e sociedade* 4:143–69.

BIBLIOGRAPHY

Skidmore, Thomas E. 1993. "Bi-racial U.S.A. vs. Multi-racial Brazil: Is the Contrast Still Valid?" *Journal of Latin American Studies* 25:373–86.

Smith, Robert J. 1975. *The Art of the Festival as Exemplified by the Fiesta to the Patroness of Otuzco: La Virgen de la Puerta.* Lawrence: University of Kansas Publications in Anthropology, no. 6.

Spencer, Jonathan. 1997. "Post-colonialism and the Political Imagination." *Journal of the Royal Anthropological Institute* 3 (4): 1–19.

Stein, Stanley J. 1990. *Vassouras: Um município brasileiro do café, 1850–1900.* Rio de Janeiro: Nova Fronteira.

Stewart, Michael. 1989. "'True Speech': Songs and Moral Order of a Hungarian Vlach Gypsy Community." *Man* 24 (1): 79–101.

Stokes, Martin. 1994. "Introduction: Ethnicity, Identity and Music." In *Ethnicity, Identity and Music: The Musical Construction of Place,* ed. Martin Stokes, 1–27. Oxford: Berg.

Stolcke, Verena. 1993. "A família que não é sagrada." In *Colcha de retalhos: Estudos sobre a família no Brasil,* ed. Antonio Augusto Arantes, Bela Feldmann-Bianco, Carlos Rodrigues Brandão, et al., 61–114. Campinas: Ed. da UNICAMP.

Sugarman, Jane C. 1988. "Making Muabet: The Social Basis of Singing among Prespa Albanian Men." *Selected Reports in Ethnomusicology* 7:1–42.

Sullivan, Lawrence. 1997. "Enchanting Powers: An Introduction." In *Enchanting Powers: Music in the World's Religions,* ed. Lawrence E. Sullivan, 1–14. Cambridge, Mass.: Harvard University Press.

Tambiah, Stanley J. [1981] 1985. "A Performance Approach to Ritual." In *Culture, Thought and Social Action: An Anthropological Perspective,* ed. Stanley J. Tambiah, 113–69. Cambridge, Mass.: Harvard University Press.

Taussig, Michael T. 1980. *The Devil and Commodity Fetishism in South America.* Chapel Hill: University of North Carolina Press.

Tinhorão, José Ramos. 1994. *Fado, dança do Brasil, cantar de Lisboa: O fim de um mito.* Lisbon: Caminho da Música.

Toledo, Roberto Pompeu de. 1992. "O charme do 1,8%." *Veja* 25 (4): 58–63.

Travassos, Elizabeth. 2000. ""Ethics in the Sung Duels of North-Eastern Brazil: Collective Memory and Contemporary Practice." *British Journal of Ethnomusicology* 9 (1): 61–94.

Turino, Thomas. 1989. "The Coherence of Social Style and Musical Creation among the Aymara in Southern Peru." *Ethnomusicology* 33 (1): 1–30.

———. 1993. *Moving Away from Silence: Music of the Peruvian Altiplano and the Experience of Urban Migration.* Chicago: University of Chicago Press.

Turner, Victor. 1967. *The Forest of Symbols: Aspects of Ndembu Ritual.* Ithaca, N.Y.: Cornell University Press.

———. 1974. *The Ritual Process.* Harmondsworth, England: Penguin Books.

Wade, Peter. 1997. *Race and Ethnicity in Latin America.* London: Pluto Press.

Wagley, Charles. 1964. *Amazon Town: A Study of Man in the Tropics.* New York: Alfred Knopf.

———. 1971. *An Introduction to Brazil.* New York: Columbia University Press.

Watson, Graham. 1991. "Rewriting Culture." In *Recapturing Anthropology: Working in the Present,* ed. Richard G. Fox, 73–92. Santa Fe, N.Mex: School of American Research Press.

Weber, Max. [1922] 1963. *The Sociology of Religion.* Translated by Ephraim Fischoff. New York: Beacon Press.

BIBLIOGRAPHY

———. 1958. *From Max Weber.* Edited by Hans Gerth and C. Wright Mills. New York: Oxford University Press.

Whitehouse, Harvey. 1995. *Inside the Cult: Religious Innovation and Transmission in Papua New Guinea.* Oxford: Clarendon Press.

Willems, Emilio. 1961. *Uma vila brasileira.* São Paulo: Difusão Européia do Livro.

Winant, Howard. 1992. "Rethinking Race in Brazil." *Journal of Latin American Studies* 24:173–92.

Zaluar, Alba. 1980. "Milagre e castigo divino." *Religião e sociedade* 5:161–87.

———. 1983. *Os homens de Deus: Um estudo dos santos e das festas no catolicismo popular.* Rio de Janeiro: Zahar.

Zuhur, Sherifa, ed. 1998. *Images of Enchantment: Visual and Performing Arts of the Middle East.* Cairo: American University in Cairo Press.

Index

accordion, 43, 70, 94, 102, 153, 217, 240n. 2
Adoration of the Wise Men, xii, 29, 64, 125, 139, 143, 149, 156–57, 184, 238n. 9
adorations, *folia,* 75, 130, 147–51, 165–96, 205–6, 208. *See also* verses: adoration
adufo, 233n. 16
ajudante, 33–34, 36, 39, 48, 70, 97–99, 101
alcohol consumption, 58, 64–65, 94, 117–18, 120, 125, 178, 206, 208. *See also mé*
alféres, 235nn. 6, 8
altars, xii, 123–26, 128–30, 139, 144, 149–50, 165
Alvarenga, Oneyda, 30, 64
amulets, 136
Andrade, Mário de, xiv, 233n. 5
Annunciation, 125
Anthony, Saint, 6, 123
apocryphal texts, 151, 237n. 7
apresentações. See performance: staged
Araújo, Alceu Maynard de, 30, 32–33, 233nn. 6, 7, 235n. 6
Arceburgo, 37, 59, 74, 163, 190, 194–95, 197, 199, 206–7
associations. *See* resonance, associative; webs of association
Austin, J., 129
authenticity, 202

back singers, 34, 36, 48–49, 95, 98–99, 132–33
bad boss, 164
baiano style, 41–42, 234n. 17
baião, 240n. 2
baile, 194
bairros, 47–54, 152, 220
Baltazar, 67, 151, 155–56, 160
Balthasar, 151
bandas de pifes, 41
bandeira dos santos reis. See banner

bandeiras (militia companies), 64, 234n. 19
bandeiras de santo reis (musical ensemble), 64
bandeireiro, 65, 78
bandolins, 43, 102–3, 217
banner, 64, 123–25, 127–28, 136, 139–42, 186–88, 197, 237n. 2; and *bandeireiros,* 78; and *bastião,* 73–74, 76; capturing of, 67; and *donos,* 65. 81; and promises, 179–80; and protection rites, 136; and the dead, 113, 176; at rehearsals, xii, 95
barroco mineiro, 46
bastião, xiii, 65, 69, 71–78, 133–36, 142, 157, 212, 215, 235n. 6, 237n. 6; in *folia* ritual, xiii, 5, 67, 125–26, 144, 147–50, 168, 170, 173, 176, 192–93, 197, 206. *See also* clowns
bastiãozinho, 73, 84, 180, 182
Bauman, Richard, 11–12, 128
Béhague, Gerard, 9, 29
Bell, Catherine, 12, 128, 211
Belquior, 151
Benedict the Moor, Saint, 6, 85
benzimentos, 184
Bible, 83, 151. *See also* Holy Scriptures
black King, 144, 151, 156, 159–60, 173, 238n. 9
Blacking, John, 14–15, 90, 214, 220, 236n. 6
Blechó or Blechió, 67, 151, 155–56
blessings, xiii, 5, 129–30, 139–41, 172–77, 185–89, 197, 210, 218, 237n. 9; performance of, 126, 166–72, 194. *See also* verses: blessing or family
Bloch, Maurice, 134, 236n. 6, 237n. 8
blocos afro, 86
body language, 110–11, 120
Bohlman, Philip, 10
bóias-frias (rural day laborers), 55
bom patrão. See good boss
bonés (traditional headgear), 57
Brandão, Carlos Rodrigues, 6, 10,176–79, 182, 202–3, 231n. 4, 233nn. 5, 6, 7, 237n. 3, 240n. 2

INDEX

Brechó, 151
Bruner, Edward M., 214

caboclos, 60
cacetero, 39, 98–99, 233n. 14
caderneta (notebook), 79, 119
caipira, 56, 152
caixa, 5, 29, 42, 70–72, 94, 96, 100, 103, 105, 107, 117, 184, 217. *See also* drums
Canaan (son of Noah), 238n. 9
candomblé. See possession cults
cantadores, 235n. 4
capacetes, 73
capelão, 125
carnival, 65
Caspar, 151. *See also* Gaspar
castigos divinos. See punishments, divine
cateretê, 29, 43, 232n. 1
Catholic Church, 6–8, 86, 152, 198, 211–13, 231nn. 4, 5, 241n. 2
Catholicism, 8, 21, 152, 154, 205, 211; popular, 2–3, 6–10, 22, 64, 86, 178, 198, 212–13, 215, 231nn. 4, 6. *See also* traditions, popular Catholic
catira, 232n. 1
cavaquinho, 43, 84, 102–3, 217
cebolão (*viola* tuning), 101
CEBs. *See* Christian base communities
charismatic movement, 8, 241n. 1
choirs, 201
choro, 217, 236n. 4
Christ. *See* Jesus
Christian base communities, xiv, 8, 231n. 5
Christian tradition, 22, 150–52, 161, 238n. 9; in ethnographic representation, 22–23; in *folia* representations, xii, 64, 144, 149, 151–52, 154, 160–61. *See also* Catholicism
Christmas season, xi, 1, 29, 31, 41, 120, 122, 200–201, 204
chula, 74
church. *See* Catholic Church
civilizing process, 120, 208, 211
clientelism, 164, 234n. 25. *See also* patronage
closures, 136–38
clowning, ritual, 134
clowns, 5, 31, 65, 134–35, 221, 237n. 7. *See also bastião*
colonato, 52, 238n. 9
colônia, 52–53
communitas, 16
community studies, 8, 10
companhias de reis, xi, 30–31. *See also folia de reis*
competition, 68–69, 74, 76, 116–17

conceptual frameworks, 90, 115–16, 120–21, 212, 235n. 1
confraternities, 30, 45–46
congados, 6, 41, 85–87, 202, 235n. 3, 240n. 1
Connerton, Paul, 129
contra-tipe, 36, 39, 70–71, 98–99
contrato, 36–37, 70–72, 98–99, 111–12, 119, 233n. 13
coordinator, 78–80
corta-jaca, 74
crèche. *See* manger scene
crib. *See* manger scene
crosses, three, 76
cultural administrators, 79–80, 87, 203–6, 208–9

daMatta, Roberto, 22, 65, 232n. 14
dança de São Gonçalo. See dance: Saint Gonçalo
dance, 5–6, 15, 85–87, 130, 194–96, 217, 236n. 7; Saint Gonçalo, 6, 43, 232n. 1, 240nn. 3, 1
Débret, Jean Baptiste, 30
decision making, 94–95, 115, 121, 218
defamiliarization, 22–23
demolitions, 136
Department of Culture, xii, 80, 86, 117, 190–91, 199, 201, 204–6
departure of the banner, 5, 122–30, 136, 138–42, 216
desmanches, 136–38
devotion, 6, 31, 125, 138–39, 141, 147–48, 186, 203, 207, 211, 216, 218
dignity, 20–21, 135, 155, 198, 208, 212, 222
Divine Holy Spirit, 21, 40, 85
divine intervention, 161
divine mandate, 49, 182, 220
dom. See gift
dona da bandeira, 65
donations, xi, 5, 64, 76, 79, 134, 172, 174, 176–77, 180, 185–86, 188–89, 197, 210, 216, 218
dono da bandeira, 59, 65, 80–81, 88
dono da festa, 65
Douglas, Mary, 135
drums, 6, 32, 41–42, 94, 105, 236n. 9, 240n. 2. *See also caixas*
duplas sertanejas, 200
Durham, Eunice, 48, 55, 56, 184, 232n. 15

egalitarianism, 49, 54, 112, 115–16, 220
embaixada, xiii, 118–19; and the *embaixador,* 66–67, 83, 100, 112, 216; in *folia* performances, 125, 129–30, 132–33, 136, 139–40, 143–44, 150, 167, 175, 177, 191–93; instructions in, 97, 207
embaixador, 66–72, 74, 80–83,85, 110–12, 114, 121, 174, 216; in *folia* rituals, 137, 148, 174, 196–97,

207; in the *mineiro* style, 36, 39–40, 97–98, 100; in the *paulista* style, 34, 48; and the *viola,* 70, 100–101
enchantment, 3–4, 13–14, 16–17, 210, 219, 231n. 3; in *folia* rituals, 21, 49, 128, 141–42, 165, 185–86, 189, 221–22; in music making, 15–16, 219
encontros. See encounters
encounters (confrontations), 31, 67–69, 76–77, 201, 207
encounters (state-sponsored events), 201
endo-ethnography, 22
ensaio. See rehearsals
entextualization, 11–13, 213
Epiphany, 30
equality, 49, 77, 98, 160–62, 212, 234n. 22
estilo baiano. See baiano style
estilo mineiro. See mineiro style
estilo paulista. See paulista style
estribilho, xii, 43, 70–71, 95, 102–3, 110, 191, 193
ethnographic representation, 23
evil eye, 136
exchange, 5, 68, 128, 133–34, 157, 161, 177–78,183–68, 212, 222; at the Adoration, 5, 133, 157, 161, 212; asymmetrical, 161, 239n. 14; in *folia* rituals, xi, 5, 134, 172, 177–78, 210; between humans and saints, 128, 134, 178, 222; interhousehold, 48, 53, 218; in popular Catholicism, 178; reciprocal, 50, 157, 161, 222. *See also* reciprocity
experience, 3–4, 11–17, 131, 141, 186–89, 211–22; bodily, 120–21, 141, 186, 213, 218; music-making, 3–4, 15–16, 89, 90, 111–13, 115, 133, 185; performance, 53; subaltern, 20, 155–56, 159–65, 212; urban, 6, 17, 56, 87
expulsion, 54–55, 221
ex-voto, 179–80

false consciousness, 86
family, 140–41, 172–77, 183, 198, 210, 215; and blessings, 71, 130, 166–67; and *folia* membership, 84; of God, 141, 150, 157, 165, 185–86, 210; and the Holy Family, 150; organization of, 47–48, 51–55, 162–65; symbolic extension of, 197–98, 210. *See also* household; relations: family
fanfarras, 201
farda, 73, 79–80, 123. *See also* uniforms
favelas, 55–56
favores (favors), 51
fazendas. See plantations
fechamento. See closures
fellow townsmen, 55, 59–60, 197
Fernandes, Vasco, 238n. 9

Fernandez, James, 11–13, 130, 231n. 7
festa da chegada. See festival of the arrival
festeira, 66, 124–28, 190
festeiro, 5, 65–66, 78, 80–81, 122–23, 138, 180, 190–92, 195, 216
festival of the arrival, xi, 5, 66, 81, 83, 122, 155, 186, 189, 193–99, 210–11, 216
festivals: folklore, 202, 205; Pentecost (*Festa do Divino*), 21, 40, 85; popular Catholic, 6, 30, 45–46, 48–49, 53, 85–87, 202, 240n. 4; *sertanejo,* 200
final chord, 33, 35–36, 39–40, 98–100, 132–33, 141–44, 210, 218, 237n. 2
Finnegan, Ruth, 89
Folia do Baeta Neves, 37, 44, 58–60, 78, 80–81, 88, 98–99, 102, 113, 117–18, 120, 149, 172, 175, 187, 190, 196–97, 199–201, 203–9; performances of, 122, 124, 143, 167
Folia do Seu Alcides, 43, 58, 60–61, 105, 148, 196
Folia do Zé dos Magos, 58, 60, 63, 86, 116, 167, 173, 175–76, 196–97
Folia do Zé Machado, 36, 58, 61, 96, 113, 183, 195
Folia do Zé Quatorze, 36, 58, 93, 122, 173
folia, 30
folias de reis, xi–xii, 1–3, 5–6, 21, 29–31, 177–78, 233nn. 5, 6, 7; discord in, 138–39, 142, 157; instrumentation of, 5, 32, 42–44, 70, 216–17; organization and hierarchy of, 31, 65–81, 115–16; origin myths of, 5, 27–29; recruitment to, 82–85, 219; in São Bernardo, 35, 58–61, 79, 81, 88, 122, 204, 208; in the urban context, xi, 5–6, 18–20, 58–62, 78–80, 85–89, 117–18, 166–67, 197–98, 216; women in, 84, 89, 96, 235n. 3, 235n. 7
folias do divino, 33, 40, 114, 136n. 8
foliões, xii, 1, 215; as defenders of the banner, 68, 197; musical knowledge of, 95, 99–102, 107, 112, 116; and offense, 113–14; and outsiders, 190, 203–5; political activity of, 18–19, 164; socialization of, 78, 83–84, 111
folk groups, 80, 200, 202–3, 209
folklore, 5, 9–10, 20, 86, 198, 200–202, 205, 208
food, xi, 5–6, 13, 55, 66, 95, 130, 143, 177–78, 185–86, 190, 194–96, 216, 221
formalization, 113, 132, 149–50, 153, 236n. 5
forró, 194, 217
Franco, Maria Sylvia de Carvalho, 49
Freyre, Gilberto, 50, 234n. 20, 239n. 13
front singers, 33–34, 36, 48–49, 97–99, 132, 193

ganzá, 43
Gaspar, 27, 29, 67, 151, 155–56, 160. *See also* Caspar

INDEX

generosity, 51, 53, 142, 174, 176–77, 195, 197, 207–8, 222

George, Saint, 123

gift (talent), 66, 82, 84

gift. *See* exchange; Three Kings: and gifts

giros, 5, 120

gold era, 45–47

Gonçalo, Saint, 123

good boss, 53, 164, 221

Goody, Jack, 211, 241n. 1

Gramsci, Antonio, 9–10, 20, 155

Great ABC, 17

grupos folclóricos. See folk groups

guincho, 233n. 8

guitars, 43, 70, 82–83, 102–3, 217, 235nn. 5, 4

Hail Mary. *See* prayer

half-moons, 191, 240n. 1

hat game, 194

heaven. *See* sacred sphere

Herod, King, 27–28, 134, 151, 154, 157–59, 161–64, 179, 212, 221, 239n. 14; emissaries of, 72–74, 77

Herods (dangers), 1, 66–67, 95, 122, 125, 136–37, 157

hidden transcripts, 20, 23, 155, 157, 159, 164

Holy Family, 143, 150, 161, 210

Holy Scriptures, 146, 150. *See also* Bible

hospitality, 177–78, 185

households, xiii, 47–49, 51–55, 121, 176–78, 183–84, 210, 216, 218, 240n. 2; head of, 162–63, 167–71, 173–75, 177. *See also* family

humanity, 11, 49, 133–35, 141, 157, 161, 185–86, 211–12, 222

humans, 48–49, 135, 141–42, 153, 157, 177–78, 180, 185, 212, 222; as bodily beings, 213; and the dead, 176; as historical agents, 9; and morality, 11, 197; and the saints, 128–29, 173, 181

humiliation, 79–80, 113, 159, 164, 199, 209, 222

hybridization, 53

iconography, 46, 139, 180

ideal types, 213

identity, 218; ethic, 161; male, 49; moral, 2; national, 239n. 13; personal, 140; subaltern, 197

illness, 19, 83, 124, 142, 163, 168, 174, 179, 184

immigration, 51–52, 238n. 9

improvisation: musical, 100, 103, 105, 107–9; verse, xiii, 32, 57, 66–68, 97, 111–12, 121, 132, 140, 175

industry, xi, xiv, 17–18, 45

infant mortality, 162

inflation, 18, 56

infrapolitics, 20, 198, 222

initiation, 77, 107

inscriptions, 67, 75, 191, 196, 237n. 2

integrity, 220–21; cultural, 2, 21, 23; of the *embaixador,* 67; of the *folia,* 64, 76, 116, 136, 138; human, 56; moral, 199, 212, 222; musical, 114–15, 133; personal, 49, 53, 69, 93–94, 113, 116, 120

interior, the, 197, 240n. 3

intervals (musical), 235n. 3

invented traditions, 202, 205, 209

irmandades. See confraternities

itinerant ensembles, 29

janeiras, 30

Japheth (son of Noah), 238n. 9

Jesus, 27–28, 41, 72–74, 135, 143–46, 149–50, 152, 156–60, 173

John the Baptist, 6, 123

jornadas. See journeys

journey of the Magi, 40, 67–68, 75, 125, 149–54, 158–60, 237n. 7; and *folia* practice, xi, 5, 11, 120, 139–40, 153–54

journeys (*folia*), 1–5, 10–11, 120, 128–29, 139, 141, 203, 210, 221–22; adorations during, 147; and danger, 1, 66, 128n, 128, 136–38, 142, 157; and *donos,* 65; and promises, 81; and the church, 2; and the journey of the Wise Men, xi, 5, 185, 218; expenses of, 123; in the urban context, 197; itinerary of, 1, 65, 123, 153

justice, 20, 159, 161–62

King of the Congo, 160, 173

Kings' Day, xi, 5, 30, 193, 237n. 4

Koestler, Arthur, 134

Koskoff, Ellen, 89–90

Kuipers, Joel, 12

labor unions, xiv, 18, 79, 200

Land Labor Statute, 54

lapa/lapinha, 237n. 1. *See also* manger scenes

Law of the Land, 50

Leach, Edmund, 16, 154, 238n. 7

leaders, 115–18, 120, 215, 217; in decision making, 94–95, 121; in *folias,* 80–81; and offense, 113, 117; and outsiders, 200–201, 204; in popular Catholicism, 48

letreiros. See inscriptions

levantamento do mastro, 195

liberation theology, 7, 86, 231n. 5

linhas (verse couplet), 32–33, 37–38, 97, 103

litany, 32

262

INDEX

Lord, Albert, 66
Lord's Prayer. *See* prayer
LP, xii, 80, 199–202, 204, 206–7

magi, 151–53, 237n. 6, 238nn. 7, 8. *See also* Three
    Kings
manger scene, xiii, 5, 123, 143–44, 147–50, 165, 191,
    196, 204–5, 210, 237n. 1
marcadora, 79
marching bands, 201
marginality, 2, 7, 20, 173, 198, 205, 221–22
Martins, José de Souza, 52, 200, 234n. 23
marungo, 235n. 6
Mary. *See* Our Lady
masks, 73, 75, 135–36, 144, 147, 170
massacre of the innocents, 72–74, 151, 157–58, 162–
    63, 179, 238n. 10
mater dolorosa, 162, 179
Matthew, Saint, 150
Maués, Raymundo Heraldo, 10, 179–80, 231n. 4
mau-olhado, 136
mau patrão. See bad boss
Mauss, Marcel, 177, 189
mé, 63, 81, 125, 147. *See also* alcohol consumption
meia-luas, 191
meião, 36, 99
melê, 43
Melkon, 151
Mello e Souza, Antônio Cândido de, 8, 35
Mello Morais Filho, Alexandre José de, 30
Melquior, 151, 156
memory, 10, 132; and affective experience, 12; bod-
    ily, 129; collective, 216; and musical style, 54; rit-
    ual and the rekindling of, 135, 140, 144, 176, 188,
    214
metonyms of narrative, 153
midnight mass, 122
migration, 17–18, 55–56, 184, 207–8, 216
mineiro style, xiii, 35–41, 46, 53–54, 56–58, 132, 170,
    210, 216, 218, 220, 237n. 9
minimal needs, 35, 47
minimum wage, 18, 232n. 10
miracles, 179–80
miraculous conception, 151
misfortune, 73, 78, 179, 182–83
missa do galo, 237n. 4. *See also* midnight mass
mobility, 44–45, 52–53, 55, 113, 221
moçambiques, 6, 41, 85, 202, 240n. 1
modas (melodic structures), 33
modernization, 57–58, 86, 117–18, 208–9, 216
money, xi, 73, 76, 79, 176, 178, 216

moral capital, 198
moral community, 2, 11, 21, 197–98
moral economy, 161
morality, 3, 9–11, 135, 141, 155–57, 160–61, 165, 186,
    208, 211, 213, 222
moral order, 3, 12, 17, 139, 197, 208, 212, 219
mothers, xiv, 83, 135, 158, 162, 175, 179, 181
motif clusters, 131–32, 141–42, 150, 165, 173, 187
motifs, 13–14, 130–32, 213, 215–17; in the *folia* reper-
    toire, 142, 148–49, 151–53, 155
music, 3–4, 16, 219–20, 235n. 1; conceptions of, 89–
    90, 102, 110–15, 118, 219; and emotion, 186; and
    migration, 207; research on Brazilian, 29–30; and
    ritual experience, 141, 188, 218; and the saints,
    132–33, 142, 185, 212
musical styles, 3, 171–73; antiphonal, 32, 35, 41, 49;
    cumulative, xiii, 32–33, 35, 218, 220; *folia,* 31–33,
    53–54, 132, 172–73, 220–21; participatory, 112, 114;
    of popular Catholic traditions, 32–33; urban, 208;
    and urban *folias,* 62
music making, 3–4, 14–16, 84, 89, 90, 109, 110, 112–
    13, 121, 125, 128, 130, 132–33, 185–86, 215, 217–20;
    orientations toward, 88–90, 96, 109, 112, 114–15,
    117, 219, 235n. 1; participatory, 217, 219–20; and
    social harmony, 185
mutirões, 48

Nativity, 125, 131, 144, 148–52, 154, 239n. 11
natural law, 9, 17, 49, 155, 161–62, 165, 185, 189, 211–
    12, 219, 221
natural tuning, 101
networks, social, 2, 21, 55, 91, 93, 95, 141, 167, 174,
    182–86, 188, 231n. 2

obligations, 49, 177, 184–86, 189, 194, 221; to cul-
    tural administrators, 203–4; family, 47–48, 185;
    mutual, 2, 49, 58, 141, 181–83, 185, 198, 208, 220–
    21; and promises, 73, 81, 181–84; to the saints, 49,
    60, 62, 124, 132, 173, 175, 181, 207
offense, 95, 113, 116, 161
offerings. *See* donations
organic ideologies, 10
original sin, 212
orthodoxy, 151, 153–54, 160–61, 211–12
Our Father. *See* prayer
Our Lady of the Rosary, 6, 85–86
Our Lady, 5, 27–26, 74, 123, 162, 179

palhaço, 235n. 6
pandeiro. See tambourine
parallel sixths, 32, 233n. 9, 235n. 2

263

INDEX

parallel thirds, 31, 33, 36, 43, 97–98, 100–102, 233n. 9, 235n. 3

Parkin, David, 13, 129, 236n. 6

participatory discrepancies, 236n. 7

pastoril, 29, 30

patrão, 72. *See also* household: head of

patronage, 31, 80, 123, 164, 190, 199, 202–3

paulista style, 33–35, 48–49, 53–54, 132, 216, 220

paulistinhas, 46

Pentecostalism, 8, 59, 167, 181

Pereira de Queiroz, Maria Isaura, 54

performance: and modernization, 57–58; *folia,* 5, 66, 147–48, 178, 189, 193, 195–97, 213, 215–16, 218; practice, 16, 90, 220; requirements, 14–15, 90, 110, 220; ritual, 13, 128, 213–16, 218; staged, 80, 117, 199–205; urban style of, 207–8. *See also* music making

performatives, 129–30

persecutions, 136

personhood, 49, 140, 218

pífanos, 31

pifes, 31

plantations, 50–54, 220–21

political, the, 198, 202–3, 220

possession cults, 8, 60, 167, 235n. 3

pousos, 31, 65, 67, 73, 134, 143, 206

poverty, 2, 17–18, 20, 45, 55–56, 113, 156, 164, 179, 196, 211

prayer, 32, 128, 171, 137, 236n. 1

Presentation in the Temple, 125, 146, 151

presépio, 237n. 1

processional bands, 201, 240n. 4

profecia. See prophecies

promessa. See promise

promise, 128, 178–82, 185, 240nn. 5, 6, 7; and the banner, 64; for children, xiv, 73, 83, 135; and *folia* participants, 60–61, 66, 73, 81, 83, 124, 139

prophecies, xiii, 75, 144, 147–50, 152, 206

protection rites, 122, 124–26, 128, 136. *See also* closures

PT, 18–19, 79–80, 232n. 13

public presentations. *See* performance: staged

public transcripts, 22–23

punishments, divine, 73, 78, 181–82, 240n. 7

quermesses, 85–86

radical empiricism, 24

reciprocity, 161, 178, 182–83, 185–86, 189, 212; and the *bastião,* 134; and the *folia* ethos, 31, 165; during *folia* journeys, 147, 176–78; and the good

boss, 221; between humans and saints, 134, 139; negative, 161, 240n. 7; and outsiders, 204; in rural neighborhoods, 47, 49

reco-reco, 43

reenchantment, 185, 212, 222

rehearsals, xi, 65, 88–95, 121

reification, 114–15, 118

reis (supernatural being), 155, 233n. 11

religion, 11–12, 16, 186, 211–15; vernacular, 3–4, 10, 13, 211–13, 215. *See also* Catholicism

repetition, xii, 32–35, 49, 89, 95, 111, 113, 121, 132, 150, 236n. 6, 237n. 5

repico (drum), 105

representations, 4, 186, 188, 214–15, 217, 221; ethnographic, 23; in the *folia* repertoire, xii, 101, 149–50, 152, 154–55; in popular Catholicism, 10, 22, 139, 212–13

requinta, 179

resonance, associative,13–14, 131–32, 153, 160, 186–87, 214, 217–18; in the *folia* context, 132, 135, 137, 140–42, 162, 173, 217–18, 221

resposta, 34, 37, 39, 48, 99, 101

revitalization movements, 11, 13, 214–15

revival movements. *See* revitalization movements

rezador, 125

rio abaixo (*viola* tuning), 101

rite of passage, 77

ritual, 11–14, 16, 128, 211–17

ritual clowning. *See* clowning, ritual

ritual script, 13, 130–32, 139, 147, 172–73, 176, 186, 215, 218

Romanization, 7, 211

Rosaldo, Renato, 153, 189

rosary, 32, 122, 125, 126, 129, 138, 193, 196, 236n. 1

Rugendas, Johann M. 30

rural neighborhoods. *See bairros*

sacraments, 8, 211

Sacred Heart of Jesus, 124

sacred sphere, 11–12, 16–17, 128–29, 134, 140–41, 173, 176, 211

sacrifice, 94, 155, 179–80, 217

saída da bandeira. See departure of the banner

Saint Gonçalo dance. *See* dance: Saint Gonçalo

saints, 6, 49–50, 135, 140, 165–66, 185, 211–12, 222; and confraternities, 45; humanization of, 180, 222; and humans, 48–49, 128, 142, 177–83, 189; iconography of, 123; and music, 142; and *reis,* 155; and the *viola,* 102

sala dos milagres, 180

samba schools, 86

264

INDEX

sanfona. *See* accordion

São Bernardo do Campo, xi, xiv, 17–18, 42, 58–62, 86, 91, 118, 122, 183, 195, 199–200, 205–9

São Paulo, 17–18, 20, 87, 164, 206

Scheper-Hughes, Nancy, 23, 162, 164, 183, 234n. 25, 235n. 11

Schutz, Alfred, 15

Scott, James, 20, 22, 155, 162, 198

Sebastian, Saint, 61, 195

segunda, 33

self-esteem, 20, 198–99, 208–9, 222

senzalas (slave quarters), 51

serestas, 217

sharecroppers, 50–51, 53

Shem (son of Noah), 238n. 9

slaves, 50–51, 155, 156–57, 239n. 13

sociability, 2, 10, 15–16, 48, 53, 55, 62, 94, 121, 153, 221; in music making, 90, 110, 112, 114, 121, 219

social ascent, 52, 55–56, 58, 184, 208

social harmony, 11, 14, 17, 49, 133–34, 157, 185, 212, 222; disruptions of, 136, 139; and the final chord, 142, 218

social ideal, 3, 10, 15–16, 133, 138–39, 219

social relations, 133, 220; dyadic, 51, 121, 183; equivalent transient, 234n. 22; family, 56, 140, 198, 218; interclass, 9, 96, 113–14, 163–65, 198, 205, 220–21, 235n. 11; interhousehold, 48, 175; intraclass, 45, 51, 54; of musical production, 15–16, 90, 110–11, 114–15, 117; racial, 159–60, 198, 239n. 13

solidarity, 2, 47–49, 51, 141, 183–84, 198

song, 130, 132, 134, 150, 207, 237n. 8; texts of, 4, 14

speech, 12, 129, 132, 134, 149, 237n. 8

spokesmen of the Kings. *See* voices of the Magi

Stokes, Martin, 11

stories, 4–5, 138, 148, 151, 153–57, 159–62, 181, 212–13, 217

subalternity, 2, 9–10, 20, 23, 178, 198, 203, 212–13, 222

Sugarman, Jane, 109, 134, 232n. 9, 237nn. 5, 8

symbolic capital, 196–97

tala, 36, 39, 70, 99–100, 107, 112, 233n. 12

tambourine, 5, 29, 42– 43, 70, 100, 105, 184, 196, 217

telegraphic narration, 140, 153, 155

terço. *See* rosary

ternos de congos, 233n. 15

thanksgiving, 36, 166, 169–70, 171–74, 176–77. *See also* verses: thanksgiving

theatricality, 148, 173,196

Three Kings, 27–29, 128–29, 144, 150–61, 210, 212,

237–38n. 7; and the banner, 64, 139–40; and Christian tradition, 150–51; ethnic origins of, 156, 238n. 9; as a *folia,* 41; and *folia* practice, 42–43, 70, 80, 94, 143, 149, 153, 157, 184–85, 210, 217; and gifts, 5, 133, 139, 151, 156–57, 161, 238n. 7; as Herod's slaves, 27–28, 155; human encounters with, 173, 222; humanization of, 153, 156; iconography of, 144, 154; inscriptions of, 67; instruments of, 32, 42, 70, 94, 153, 157, 184, 217; messages from, 66; moral principles of, 64, 135, 197; and music, 5, 132–33, 142, 184–85, 212; as musicians, 5, 152; offense to, 78, 120; promises to, 60, 66, 69, 73, 81, 83–84, 135, 139, 174, 179. *See also* magi

timeline, 41–42, 204n. 2

tipe, 36, 39, 70, 98–99, 233n. 12

toadas (melodic structures), xii–xiii, 32–36, 39, 67, 88–90, 95–96, 98–103, 107, 109–11, 132–33, 173, 210, 237n. 9; of the King of the Congo, 173; thanksgiving, 36, 39, 169, 174

total social fact, 2

trabalhos (works of magic), 136

traditions, popular Catholic, 31–33, 40–41, 48–49, 53, 61, 85–86, 197–98, 202, 205, 211, 213, 215

triangle, 43, 240n. 2

Turino, Thomas, 16, 89, 90, 231n. 2, 235n. 1, 236n. 5

Turner, Victor, 14, 16, 77, 222, 241n. 1

umbanda. *See* possession cults

uniforms, 79, 123, 190–91, 197, 204, 206–7, 209, 235n. 9

urbanization, 17, 216

variations, 95, 99, 102–3, 111–12, 149

Vatican II, 6

verses, 33, 67, 111, 130, 216; adoration, xiii, 130, 144, 148–55, 158; at arrivals, 192–96; blessing or family, 67, 126–27, 130, 140–41, 166, 171–76, 185, 187, 218; closure, 68, 136; for the dead, 130, 170–71, 176; encounter, 130; formulaic character of, 66, 97, 103, 153; instructions in, 97; mission, 122, 125–26, 129, 130, 132, 138–39; and modernization, 208; thanksgiving, xiii, 122, 127, 130, 171, 173, 176–77, 188

viola, 5, 29, 33, 42–43, 70, 83, 100–103, 184, 217, 235n. 5, 236n. 4

violins, 43, 102

violões. *See* guitars

Virgin Mary. *See* Our Lady

visions, 4, 11, 21, 133, 142, 155, 161, 185–86, 210, 219–22

INDEX

visitations, xi, 5, 31, 166–67, 172–78, 186, 189, 210, 237n. 3; *bastião* at, 75, 134; and the dead, 113; *folia* performances of, 167–72, 206–7; inscriptions at, 67

voices of the Magi, 48, 64, 128–29, 132, 141, 185, 187, 218, 221-22

voluntary associations, 31, 113, 116

weapons of the weak, 198

Weber, Max, 3–4, 10, 241n. 1

webs of association, 13–14, 130–31, 141–42, 217–19

Whitehouse, Harvey, 12, 211–14

wholeness, 11–12, 14, 213, 218

Wise Men. *See* magi; Three Kings

women, 47, 52, 162; in administrative roles, 65, 79; during *folia* activities, xii–xiii, 66, 89, 123, 125, 194, 196; in *folias,* 59, 84, 93, 96, 113, 216, 235nn. 3, 7; in Portuguese choruses, 46

Workers' Party. *See* PT

zabumbas, 41, 240n. 2

Zaluar, Alba, 10, 53, 179

This book belongs to

ANIMATED CLASSICS

Disney

The Lion King

Acknowledgments
Special thanks to the staff at the Walt Disney Animation Research Library and the Walt Disney Archives for their invaluable assistance and for providing the artwork for this book.

First published in the UK in 2019 by Studio Press Books,
an imprint of Bonnier Books UK,
The Plaza, 535 King's Road,
London, SW10 0SZ

studiopressbooks.co.uk
bonnierbooks.co.uk

Copyright © 2019 Disney Enterprises, Inc.
All rights reserved. No part of this publication may be reproduced or transmitted in any form or by any means, electronic, or mechanical, including photocopying, recording, or by any information storage and retrieval system, without permission in writing from the publisher.

Printed in China
2 4 6 8 10 9 7 5 3 1

All rights reserved
ISBN 978-1-78741-532-4

Text adapted by Lily Murray
Edited by Frankie Jones
Designed by Nia Williams
Cover designed by Rob Ward
Cover illustrated by Chellie Carroll

The Lion King hit theatres in June 1994. I was eight years old and already had a healthy love of drawing, inspired largely by Disney's library of animated films.

But something about this movie was different for me. Before the movie was even released, I saw the trailer in theatres and it stuck with me for a long, long time. I can't recall any one reason that *The Lion King* resonated with my young self as much as it did. Perhaps it was the music, or the rich visuals, or the fact that it transported me to a place that no fairy tale had up to that point. The emotions of the film, the choices the characters make and the journey they go on certainly touch something inside all of us. I'm sure the talking animals were a big selling feature for me as well. But I do recall feeling, although the exact thought wasn't fully formed in my head, "I want to make something like this."

It didn't take long for that thought to crystallise. I was nine years old when I saw a behind-the-scenes TV special about rough animation. I saw an animator flipping sheets of paper and it clicked for me: "Oh! You can make a movie with drawings!" I knew then that I wanted to work in animation.

I spent hours poring through *The Art of The Lion King* book. I studied the different art styles until I could name the artist just by looking at a drawing. Seeing the names of female story artists, such as Lorna Cook and Brenda Chapman, was no doubt of great significance, but I had no idea how noteworthy that was at the time.

It's a bizarre and beautiful thing to have wound up with the job I wanted when I was nine. I've had the pleasure of knowing and working with some of the people whose names I memorised from that art book. Much about the way we make movies has changed, but the core of the films, the artistry and storytelling – all the things that make *The Lion King* the masterpiece it is – is still here in spades. I hope anyone reading this book finds their "Lion King" and is inspired to go out and make awesome things.

Lissa Treiman

Walt Disney Animation Studios

Disney *The Lion King*

The sun rose over the savanna, huge and yellow in the vast sky. One by one, the animals raised their heads to the sun and began to move.

Impala leaped, zebras galloped and elephants swayed across the plains. Large and small, they swam, flew and marched to Pride Rock, where Mufasa, their king, stood proud and tall.

Then, leaning on his walking stick, came Rafiki, a wise old friend of the king. The crowds parted before him and he climbed Pride Rock until he reached Mufasa, and hugged him.

Mufasa smiled and strode over to his wife, Sarabi. Nestled in her paws was their tiny cub.

Rafiki smeared red juice and scattered dust across the cub's forehead. Then he carried the cub to the edge of Pride Rock, holding him high above his head for all to see – Simba, their new prince and future king.

Animated Classics

Across the plains, Mufasa's brother, Scar, was still in his lair. "Life's not fair, is it?" he said, trapping a helpless mouse under his paw. "You see, I shall never be king. And you," he went on, dangling the mouse over his mouth, "shall never see the light of another day."

"Didn't your mother ever tell you not to play with your food?" the king's adviser, Zazu, interrupted.

"What do you want?" Scar demanded.

"I'm here to announce that King Mufasa's on his way," said Zazu, "so you'd better have a good excuse for missing the ceremony this morning."

"Oooh," said Scar sarcastically. "I quiver with fear." He pounced on Zazu, trapping him in his mouth.

"Scar!" Mufasa shouted from the entrance of the lair. "Drop him."

"Impeccable timing, Your Majesty," said Zazu.

Mufasa strode towards Scar. "Sarabi and I didn't see you at the presentation of Simba."

Zazu hopped forwards. "As the king's brother, you should have been first in line."

"Well I was first in line until the little hairball was born," replied Scar.

"That hairball is my son and your future king," said Mufasa.

"Oh, I shall practise my curtsy," said Scar, turning away.

"Don't turn your back on me, Scar."

"Oh, no, Mufasa. Perhaps you shouldn't turn your back on me," hissed Scar.

"Is that a challenge?" roared Mufasa.

"I wouldn't dream of challenging you. As far as brains go, I got the lion's share. But when it comes to brute strength, I'm afraid I'm at the shallow end of the gene pool."

And on those words, Scar stalked away.

•• •••• ••

That night, as the rains fell and lightning crackled through the sky, Rafiki stood beneath the branches of a tree, painting a picture of a lion cub on the bark.

"Simba," he said with a smile.

As the months passed, Simba grew into a curious cub, running all over Pride Rock. One morning, before dawn, he rushed to his father. "Dad! Dad! Dad! Dad!" he called, nudging him. "Come on, Dad! You promised!"

"OK, OK, I'm up, I'm up," said Mufasa.

He led Simba to the edge of Pride Rock, to watch the dawn light break across the sky. "Look, Simba. Everything the light touches is our kingdom," said Mufasa. "A king's time as ruler rises and falls like the sun. One day, Simba, the sun will set on my time here and will rise with you as the new king."

"And this'll all be mine?" gasped Simba.

"Everything," said Mufasa.

"What about that shadowy place?" asked Simba.

"That's beyond our borders," Mufasa replied. "You must never go there, Simba."

Animated Classics

Together, father and son began to walk across the plains with Zazu flying behind them. "Everything you see exists together in a delicate balance," explained Mufasa. "As king, you need to understand that balance and respect all the creatures, from the crawling ant to the leaping antelope."

"But, Dad, don't we eat the antelope?"

"Yes, Simba, but let me explain. When we die, our bodies become the grass and the antelope eat the grass. And so we are all connected in the great circle of life."

"Sire!" called Zazu urgently. "Hyenas in the Pride Lands!"

Mufasa tensed. "Zazu, take Simba home," he ordered. Without a moment's delay, he ran towards the Pride Lands.

"I never get to go anywhere," grumbled Simba, watching his father leave.

✣ *Animated Classics* ✣

While Mufasa dealt with the hyenas, Simba visited his uncle Scar at his rocky lair.

"I'm gonna be King of Pride Rock," he announced. "My dad just showed me the whole kingdom... and I'm gonna rule it all."

"So your father showed you the whole kingdom, did he?" asked Scar.

"Everything," said Simba.

"He didn't show you what's beyond that rise at the northern border?"

"Well, no," admitted Simba. "He said I can't go there."

"And he's absolutely right. It's far too dangerous," agreed Scar. "Only the bravest lions go there."

"Well, I'm brave," said Simba. "What's out there?"

"I'm sorry, Simba. I just can't tell you. An elephant graveyard is no place for a young prince. Oops!" Scar clapped his paw over his mouth.

"Whoa!" said Simba.

"Promise me you'll never visit that dreadful place," said Scar. "You run along now and have fun. And remember, it's our little secret."

As Simba left, an evil smile crept across Scar's face.

Simba ran to his friend, Nala. "Come on. I just heard about this great place," he said. "It's really cool."

"So, where is this really cool place?" asked Sarabi, listening in.

"Oh," said Simba. "Around the water hole..."

Both Nala and Simba looked at their mothers, pleading to be allowed to go.

"As long as Zazu goes with you," said Sarabi.

"So, where are we really going?" whispered Nala as they began their journey with Zazu.

"An elephant graveyard," Simba whispered back.

"Wow!" said Nala. "So, how are we going to ditch the dodo?"

Simba grinned. While Zazu was busy talking, the cubs created a distraction, darting between a herd of elephants and zebras.

"We lost him!" said Nala.

"I… am a genius," Simba boasted.

"Hey, genius," Nala replied. "It was my idea." She pounced on Simba, playfully pinning him to the ground.

Animated Classics

They began tumbling over each other, down a rocky slope, until they landed with a thud in the elephant graveyard.

"It's really creepy," said Nala.

"Yeah," agreed Simba. "Let's go check it out."

But at that moment, Zazu flew down. "The only checking out you will do will be to check out of here. We're way beyond the boundary of the Pride Lands," he squawked. "Right now, we are all in very real danger."

"Danger? Ha!" said Simba. "I walk on the wild side. I laugh in the face of danger." He let out a laugh.

But he was drowned out by three hyenas cackling.

"Well, well, well," said Shenzi. "What have we got here?"

"A trio of trespassers!" replied Banzai as the third hyena, Ed, continued to laugh. Then she turned on Zazu. "I know you. You're Mufasa's little stooge."

"It's time to go!" insisted Zazu.

"What's the hurry?" asked Shenzi. "We'd love you to stick around for dinner."

"Yeah," said Banzai. "We could have whatever's 'lion' around!"

With that, Nala and Simba ran. On and on they raced until they came to a wall of rock, which blocked their escape. They turned to see the hyenas stalking towards them.

Disney *The Lion King*

Suddenly, Mufasa leaped down, pinning the hyenas to the ground.

"If you ever come near my son again…" Mufasa growled.

The hyenas fled. They were no match for Mufasa.

"Dad, I–" Simba began.

"You deliberately disobeyed me. Let's go home," Mufasa said sternly.

Animated Classics

While Zazu took Nala home, Mufasa turned to his son. "Simba, I'm very disappointed in you."

"I was just trying to be brave, like you," said Simba.

"I'm only brave when I have to be," explained Mufasa.

"But you're not scared of anything."

"I was today," said Mufasa. "I thought I might lose you."

"I guess even kings get scared, huh?"

Mufasa smiled down at his son. "Come here, you," he said. He picked Simba up, ruffling his fur. Then they rolled together through the moonlit grass.

"Dad?" said Simba. "We're pals, right?"

"Right," answered Mufasa.

"And we'll always be together, right?"

Mufasa paused for a moment. "Let me tell you something that my father told me. Look at the stars. The great kings of the past look down on us from those stars. So whenever you feel alone, just remember that those kings will always be there to guide you. And so will I."

Meanwhile, Scar visited the hyenas.

"Hey, did you bring us anything to eat?" asked Banzai.

"I don't think you really deserve this," said Scar, holding up a zebra's leg. "I practically gift-wrapped those cubs for you and you couldn't even dispose of them."

"It wasn't exactly like they were alone, Scar," said the hyenas. "What were we supposed to do? Kill Mufasa?"

"Precisely," said Scar.

Disney *The Lion King*

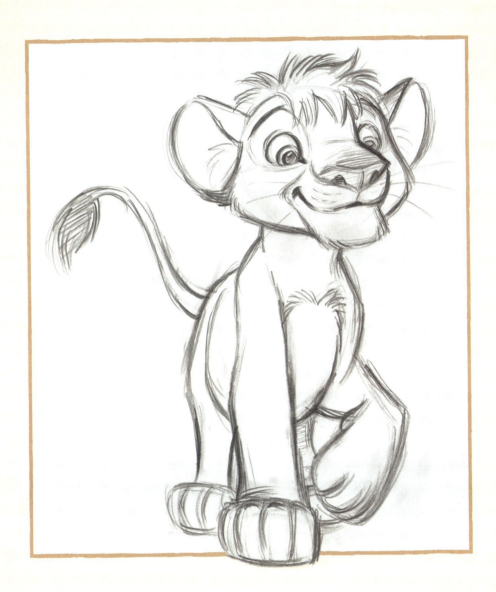

The next day, Scar took Simba down to the gorge. "Now, you wait here," he instructed. "Your father has a marvellous surprise for you."

"Hey, Uncle Scar. Will I like this surprise?"

"Simba," said Scar as he turned to leave. "It's to die for."

High above the gorge, a herd of wildebeest peacefully chewed the grasses. The hyenas lay hidden behind a rock. On Scar's signal they startled the wildebeests, driving them down into the gorge.

The first thing Simba felt was the ground trembling beneath him. Then he saw the powerful stampede rushing towards him. In terror, he ran.

Scar called out to Mufasa. "Quick! Stampede in the gorge. Simba's down there!"

As Mufasa ran to save his son, Simba clung to a low branch. The stampede raced past him.

"Your father is on the way," Zazu cried. "Hold on!"

But Simba's branch was beginning to break. "Dad!" he screamed.

Animated Classics

Mufasa leaped into the gorge and ran through the stampede. He grabbed his son and placed him on a rocky ledge. Suddenly, Mufasa was struck by a wildebeest and dragged into the stampede.

Mufasa clawed his way back up the rocks. When Mufasa reached the top, he called out to Scar for help.

Scar reached down and gouged his claws into Mufasa's outstretched paws. "Long live the king," he whispered with menace as he threw Mufasa back down into the gorge.

"No!" cried Simba.

Disney *The Lion King*

By the time Simba reached the bottom of the gorge, the herd was gone. In the dusty air, he found his father, lying on the ground.

"You've got to get up," cried Simba. But Mufasa did not move.

🦁 Animated Classics 🦁

"Help!" called Simba as tears slid down his face. "Somebody, anybody, help."

He crept under his father's paw and lay there until Scar arrived.

"Simba," said Scar. "What have you done? The king is dead. And if it weren't for you, he'd still be alive. What will your mother think?"

"What am I going to do?" asked Simba, sobbing.

"Run away, Simba," said Scar. "Run. Run away and never return."

And on those words, Simba ran.

Disney *The Lion King*

Behind Scar, the hyenas were waiting.

"Kill him," commanded Scar.

The hyenas chased Simba until they came to a large patch of thorny bushes. Only Simba could fit through without getting scratched.

"There ain't no way I'm going in there," said Shenzi, not wanting to get pricked by the thorns. "He's as good as dead out there anyway. And if he comes back, we'll kill him."

On Pride Rock, Scar stood before the other lions.

"Mufasa's death is a terrible tragedy," he said. "But to lose Simba, who had barely begun to live… for me, it is a deep, personal loss. So it is with a heavy heart that I assume the throne. Yet out of the ashes of this tragedy we shall rise, to greet the dawning of a new era, in which lion and hyena come together in a great and glorious future."

Disney *The Lion King*

As he spoke, the hyenas crowded onto Pride Rock, their howling laughter echoing over the land.

Standing beside his tree, Rafiki shook his head in sorrow. Then he raised his paw and smeared his picture of Simba.

Animated Classics

Far away, on dry, cracked ground, Simba lay sleeping, encircled by vultures. Then the sound of hooves filled the air as Pumbaa, the warthog, and his friend Timon, barreled into them.

"I love it! Bowling for buzzards!" said Pumbaa as the vultures scattered. "Hey, Timon, you better come look. I think it's still alive."

Timon sniffed Simba and lifted his paw. "Geez, it's a lion!" he cried. "Run, Pumbaa. Move it!"

"Hey, Timon, it's just a little lion. Look at him. He's so cute and all alone. Can we keep him?"

"Lions eat guys like us!"

"Maybe he'll be on our side!" said Pumbaa.

"Hey! I got it!" said Timon. "What if he's on our side? You know, having a lion around might not be such a bad idea."

Pumbaa bent down, scooped up the sleeping Simba with his tusks, and carried him away.

Animated Classics

They laid Simba down beneath a tree and splashed him with water until he awoke.

"I saved you," said Timon. "Well, Pumbaa helped. A little."

"Thanks for your help," said Simba and he began to walk away.

"Hey, where you going?" asked Timon.

"Nowhere," said Simba.

"So, where you from?" asked Timon, running after him.

"Who cares?" said Simba. "I can't go back."

"You're an outcast," said Timon. "That's great, so are we."

"What did you do, kid?" asked Pumbaa.

"Something terrible. But I don't want to talk about it."

Animated Classics

"You know, kid," said Pumbaa, "in times like this, my buddy Timon here says, 'You got to put your behind in your past.'"

"No, no, no! Amateur! Lie down before you hurt yourself. It's, 'You got to put your past behind you,'" said Timon. "Repeat after me, *hakuna matata*."

"What?"

"It means 'no worries'," explained Pumbaa.

Disney *The Lion King*

Simba followed his new friends to their home. When it was time to eat, Timon offered a slimy grub to Simba, who took it reluctantly.

"Oh, well," said Simba, holding up the grub. "*Hakuna matata.*"

The days passed, and then the months and the years. Soon, Simba was a fully-grown lion, living in a worry-free paradise with his friends.

But back at Pride Rock, the animals were living through dark days. Even the hyenas were complaining.

"Scar," said Shenzi. "There's no food, no water."

"I thought things were bad under Mufasa," said Banzai.

"What did you say?" snarled Scar. "Get out!"

Disney *The Lion King*

Meanwhile, Simba, Pumbaa and Timon were lying on their backs gazing up at the starry night sky.

"Ever wonder what those sparkly dots are up there?" asked Pumbaa.

"Well," said Simba reluctantly, "somebody once told me that the great kings of the past are up there, watching over us."

"You mean a bunch of royal dead guys are watching us?" said Timon. He and Pumbaa started to laugh.

"Yeah," said Simba, pretending to laugh with them. "Pretty dumb, huh?" He walked over to a ledge and flopped down, sending a cloud of dust swirling away on the breeze.

On the other side of the plains, Rafiki caught the dust in his hands and gazed at it. "Simba?" he said. "He's... he's alive? He's alive!" Then he painted a new picture of Simba on the trunk of his tree. "It is time," he announced.

Unaware of Rafiki's discovery, Nala, now a fully-grown lioness, was searching beyond the Pride Lands for food. As she stalked through the grasses, she scented Pumbaa and gave chase. But as she pounced to catch him, Simba leaped at her with a roar.

They rolled over and over, until Nala pinned Simba to the ground, just as she had when they were cubs.

"Nala?" said Simba. "Is it really you?"

Nala drew back. "Who are you?" she asked.

"It's me. Simba."

For a moment she froze, then she smiled. "Whoa! How did you...? Where did you come from?" she said.

"It's great to see you," said Simba.

"Hey! What's goin' on here?" cried Timon, coming between them.

"Timon, this is Nala. She's my best friend."

"Wait till everyone finds out you've been here all this time," said Nala. "And your mother... what will she think?"

"She doesn't have to know," said Simba. "Nobody has to know."

"Of course they do. Everyone thinks you're dead. Scar told us about the stampede."

"He did? What else did he tell you?"

"What else matters? You're alive. And that means... you're the king," said Nala. "You don't know how much this will mean to everyone. What it means to me. I've really missed you."

"I've missed you, too," said Simba.

And they walked off together, drinking from pools and bounding through the grasses.

Disney *The Lion King*

🦁 *Animated Classics* 🦁

"We've really needed you at home," said Nala. "You're the king."

"I'm not the king. Scar is," replied Simba.

"Simba, he let the hyenas take over the Pride Lands. Everything's destroyed. There's no food. No water. If you don't do something soon, everyone will starve."

"I can't go back," Simba said. "Look, sometimes bad things happen and there's nothing you can do about it. So why worry?"

"Because it's your responsibility," Nala explained. "Don't you understand? You're our only hope."

"Sorry," said Simba, hanging his head.

"What's happened to you? You're not the Simba I remember."

Disney *The Lion King*

"Listen," Simba said angrily. "You think you can just show up and tell me how to live my life? You don't even know what I've been through."

He walked away from Nala.

As darkness covered the sky, he gazed up at the stars. "You said you'd always be there for me. But you're not. And it's because of me. It's my fault," he said, choking back the tears.

Then Simba heard chanting coming from the treetops.

"I know who you are," said Rafiki, leaping down from the tree. "You're Mufasa's boy."

Simba turned to Rafiki in wonder.

"He's alive!" said Rafiki. "And I'll show him to you." And with that, Rafiki darted away. Simba raced after him through twisted tree branches and vines.

Animated Classics

Rafiki suddenly stopped at a pool of water. Simba looked down at his reflection.

"Look harder," said Rafiki.

This time, Mufasa gazed back at Simba. "You see," said Rafiki. "He lives in you."

"Simba," called Mufasa's voice from the clouds.

Simba looked up at the sky and there was Mufasa, surrounded by a billowing cloud.

"Look inside yourself, Simba. You are more than what you have become. You must take your place in the circle of life," Mufasa said. "Remember who you are. You are my son and the one true king."

Disney *The Lion King*

Then his image faded into the clouds and Simba was alone again with Rafiki.

"I know what I have to do, but going back means I'll have to face my past," Simba told Rafiki.

Rafiki took his stick and whacked Simba on the head.

"Ow! Geez, what was that for?" Simba asked.

"It doesn't matter, it's in the past," Rafiki explained.

"Yeah, but it still hurts."

"Oh, yes, the past can hurt," said Rafiki. "But the way I see it, you can either run from it, or learn from it." And with that he went to whack Simba on the head again, only this time, Simba avoided it.

Simba knew what he had to do. He ran all the way back to the Pride Lands with Nala, Timon and Pumbaa following close behind.

When he arrived, he looked in shock at the barren land.

"It's awful, isn't it?" said Nala, joining him. "What made you come back?"

"This is my kingdom," said Simba. "If I don't fight for it, who will?"

As they neared Pride Rock, Pumbaa and Timon distracted the hyenas while Simba and Nala sneaked past them.

Simba saw his mother standing before Scar. "There is nothing left," Sarabi told Scar. "We have only one choice. We must leave Pride Rock."

"We're not going anywhere," said Scar.

"Then you have sentenced us to death."

"I am the king," replied Scar. "I can do whatever I want."

Animated Classics

"If you were half the king Mufasa was…" Sarabi began, but Scar knocked her to the ground before she could finish.

"I am ten times the king Mufasa was!"

There was a snarling sound and Scar looked up to see Simba. He raced down to his mother.

"Simba?" said Sarabi.

"I'm home," said Simba, touching his head to hers.

"Simba…" purred Scar. "I'm a little surprised to see you… alive."

"Step down, Scar," demanded Simba.

"There is one little problem," said Scar. "You see them?" He pointed to the hyenas. "They think I'm king."

"Well we don't," said Nala, flanked by the lionesses. "Simba's the rightful king."

"Ah," said Scar, circling Simba. "So, you haven't told them your little secret. Well, Simba, now's your chance to tell them. Tell them who is responsible for Mufasa's death," said Scar.

"I am," said Simba.

"You see? He admits it. Murderer!" cried Scar.

"No, it was an accident," explained Simba.

Animated Classics

"If it weren't for you, Mufasa would still be alive," retorted Scar. "It's your fault he's dead. Do you deny it?"

"No," replied Simba.

"Then you're guilty," Scar seethed.

Scar drove Simba back towards the edge of the rock.

Disney *The Lion King*

"Oh, Simba," he continued. "You're in trouble again. But this time, Daddy isn't here to save you and now everyone knows why!"

Simba slipped and fell. He clung to the edge of the rock. A spark of lightning struck the dry grasses below him, which burst into flames.

"Now, this looks familiar," said Scar. "This is just the way your father looked before he died." Then he bent down close. "And here's my little secret," he whispered. "I… killed… Mufasa."

Simba sprung up, pinning Scar to the ground while the hyenas and lionesses watched. "Murderer!" he shouted. "Tell them the truth."

"I did it," Scar whispered.

"So they can hear you," demanded Simba.

"I killed Mufasa," admitted Scar.

Realising the moment had come, the hyenas sprang at the lionesses, who fought back with the help of Simba's friends.

Animated Classics

Simba gave chase to Scar, who tried to run away.

"Murderer," growled Simba. "You don't deserve to live."

"But, Simba, I am family. It's the hyenas who are the real enemy. It was their fault. It was their idea."

"Why should I believe you? Everything you ever told me was a lie," replied Simba.

"What are you going to do? You wouldn't kill your own uncle."

Disney *The Lion King*

"No, Scar. I'm not like you," said Simba. "Run. Run away, Scar, and never return."

But as Scar prowled past him, he threw burning coals into Simba's eyes and leaped at him.

The two lions fought, pounding with their paws and slashing with their claws. At last, Simba sent Scar tumbling over the cliff edge.

Scar rose slowly to his feet, just as the hyenas approached him. "My friends," said Scar.

"Friends?" said Shenzi. "I thought he said we were the enemy."

Then they set upon him as flames consumed the land.

Animated Classics

Soon, rain fell from the sky, extinguishing the flames. Simba and the lionesses gathered together beneath Pride Rock.

"It is time," said Rafiki to Simba.

Simba walked to the top of Pride Rock. He gazed up at the rain clouds. "Remember," his father's voice boomed.

Then Simba let out a deep-throated roar that echoed across the plains. He had taken his place as king.

In time, the Pride Lands became green again. The herds returned. Simba stood on Pride Rock with Nala, Timon and Pumbaa beside him while Zazu circled above. The animals of the Pride Lands bowed low before them. Rafiki walked to the edge of Pride Rock, holding Simba and Nala's lion cub in his hands. He held the lion cub high above his head in celebration of the circle of life.

Disney *The Lion King*

Simba and his pride lived
happily ever after.

The End

Animated Classics

The Art of Disney The Lion King

The Lion King was Disney's first original feature animation not based on source material. The concept for a coming-of-age tale set in Africa was born on a plane ride and, through research trips and intensive brainstorming sessions, the film we now know began to emerge. The artists working on the film were inspired by African art, as well as by the actors cast in the film. Animators attended lectures on animal movement and behaviour, and had the opportunity to sketch from live animals brought into the studio. *The Lion King* is often praised for its artistic brilliance, and throughout this book you can see concept art, animation drawings and story sketches from the following Disney studio artists.

Disney *The Lion King*

Greg Drolette

Greg Drolette worked at the Walt Disney Studios during the 1980s and 1990s, creating background paintings for some of the biggest films of this period including *The Little Mermaid, Beauty and the Beast, Aladdin, The Lion King, Hercules* and *Atlantis: The Lost Empire*.
Background painting on pages 2-3 and 70-71; colour key on page 64.

Thom Enriquez

Thom Enriquez is a storyboard artist and animator who contributed to the story development of films such as *The Lion King, Hercules, Mulan* and *Brother Bear*. Enriquez has also worked on *Beauty and the Beast, The Hunchback of Notre Dame* and *The Little Mermaid*.
Concept art on page 4; story sketch on page 31.

Hans Bacher

Hans Bacher, born in Germany, is a well-known and respected animation artist. He began his Disney career in 1987 and has worked as a production designer, visual development artist, storyboard artist and character designer on films including *Aladdin, Beauty and the Beast, The Lion King, Hercules* and *Mulan*.
Concept art on page 7.

Andreas Deja

Polish-born animator Andreas Deja joined the Walt Disney Studios animation department in 1980 and quickly established himself as a supervising animator for some of the most memorable Disney villains. He has animated Gaston in *Beauty and the Beast*, Jafar in *Aladdin* and Scar in *The Lion King*. Deja doesn't always animate the bad guys! For *The Little Mermaid*, Deja animated King Triton as well as the titular character from *Hercules*, Lilo in *Lilo & Stitch* and Tigger in the 2011 animated feature *Winnie the Pooh*. In 2015, Deja was named a Disney Legend.
Concept art on pages 10, 28, 34 and 56; rough animation drawing on page 44.

Ellen Woodbury

Joining Disney in the 1980s, Ellen Woodbury spent twenty years of her career working as an animator across many of Disney's biggest films of the period. Following an MFA in Experimental Animation at CalArts and a short stint at another studio, Woodbury joined the Walt Disney Studios and apprenticed under Mike Gabriel, Hendel Butoy and Mark Henn. Woodbury became the first female supervising animator, a role that she began on *The Lion King*, supervising the animation of Zazu.
Animation drawing on page 12.

Animated Classics

Dan Cooper

After graduating from the Art Center College of Design and a stint in advertising, Dan Cooper joined the Walt Disney Studios in 1990 working on films such as *Aladdin*, *The Lion King* and *Pocahontas* as a background artist. Cooper now works as a visual development artist and has contributed to some of Disney's most recent animated films including *Tangled*, *Moana*, *Wreck-It Ralph* and *Ralph Breaks the Internet*.
Background painting on page 13.

Bob Smith

Bob Smith is a California native. He's worked for the U.S. Navy and as a fine artist, but he spent more than forty years in animation. Smith joined the Walt Disney Studios as a layout artist and character designer on films including *Oliver & Company*, *The Rescuers Down Under* and *The Lion King*.
Concept art on page 14.

Roger Allers

Inspired by a childhood love of Disney, Roger Allers joined the Walt Disney Studios in 1985 as a storyboard artist for *Oliver & Company*. Allers continued to work on storyboarding for films such as *The Little Mermaid* and *The Rescuers Down Under* before undertaking the role of head of story on *Beauty and the Beast*. In 1991, Allers signed on to co-direct a project titled *King of the Jungle*, which later became *The Lion King*. Allers went on to co-write the libretto for *The Lion King* on Broadway, for which he received a Tony Award nomination.
Story sketch on page 17.

Chris Sanders

A CalArts alumni, Chris Sanders joined the Walt Disney Studios shortly after graduation in 1984. Sanders has worked as a character designer, storyboard artist, artistic director and production designer across projects such as *Beauty and the Beast*, *The Lion King* and *Mulan*. Sanders directed the 2002 animation *Lilo & Stitch* and also provided the voice of Stitch for many of the Western releases of the film.
Concept art on pages 18, 36 and 39; story sketch on page 53.

Rick Maki

Canadian-born animator Rick Maki joined the Walt Disney Studios to work in the story department for *The Lion King*. Maki has worked as a character designer and visual development artist on many Disney features including *Hercules*, *Tarzan* and *The Princess and the Frog*.
Concept art on page 19.

Disney *The Lion King*

Don Moore

Don Moore is principally a background artist who has contributed to many Disney animated features including *The Lion King*, *Pocahontas*, *The Hunchback of Notre Dame*, *Hercules* and *Tarzan*. *Colour key on page 22.*

Dave Burgess

Animator Dave Burgess has worked on many Disney films, animating characters such as Genie in *Aladdin*, Gaston in *Beauty and the Beast*, Jane in *Tarzan* and Milo in *Atlantis: The Lost Empire*. For *The Lion King*, Burgess worked as the supervising animator for the hyenas. *Concept art on page 23.*

Lorna Cook

Lorna Cook worked as an animator and storyboard artist at the Walt Disney Studios throughout the 1980s and 1990s, contributing to films such as *The Fox and the Hound*, *Beauty and the Beast* and *Mulan*. For *The Lion King*, Cook helped animate adult Simba. *Story sketches on pages 24 and 26.*

Andy Gaskill

At twenty-one, Andy Gaskill joined the Walt Disney Studios straight from art school, where he enrolled in the first animation training programme, supervised by Disney veteran Eric Larson. He first worked as an animator on *Winnie the Pooh and Tigger Too*, *The Rescuers* and *The Fox and the Hound* before moving into roles such as storyboard artist for *TRON*, visual development artist for *The Little Mermaid*, and art director for *The Lion King*, *Hercules* and *Treasure Planet*. Gaskill also worked for Walt Disney's Imagineering, creating designs for attractions at the Walt Disney Parks and Resorts. *Story sketches on pages 27, 52 and 54; storyboard thumbnail on page 55.*

Mark Henn

In 1978, Mark Henn studied in the Walt Disney Character Animation Program at CalArts and was hired at the Walt Disney Studios in 1980. His first big assignment was to animate Mickey Mouse in *Mickey's Christmas Carol* – since then he has worked on dozens of Disney's biggest films, specialising in animating female characters such as Ariel in *The Little Mermaid*, Belle in *Beauty and the Beast*, Jasmine in *Aladdin*, the titlular character of *Mulan*, Tiana in *The Princess and the Frog* and Anna in *Frozen*. For *The Lion King*, Mark worked as the supervising animator for young Simba. *Concept art on page 29.*

Doug Ball

Working as a background artist and visual development artist, Doug Ball has contributed to some of Disney's most popular films of the 1990s and 2000s, including *Beauty and the Beast*, *The Lion King*, *Enchanted* and *The Princess and the Frog*. *Colour key on page 30; concept art on pages 46 and 49.*

Animated Classics

Barry Johnson

Storyboard and visual development artist Barry Johnson has worked across many Disney films including *The Lion King* and *Mulan*. Most recently, Johnson has contributed to *Big Hero 6*, *Wreck-It Ralph*, *Frozen*, *Moana* and Pixar Animation Studios' *Brave*.
Story sketches on pages 32, 40 and 45.

Burny Mattinson

Working with the Walt Disney Studios for more than sixty-five years, Burny Mattinson has almost done it all. Starting with the company in 1953, Mattinson has been an animator, story artist, writer, director and producer for over half a century of Disney classics such as *Sleeping Beauty*, *The Jungle Book*, *The Rescuers*, *Mickey's Christmas Carol*, *The Great Mouse Detective*, *The Little Mermaid*, *Aladdin*, *The Lion King* and *Big Hero 6*, among others. His continuing love of the medium of animation and for the simple joys of storytelling are an inspiration to filmmakers and audiences around the world.
Story sketches on pages 35 and 41.

Tony Bancroft

Best known for co-directing *Mulan*, Tony Bancroft has animated some of Disney's most memorable sidekicks including Cogsworth in *Beauty and the Beast*, Iago in *Aladdin*, Pumbaa in *The Lion King* and Kronk in *The Emperor's New Groove*.
Concept art on page 38.

Michael Surrey

Michael Surrey moved to California from Canada following the release of *The Little Mermaid* to join the Walt Disney Studios. He was hired as an assistant animator on *Beauty and the Beast* and went on to assist Glen Keane in his animation of the titular character of *Aladdin*. For *The Lion King*, Surrey was assigned as supervising animator for the meerkat, Timon. Following that success, Surrey worked as a supervising animator on many Disney characters including Terk in *Tarzan* and Ray in *The Princess and the Frog*.
Concept art on page 38.

Anthony DeRosa

Anthony "Tony" DeRosa has worked at the Walt Disney Studios since 1985, working as an animator on films such as *The Little Mermaid*, *Beauty and the Beast* and *Aladdin*. For *The Lion King*, DeRosa was the supervising animator for adult Nala.
Concept art on page 47.

Kelvin Yasuda

Joining the Walt Disney Studios in the 1980s, Kelvin Yasuda contributed to many Disney films of the 1980s, 1990s and 2000s as an effects animator. Yasuda worked on *The Black Cauldron*, *Oliver & Company*, *The Little Mermaid*, *Beauty and the Beast*, *The Lion King* and *Fantasia/2000*.
Concept art on page 60.

Disney *The Lion King*

Tom Shannon

Tom Shannon worked as a layout artist for two decades at the Walt Disney Studios, contributing to films such as *The Rescuers Down Under*, *Beauty and the Beast*, *Aladdin*, *The Lion King*, *Mulan* and *Tarzan*. Concept art on page 61.

Glossary

Animation drawing: an illustration created for the final animation, ready to be traced on to a cel or scanned into a computer for digital inking and painting.

Background painting: establishes the colour, style and mood of a scene. They're combined with cels for cel set-ups or for the finished scene.

Colour key: establishes the look and feel of a background painting and the overall colour of a scene. Colour keys help animators to avoid any colour overlaps or clashes when placing characters and objects on backgrounds.

Concept art: drawings, paintings or sketches prepared in the early stages of a film's development. Concept art is often used to inspire the staging, mood and atmosphere of scenes.

Rough animation drawing: a drawing created very early in the animation process to test an animation.

Story sketch: shows the action that's happening in a scene, as well as presenting the emotion of the story moment. Story sketches help to visualise the film before expensive resources are committed to its production.

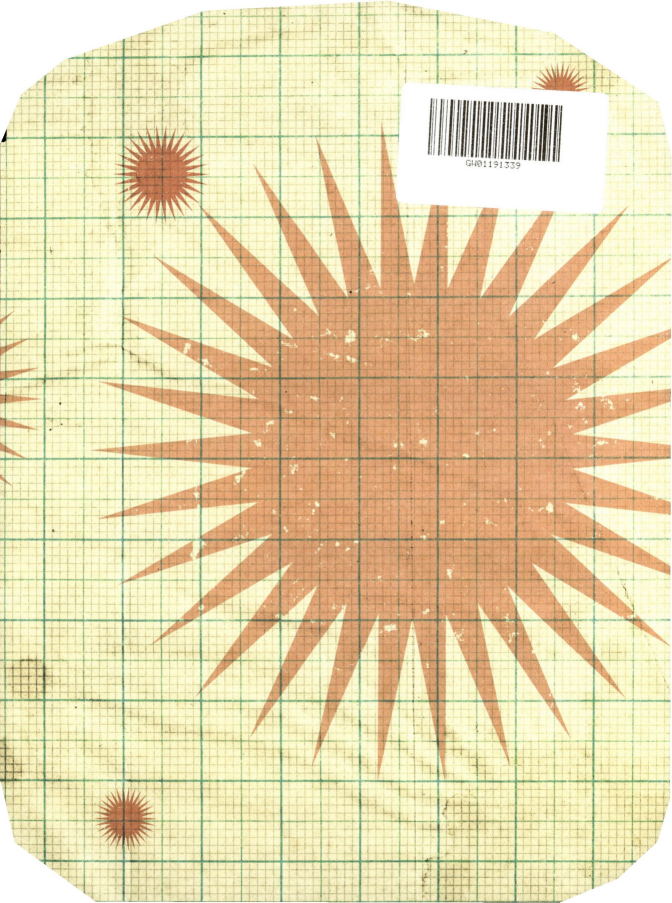

MAN-UP
YOUR MEALS

This edition published by Parragon Books Ltd in 2014
LOVE FOOD is an imprint of Parragon Books Ltd

Parragon Books Ltd
Chartist House
15—17 Trim Street
Bath BA1 1HA, UK
www.parragon.com/lovefood

Copyright © Parragon Books Ltd 2014

LOVE FOOD and the accompanying heart device is a registered trademark of
Parragon Books Ltd in Australia, the UK, USA, India and the EU.

All rights reserved. No part of this publication may be reproduced, stored in
a retrieval system or transmitted, in any form or by any means, electronic,
mechanical, photocopying, recording or otherwise, without the prior permission
of the copyright holder.

ISBN: 978-1-4723-4541-7

Printed in China

Project Managed by Kerry Starr
Cover and Internal Design by Lexi L'Esteve
New Recipes and Home Economy by Lincoln Jefferson
New Photography by Mike Cooper
Introduction and Incidental Text by Dominic Utton

Notes for the Reader
This book uses both metric and imperial measurements. Follow the same units of
measurement throughout; do not mix metric and imperial. All spoon measurements
are level: teaspoons are assumed to be 5 ml, and tablespoons are assumed to
be 15 ml. Unless otherwise stated, milk is assumed to be full fat, eggs and
individual vegetables are medium, and pepper is freshly ground black pepper.
Unless otherwise stated, all root vegetables should be peeled prior to using.

Garnishes, decorations and serving suggestions are all optional and not
necessarily included in the recipe ingredients or method.
The times given are an approximate guide only. Preparation times differ
according to the techniques used by different people and the cooking times
may also vary from those given. Optional ingredients, variations or serving
suggestions have not been included in the time calculations.

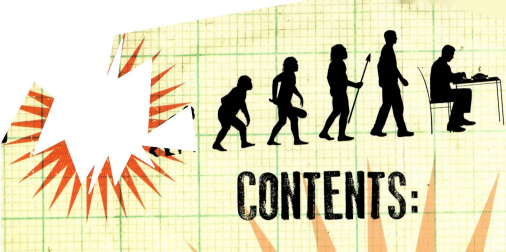

CONTENTS:

INTRODUCTION...6

CHAPTER 1 **SNACK ATTACK**...08

CHAPTER 2 **HUNGER-BUSTING MAN MEALS**...40

CHAPTER 3 **MEGA PUDS**......70

CHAPTER 4 **GET SET TO IMPRESS**...100

INDEX......128

What `Real` Man Food is...

Men — we're under threat. Assailed by the forces of metrosexuality on the one front and the relentless march of domesticity on the other. If we're not moisturizing, we're comparing colour swatches. If we're not exfoliating, we're shopping for scatter cushions. We're in danger of losing our last X chromosome. And now, worst of all, it seems they're coming for our food.

Tiny portions? Low-fat options? Quinoa, for crying out loud? What happened to men eating like, well, men?

It used to be so different. Once upon a golden age, the relationship between men and food was simple. The way to a man's heart was through his stomach. We were what we ate. And what we ate was usually something big and hearty and carb-heavy and probably spicy and more often than not once possessed of a heart and a stomach itself.

We were men! We were hunters, gatherers, providers, and protectors. And we needed the kind of food that could fuel such activities that could sustain and strengthen and empower us to fulfill our destinies. Man food was manly food — full of energy and power and purpose. Like us, in fact.

So what happened? Progress happened. Progress in technology, in lifestyle, in medicine and health, in social equality. And somehow, somewhere along the line, amidst all of the undeniably great things about that progress, something was lost. Some essential part of our masculinity was lost.

Well this is where the balance gets redressed. Yes, we may moisturize occasionally. Sure, we may know one end of a home furnishings store from the other, fine, we're happy to use sunscreen and lip balm and understand the importance of not wearing the same pants for three consecutive days… but that doesn't mean we're about to surrender our gender altogether. It doesn't mean we can't at least eat like real men.

And so right here, gentlemen, is where the buck stops. This is where we make our stand, knife and fork and griddle in hand. This is a recipe book for men, by men, full of real man food.

Inside these pages you're going to find a kind of culinary manifesto (pun intended). A feast for the eyes, for the mind, for the belly… and for the X in our chromosomes that sets us apart from the other 50 per cent of the human race.

But don't get us wrong. We're not advocating sexism, or chauvinism, or general bare-chested idiocy. We're not Neanderthals.

Eating like a man doesn't mean a return to less-enlightened times. It doesn't mean a diet of gut-busting fry-ups, grease-soaked butties or even freshly-speared barbecued woolly mammoth burgers (delicious though the last one sounds).

Eating — and cooking — man food doesn't mean living unhealthily any more than it means having to hunt and kill your own breakfast.

Nor does it mean flame-grilling everything over a self-built fire in the wilderness while simultaneously whittling your own Native American canoe with one hand and splicing together a bivouac with the other. (Although, again, if you fancy it, by all means have a go.)

And, most crucially of all, it doesn't mean excluding the ladies altogether.

What it does mean, however, is a re-embracing of the kind of properly-proportioned, fantastically tasty, seriously masculine eating that's been sadly lacking from our diet in recent times. This book is about saying: not only is it ok to eat like a man, but, you know what? It's better. It's preferable.

Man food is about carbs. It's about meat. It's about proper portion sizes. It's about taste: real taste — and that means heat, spice, zing, va-va-voom!

It means that the next time the boys are round and looking for a snack-sized pick-me-up, you don't reach for the macrobiotic yoghurt dips and rabbit-food nutrition bars but instead show your real credentials by whipping up some proper munch-busters: Triple-Cooked Fries, Mighty Meatball Sub, Blazin' Beef Tacos.

It means knowing the right way to go about fulfilling the appetite of a man living a proper man's life. We're talking creating Double-Decker Burgers from scratch; putting together the kind of Meatloaf or Chilli that won America the West; sorting out Colossal Kebabs, Buffalo Wings, Giant Meat Feast Pizza, Super Surf 'n' Turf…

And let's not forget a grill. Every man should know how to create the perfect mixed grill. Steaks, chops, sausages, chorizo, eggs, mushrooms, tomatoes — turn to page 46 and we defy you not to start drooling.

Satisfied yet? Thought not. Real men eat pudding too: and so we've got killer recipes for making your own Boozy Chocolate Cheesecake, Beeramisu, Cookie Dough Ice Cream, Sticky Toffee Pudding, and so much more…

We've also got a section on brewing your own beer. We've got nothing against wine, of course, but when you make it yourself… well, then beer becomes something more than just a drink: it becomes a craft.

And, just in case you're unsure about which delicious recipe to try due to your busy schedule or choice of dinner companion ('friends night' or 'date night'?) let our handy difficulty rating at the top of each recipe guide you. Ranging from 1 (easy) to 6 (more complex) it will give you a helpful indication to the effort and skill involved.

But enough waffle (oh, that reminds us: Beer Waffles with Ham & Cheese — page 14): you're not here to be told how to be a man. You already know how to be a man. You are a man! All you have to do now is start eating like one again…

Enjoy!

Chapter 1
SNACK ATTACK

TRIPLE-COOKED CHIPS 10

BACON & CHEESE CHIPS 12

BEER WAFFLES WITH
HAM & CHEESE 14

THE BEST
BACON BUTTY 16

JUMBO POTATO
WEDGES WITH DIPS 18

ULTIMATE NACHOS
WITH BEEF 20

BLAZIN' BEEF TACOS 22

MIGHTY MEATBALL SUB 24

RUMP STEAK SANDWICHES 26

QUICK & EASY CORN DOGS 28

HOW TO BREW YOUR OWN BEER 30

TUNA MELT BAGELS 32

FIERY FISH FINGER SANDWICH
WITH RUSSIAN DRESSING & ROCKET 34

SPICY BAKED EGGS WITH
TOMATO & BACON SAUCE 36

MIGHTY 5 EGG OMELETTE
WITH CHORIZO, RED ONION & BLUE CHEESE 38

TRIPLE-COOKED CHIPS

DIFFICULTY

Ingredients

900 g/2 lb potatoes

1 litre/1¾ pints vegetable oil

sea salt

1. Cut the potatoes into 5 x 5-mm/¼-inch sticks. Soak the cut potatoes in a bowl of cold water for 5 minutes, then drain and rinse.

2. Bring a medium-sized saucepan of lightly salted water to the boil over a high heat. Add the potatoes, bring back to the boil and cook for 3—4 minutes, until the potatoes begin to soften. Drain the potatoes and spread on a baking sheet lined with kitchen paper. Refrigerate for 1 hour or overnight.

3. Place the oil in a large, heavy-based saucepan or a deep-fryer. If using a saucepan, attach a deep-frying thermometer. Heat the oil to 180—190°C/350—375°F, or until a cube of bread browns in 30 seconds. Carefully add the cut potatoes, in batches, if necessary, to avoid overcrowding. Cook for about 3—4 minutes, until beginning to brown. Remove using tongs and drain on a plate lined with kitchen paper.

4. Return the oil to 180—190°C/350—375°F, then add the potatoes again and fry for about 3—5 minutes, until golden brown and crisp. Remove from the oil and drain on a plate lined with kitchen paper. Season generously with sea salt and serve immediately.

BACON & CHEESE CHIPS

DIFFICULTY

Ingredients

3 streaky bacon rashers

3 tbsp butter

½ onion, diced

1 garlic clove, finely chopped

3 tbsp plain flour

350 ml/12 fl oz milk

280 g/10 oz mature Cheddar cheese, grated

55 g/2 oz freshly grated Parmesan cheese

125 ml/4 fl oz soured cream

2 tsp Dijon mustard

½ tsp salt

freshly cooked Triple-Cooked Chips (see page 10)

2 tbsp snipped fresh chives, to garnish

1. Fry the bacon in a dry frying pan until crisp, then remove and drain on kitchen paper. Crumble and set aside.

2. Melt the butter in a saucepan over a medium heat. Add the onion and cook, stirring, for about 4 minutes, until soft. Add the garlic and cook for a further minute. Whisk in the flour and cook for a further 30 seconds. Slowly add the milk and cook over a medium heat, whisking constantly, for a further 3 minutes, until the sauce thickens. Reduce the heat to low and add the Cheddar cheese and Parmesan cheese 25 g/1 oz at a time, stirring after each addition, until the cheese is completely melted. Stir in the soured cream, mustard and salt. Keep the sauce warm until ready to serve.

3. Place the chips in a large bowl or on a serving platter and pour over the sauce. Sprinkle with the crumbled bacon and chives and serve immediately.

BEER WAFFLES WITH HAM & CHEESE

PREP: 20 mins
SERVES 4
COOK: 15 mins

DIFFICULTY

Ingredients

150 g/5½ oz plain white flour

1½ tsp baking powder

pinch of salt

2 tsp English mustard powder

250 ml/9 fl oz beer or lager

1 large egg

2 tbsp sunflower oil, plus extra for greasing

Topping
8 thin slices smoked ham

140 g/5 oz Gruyère cheese or Cheddar cheese, coarsely grated

1. Sift the flour, baking powder, salt and mustard powder into a bowl. Add the beer, egg and oil and whisk to a smooth batter. Leave to stand for 5 minutes.

2. Lightly grease a waffle maker and heat until hot. Pour the batter into the waffle maker and cook until golden brown. Repeat, using the remaining batter, while keeping the cooked waffles warm.

3. Preheat the grill to high. Place the waffles on a baking sheet and arrange the ham on top. Sprinkle with the grated cheese and grill until melted. Serve immediately.

TOP TIP

If you do not have a waffle-maker, you can find packaged waffles in all good supermarkets. Choose a variety with indentations (Belgian waffles are the best), as these will hold the delicious fillings better.

THE BEST BACON BUTTY

DIFFICULTY

Ingredients

1 large French stick

4 tbsp mayonnaise

500 g/1 lb 2 oz smoked streaky bacon

4 tbsp vegetable oil

4 eggs

10 Swiss cheese slices

chipotle chilli sauce, to taste

1. Preheat the grill to high.

2. Cut the French stick in half lengthways, spread with the mayonnaise and set aside.

3. Grill the bacon on both sides until crispy or cooked to your liking, then put aside in a warm place.

4. In a medium-sized frying pan heat the oil over a medium-low heat and crack the eggs in one at a time and cook to your liking.

5. Place the cheese slices on one half of the French stick and top with the bacon, fried eggs and chipotle chilli sauce.

6. Press the two halves of the French stick together gently. Cut in half and serve immediately.

TOP TIP

If you can't get your hands on a French stick use thick-cut slices of white bread. Lightly toast and butter the bread for the perfect sandwich alternative.

JUMBO POTATO WEDGES WITH DIPS

PREP: 15 mins
SERVES 2
COOK: 35 mins

DIFFICULTY

Ingredients

- 6 large jacket potatoes
- 6 tbsp olive oil
- 1 tbsp paprika
- 1 tsp dried oregano
- small bunch fresh thyme
- 3 garlic bulbs, tops cut off
- 4 tbsp mayonnaise
- 4 tbsp soured cream
- 2 tbsp creamed horseradish
- small bunch fresh chives, chopped
- salt and pepper

1. Preheat the oven to 200°C/400°F/Gas Mark 6.

2. Cut each potato in half then cut each half into three and place in a large bowl. Season to taste with salt and pepper and add in the olive oil, paprika, oregano, thyme and garlic bulbs. Mix gently until all of the potatoes and garlic are covered.

3. Line a large baking tray with baking paper and add the potatoes and garlic, making sure that you scrape everything out of the bowl. Cook in the preheated oven for 20 minutes, or until the garlic feels soft when pressed. Remove the garlic and set aside and turn the wedges over. Return the wedges to the oven and cook for an additional 15 minutes.

4. Meanwhile, put the mayonnaise and soured cream in separate bowls. Add the creamed horseradish and chives to the soured cream and mix well then set aside.

5. When the potatoes are cooked, remove from the oven and leave to cool for 5 minutes. Place the slightly cooled garlic bulbs on a clean surface and scrape out the cooked flesh with a knife, discarding the skin, then roughly chop and add to the mayonnaise.

6. Serve the wedges immediately with the dips.

ULTIMATE NACHOS WITH BEEF

PREP: 10 mins | SERVES 2 | COOK: 30 mins

DIFFICULTY

Ingredients

- 2 tbsp olive oil
- 1 onion, chopped
- 200 g/7 oz fresh beef mince
- 1 tbsp dried oregano
- 1 tbsp paprika
- 1 tbsp cumin
- 400 g/14 oz passata
- 225 ml/8 fl oz water
- 30 g/1 oz butter
- 30 g/1 oz plain flour
- 450 ml/16 fl oz milk, warmed
- 100 g/3½ oz Cheddar cheese, grated
- 100 g/3½ oz Monterey Jack cheese, grated
- 1 tbsp American mustard
- 55 g/2 oz Parmesan cheese
- 200 g/7 oz tortilla chips
- 1 ripe avocado
- 100 g/3½ oz pickled jalapeños, drained
- 1 small red onion, finely chopped
- salt and pepper

1. In a medium-sized pan, heat the oil over a medium-high heat and add the onion. Cook for 5 minutes, or until translucent and slightly golden. Add the mince and cook for a further 5 minutes, breaking up the meat with a wooden spoon until it starts to brown.

2. Add the oregano, paprika, cumin, passata and water, and cook over a low heat for 20 minutes, or until reduced by half. Season to taste with salt and pepper and set aside.

3. Meanwhile, melt the butter in a medium-sized pan, add the flour and mix well with a wooden spoon. Slowly add the warm milk, trying to avoid any lumps forming, until the sauce thickens and starts to boil. Turn off the heat and add the Cheddar cheese, Monterey Jack cheese, American mustard and half the Parmesan cheese. Stir until smooth, season to taste with salt and pepper and set aside.

4. On a large serving platter, ladle over half of the mince. Place tortilla chips on top, followed by the rest of the mince, then top with the cheese sauce.

5. Cut the avocado in half, remove the stone, peel and chop into small pieces. Scatter the avocado pieces over the nachos along with the jalapeños, chopped red onion and the remaining Parmesan cheese. Serve immediately.

BLAZIN' BEEF TACOS

PREP: 20 mins
SERVES 2
COOK: 25 mins

DIFFICULTY

Ingredients

- 2 tbsp corn oil
- 1 small onion, finely chopped
- 2 garlic cloves, finely chopped
- 280 g/10 oz fresh beef mince
- 1½ tsp hot chilli powder
- 1 tsp ground cumin
- 8 taco shells
- 1 avocado
- 2 tbsp lemon juice
- ¼ head of lettuce, shredded
- 4 spring onions, thinly sliced
- 2 tomatoes, peeled and diced
- 125 ml/4 fl oz soured cream
- 115 g/4 oz Cheddar cheese, grated
- salt and pepper

1. Heat the oil in a frying pan. Add the onion and garlic and cook over a low heat, stirring occasionally, for 5 minutes, until softened. Add the beef, increase the heat to medium and cook, stirring frequently and breaking it up with a wooden spoon, for 8–10 minutes, until evenly browned. Drain off as much fat as possible.

2. Stir in the chilli powder and cumin, season to taste with salt and pepper and cook over a low heat, stirring frequently for a further 8 minutes, then remove from the heat.

3. Heat the taco shells according to the packet instructions. Meanwhile, peel, stone and slice the avocado and gently toss with the lemon juice in a bowl.

4. Divide the lettuce, spring onions, tomatoes and avocado slices among the taco shells. Add a tablespoon of soured cream to each, then divide the beef mixture among them. Sprinkle with the cheese and serve immediately.

MIGHTY MEATBALL SUB

DIFFICULTY

Ingredients

Meatballs
450 g/1 lb lean beef mince

1 small onion, grated

2 garlic cloves, crushed

25 g/1 oz fine white breadcrumbs

1 tsp hot chilli sauce

salt and pepper

wholemeal flour, for dusting

groundnut oil, for shallow frying

1 tbsp olive oil

1 small onion, sliced

4 sub rolls or small baguettes

4 tbsp mayonnaise

55 g/2 oz sliced jalapeños (from a jar)

2 tbsp American mustard

1. Place the beef, onion, garlic, breadcrumbs and chilli sauce into a bowl. Season to taste and mix thoroughly. Shape the mixture into 20 small equal-sized balls using floured hands. Cover and chill in the refrigerator for 10 minutes or until required.

2. Heat a shallow depth of oil in a wok or heavy frying pan until very hot, then fry the meatballs in batches for 6–8 minutes, turning often, until golden brown and firm. Remove with a slotted spoon, drain on kitchen paper and keep hot.

3. To make the sandwich, heat the olive oil in a clean pan and fry the onions on a moderate heat, stirring occasionally, until soft and golden brown.

4. Split the rolls lengthways and spread with mayonnaise. Arrange the onions, meatballs and jalapeños over the bottom half, squeeze the mustard over and top with the other half. Serve immediately.

MAN UP
Go large by swapping one sub roll for a halved French stick. All the better for cramming in even more meatballs.

RUMP STEAK SANDWICHES

PREP: 10 mins
SERVES 4
COOK: 25 mins

DIFFICULTY

Ingredients

- 8 slices thick white bread
- butter, softened, for spreading
- 2 handfuls mixed salad leaves
- 3 tbsp olive oil
- 2 onions, thinly sliced
- 675 g/1 lb 8 oz rump steak, 2.5 cm/1 inch thick
- 1 tbsp Worcestershire sauce
- 2 tbsp wholegrain mustard
- 2 tbsp water
- salt and pepper

1. Spread each slice of bread with some butter and add a few salad leaves to the four bottom slices.

2. Heat 2 tablespoons of the oil in a large frying pan over a medium heat. Add the onions and cook, stirring occasionally, for 10–15 minutes, or until softened and golden brown. Using a slotted spoon, transfer to a plate and set aside.

3. Increase the heat to high and add the remaining oil to the pan. Add the steak, season to taste with pepper and seal on both sides. Reduce the heat to medium and cook for 2½–3 minutes on each side for rare, or until cooked to your liking (see page 62). Transfer the steak to the plate with the onions.

4. Add the Worcestershire sauce, mustard and water to the pan. Use a wooden spoon to scrape the sediment from the base of the pan. When the liquid has deglazed the pan, add the onions and stir. Season to taste with salt and pepper.

5. Thinly slice the steak across the grain, divide between the four bottom slices of bread and cover with the onion and mustard dressing. Cover with the top slices of bread and press down gently. Serve immediately.

QUICK & EASY CORN DOGS

DIFFICULTY

Ingredients

- oil for deep-frying
- 100 g/3½ oz plain flour, sifted, plus 4 tbsp for dusting
- 300 g/10½ oz fine polenta
- 2 tbsp caster sugar
- 1 tsp smoked paprika
- 2 tsp mustard powder
- 1 tsp salt
- 1 tsp baking powder
- 2 large eggs
- 300 ml/10 fl oz buttermilk
- 150 ml/5 fl oz water
- 10 large frankfurters
- mustard and ketchup, to serve

1. Heat enough oil for deep-frying in a large pan or deep-fryer to 180—190°C/350—375°F, or until a cube of bread browns in 30 seconds.

2. Meanwhile, in a medium-sized bowl mix together the flour, polenta, sugar, smoked paprika, mustard powder, salt and baking powder. Beat in the eggs using a wooden spoon then gradually add in the buttermilk and water and continue to beat until smooth and the consistency of double cream.

3. Insert a wooden skewer about three quarters of the way up each frankfurter. Place the remaining 4 tablespoons of flour in a bowl. Roll each frankfurter in the flour and then dip into the batter, turning to get an even coating and letting any excess batter drip off.

4. Lower the corn dogs into the hot oil in batches of two and cook for 5 minutes, or until golden brown. Remove, drain on kitchen paper and keep warm. Repeat until all the corn dogs are cooked.

5. Serve immediately with the mustard and ketchup.

HOW TO BREW YOUR OWN BEER

It was no less a man than the great Benjamin Franklin who said: 'Beer is proof that God loves us and wants us to be happy'. (Some scholars dispute whether or not it really was Ben Franklin who first said that, but the way we figure it is, either way he's correct, and anyway, we're not about to argue with one of the Founding Fathers of America, right?)

But the problem with beer is: it can be expensive. And you need to go to the shops to buy it. And there's only so much you can carry home anyway. What's needed is some sort of method of making sure you've got plenty of the stuff, always on tap, and at a fraction of the price you'd pay for a six-pack or two…

Brewing beer used to have a bit of a bad rep. It was either the preserve of oddly-bearded gentlemen in knitwear and sensible shoes, or else desperate students eager to get any old slop down their necks in the cause of getting blotto. To put it bluntly: normal guys didn't brew their own beer.

Well that's all changed.

'Craft' beer — real ale created with natural products by skilled, dedicated brewers and drunk by a hipper, younger, more sophisticated crowd — has never been more popular. And the natural consequence of drinking craft beer is that it leaves you wondering just how easy it might be to create craft beer ourselves.

Brilliantly, the answer is: easier than you think.

Today, more and more men are turning to homebrew — and, crucially, the quality of the product they're making has improved dramatically. Homebrew organizations, websites and suppliers are all reporting a massive upsurge in interest — and those getting involved range from bridegrooms looking to provide their own bespoke wedding ales to family guys supplying cheap and plentiful booze for everything from summer street parties to Christmas get-togethers and of course, ordinary, regular men who fancy the idea of something fun, creative, and, well, beer-like as a hobby.

Gone are the days of homebrew that requires a cast-iron stomach to handle — now just about every man with a taste for a good pint can knock out something delicious, inexpensive, and reassuringly potent.

There are three basic methods of brewing your own beer — meaning that not only can the complete novice get to grips with it, but that as you grow in confidence, you can start to create wholly original ales of your own.

The first, and simplest, is to start with a kit. You may need to search around a few hardware shops — but there's a wide range available on the internet. Everything you need to make around five gallons (or 40 pints) will be contained within them — and it's just a matter of following the instructions.

A word of warning, however — do follow those instructions! Beer brewing is a pretty exact science and any experimentation at this stage is likely only to lead to something undrinkable. Pay special attention to sterilization — everything must be scrupulously clean. If not, you're going to end up with 40 pints of vinegar at best. (And no, that doesn't mean you can use it as vinegar either…)

Making up a batch of beer this way will take about four weeks from start to finish — that time being divided as follows:

Preparation, cleaning and mixing of the ingredients — a couple of hours.
Fermentation — where you leave it to work its magic — two weeks.
Decanting into bottles — an hour or so.
Final conditioning — another two-three weeks.

With such a wide range of different kits available, it's worth experimenting with a few and then staggering the process so you always have a ready supply fermenting, conditioning, and available for drinking.

For the more adventurous, however, 'extract brewing' gives the opportunity to better tailor your beer to your own tastes.

Where a homebrew kit will contain all the ingredients pre-measured for you, extract brewing means adding your own hops and yeast separately — meaning you have far more control over the flavour.

The ready mashed 'syrup' or malt extract is bought as usual — but you will need to steep your hops in a big pot (20 litres or more) before adding them to the mix along with the yeast. There is a wealth of information online about different types and proportions of hops (or grain) to use — and even small changes in your recipe can make for intriguingly different flavoured beers.

Fermentation is usually quicker than with a kit — typically one week instead of two — after which the ale is decanted into bottles as usual. The result can be so much more satisfying: where kits are quick, easy and convenient, extract brewing gives you far more of the feel of a real brewer.

For the really confident, however, full-mash (or 'all grain') brewing basically replicates the exact process professional beer producers use. Every ingredient is bought in its raw state and the brewer needs to steep, boil, mash and ferment it accordingly to produce a beer.

Some specialist equipment will be needed — most notably several very large boiling pots, plus a hydrometer to monitor the extraction process — but by and large, if you've successfully made a few batches using extract brewing, you should give it a go. Again, the internet is your friend — there are a wealth of recipes online.

Another great tip is to keep a detailed notebook — this will not only help pinpoint where you might have gone wrong but also serve as a valuable record of how you did things right!

And finally, remember: it's supposed to be fun. Obviously the drinking bit's fun but with a little practise and a bit of dedication, creating your own brew can prove pretty satisfying too…

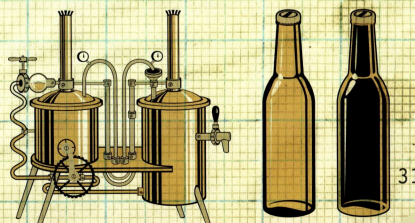

TUNA MELT BAGELS

PREP: 50 mins + rising
MAKES 8
COOK: 40 mins

DIFFICULTY

Ingredients

500 g/1 lb 2 oz strong white flour, plus extra for dusting

1 sachet easy-blend dried yeast

1 tbsp caster sugar

1½ tsp salt

325 ml/11 fl oz lukewarm water

olive oil, for greasing

55 g/2 oz poppy seeds

375 g/13 oz canned tuna in brine, drained and flaked

3 tbsp mayonnaise

2 tbsp snipped fresh chives, plus extra to garnish

200 g/7 oz Cheddar cheese, grated

1. Mix the flour, yeast, sugar and salt in a large bowl. Make a well in the centre and stir in just enough of the water to mix to a soft dough.

2. Turn out the dough onto a lightly floured work surface and knead for about 10 minutes until smooth. Cover and leave in a warm place for about 1 hour, or until doubled in size.

3. Turn out the dough onto a lightly floured work surface and lightly knead until smooth. Divide into eight pieces and roll each piece into a smooth ball. Make a hole in the centre of each ball with a floured finger, then swirl your finger around to stretch and open out the ball to a ring. Cover and leave to stand for 20 minutes.

4. Preheat the oven to 220°C/425°F/Gas Mark 7 and grease a baking sheet. Bring a large saucepan of water to the boil, then lower the bagels into the water in batches and cook, turning once, for about 2 minutes until they puff up.

5. Put the poppy seeds into a shallow bowl. Lift out the bagels with a slotted spoon and press them into the poppy seeds. Place the bagels on the prepared baking sheet and bake in the preheated oven for 20—25 minutes until golden brown and firm. Transfer to a wire rack and leave to cool.

6. Preheat the grill to high. Mix the tuna with the mayonnaise and chives. Split the bagels in half and top with the tuna mixture. Sprinkle with the cheese, place on the grill rack and cook under the preheated grill until the cheese is melted. Replace the bagel lids and serve immediately sprinkled with chives.

FIERY FISH FINGER SANDWICH
WITH RUSSIAN DRESSING & ROCKET

DIFFICULTY

Ingredients

oil for deep-frying

20 fish fingers

4 large slices white bread

100 g/3½ oz rocket

Russian Dressing
2 tbsp mayonnaise

1 tbsp creamed horseradish

1 tbsp tomato ketchup

1 tbsp soured cream

1 tbsp sriracha hot chilli sauce

1 tsp Worcestershire sauce

½ tsp smoked paprika

1. Heat enough oil for deep-frying in a large pan or deep-fryer to 180–190°C/350–375°F, or until a cube of bread browns in 30 seconds.

2. Meanwhile, mix together all of the Russian dressing ingredients in a small bowl and set aside.

3. Deep-fry the fish fingers in batches of ten for 5 minutes or until golden, then remove with a slotted spoon, drain on kitchen paper and leave in a warm place while you cook the remaining fish fingers.

4. Spread some of the dressing on 2 of the bread slices. Divide the fish fingers between two slices of bread and drizzle over the rest of the dressing. Top with the rocket and the remaining bread slices and serve immediately.

CULT CLASSIC
This is a cult classic with a pimped-up version of Thousand Island Dressing.

SPICY BAKED EGGS WITH TOMATO & BACON SAUCE

PREP: 20 mins
SERVES 4
COOK: 1 hr

DIFFICULTY

Ingredients

- 25 g/1 oz butter
- 2 tbsp olive oil
- 1 onion, finely chopped
- 2 garlic cloves, finely chopped
- 1 celery stick, finely chopped
- 225 g/8 oz lean bacon, diced
- 1 red pepper, deseeded and diced
- 500 g/1 lb 2 oz plum tomatoes, peeled, cored and chopped
- 2 tbsp tomato purée
- brown sugar, to taste
- 1 tbsp chopped fresh parsley
- pinch of cayenne pepper
- 100 ml/3½ fl oz water
- 225 g/8 oz canned sweetcorn, drained
- 4 large eggs
- salt and pepper

1. Melt the butter with the oil in a saucepan. Add the onion, garlic and celery and cook over a low heat, stirring occasionally, for 5 minutes, until softened. Add the bacon and red pepper and cook, stirring occasionally, for a further 10 minutes.

2. Stir in the tomatoes, tomato purée, sugar to taste, parsley, cayenne pepper and water and season to taste with salt and pepper. Increase the heat to medium and bring to the boil, then reduce the heat and simmer, stirring occasionally, for 15 minutes, until thickened. Meanwhile, preheat the oven to 180°C/350°F/Gas Mark 4.

3. Stir the sweetcorn into the sauce and transfer the mixture to an ovenproof dish. Make four small hollows with the back of a spoon and break an egg into each.

4. Bake in the preheated oven for 25–30 minutes, until the eggs have set. Serve immediately.

MIGHTY 5 EGG OMELETTE
WITH CHORIZO, RED ONION & BLUE CHEESE

DIFFICULTY

Ingredients

- 1 tbsp olive oil
- 1 tbsp butter
- 200 g/7 oz chorizo, diced
- 1 large red onion, chopped
- 5 large eggs, beaten
- 150 g/5½ oz blue cheese, crumbled
- salt and pepper

1. Preheat the grill to high.

2. In a large frying pan heat the oil and butter over a medium heat. Add the chorizo and red onion and fry for 8–10 minutes, or until golden.

3. Pour in the eggs and season to taste with salt and pepper. Using a spatula, scrape the eggs away from the edges of the pan in a circular motion until the omelette starts to set. Scatter over the cheese and place under the preheated grill for 5 minutes, or until golden and bubbling.

4. Remove from the grill and leave to cool for 5 minutes before serving.

HUNGRY? Really hungry? Serve this mighty omelette with a bowl of Triple-cooked Chips (see page 10).

Chapter 2
HUNGER-BUSTING MAN MEALS

CHILLI-FLAVOURED SPARE RIBS 42

MONSTER HOT DOGS 44

MEGA MIXED GRILL 46

FETTUCINE ALFREDO 48

FOUR CHEESE MACARONI 50

MEATLOAF 52

TEXAS LONE STAR CHILLI 54

GIANT MEAT FEAST PIZZA 56
DOUBLE-DECKER BURGERS 58
LOADED CHICKEN FAJITAS 60
HOW TO COOK THE PERFECT STEAK 62
CHICKEN WINGS WITH HOT SAUCE 64
PIRI CHICKEN 66
SAL LAMB KEBAB WITH HOT CHILLI SAUCE 68

CHILLI-FLAVOURED SPARE RIBS

PREP: 30 mins
SERVES 4
COOK: 1–1½ hrs

DIFFICULTY

Ingredients

Smoky Rub
2 tbsp mild chilli powder
2 tsp smoked paprika
2 tsp mild paprika
4 tsp dried oregano
2 tsp onion powder
2 tsp salt

1.8–2.25 kg/4–5 lb pork spare ribs
mashed potato, to serve
spring greens or cabbage, to serve

1. To make the smoky rub, combine the chilli powder, smoked paprika, mild paprika, oregano, onion powder and salt in a small bowl. Rub the mixture all over the ribs and set aside for 15 minutes to marinate.

2. Preheat the oven to 160°C/325°F/Gas Mark 3 and line a roasting tin with foil. Put a rack in the roasting tin. Place the ribs on the rack and roast for 1-1½ hours, or until cooked through and the meat is tender.

3. Remove the ribs from the oven, cut into serving portions and serve with mashed potato and spring greens.

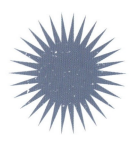

MONSTER HOT DOGS

DIFFICULTY

Ingredients

2 tbsp vegetable oil

2 large onions, sliced

4 large frankfurters

4 hot dog rolls

To Serve
dill pickles, sliced

American mustard

sweet pickle relish

Cheddar cheese, grated

1. In a medium-sized pan heat the oil over a medium heat and gently fry the onions for 20 minutes, or until soft and caramelized. Remove and set aside in a warm place.

2. Meanwhile, cook the frankfurters according to the packet instructions.

3. To serve, split the hot dog rolls and divide the frankfurters between them. Top with the onions, pickles, mustard, relish and grated Cheddar cheese. Serve immediately.

45

MEGA MIXED GRILL

PREP: 5 mins
SERVES 1
COOK: 20 mins

DIFFICULTY

Ingredients

1 fillet steak, about 225 g/8 oz
2 small lamb chops
2 large field mushrooms
1 large beef tomato, cut in half
6 tbsp vegetable oil
2 pork sausages
1 gammon steak, about 225 g/8 oz
55 g/2 oz chorizo, sliced
2 eggs
salt and pepper
freshly cooked Triple-Cooked Chips (see page 10), to serve

1. Season the fillet steak, lamb chops, mushrooms and tomato with salt and pepper to taste.

2. Heat 4 tablespoons of the oil over a high heat in a large frying pan. When the oil starts to smoke, add the lamb chops and sausages to the pan and cook the chops for 2 minutes on each side until seared and brown. Reduce the heat and continue to cook the chops until done to your liking. Remove the chops from the pan and keep warm on a large plate.

3. Return the heat to high and add the gammon steak and fillet steak. Cook the gammon for 3-4 minutes on each side and the fillet steak for 2 minutes on each side, or until cooked to your liking (see page 62). Turn the sausages every now and then to ensure even cooking.

4. Remove all of the meat from the pan, apart from the sausages, and add to the warm plate. Add the chorizo, mushrooms and tomato to the pan and cook on each side for 4 minutes, then add to the plate, again, apart from the sausages.

5. Heat the remaining 2 tablespoons of oil over a medium heat in a non-stick frying pan and fry the eggs to your liking. Add to the warmed plate.

6. Remove the sausages from the large frying pan, slicing one open to ensure that no traces of pink remain. Add to the plate and serve the mixed grill immediately with the chips.

FETTUCINE ALFREDO

DIFFICULTY

Ingredients

400 g/14 oz dried fettucine

85 g/3 oz unsalted butter, diced

2 garlic cloves, finely chopped

400 ml/14 fl oz double cream

175 g/6 oz freshly grated Parmesan cheese, plus extra to serve

salt and pepper

1. Bring a large saucepan of lightly salted water to the boil. Add the pasta, bring back to the boil and cook for 8–10 minutes, until tender but still firm to the bite.

2. Meanwhile, melt the butter in a large frying pan over a medium heat. Add the garlic and stir for 1 minute, taking care that it doesn't brown. Stir in the cream and bring to the boil. Add half of the cheese and stir until melted, then reduce the heat to very low and season to taste with salt and pepper.

3. Drain the pasta without shaking and reserve a little of the cooking liquid. Immediately add the hot pasta and the remaining cheese to the cream sauce, using two forks to toss until well coated. If the sauce seems too thick, add a little of the reserved cooking liquid to thin it, then toss again.

4. Divide between warmed bowls and serve immediately, with extra cheese.

TOP TIP
This dish doesn't have to be meat-free, serve with shredded left-over Roast Chicken (see page 106), or — if you have any left — bite-sized pieces of chuck steak (see page 110).

FOUR CHEESE MACARONI

DIFFICULTY

Ingredients

- 85 g/3 oz freshly grated Parmesan cheese
- 55 g/2 oz fine dry breadcrumbs
- 400 g/14 oz dried macaroni
- 40 g/1½ oz butter, plus extra for greasing
- 40 g/1½ oz plain flour
- 450 ml/16 fl oz lukewarm milk
- freshly grated nutmeg, to taste
- 85 g/3 oz dolcelatte cheese, finely chopped
- 85 g/3 oz provolone or Taleggio cheese, grated
- 55 g/2 oz mozzarella cheese, diced
- olive oil, for drizzling
- salt and pepper

1. Preheat the oven to 200°C/400°F/Gas Mark 6. Lightly grease a large baking dish with butter, then set aside. Mix a third of the Parmesan cheese with the breadcrumbs and set aside.

2. Bring a large saucepan of lightly salted water to the boil, add the macaroni, bring back to the boil and cook for 2 minutes less than specified in the packet instructions. Drain well, rinse with cold water, drain again and set aside.

3. Meanwhile, melt the butter in a saucepan over a medium heat. Sprinkle over the flour and stir for 2 minutes, until blended. Remove the pan from the heat and stir in the milk, stirring constantly to prevent lumps forming.

4. Return the pan to the heat, stir in the nutmeg and season to taste with salt and pepper. Slowly bring to the boil, stirring, until the sauce thickens. Stir in the remaining Parmesan cheese, the dolcelatte cheese and the provolone cheese and continue stirring until the cheese melts and is blended. Stir in the mozzarella cheese.

5. Add the macaroni and stir to coat in the sauce. Adjust the seasoning, if necessary. Tip the mixture into the prepared dish and smooth the surface. Sprinkle the breadcrumb mixture over the top and drizzle with oil.

6. Place the dish on a baking sheet and bake in the preheated oven for 20–25 minutes, until golden brown on top. Leave to stand for a few minutes, then serve straight from the dish.

51

MEATLOAF

DIFFICULTY

Ingredients

- 25 g/1 oz butter
- 1 tbsp olive oil, plus extra for brushing
- 3 garlic cloves, finely chopped
- 100 g/3½ oz carrots, very finely diced
- 55 g/2 oz celery, very finely diced
- 1 onion, very finely diced
- 1 red pepper, deseeded and very finely diced
- 4 large white mushrooms, very finely diced
- 1 tsp dried thyme
- 2 tsp finely chopped fresh rosemary
- 1 tsp Worcestershire sauce
- 6 tbsp tomato ketchup
- ½ tsp cayenne pepper
- 1.1 kg/2 lb 8 oz beef mince, chilled
- 2 eggs, beaten
- 55 g/2 oz fresh breadcrumbs
- 2 tbsp brown sugar
- 1 tbsp Dijon mustard
- salt and pepper

1. Melt the butter with the oil and garlic in a large frying pan. Add the vegetables and cook over a medium heat, stirring frequently, for 10 minutes until most of the moisture has evaporated.

2. Remove from the heat and stir in the herbs, Worcestershire sauce, 4 tablespoons of the tomato ketchup and cayenne pepper. Leave to cool.

3. Preheat the oven to 160°C/325°F/Gas Mark 3. Brush a loaf tin with oil.

4. Put the beef into a large bowl and gently break it up with your fingertips. Add the vegetable mixture, eggs and salt and pepper to taste and mix gently with your fingers. Add the breadcrumbs and mix.

5. Transfer the meatloaf mixture to the loaf tin. Smooth the surface and bake in the preheated oven for 30 minutes.

6. Meanwhile, make a glaze by whisking together the sugar, the remaining 2 tablespoons of tomato ketchup, mustard and a pinch of salt.

7. Remove the meatloaf from the oven and spread the glaze evenly over the top. Return to the oven and bake for a further 35–45 minutes until cooked through and the meat is no longer pink.

8. Remove from the oven and leave to rest for at least 15 minutes. Slice thickly to serve.

53

TEXAS LONE STAR CHILLI

PREP: 30 mins
SERVES 4
COOK: 2¼ hrs

DIFFICULTY

Ingredients

- 2 tbsp vegetable oil
- 1.3 kg/3 lb stewing steak, cut into 1-cm/½-inch cubes
- 1 large onion, diced
- 3 garlic cloves, very finely chopped
- 2 green bird's eye chillies, deseeded and very finely chopped
- 2 red jalapeño peppers, deseeded and very finely chopped
- 2 tbsp hot chilli powder, or to taste
- 1 tbsp ground cumin
- 1 tsp dried oregano
- 1½ tsp salt
- ½ tsp pepper
- ¼ tsp cayenne pepper
- 700 ml/1¼ pints beef stock
- 280 g/10 oz chopped tomatoes
- 1 tbsp polenta
- water as needed
- diced white onion and freshly chopped coriander, to garnish (optional)

1. In a flameproof casserole or large heavy-based pan, heat the oil over a high heat and add the beef, in batches if necessary, and sear until well browned. Add the onion to the pan, reduce the heat to medium and fry for 5 minutes. Add the garlic and cook for a further 1 minute.

2. Add all the remaining ingredients, except the polenta, and bring to the boil and reduce the heat to low, cover and simmer for 1 hour, stirring occasionally. Uncover and stir in the polenta. Continue cooking uncovered, stirring occasionally, for a further 1 hour or until the meat is very tender. Add the water during the cooking to adjust the thickness if necessary, and to occasionally skim off any scum that floats to the surface.

3. Taste and adjust the seasoning, if necessary. Serve the chilli immediately, garnished with white onions and coriander, if liked.

SPICY
You can make this chilli super-spicy by upping the quantity of fresh chillies, jalapeños, chilli powder and cayenne! Why not test your endurance of the Scoville scale by making this dish an Ultimate Food Challenge (see page 118).

54

GIANT MEAT FEAST PIZZA

PREP: 30 mins + rising
MAKES 1
COOK: 40 mins

DIFFICULTY

Ingredients

Pizza Base
400 g/14 oz strong bread flour, plus extra for dusting
1 tsp dry active yeast
1 tsp caster sugar
4 tbsp olive oil
1 tsp salt
250 ml/9 fl oz warm water

Meat Sauce
2 tbsp olive oil
3 garlic cloves, sliced
100 g/3½ oz lean beef mince
200 ml/7 fl oz passata
½ tsp dried oregano
100 ml/3½ fl oz water
salt and pepper

Topping
200 g/7 oz mozzarella, crumbled
4 slices Parma ham
4 slices wafer-thin ham
40 g/1½ oz diced pancetta
100 g/3½ oz chorizo, sliced
40 g/1½ oz freshly grated Parmesan cheese

1. In a large bowl sift together the flour, yeast and caster sugar. Using a wooden spoon, slowly mix in the olive oil, salt and warm water. When a loose dough starts to form, tip out onto a floured surface and knead for 10 minutes, until smooth and elastic. Put the dough in a clean bowl, cover with clingfilm and leave in a warm place for 1½ hours, or until the dough has doubled in size.

2. Meanwhile, in a medium-sized pan heat the olive oil and garlic and fry until the garlic starts to brown a little. Add the mince and cook for 10 minutes until the meat starts to brown. Add the passata, dried oregano and water and cook for 20 minutes, or until the sauce has reduced by half. Season to taste with salt and pepper and set aside.

3. Preheat the oven to 220°C/425°F/Gas Mark 7.

4. Once the dough has risen, knock back slightly and turn out onto a floured surface. Using a rolling pin, lightly roll the dough to fit a 12–15-cm/30–38-inch rectangular non-stick baking tray. Lay the dough on the baking tray and push to the edges, if necessary.

5. Spread the meat sauce over the base of the pizza, leaving a 2.5-cm/1-inch border around the edges. Scatter over the mozzarella and then top with the rest of the meats and the Parmesan cheese.

6. Cook in the preheated oven for 10 minutes, or until golden and bubbling. Serve immediately.

DOUBLE - DECKER BURGERS

PREP: 20 mins
MAKES 4
COOK: 10 mins

DIFFICULTY

Ingredients

- 900 g/2 lb fresh beef mince
- 2 tsp salt
- ½ tsp pepper
- vegetable oil, for frying
- Cheddar cheese slices
- 4 soft burger buns, split
- lettuce leaves
- tomato slices
- red onion slices
- gherkins, halved lengthways

1. Place the beef in a medium-sized bowl with the salt and pepper and mix gently to combine. Divide into eight equal-sized portions and shape each portion into a patty no thicker than 1 cm/½ inch — the thinner the better for these burgers.

2. Place a large griddle pan over a medium–high heat. Add enough oil to coat the base of the pan. Add the patties and cook for about 4 minutes, without moving, until the burgers are brown and release easily from the pan. Turn and cook on the other side for 2 minutes, then put a slice of cheese on top of each burger and cook for a further 2 minutes, or until cooked to your liking.

3. Place a burger on each bun base, then place a second burger on top. Add the lettuce leaves, tomato slices, onion slices and gherkins and serve immediately.

MAN UP

Double-decker?! Pah! Why not make it a triple-decker — or more? The sky is quite literally the limit with this beast of a burger!

LOADED CHICKEN FAJITAS

PREP: 20 mins + marinating
SERVES 4
COOK: 15 mins

DIFFICULTY

Ingredients

3 tbsp olive oil, plus extra for drizzling

3 tbsp maple syrup or honey

1 tbsp red wine vinegar

2 garlic cloves, crushed

2 tsp dried oregano

1–2 tsp dried red pepper flakes

4 skinless, boneless chicken breasts

2 red peppers, deseeded and cut into 2.5-cm/1-inch strips

8 tortillas, warmed

salt and pepper

1. Place the oil, maple syrup, vinegar, garlic, oregano, pepper flakes and salt and pepper to taste in a large, shallow dish or bowl and mix together.

2. Slice the chicken across the grain into 2.5-cm/1-inch thick slices. Toss in the marinade until well coated. Cover and chill in the refrigerator for 2–3 hours, turning occasionally.

3. Heat a griddle pan until hot. Lift the chicken slices from the marinade with a slotted spoon, lay on the griddle pan and cook over a medium-high heat for 3–4 minutes on each side, or until cooked through. Remove the chicken to a warmed serving plate and keep warm. Add the peppers, skin-side down, to the griddle pan and cook for 2 minutes on each side. Transfer to the serving plate. Serve immediately with the warmed tortillas to be used as wraps.

HOW TO COOK THE PERFECT STEAK

BLUE Prepare the steak as instructed, then place in the preheated pan and seal both sides of the meat. The steak should be browned on the outside, but still raw in the middle. When pressed it should bulge slightly, and the indentation should remain in the meat.

RARE Prepare the steak as instructed, then place in the preheated pan and seal both sides of the meat. The steak should be warm through the middle, browned on the outside, but still pink in the centre. It will be slightly more resistant to the touch than a blue steak.

*Cooking times will vary depending on the type and thickness of the steak, and how hot your pan is.

MEDIUM Prepare the steak as instructed, then place in the preheated pan and seal both sides of the meat. The steak should be more brown than pink, but still slightly pink in the centre. When pressed, a medium steak will offer some resistance and the indentation will spring back into place.

MEDIUM RARE Prepare the steak as instructed, then place in the preheated pan and seal both sides of the meat. The steak should be browned on the outside, but still slightly pink in the centre. When pressed, the indentation should remain, but will quickly pool with cooking juices.

WELL DONE Prepare the steak as instructed, then place in the preheated pan and seal both sides of the meat. The steak should be brown all the way through. When pressed, the steak will offer a good deal of resistance and will spring immediately back into place.

CHICKEN WINGS WITH HOT SAUCE

DIFFICULTY

Ingredients

- 1.8 kg/4 lb chicken wings, thawed if frozen, and patted dry
- 1 tbsp vegetable oil
- 1 tbsp plain flour
- 1 tsp salt
- 150 ml/5 fl oz Frank's hot red cayenne pepper sauce
- 115 g/4 oz cold unsalted butter, cut into 2.5-cm/1-inch slices
- 1½ tbsp white vinegar
- ¼ tsp Worcestershire sauce
- 1 tsp Tabasco
- ¼ tsp cayenne pepper
- pinch of garlic powder
- salt to taste
- blue cheese dressing, to serve

1. Preheat the oven to 220°C/425°F/Gas Mark 7.

2. If using whole wings, cut each into two pieces. (The small wing tips can be discarded or saved for stock.) In a large mixing bowl, toss the wings with the oil, flour and salt until evenly coated.

3. Line two baking trays with lightly greased foil or silicon baking mats. Divide the wings between the trays and spread them out evenly — do not crowd. Bake in the preheated oven for 25 minutes.

4. Meanwhile, mix all the sauce ingredients in a saucepan. Bring to a simmer, whisking, over a medium heat. Remove from the heat and set aside. Taste and adjust the seasoning and spices, if necessary.

5. Remove the chicken wings from the oven, turn the wings over, then return them to the oven and cook for a further 20—30 minutes, depending on the size of the wings, until well browned and cooked through. When fully cooked the juices will run clear when a skewer is inserted into the thickest part of the meat. Transfer to a large mixing bowl.

6. Pour the warm sauce over the hot wings and toss with a spoon or palette knife to completely coat. Leave to rest for 5 minutes. Before serving, toss again and serve with blue cheese dressing.

PIRI PIRI CHICKEN

DIFFICULTY

Ingredients

- 8 chicken drumsticks
- 1½ tsp crushed dried red chillies
- 2 garlic cloves, crushed
- 1 tsp dried oregano
- 2 tsp smoked paprika
- juice of ½ lemon
- salt and pepper

To Serve
- lemon wedges
- mixed salad leaves
- tortillas

1. Preheat the oven to 220°C/425°F/Gas Mark 7. Cut deep slashes into the thickest parts of the meat.

2. Place the chillies, garlic, oregano, paprika and lemon juice in a large mixing bowl. Season to taste with salt and pepper and mix together. Add the chicken and turn to coat evenly.

3. Arrange the chicken in a single layer in a large, shallow roasting tin. Bake in the preheated oven for 20—25 minutes, turning occasionally. Check the chicken is tender and the juices run clear when a skewer is inserted into the thickest part of the meat.

4. Transfer to serving plates. Serve with lemon wedges, mixed salad leaves and tortillas.

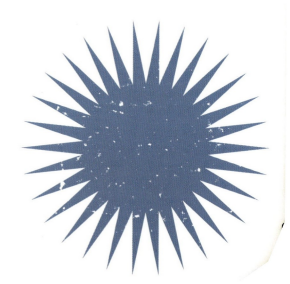

COLOSSAL LAMB KEBAB
WITH HOT CHILLI SAUCE

DIFFICULTY

Ingredients

500 g/1 lb 2 oz leg of lamb, diced

2 tbsp olive oil

1 tsp dried thyme

1 tsp paprika

1 tsp ground cumin

1 large flatbread

1 small red onion, sliced

1 tomato, chopped

small bunch fresh coriander, chopped

½ lemon

salt and pepper

sriracha or other hot chilli sauce and natural yogurt, to serve

1. In a medium-sized bowl mix the lamb with the olive oil, thyme and spices and season to taste with salt and pepper.

2. Preheat a large griddle pan or barbecue.

3. Thread the lamb onto two large skewers, and cook in the preheated pan for 4-5 minutes on each side, or until cooked to your liking.

4. Heat a large, dry frying pan and cook the flatbread for a few seconds on both sides until soft.

5. Remove the lamb from the skewers, place on the flatbread and top with the onion, tomato and coriander. Squeeze over the lemon and serve immediately with the sriracha and natural yogurt.

TOP TIP
You can use any meat to make up this king of kebabs. Equally good is using the meat-free alternative of falafels for a tasty change.

Chapter 3
MEGA PUDS

CHOCOLATE MOUSSE WITH A CHILLI KICK 72

BOOZY CHOCOLATE CHEESECAKE 74

CHOCOLATE CHIP COOKIES & ICE CREAM CAKE 76

ROCKY ROAD DOUGHNUTS 78

DON'T FORGET THE GYM! 80

BANANA BREAKFAST SHAKE 81

AWESOME APPLE TURNOVER 82

STICKY TOFFEE PUDDING 84

EASY SOURED CREAM PUMPKIN PIE 86

PEANUT BUTTER S'MORES 88

BEERAMISU 90

PANCAKE PEAK 92

BIG BANANA SPLIT 94

COOKIE DOUGH ICE CREAM 96

CHUNKY CHOCOLATE BREAD & BUTTER PUDDING 98

CHOCOLATE MOUSSE WITH A CHILLI KICK

DIFFICULTY

Ingredients

150 g/5½ oz 70% dark chocolate, broken into pieces

pinch of salt

4 large eggs, separated

55 g/2 oz caster sugar

150 ml/5 fl oz double cream

1 tsp chipotle powder

2 tsp orange zest

100 g/3½ oz sour cherries

100 ml/3½ fl oz dark rum

55 g/2 oz roasted hazelnuts

1. Place the chocolate pieces in a large heatproof bowl set over a pan of gently simmering water and heat, stirring occasionally, until melted. Remove from the heat and set aside to cool.

2. Once the chocolate has cooled, beat in the salt, egg yolks and sugar.

3. In a separate bowl whisk the double cream until it has thickened slightly.

4. In a clean bowl whisk the egg whites until stiff peaks have formed.

5. Add the chipotle powder and 1 teaspoon of the orange zest to the chocolate mixture, then fold in the cream, followed by the egg whites. Divide between four glasses and place in the refrigerator for 2 hours to set.

6. Meanwhile, soak the sour cherries in the rum and roughly chop the hazelnuts.

7. Just before serving remove the mousse from the refrigerator and top with the rum-soaked sour cherries, the hazelnuts and the remaining orange zest.

BOOZY CHOCOLATE CHEESECAKE

PREP: 30 mins + chilling
SERVES 8
COOK: 10 mins

DIFFICULTY

Ingredients

vegetable oil, for oiling

175 g/6 oz chocolate chip cookies

55 g/2 oz unsalted butter

crème fraîche and fresh fruit, to serve

Filling

225 g/8 oz plain chocolate, broken into pieces

225 g/8 oz milk chocolate, broken into pieces

55 g/2 oz golden caster sugar

350 g/12 oz cream cheese

425 ml/15 fl oz double cream, lightly whipped

3 tbsp Irish Cream liqueur

1. Line the base of a 20-cm/8-inch round springform cake tin with baking paper and brush the sides with oil. Place the cookies in a polythene bag and crush with a rolling pin. Put the butter in a saucepan and heat gently until melted. Stir in the crushed cookies. Press into the base of the prepared cake tin and chill in the refrigerator for 1 hour.

2. Put the plain and milk chocolate into a heatproof bowl set over a saucepan of gently simmering water until melted. Leave to cool. Put the sugar and cream cheese in a bowl and beat together until smooth, then fold in the cream. Fold the melted chocolate into the cream cheese mixture, then stir in the liqueur.

3. Spoon into the cake tin and smooth the surface. Leave to chill in the refrigerator for 2 hours, or until quite firm. Transfer to a serving plate and cut into slices. Serve with crème fraîche and fresh fruit.

WHY NOT?

Up your cream liqueur intake by serving this cheesecake with a glass of cream liqueur on the side or an Irish coffee on a cold day.

CHOCOLATE CHIP COOKIES & ICE CREAM CAKE

DIFFICULTY

Ingredients

175 g/6 oz butter, softened, plus extra for greasing

200 g/7 oz dark brown sugar

100 g/3½ oz caster sugar

1 egg

1 egg yolk

1 tsp vanilla extract

250 g/9 oz plain flour

½ tsp salt

½ tsp bicarbonate of soda

325 g/11½ oz dark chocolate, broken into pieces

2 litres/3½ pints vanilla ice cream

1. Using a food processor on high, cream together the butter and sugars until pale and doubled in size, this will take approximately 8 minutes. Reduce the speed of the food processor slightly and gradually add the egg, egg yolk and vanilla extract until well combined. Turn off the food processor and sift in the flour, salt and bicarbonate of soda. With the food processor on low, process the mixture until well combined, then add the chocolate pieces and mix briefly. Place the dough in the refrigerator for 30 minutes.

2. Preheat the oven to 180°C/350°F/Gas Mark 4.

3. Remove the dough from the refrigerator and divide into three equal-sized pieces.

4. Grease and line three 23-cm/9-inch round cake tins and press the dough into the bottom of the tins, making sure the dough is even and goes right to the edges.

5. Cook in the preheated oven, in batches if necessary, for 15 minutes, or until just turning golden. Remove and leave to cool in the tins.

6. Meanwhile, remove the ice cream from the freezer and allow to soften.

7. Remove two cookies from their tins. Keep the third cookie in its tin as the cake base and build your cake with alternate, equal-sized layers of ice cream and cookie, finishing with the final — and best-looking — cookie on top. Push down gently to make sure the ice cream comes to the sides of the tin.

8. Place in the freezer for 4 hours. Remove from the freezer 10 minutes before serving.

ROCKY ROAD DOUGHNUTS

DIFFICULTY

Ingredients

175 ml/6 fl oz milk

40 g/1½ oz butter

280 g/10 oz strong white flour, plus extra for dusting and kneading

2 tbsp cocoa powder

¼ tsp salt

1½ tsp easy-blend dried yeast

2 tbsp caster sugar

1 large egg, beaten

oil, for deep-frying and greasing

Topping
115 g/4 oz milk chocolate, broken into pieces

40 g/1½ oz unsalted butter

3 tbsp chopped mixed nuts

40 g/1½ oz mini pink and white marshmallows

25 g/1 oz glacé cherries, chopped

---

1. Put the milk and butter into a small saucepan over a low heat and heat until the butter has melted. Leave to cool for 5 minutes.

2. Sift together the flour and cocoa powder into a large bowl and stir in the salt, yeast and sugar. Pour in the milk mixture and the egg and mix to a soft dough. Turn out the dough onto a floured surface and knead for 5–6 minutes, until smooth and elastic, adding a little more flour if needed.

3. Place the dough into a bowl, cover and leave in a warm place for 1–1½ hours, or until doubled in size. Line a large baking sheet with baking paper.

4. Knock back the dough and roll out on a lightly floured surface to a thickness of 1½ cm/⅝ inch. Using a 9-cm/3½-inch doughnut cutter, stamp out 6 doughnuts. Lightly re-knead the trimmings, roll out and stamp out another 2 doughnuts. Place on the prepared baking sheet. Cover with lightly oiled clingfilm and leave in a warm place for 10 minutes, until puffy.

5. Heat enough oil for deep-frying in a large saucepan or deep-fryer to 180–190°C/350–375°F, or until a cube of bread browns in 30 seconds. Add the doughnuts, a few at a time, and fry on each side for 1–2 minutes, or until golden. Remove with a slotted spoon and drain on kitchen paper. Leave to cool.

6. To make the topping, put the chocolate and butter into a heatproof bowl set over a saucepan of gently simmering water and heat until melted. Stir until smooth, then leave to cool for 5 minutes. Dip each doughnut in the chocolate glaze and place on a wire rack. Top with the nuts, marshmallows and cherries and drizzle over any remaining chocolate sauce. Leave to set.

DON'T FORGET THE GYM!

The benefits of man food are obvious. There's the taste, of course, the properly-sized portions, the sense of achievement cooking it gives you, the taste, the smell, the look, the taste…

But then there may be, if we're being totally honest, the potential for one minor drawback to chowing down on all this carb-heavy, protein-rich, mammoth-sized meaty goodness. Some might say that such a diet might require a little regular exercise to help keep things properly proportioned.

To which we say: bring it on! Working up a sweat never did anyone any harm (within reason) — and it's not as if we're about to go crazy with the bench presses and rowing machines or anything. A sensible amount of exercise can prove complementary to eating like a real man… and one of the side effects is that our kind of diet is going to fuel a workout — and help develop muscle while we're about it.

Keeping fit doesn't necessarily mean joining a gym. Getting together with the boys every Sunday for a game of football will go a long way to keeping you in condition — or if you can't find enough willing players, an hour or two of one-on-one basketball every week should get a good sweat on.

For the lone-wolf exercisers, running, swimming or cycling are excellent at working the whole cardiovascular system — again, you don't need to make any pretense at elite athleticism but a half-hour jog, swim or cycle a couple of times a week will work wonders.

Keen for more? Try the following — again, you can do them all in the comfort of your own home…

Press ups: these will work every major muscle group in your body. Start by pushing against a wall, progress to a kneeling position, and once you can manage it, on the floor.

Lunges: great for your thighs and glutes — keeping your back straight, put your feet together and take a big stride forward, bending your front leg so it's at 90 degrees. Repeat with the other leg.

Squats: work your core (i.e., your belly) by slowly lowering yourself as if you're sitting on an imaginary chair. Keep your back straight and hold the position for a second before straightening up again.

Crunches: another great core exercise — lie flat on your back with your knees bent and your arms behind your head and slowly lift your head forwards until your shoulder blades are off the ground. Keep your arms behind your head, hold for a moment, then relax.

And after all that? Mix yourself up a tasty protein shake and start planning your next meal completely guilt-free!

Banana Breakfast Shake

INGREDIENTS
2 large ripe bananas
2 tbsp oat bran
2 tbsp honey
1 tbsp lemon juice
300 ml/10 fl oz soya milk
ground cinnamon, to sprinkle

1. Peel and roughly chop the bananas and place in a large jug with the oat bran, honey and lemon juice. Add the soya milk.

2. Blend the ingredients with an electric hand blender, or tip into a food processor or blender and process until smooth and bubbly.

3. Pour the shake into tall glasses and sprinkle with cinnamon. Serve immediately.

AWESOME APPLE TURNOVER

DIFFICULTY

Ingredients

1.3 kg/3 lb cooking apples, peeled, cored and chopped

55 g/2 oz butter, plus extra for greasing

100 g/3½ oz soft light brown sugar

100 g/3½ oz sultanas

1½ tbsp cornflour, mixed with 2 tablespoons of water

1 kg/2 lb 4 oz ready-made puff pastry

plain flour, for dusting

1 egg, beaten with 1 tbsp water

2 tbsp demerara sugar

1. Grease a large baking sheet and set aside. Put the apples, butter, brown sugar and sultanas into a large, deep frying pan and heat over a low heat, stirring, until the butter has melted and the sugar has dissolved. Cover and simmer for 10—15 minutes, until the apples are tender.

2. Stir the cornflour mixture until it forms a smooth paste and add into the pan. Simmer for a further 5 minutes, stirring constantly, until the liquid has thickened. Remove from the heat and leave to cool.

3. Roll out half the pastry on a lightly floured surface to a thickness of about 8 mm/⅜ inch. Cut the pastry into a triangle shape, around 33 cm/13 inches along the two short sides and 40 cm/16 inches along the long side. Sprinkle the prepared baking sheet with a little cold water and place the pastry triangle on it. Preheat the oven to 220°C/425°F/Gas Mark 7.

4. Spoon the cold apple filling on top of the pastry, leaving a 3-cm/1¼-inch border all around. Brush the border with cold water.

5. Roll out the remaining pastry to a slightly larger triangle and drape over the filling. Firmly press the edges of the pastry together to seal, trim with a sharp knife and crimp with your fingertips. Brush the top of the turnover with the beaten egg mixture and sprinkle with the demerara sugar. Pierce three small holes in the pastry to allow the steam to escape.

6. Bake the turnover in the preheated oven for 35—45 minutes, until risen and golden brown. Cover loosely with foil if the pastry starts to over brown. Serve warm or cold.

STICKY TOFFEE PUDDING

PREP: 40 mins
SERVES 4
COOK: 35–40 mins

DIFFICULTY

Ingredients

Pudding
75 g/2¾ oz sultanas

150 g/5½ oz stoned dates, chopped

1 tsp bicarbonate of soda

25 g/1 oz butter, plus extra for greasing

200 g/7 oz soft light brown sugar

2 eggs

200 g/7 oz self-raising flour, sifted

Sticky Toffee Sauce
25 g/1 oz butter

175 ml/6 fl oz double cream

200 g/7 oz soft light brown sugar

zested rind of 1 orange, to decorate

freshly whipped cream, to serve (optional)

1. To make the pudding, put the sultanas, dates and bicarbonate of soda into a heatproof bowl. Cover with boiling water and leave to soak.

2. Preheat the oven to 180°C/350°F/Gas Mark 4. Grease a round cake tin, 20 cm/8 inches in diameter.

3. Put the butter in a separate bowl, add the sugar and mix well. Beat in the eggs then fold in the flour. Drain the soaked fruit, add to the bowl and mix. Spoon the mixture evenly into the prepared cake tin.

4. Transfer to the preheated oven and bake for 35–40 minutes. The pudding is cooked when a skewer inserted into the centre comes out clean.

5. About 5 minutes before the end of the cooking time, make the sauce. Melt the butter in a saucepan over a medium heat. Stir in the cream and sugar and bring to the boil, stirring constantly. Reduce the heat and simmer for 5 minutes.

6. Turn out the pudding onto a serving plate and pour over the sauce. Decorate with zested orange rind and serve with whipped cream, if using.

85

EASY SOURED CREAM PUMPKIN PIE

DIFFICULTY

Ingredients

Pastry
150 g/5½ oz plain flour, plus extra for dusting

¼ teaspoon salt

75 g/2¾ oz vegetable fat, diced

4–5 tbsp ice-cold water

Pumpkin Filling
150 g/5½ oz caster sugar

55 g/2 oz soft light brown sugar

½ tsp ground cinnamon

½ tsp ground nutmeg

¼ tsp ground ginger

generous pinch of salt

900 g/2 lb pumpkin or butternut squash, peeled, seeded, cooked and mashed (about 450 g/1 lb prepared weight)

225 g/8 oz soured cream

3 eggs, separated

whipped cream, to serve

1. Combine the flour and salt in a bowl and mix in the vegetable fat with a pair of knives until the mixture resembles coarse breadcrumbs.

2. Sprinkle the ice-cold water, 1 tablespoon at a time, evenly over the surface, while stirring with a fork, until all the dry ingredients are moistened. Shape the dough into a ball, cover and refrigerate until chilled.

3. Preheat the oven to 200°C/400°F/Gas Mark 6. Roll the dough out to 8-mm/⅜-inch thickness on a lightly floured surface. Line a 23-cm/9-inch pie dish with the pastry, pressing it into place, and trim the edges.

4. Combine the caster sugar, brown sugar, cinnamon, nutmeg, ginger and salt, stirring well. Add the pumpkin and soured cream, stirring well.

5. Beat the egg yolks until thick, then stir them into the pumpkin mixture. Beat the egg whites on medium speed with an electric hand-held mixer until forming stiff peaks. Fold the egg whites into the pumpkin mixture.

6. Pour the filling into the pastry case. Bake in the preheated oven for 10 minutes, then reduce heat to 180°C/350°F/Gas Mark 4 and bake for 45–50 minutes or until set.

PACKS A PUNCH

This pie may look basic but its pumpkin filling packs a real taste-punch.
Serve with lashings of whipped cream and devour.

PEANUT BUTTER S'MORES

DIFFICULTY

Ingredients

115 g/4 oz smooth peanut butter

6 graham crackers or digestive biscuits

85 g/3 oz plain chocolate, broken into squares

1. Preheat the grill to high. Spread the peanut butter on one side of each cracker.

2. Place the chocolate pieces on four of the crackers and invert the remaining crackers on top.

3. Toast the s'mores under the preheated grill for about 1 minute until the filling starts to melt. Turn carefully using tongs. Leave to cool slightly, then serve.

TOP TIP

For an extra layer, try adding toasted marshmallows to your s'mores stack. Serve with whipped cream or ice cream if you're really in need of a dessert to die for.

BEERAMISU

DIFFICULTY

Ingredients

750 g/1 lb 10 oz mascarpone cheese

600 ml/1 pint double cream

300 g/10½ oz caster sugar

450 ml/16 fl oz stout

1 tbsp vanilla extract

50 boudoir biscuits

2 double shots espresso

400 ml/14 fl oz Irish cream

cocoa, for dusting

1. In a large bowl beat together the mascarpone cheese, double cream and sugar until combined. Gradually add the stout and vanilla extract and beat until the mixture resembles a thick cream.

2. In a medium-sized bowl soak the boudoir biscuits in the espresso and Irish cream for around 10 seconds, and then break up the softened biscuits using a spoon.

3. In a 4-litre/7-pint dish or bowl layer the mascarpone mixture and then the soaked biscuit mixture alternately until there are four layers of each mixture. Finish off with one more layer of the mascarpone mixture.

4. Refrigerate for at least 3 hours or until needed.

5. Before serving remove from the refrigerator and dust with cocoa.

PANCAKE PEAK

PREP: 40 mins • **SERVES 6** • **COOK: 1–1½ hrs**

DIFFICULTY

Ingredients

- 1.4 kg/3 lb 2 oz plain flour
- 6 tbsp baking powder
- ½ tsp salt
- 85 g/3 oz caster sugar
- 12 large eggs
- about 2 litres/3½ pints milk
- 140 g/5 oz butter, melted and cooled, plus extra for frying
- 600 ml/1 pint maple syrup and fresh fruit, to serve

1. Sift together half the flour, half the baking powder and half the salt into a large bowl. Stir in half the sugar and make a well in the centre. Beat 6 eggs in a jug, then pour into the well. Gradually whisk the eggs into the dry mixture with a balloon whisk.

2. When some of the flour has been incorporated start gradually pouring 850 ml/1½ pints of the milk into the bowl. Continue whisking, adding more of the milk and drawing in the flour from the sides of the bowl, until a smooth, thick batter forms. Whisk in half the melted butter.

3. Repeat with the remaining batter ingredients to make another large bowl of batter. Cover both bowls of batter and leave to stand for 30 minutes. Preheat the oven to 140°C/275°F/Gas Mark 1. Line two large baking sheets with baking paper and set aside.

4. Heat a little butter in a large nonstick frying pan or pancake pan until sizzling. Pour a ladleful of batter into the pan, swirling to coat the base. Cook over a medium heat, until bubbles appear on the surface. Use a fish slice to flip the pancake and cook for 1 minute, until just cooked. Slide the pancake onto one of the prepared baking sheets and place in the oven to keep warm.

5. Repeat with the remaining batter to make about 36 pancakes in total, stacking the cooked pancakes on top of each other in the warm oven. If the batter becomes too thick whisk in a little more milk to thin.

6. Pile up the hot pancakes on a large, warmed serving platter. Pour over some of the maple syrup, top with fresh fruit and serve with the remaining maple syrup on the side.

BIG BANANA SPLIT

Ingredients

1 large banana

500 ml/18 fl oz chocolate ice cream

250 ml/9 fl oz clotted cream

100 ml/3½ fl oz caramel sauce

55 g/2 oz pecan nuts, crushed

55 g/2 oz maraschino cherries

1. Peel and split the banana lengthways then put onto an oblong serving plate.

2. Put 3 large scoops of chocolate ice cream on top then 3 scoops of clotted cream.

3. Drizzle over the caramel sauce, top with the crushed nuts and cherries and serve immediately.

MAN UP
Big Banana Split just not big enough? Add scoops of Cookie Dough Ice Cream (see page 96) and up the quantity of caramel sauce for a side-splitting banana-buster!

COOKIE DOUGH ICE CREAM

DIFFICULTY

PREP: 15 mins + freezing
SERVES 1–2
COOK: 20 mins

Ingredients

Cookie Dough
100 g/3½ oz butter, softened
55 g/2 oz light brown sugar
55 g/2 oz dark brown sugar
1½ tsp vanilla extract
175 g/6 oz plain flour
100 g/3½ oz dark chocolate chips

Ice Cream
450 ml/16 fl oz whole milk
12 egg yolks
1½ tsp vanilla extract
300 g/10½ oz caster sugar
450 ml/16 fl oz double cream

1. In a food processor beat together the butter, light brown sugar and dark brown sugar until pale and fluffy. Add the vanilla extract and all the flour, then pulse the mixture until it starts to come together. Turn the mixture onto a clean surface and fold in the chocolate chips by hand. Wrap in clingfilm and chill in the refrigerator for 30 minutes.

2. Meanwhile, slowly heat the milk in a heavy-based pan.

3. In a medium-sized heatproof bowl, whisk together the egg yolks, vanilla extract and the caster sugar.

4. When the milk comes to the boil, remove from the heat and gradually pour it into the egg mixture, whisking as you pour. Then pour the mixture back into a clean pan, stir with a wooden spoon and slowly heat until the sauce thickens, taking care that the mixture does not boil. Add the double cream and leave to cool slightly before putting in an ice-cream machine.

5. Following the manufacturer's instructions, churn the mixture until almost frozen.

6. Meanwhile, remove the cookie dough from the refrigerator and break into walnut-sized pieces.

7. Add the dough pieces to the almost-frozen ice cream and churn a couple of times to mix in the dough without breaking it up too much.

8. Transfer the mixture to a freezer-proof container and freeze for an hour, or until required.

CHUNKY CHOCOLATE
BREAD & BUTTER PUDDING

DIFFICULTY

Ingredients

- 1 large brioche loaf
- 200 g/7 oz butter, softened
- 150 g/5½ oz 70% dark chocolate, broken into large pieces
- 100 g/3½ oz chopped dried figs
- 4 large eggs
- 600 ml/1 pint whole milk
- 150 g/5½ oz caster sugar
- 1 tsp vanilla extract
- single cream, to serve

1. Preheat the oven to 160°C/325°F/Gas Mark 3.

2. Line a 900-g/2-lb loaf tin with baking paper.

3. Slice the brioche and butter each slice on one side. Sprinkle the chocolate and figs over the buttered side of the slices. Put the slices back into the shape of the loaf and fit it into the prepared tin.

4. In a medium-sized bowl whisk together the eggs, milk, sugar and vanilla extract, then pour the mixture over the brioche and allow to soak for 5 minutes.

5. Cook in the preheated oven for 35–40 minutes, or until golden and the juices have set in the middle. Remove from the oven and leave to cool for 10 minutes before serving with cream.

99

Chapter 4
GET SET TO IMPRESS

TURKEY SCHNITZEL WITH POTATO WEDGES 102

CHICKEN JALFREZI .... 10[2]

ROAST CHICKEN 106

WHOLE TANDOORI CHICKEN 108

DRUNK CHUCK STEAK 110

SPAGHETTI & MEATBALLS 112

PRIME RIB OF BEEF
WITH TRADITIONAL HORSERADISH SAUCE 114

SUPER SURF & TURF 116

THE BIG EAT CHALLENGE 118

RACK OF LAMB 120

BEER-BATTERED
FISH & CHIPS 122

PAELLA 124

ONE POT
CLAM BAKE 126

TURKEY SCHNITZEL WITH POTATO WEDGES

DIFFICULTY

Ingredients

4 potatoes, unpeeled

2 tbsp olive oil, plus extra for shallow frying

1 tbsp dried sage

55 g/2 oz fresh white breadcrumbs

40 g/1½ oz finely grated Parmesan cheese

4 thinly sliced turkey escalopes

1 egg, beaten

salt and pepper

lemon wedges, to serve

1. Preheat the oven to 220°C/425°F/Gas Mark 7. Cut each potato into eight wedges.

2. Place the potato wedges in a bowl and add the oil, 1 teaspoon of the sage, and salt and pepper to taste. Toss well to coat evenly.

3. Arrange the potatoes in a single layer on a baking sheet. Bake in the oven for about 25 minutes, until golden brown and tender.

4. Meanwhile, mix together the breadcrumbs, cheese, remaining sage, and salt and pepper to taste.

5. Dip the turkey in the beaten egg and then in the crumb mixture, pressing to coat on both sides.

6. Heat a shallow depth of oil in a frying pan over a fairly high heat, add the turkey and fry for 4–5 minutes, turning once, until golden brown and the turkey is cooked through. Serve the turkey immediately with the potato and lemon wedges.

CHICKEN JALFREZI

PREP: 25 mins
SERVES 4–6
COOK: 35–40 mins

DIFFICULTY

Ingredients

- 55 g/2 oz ghee or 4 tbsp vegetable oil or groundnut oil
- 8 skinless, boneless chicken thighs, sliced
- 1 large onion, chopped
- 2 tbsp garlic paste
- 2 tbsp ginger paste
- 2 green peppers, cored, deseeded and chopped
- 1 large fresh green chilli, deseeded and finely chopped
- 1 tsp ground cumin
- 1 tsp ground coriander
- ¼–½ tsp chilli powder
- ½ tsp ground turmeric
- ¼ tsp salt
- 400 g/14 oz canned chopped tomatoes
- 125 ml/4 fl oz water
- chopped fresh coriander, to garnish
- freshly cooked rice, to serve

1. Melt half the ghee in a kadhai, wok or large frying pan over a medium-high heat. Add the chicken pieces and stir for around 5 minutes until browned, but not necessarily cooked through, then remove from the pan with a slotted spoon and set aside.

2. Melt the remaining ghee in the pan. Add the onion and fry, stirring frequently, for 5–8 minutes until golden brown. Stir in the garlic and ginger paste and continue frying for 2 minutes, stirring frequently.

3. Add the peppers to the pan and stir around for 2 minutes.

4. Stir in the chilli, cumin, coriander, chilli powder, turmeric and salt. Add the tomatoes with their juices and the water and bring to the boil.

5. Reduce the heat to low, add the chicken and leave it to simmer, uncovered, for 10 minutes, stirring frequently, until the peppers are tender and the chicken is cooked through. Garnish with the coriander and serve immediately with freshly cooked rice.

SPICE FACTOR
Add whole green chillies to this curry classic to seriously increase the spice-factor.

ROAST CHICKEN

DIFFICULTY

Ingredients

1 chicken, weighing 2.25 kg/5 lb

55 g/2 oz soft butter

2 tbsp chopped fresh lemon thyme, plus extra sprigs to garnish

1 lemon, quartered

125 ml/4 fl oz white wine, plus extra if needed

salt and pepper

1. Preheat the oven to 220°C/425°F/Gas Mark 7. Place the chicken in a roasting tin.

2. Place the butter in a bowl, mix in the chopped thyme and season well with salt and pepper. Butter the chicken all over with the herb butter, inside and out, and place the lemon quarters inside the cavity. Pour the wine over the chicken.

3. Roast the chicken in the centre of the preheated oven for 15 minutes. Reduce the temperature to 190°C/375°F/Gas Mark 5 and continue to roast, basting frequently, for a further 1¾ hours. Cover with foil if the skin begins to brown too much. If the tin dries out, add a little more wine or water.

4. Test that the chicken is cooked by inserting a skewer into the thickest part of the meat and making sure the juices run clear. Remove from the oven.

5. Remove the chicken from the roasting tin and place on a warmed serving plate. Cover with foil and leave to rest for 10 minutes before carving.

6. Place the roasting tin on the top of the hob and simmer the pan juices gently over a low heat until they have reduced and are thick and glossy. Season to taste with salt and pepper. Serve the chicken with the pan juices and garnish with thyme sprigs.

WHOLE TANDOORI CHICKEN

DIFFICULTY

PREP: 35 mins + marinating
SERVES 4
COOK: 55 mins

Ingredients

1 chicken, 1.5 kg/3 lb 5 oz

2 tsp garam masala spice mix

300 ml/10 fl oz natural yogurt

1 onion, finely chopped

2 garlic cloves, crushed

2.5-cm/1-inch piece fresh ginger, peeled and grated

juice of 1 lemon

2 tbsp tomato purée

1 tsp chilli powder

1 tsp ground cumin

1 tsp turmeric

1 tbsp paprika (not smoked)

1 tsp salt

To Serve
basmati rice

naan bread

lime wedges

hot lime pickle

1. Cut two slits into each chicken leg and two into each thigh. They should just reach the bone. Make two shallower cuts into the fleshiest part of each breast. These are to allow the marinade to penetrate into the meat.

2. Mix all of the remaining ingredients together in a food processor and blend to a smooth paste. Place the chicken in a large, non-metallic dish and cover it in the paste, massaging it deep into the skin and flesh. Place the chicken, uncovered, in the refrigerator to marinate for as long as possible — preferably 24 hours.

3. Remove the chicken from the refrigerator an hour before cooking to warm it to room temperature. Preheat the oven to 220°C/425°F/Gas Mark 7. Place the chicken in the oven and cook, uncovered, for 20 minutes, then reduce the heat to 180°C/350°F/Gas Mark 4. Baste the chicken and cook for another 35 minutes. When fully cooked the juices will run clear when a skewer is inserted into the thickest part of the meat. Turn off the oven and open the door, leaving the chicken inside to rest for 20 minutes. Serve with rice, naan bread, lime wedges and lime pickle.

DRUNK CHUCK STEAK

DIFFICULTY

Ingredients

4 chuck steaks, 350 g/12 oz each

Marinade
4 tbsp olive oil

100 ml/3½ fl oz good quality red wine

1 small bunch fresh thyme, leaves picked

1 small bunch fresh rosemary, leaves picked

2 garlic cloves, crushed

1 tbsp Dijon mustard

1 tsp salt

1 tsp pepper

1. Place all of the marinade ingredients into a shallow non-metallic dish, large enough to hold all of the steaks in a single layer. Mix the ingredients together.

2. Add the steaks to the marinade, turning a few times to coat. Cover and chill in the refrigerator for a minimum of 4 hours, or for up to 12 hours if time allows. Turn once, mid-way through marinating.

3. Remove from the refrigerator 1 hour before cooking, to allow the meat to return to room temperature. Discard the marinade.

4. Preheat a griddle pan over a high heat and cook the steaks for 5 minutes on each side for medium-rare, or until cooked to your liking (see page 62). Cook the steaks in batches if necessary. Set aside to rest for 5 minutes before serving.

TOP TIP
Serve this steak in replacement of the classic cooked version as part of a Mega Mixed Grill (see page 46) or a Super Surf & Turf (see page 116).

SPAGHETTI & MEATBALLS

PREP: 30 mins
SERVES 2
COOK: 1¼ hrs

DIFFICULTY

Ingredients

- 2 tbsp olive oil, plus extra for brushing
- 1 onion, finely diced
- 4 garlic cloves, finely chopped
- ½ tsp dried Italian herbs
- ½ day-old ciabatta loaf, crusts removed
- 4 tbsp milk
- 900 g/2 lb beef mince, well chilled
- 2 large eggs, lightly beaten
- 5 tablespoons chopped fresh flat-leaf parsley
- 55 g/2 oz freshly grated Parmesan cheese, plus extra to serve
- 1.5 litres/2¾ pints marinara or other ready-made pasta sauce
- 450 g/1 lb thick dried spaghetti
- salt and pepper

1. Heat the olive oil in a saucepan. Add the onion, garlic and a pinch of salt, cover and cook over a medium–low heat for 6–7 minutes, until softened and golden. Remove the pan from the heat, stir in the dried herbs and leave to cool to room temperature.

2. Tear the bread into small chunks and put into a food processor, in batches depending on the size of the machine. Pulse to make fine breadcrumbs — you'll need 140 g/5 oz in total. Put the crumbs into a bowl, toss with the milk and leave to soak for 10 minutes.

3. Preheat the oven to 220°C/425°F/Gas Mark 7. Brush a baking sheet with oil.

4. Put the beef, eggs, parsley, cheese, breadcrumbs, cooled onion mixture, 2 teaspoons of salt and 1 teaspoon of pepper into a bowl. Mix well with your hands until thoroughly combined.

5. Dampen your hands and roll pieces of the mixture into balls about the size of a golf ball. Put them on the prepared tray and bake in the preheated oven for 20 minutes. Meanwhile, pour the pasta sauce into a saucepan, stir in 225 ml/8 fl oz water and bring to simmering point. When the meatballs are done, transfer them into the hot sauce, reduce the heat to very low, cover and simmer gently for 45 minutes.

6. Bring a large saucepan of lightly salted water to the boil, add the spaghetti, curling it around the pan as it softens. Bring back to the boil and cook for 10–12 minutes, until tender but still firm to the bite.

7. Drain the spaghetti in a colander and tip into a large serving dish. Ladle some of the sauce from the meatballs over it and toss to coat. Top with the meatballs and the remaining sauce, sprinkle with cheese and serve immediately.

PRIME RIB OF BEEF
WITH TRADITIONAL HORSERADISH SAUCE

DIFFICULTY

Ingredients

4 kg/9 lb standing rib roast, trimmed and tied

2½ tbsp softened butter (or ½ tbsp per rib bone)

salt and pepper

Horseradish Sauce
6 tbsp creamed horseradish

6 tbsp soured cream

1. To make the sauce, mix the horseradish and soured cream together in a small bowl. Cover with clingfilm and chill until required.

2. Place the beef in a large roasting tin. Rub the entire surface of the meat with butter and season generously with salt and pepper. Leave to stand at room temperature for 2 hours.

3. Meanwhile, preheat the oven to 230°C/450°F/Gas Mark 8. Put the meat in the preheated oven and roast for 20 minutes to seal the outside. Then reduce the oven temperature to 160°C/325°F/Gas Mark 3 and roast for 2 hours, until the temperature of the meat reaches 43–46°C/110–115°F when tested with a meat thermometer, for medium-rare, or until cooked to your liking.

4. Set aside to rest for 30 minutes before serving. While resting the meat will continue to cook — for medium-rare the final internal temperature will be approximately 54–57°C/130–135°F. Slice and serve with the horseradish sauce.

SUPER SURF & TURF

PREP: 10 mins
SERVES 2
COOK: 25 mins

DIFFICULTY

Ingredients

500 g/1 lb 2 oz new potatoes, cut into large slices

8 tbsp olive oil

1 garlic bulb, broken into cloves

few sprigs fresh rosemary, picked

2 rib-eye steaks, about 350 g/ 12 oz each, seasoned

25 g/1 oz butter

500 g/1 lb 2 oz large raw prawns, shell on

3 garlic cloves, sliced

juice of ½ lemon

salt and pepper

1. Preheat the oven to 200°C/400°F/Gas Mark 6.

2. In a large bowl mix together the potatoes, 4 tablespoons of olive oil, the garlic cloves and rosemary, and season to taste with salt and pepper. Tip the potato mixture onto a large non-stick baking tray and cook in the preheated oven, turning at least once, for 25 minutes, or until golden and soft.

3. When the potatoes have been in the oven for 15 minutes, heat a large non-stick frying pan and add the remaining 4 tablespoons of olive oil. When the oil starts to smoke, add the steaks and butter. Cook the steaks on each side for 2 to 3 minutes or until cooked to your liking (see page 62). When the steaks are cooked, remove from the pan and set aside in a warm place to rest.

4. Return the hot frying pan to the heat and add the prawns and garlic. Cook the prawns on each side for 2 minutes, or until they turn pink. Add the lemon juice and season to taste with salt and pepper. Remove from the heat.

5. Serve the steaks immediately with the prawns and potatoes.

MAN UP
Replace the large prawns with lobster for a really impressive twist on this hearty dish.

THE BIG EAT CHALLENGE

Every man loves a challenge. It's in our genes. If we see a mountain, we have to climb it. If we see a goal, we have to kick a ball at it. If we see a restaurant menu defying us to eat a 72 ounce steak or a two-foot-long burrito or the hottest chillies in the World our natural reaction is: hell yeah!

The good news? Big eat challenges have never been more popular. The bad news? They've also never been so challenging. With prizes ranging from t-shirts to free meals (and the ubiquitous place on the Wall of Fame), most eateries aren't about to make it easy for us.

Food challenges tend to fall into the same three basic categories. They're either about size (putting away a massive portion), heat (coping with some seriously evil chilli sauce) or time (getting through a certain amount of food before the klaxon sounds). Some, of course, involve a combination of all three.

So how do you go about taking on such a task? The same way you would to scale that mountain, or score that goal. With training.

Step 1: Identify your challenge. Research is the key here. Make a note of exactly what it is you have to do, how long you have to do it, and how many have successfully done it before.

Step 2: Recreate the challenge.

Size challenges: Whether it's tackling a monster steak, working your way through a 30-inch pizza or devouring an enormous plate of fish and chips, these are all easily replicated at home. Simply find the appropriate recipe in this book, scale everything up accordingly, and get stuck in. And remember: practise makes perfect.

Heat challenges: The crucial point here is not to dive straight in with the hottest curries or spiciest sauces you can handle. Build up a tolerance, push your limits slowly, and develop stamina. Think of yourself like an athlete training at altitude — you're not going to win anything without proper acclimatization.

Time challenges: Twenty hot dogs in two minutes? Two-dozen king prawns in sixty seconds? Thirty-six chicken wings in half an hour? All eminently doable, gentlemen, and all easy to train for. A bit of preparation, a big kitchen table and a stopwatch is all that's needed (if you haven't got a stopwatch, stick something in the microwave and set it going).

Step 3: Get in there and show 'em who's boss. Remember: you're a man!

BIG EAT CHALLENGE TIPS

- Never drink water when eating chillies — it will only spread the heat around. Drink milk, instead. Lots of milk.
- It takes around 20 minutes for your stomach to tell your brain it's full. So forget about going slow and steady — pack as much in as you can before your brain catches up.
- If there's an aspect of the challenge you're most dreading, tackle that first. Leave the tastiest bits to last, when you'll need all the help you can get.
- Take any medical waivers you have to sign seriously. If you have a condition that may be affected by whatever you're about to do, our advice is, don't do it!

RACK OF LAMB

PREP: 15 mins
SERVES 2
COOK: 40–55 mins

DIFFICULTY

Ingredients

1 trimmed rack of lamb, weighing 500 g/1 lb 2oz

salt and pepper

Sauce
1 tbsp extra virgin olive oil

1 small onion, finely chopped

1 garlic clove, crushed

1–2 tbsp redcurrant jelly

1 tbsp soy sauce

200 ml/7 fl oz sanguinella or orange juice

150 ml/5 fl oz red wine

1 fresh rosemary sprig

salt and pepper

1. To make the sauce, heat the oil in a small saucepan. Add the onion and garlic and cook for 3 minutes, stirring occasionally. Add the redcurrant jelly, soy sauce, sanguinella juice, wine and rosemary and bring to the boil, stirring until the jelly has dissolved. Reduce the heat and simmer for 20 minutes, or until the sauce has reduced by half and is slightly syrupy. Season to taste with salt and pepper.

2. Preheat the oven to 200°C/400°F/Gas Mark 6. Season the meat lightly with salt and pepper and sear on all sides in a hot frying pan. Transfer the meat to a roasting pan and brush with some of the sauce. Roast in the preheated oven for 8 minutes for medium-rare, 15 minutes for medium and 20–25 minutes for well done. Remove the meat from the oven and transfer to a board. Cover loosely with foil and leave to stand for 10 minutes.

3. Meanwhile strain the sauce and reheat. Slice the rack through into individual chops and arrange on serving plates. Drizzle with the sauce and serve immediately.

BEER-BATTERED FISH & CHIPS

DIFFICULTY

Ingredients

Batter
225 g/8 oz self-raising flour, plus extra for dusting

½ tsp salt

300 ml/10 fl oz cold lager

Mushy Peas
350 g/12 oz frozen peas

30 g/1 oz butter

2 tbsp single cream

salt and pepper

vegetable oil, for deep-frying

6 large floury potatoes, such as King Edward, Maris Piper or Desirée, cut into chips

4 thick cod fillets, about 175 g/6 oz each

salt and pepper

lemon wedges, to serve

1. Sift the flour into a bowl with a little salt and whisk in most of the lager. Check the consistency and add the remaining lager; it should be thick, like double cream. Chill in the refrigerator for half an hour.

2. Cook the peas in lightly salted boiling water for 3 minutes. Drain and mash to a thick purée, add the butter and cream and season with salt and pepper to taste. Set aside and keep warm.

3. Heat the oil to 120°C/250°F in a thermostatically controlled deep fat fryer or a large saucepan using a thermometer. Preheat the oven to 150°C/300°F/Gas Mark 2.

4. Fry the chips for about 8–10 minutes until softened but not coloured. Remove from the oil, drain on kitchen paper and place in a dish in the warm oven. Increase the temperature of the oil to 180°C/350°F.

5. Season the fish with salt and pepper to taste and dust lightly with a little flour. Dip one fillet in the batter and coat thickly.

6. Carefully place in the hot oil and repeat with the other fillets (you may need to cook 2 at a time if your pan is small). Cook for 8–10 minutes, turning them over halfway through. Remove the fish from the oil, drain and keep warm.

7. Reheat the oil to 180°C/350°F and recook the chips for a further 2–3 minutes until golden brown. Drain and season with salt and pepper to taste. Serve the chips immediately with the fish, mushy peas and lemon wedges for squeezing over.

PAELLA

PREP: 30 mins
SERVES 6–8
COOK: 45 mins

DIFFICULTY

Ingredients

- 6 tbsp olive oil
- 6–8 boned chicken thighs
- 140 g/5 oz chorizo, diced
- 2 large onions, chopped
- 4 large garlic cloves, crushed
- 1 tsp mild or hot paprika
- 350 g/12 oz paella rice, rinsed and drained
- 100 g/3½ oz French beans, chopped
- 125 g/4½ oz frozen peas
- 1.3 litres/2¼ pints fish stock
- ½ tsp saffron threads, soaked in 2 tbsp hot water
- 16 live mussels, scrubbed, debearded and soaked in salted water for 10 minutes
- 16 raw prawns, peeled and deveined
- 2 red peppers, halved and deseeded, then grilled, peeled and sliced
- salt and pepper
- freshly chopped parsley, to garnish

1. Heat 3 tablespoons of the oil in a 30-cm/12-inch paella pan or casserole. Cook the chicken over a medium–high heat, turning frequently, for 5 minutes, or until golden and crisp.

2. Using a slotted spoon, transfer to a bowl.

3. Add the chorizo to the pan and cook, stirring, for 1 minute, or until beginning to crisp, then add to the chicken.

4. Heat the remaining oil in the pan, add the onions and cook, stirring, for 2 minutes. Add the garlic and paprika and cook for a further 3 minutes, or until the onions are soft but not brown.

5. Add the rice, beans and peas and stir until coated in oil. Return the chicken and chorizo and any accumulated juices to the pan. Stir in the stock, saffron and its soaking liquid, and salt and pepper to taste and bring to the boil, stirring. Reduce the heat to low and simmer, uncovered, for 15 minutes.

6. Discard any mussels with broken shells and any that refuse to close when tapped. Arrange the mussels, prawns and peppers on top. Cover and simmer for 5 minutes until the prawns turn pink and the mussels open. Discard any mussels that remain closed. Ensure the chicken is cooked through and the juices run clear by inserting a skewer into the thickest part of the meat.

7. Garnish with the parsley and serve immediately.

ONE POT CLAM BAKE

DIFFICULTY

Ingredients

2 tbsp olive oil

25 g/1 oz butter

4 shallots, finely chopped

4 garlic cloves, chopped

4 celery sticks, finely chopped

1 tbsp smoked paprika

450 ml/16 fl oz apple cider

2 litres/3½ pints hot chicken stock

500 g/1 lb 2 oz new potatoes

2 corn cobs, each cut into 3

200 g/7 oz smoked sausage, sliced

1 kg/2 lb 4 oz live clams, scrubbed

1 kg/2 lb 4 oz large raw prawns, shells on

small bunch fresh parsley, chopped

salt and pepper

fresh crusty bread, to serve

1. Add the olive oil, butter, shallots, garlic and celery to a large casserole with a tight-fitting lid. Cook uncovered over a medium-low heat for 10 minutes, or until the shallots are translucent.

2. Add the smoked paprika, cider and hot chicken stock, bring to the boil and add the new potatoes. Cover and simmer for 10 minutes, then add the corn cobs and smoked sausage. Cook for a further 10 minutes, until the potatoes are almost soft.

3. Discard any clams with broken shells and any that refuse to close when tapped. Add the clams and prawns to the casserole, and cook for a further 2 minutes, until the clams have opened and the prawns have turned pink. Discard any clams that remain closed.

4. Remove from the heat and leave for a couple of minutes, then add the chopped parsley and season with salt and pepper to taste. Transfer to a large serving dish and serve immediately with fresh crusty bread.

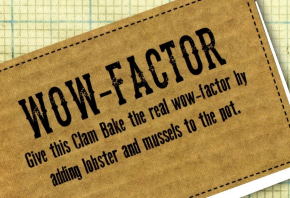

WOW-FACTOR
Give this Clam Bake the real wow-factor by adding lobster and mussels to the pot.

apples: Awesome Apple
  Turnover 82
avocados
  Blazin' Beef Tacos 22
  Ultimate Nachos with
  Beef 20

bacon
  Bacon & Cheese Chips 12
  Spicy Baked Eggs with
  Tomato & Bacon Sauce 36
  The Best Bacon Butty 16
bananas
  Banana Breakfast Shake
  81
  Big Banana Split 94
beef
  Blazin' Beef Tacos 22
  Double-decker Burgers 58
  Drunk Chuck Steak 110
  Giant Meat Feast Pizza
  56
  How to cook the perfect
  steak 62–63
  Meatloaf 52
  Mega Mixed Grill 46
  Mighty Meatball Sub 24
  Prime Rib of Beef with
  Traditional Horseradish
  Sauce 114
  Rump Steak Sandwiches 26
  Spaghetti & Meatballs
  112
  Super Surf & Turf 116
  Texas Lone Star Chilli
  54
  Ultimate Nachos with
  Beef 20
beer
  Beer Waffles with Ham &
  Cheese 14
  Beer-battered Fish &
  Chips 122
  Beeramisu 90
  home brewing 30–31
  big eat challenges
  118–119

cheese
  Bacon & Cheese Chips 12
  Beer Waffles with Ham &
  Cheese 14
  Blazin' Beef Tacos 22
  Double-decker Burgers 58
  Four Cheese Macaroni 50
  Giant Meat Feast Pizza
  56
  Mighty 5 Egg Omelette
  with Chorizo, Red Onion
  & Blue Cheese 38
  The Best Bacon Butty 16
  Tuna Melt Bagels 32
  Turkey Schnitzel with
  Potato Wedges 102
  Ultimate Nachos with
  Beef 20
  see also cream cheese

cherries
  Big Banana Split 94
  Chocolate Mousse with a
  Chilli Kick 72
  Rocky Road Doughnuts 78
chicken
  Chicken Jalfrezi 104
  Chicken Wings with Hot
  Sauce 64
  Loaded Chicken Fajitas
  60
  Paella 124
  Piri Piri Chicken 66
  Roast Chicken 106
  Whole Tandoori Chicken
  108
chilli 119
  Blazin' Beef Tacos 22
  Chicken Jalfrezi 104
  Chicken Wings with Hot
  Sauce 64
  Chilli-flavoured Spare
  Ribs 42
  Chocolate Mousse with a
  Chilli Kick 72
  Colossal Lamb Kebab with
  Hot Chilli Sauce 68
  Fiery Fish Finger
  Sandwich with Russian
  Dressing & Rocket 34
  Mighty Meatball Sub 24
  Piri Piri Chicken 66
  Texas Lone Star Chilli
  54
  Ultimate Nachos with
  Beef 20
  Whole Tandoori Chicken
  108
chocolate
  Big Banana Split 94
  Boozy Chocolate
  Cheesecake 74
  Chocolate Chip Cookies
  & Ice Cream Cake 76
  Chocolate Mousse with
  a Chilli Kick 72
  Chunky Chocolate Bread
  & Butter Pudding 98
  Cookie Dough Ice Cream
  96
  Peanut Butter S'Mores 88
  Rocky Road Doughnuts 78
chorizo
  Giant Meat Feast Pizza
  56
  Mega Mixed Grill 46
  Mighty 5 Egg Omelette
  with Chorizo, Red Onion
  & Blue Cheese 38
  Paella 124
clams: One Pot Clam Bake
  126
  Cookie Dough Ice Cream
  96
cream cheese
  Beeramisu 90
  Boozy Chocolate
  Cheesecake 74

dates & figs
  Chunky Chocolate Bread
  & Butter Pudding 98
  Sticky Toffee Pudding 84

eggs
  Mega Mixed Grill 46
  Mighty 5 Egg Omelette
  with Chorizo, Red Onion
  & Blue Cheese 38
  Spicy Baked Eggs with
  Tomato & Bacon Sauce 36
  The Best Bacon Butty 16
exercise & keeping fit 80

fish & seafood
  Beer-battered Fish &
  Chips 122
  Fiery Fish Finger
  Sandwich with Russian
  Dressing & Rocket 34
  One Pot Clam Bake 126
  Paella 124
  Super Surf & Turf 116
  Tuna Melt Bagels 32
frankfurters
  Monster Hot Dogs 44
  Quick & Easy Corn Dogs
  28

ham & gammon
  Beer Waffles with Ham
  & Cheese 14
  Giant Meat Feast Pizza
  56
  Mega Mixed Grill 46

ice cream
  Big Banana Split 94
  Chocolate Chip Cookies
  & Ice Cream Cake 76
  Cookie Dough Ice Cream
  96

lamb
  Colossal Lamb Kebab with
  Hot Chilli Sauce 68
  Mega Mixed Grill 46
  Rack of Lamb 120

marshmallows
  Peanut Butter S'Mores 88
  Rocky Road Doughnuts 78
Meatloaf 52
mushrooms
  Meatloaf 52
  Mega Mixed Grill 46
  mussels: Paella 124

nuts
  Big Banana Split 94
  Chocolate Mousse with
  a Chilli Kick 72
  Peanut Butter S'Mores 88
  Rocky Road Doughnuts 78

Paella 124
Pancake Peak 92

pasta
  Fettucine Alfredo 48
  Four Cheese Macaroni 50
  Spaghetti & Meatballs
  112
pastry
  Awesome Apple Turnover
  82
  Easy Soured Cream
  Pumpkin Pie 86
  Peanut Butter S'Mores 88
peas
  Mushy Peas 122
  Paella 124
peppers
  Chicken Jalfrezi 104
  Loaded Chicken Fajitas
  60
  Meatloaf 52
  Spicy Baked Eggs with
  Tomato & Bacon Sauce 36
Pizza 56
pork: Chilli-flavoured
  Spare Ribs 42
potatoes
  Bacon & Cheese Chips 12
  Beer-battered Fish
  & Chips 122
  Jumbo Potato Wedges with
  Dips 18
  One Pot Clam Bake 126
  Super Surf & Turf 116
  Triple-cooked Chips 10
  Turkey Schnitzel with
  Potato Wedges 102
prawns
  One Pot Clam Bake 126
  Paella 124
  Super Surf & Turf 116
pumpkin: Easy Soured
  Cream Pumpkin Pie 86

rice: Paella 124
Rocky Road Doughnuts 78

sausages
  Mega Mixed Grill 46
  One Pot Clam Bake 126
  see also chorizo;
  frankfurters
sweetcorn
  One Pot Clam Bake 126
  Spicy Baked Eggs with
  Tomato & Bacon Sauce 36

tomatoes
  Chicken Jalfrezi 104
  Giant Meat Feast Pizza
  56
  Spicy Baked Eggs with
  Tomato & Bacon Sauce 36
  Texas Lone Star Chilli
  54
  Ultimate Nachos with
  Beef 20
Tuna Melt Bagels 32
Turkey Schnitzel with
  Potato Wedges 102